# CII

# R01 – FINANCIAL SERVICES, REGULATION AND ETHICS

2015/16 edition

**Study Text**

This **Study Text** provides full coverage of the **2015/16 syllabus** for Unit R01 *Financial Services, Regulation and Ethics* of the examinations of the Chartered Insurance Institute®. The 2015/16 syllabus will be **examined from 1 September 2015 to 31 August 2016.**

**BPP**
LEARNING MEDIA

Published September 2015

ISBN 9781 4727 4150 9

British Library Cataloguing-in-Publication Data

A catalogue record for this book is available from the British Library

Published by

BPP Learning Media
BPP House, Aldine Place
London W12 8AA

www.bpp.com/learningmedia

Printed in the United Kingdom by Ricoh UK Limited
Unit 2, Wells Place, Mertham RH1 3LG

Your learning materials, published by BPP Learning Media Ltd, are
printed on paper obtained from traceable sustainable sources.

The contents of this book are intended as a guide and not professional
advice. Although every effort has been made to ensure that the
contents of this book are correct at the time of going to press, BPP
Learning Media makes no warranty that the information in this book is
accurate or complete and accept no liability for any loss or damage
suffered by any person acting or refraining from acting as a result of
the material in this book.

We are grateful to the CII® for permission to reproduce the syllabus.

*Chartered Insurance Institute® and CII® are registered trademarks. The
CII® does not endorse, promote, review or warrant the accuracy of the
products or services offered by BPP Learning Media.*

**A note about copyright**

Dear Customer

What does the © mean and why does it matter? Your market-leading BPP books, course
materials and e-learning materials do not write and update themselves. People write them:
on their own behalf or as employees of an organisation that invests in this activity.
Copyright law protects their livelihoods. It does so by creating rights over the use of the
content. Breach of copyright is a form of theft – as well being a criminal offence in some
jurisdictions, it is potentially a serious breach of professional ethics.

With current technology, things might seem a bit hazy but, basically, without the express
permission of BPP Learning Media:

- Photocopying our materials is a breach of copyright
- Scanning, ripcasting or conversion of our digital materials into different file
  formats, uploading them to facebook or emailing them to your friends is a
  breach of copyright

You can, of course, sell your books, in the form in which you have bought them – once you
have finished with them. (Is this fair to your fellow students? We update for a reason.) But
the e-products are sold on a single user license basis: we do not supply 'unlock' codes to
people who have bought them secondhand.

And what about outside the UK? BPP Learning Media strives to make our materials
available at prices students can afford by local printing arrangements, pricing policies and
partnerships which are clearly listed on our website. A tiny minority ignore this and indulge
in criminal activity by illegally photocopying out material or supporting organisations that
do. If they act illegally and unethically in one area, can you really trust them?

# Contents

## Introduction

## Chapters

## Index

# Using this Study Text

## About this Study Text

This Study Text provides comprehensive coverage for candidates sitting Unit R01 *Financial services, regulation and ethics*, an examination of the Chartered Insurance Institute®:

This Study Text contains:

- A list of topics covered in each chapter
- Clear, concise topic-by-topic coverage
- Examples to reinforce learning, confirm understanding and stimulate thought
- A roundup of the key points in each chapter
- A quiz at the end of each chapter

We recognise that most students have only limited time for study and that some study material available on the market can be very time-consuming to use. **BPP Learning Media** has prepared study material which provides you with what you need to secure a good pass in your exam if you study it fully, while making effective use of your time.

# Your exam practice and revision

How can you give yourself the best chance of success in your exam? You need to do more than work through this Study Text. The **BPP Learning Media** products described below are designed for your **exam practice** and **revision**.

## Exam practice: BPP's Practice and Revision Kit

BPP's long experience in preparing students for exams shows that **question practice** is a vital ingredient in exam success. Question practice will improve your exam technique and help to build confidence for tackling the exam itself. It can highlight problem areas and remind you of key points. BPP's **Practice and Revision Kit** includes plenty of questions for you to try. Feedback is given on answers, and there are flexible ways of using the question bank.

## Revision: BPP's Passcards

The syllabuses for your examination, which are based on the standards for Appropriate Examinations in the financial sector, are wide-ranging. In your **revision** during the run-up to the exam, you will want to focus your revision on ensuring that you recall what you have studied. BPP's **Passcards** present key facts for your subject in a visually appealing style, to remind you of key points.

## To order BPP Learning Media products

Call BPP Learning Media on +44 (0)207 061 1329 to order **Study Texts**, **Practice and Revision Kits** and **Passcards** for this and other Units for CII® examinations. For more information or to order online, visit us on the web at **www.bpp.com/learning-media**.

# Syllabus: 2015/16

## R01: Financial Services, Regulation and Ethics

In this Unit, you will investigate:

- The purpose and structure of the UK financial service industry
- How the retail customer is served by the financial service industry
- The regulatory framework, powers and responsibilities to protect the consumer
- Legal concepts and considerations relevant to financial advice
- The Code of Ethics and its impact on the business behaviours of individuals

| Syllabus learning outcome | BPP Study Text Chapter |
|---|:---:|
| **1 Understand the UK financial services industry in its European and global context** | 1 |
| 1.1 Describe the role, structure and context of the UK and international financial services markets | |
| 1.2 Explain the function and operation of financial services within the economy | |
| 1.3 Describe the role of government and the impact of the EU on UK regulation | |
| **2 Understand how the retail consumer is served by the financial services industry** | 2 |
| 2.1 Explain the obligations that the financial services industry has towards consumers | |
| 2.2 Explain consumers' main financial needs and how these may be prioritised and met | |
| **3 Understand legal concepts and considerations relevant to financial advice** | 3 |
| 3.1 Explain the concepts of legal persons, powers of attorney, law of contract and agency, and ownership of property | |
| 3.2 Explain relevant laws governing insolvency and bankruptcy | |
| 3.3 Explain relevant laws governing wills, intestacy and trusts | |
| **4 Understand the regulation of financial services** | 4 |
| 4.1 Examine the role of the PRA, FCA, HM Treasury and the Bank of England in regulating the market | |
| 4.2 Examine the role of other regulatory bodies and sources of additional oversight | |
| 4.3 Examine the statutory framework of regulation, including the role of EU regulation and key directives | |
| **5 Understand the financial regulators' responsibilities and approach to regulation** | 5 |
| 5.1 Explain the financial regulators' statutory objectives and how they are structured to achieve these objectives | |
| 5.2 Explain the main principles and rules in the PRA and FCA Handbooks | |
| 5.3 Explain the approach to risk-based supervision, discipline and enforcement, and sanctions to deal with criminal activities | |
| **6 Apply the principles and rules as set out in the regulatory framework** | 6 |
| 6.1 Apply the FCA's and PRA's regulatory principles and rules | |
| 6.2 Apply current anti-money laundering, proceeds of crime, and data protection obligations | |
| 6.3 Apply the rules of relevant dispute resolution and compensation schemes | |

| Syllabus learning outcome | BPP Study Text Chapter |
|---|---|
| **7** **Apply the regulatory framework in practice for the consumer** | **7** |
| 7.1 Apply client relationships, regulated advice standards, and the adviser responsibilities in terms of these | |
| 7.2 Monitor and review client plans and circumstances | |
| **8** **Understand the range of skills required when advising clients** | **7** |
| 8.1 Examine the range of skills required when advising clients | |
| **9** **Understand the financial regulators' use of principles and outcomes based regulation to promote ethical and fair outcomes** | **8** |
| 9.1 Examine the Principles for Businesses and the discretionary obligations these place on firms | |
| 9.2 Examine the impact of corporate culture and leadership | |
| 9.3 Examine the responsibilities of approved persons and the need for integrity, competence and fair outcomes for clients | |
| **10** **Apply the Code of Ethics and professional standards to business behaviours of individuals** | **9** |
| 10.1 Apply the Code of Ethics and the professional principles and values on which the code is based | |
| 10.2 Identify ethical dilemmas and apply the steps involved in managing ethical dilemmas | |
| **11** **Critically evaluate the outcomes that distinguish between ethical and compliance-driven behaviours** | **9** |
| 11.1 Evaluate the positive indicators of ethical behaviour | |
| 11.2 Evaluate the negative indicators of limiting behaviour to compliance within the rules | |
| 11.3 Critically evaluate the outcomes that distinguish ethical and compliant behaviours | |

# Examination format

The R01 *Financial Services, Regulation and Ethics* examination consists of **100 multiple choice questions**: **87 standard format** (choose one option from the alternatives offered in each question) and **13 multiple response format** (choose one or more options from the alternatives offered in each question).

A period of **two hours** is allowed for the examination.

Candidates will be examined on the basis of law and practice in England unless otherwise stated. You should assume that all individuals are domiciled and resident in the UK unless it is stated otherwise.

The general rule is that the new tax year and changes arising from the Finance Act will be examined from **1 September** each year. Other changes, not related to the Finance Act, will not be examined earlier than 3 months after they come into effect.

- The **2015/2016 tax year and examination syllabus** will be examined from 1 September 2015 until 31 August 2016.

- The **2016/2017 tax year and examination syllabus** will be examined from 1 September 2016 until 31 August 2017.

# Test specification

The standard number of **standard format** and **multiple response format** questions for each **Learning Outcome** in the syllabus is indicated below. However, note that the test specification has an in-built element of flexibility. It is designed to be used as a guide for study and is not a statement of actual number of questions that will appear in every exam. The number of questions testing each Learning Outcome will generally be within the range **plus or minus two** of the number indicated.

| Learning outcome | Standard format questions | Multiple response questions |
|---|---|---|
| 1  Understand the UK financial services industry in its European and global context | 6 | 0 |
| 2  Understand how the retail consumer is served by the financial services industry | 12 | 0 |
| 3  Understand legal concepts and considerations relevant to financial advice | 9 | 0 |
| 4  Understand the regulation of financial services | 6 | 0 |
| 5  Understand the financial regulators' responsibilities and approach to regulation | 29 | 0 |
| 6  Apply the principles and rules as set out in the regulatory framework | 4 | 5 |
| 7  Apply the regulatory advice framework in practice for the consumer | 5 | 8 |
| 8  Understand the range of skills required when advising clients | 4 | 0 |
| 9  Understand the financial regulators' use of principles and outcomes based regulation to promote ethical and fair outcomes | 7 | 0 |
| 10 & 11  Apply the Code of Ethics and professional standards to business behaviours of individuals, *and* Critically evaluate the outcomes that distinguish between ethical and compliance driven behaviours | 5 | 0 |
| **Total** | **87** | **13** |

# Tackling multiple choice questions

**Multiple choice questions (MCQs)** each present a number of possible answers. You have to **choose the option(s) that best answer the question**. The incorrect options are called distracters.

- In the case of **standard format** questions, **one** option must be chosen.

- For questions in **multiple response format**, you must select **all** the options that are correct to gain the mark.

Look at the **Test specification** on the previous page to see how many questions will be **standard format MCQs** and how many will be **multiple response questions**.

There is a skill in answering MCQs quickly and correctly. By practising MCQs you can develop this skill, which will give you a better chance of passing the exam.

You may wish to follow the approach outlined below, or you may prefer to adapt it to suit your own learning style and needs.

*Step 1*     **Note down how long** you should allocate to each MCQ. For example, if you have 100 questions to answer in 120 minutes, you have approximately 1.2 minutes on average to answer each question. For a group of ten questions, you have twelve minutes. You will probably not spend an equal amount of time on each MCQ. You might be able to answer some questions instantly while others will take more time to work out. Multiple response format questions may typically take longer to answer than the standard format MCQs.

*Step 2*     **Attempt each question**. Read the question thoroughly. A particular question might look familiar to you, but be aware that the detail and/or the requirement may be different from any similar question you have come across. So, read the requirement and options carefully, even for questions that seem familiar.

*Step 3*     Read all the options and see which of them match your own answer. Be careful with any numerical questions, as the distracters will generally be designed to match answers that incorporate **common errors**. Check that your calculation is correct. Have you followed the requirement exactly? Have you included every stage of the calculation?

*Step 4*     You may find that none of the options matches your answer.

- **Re-read the question** to ensure that you understand it and are answering the requirement

- **Eliminate any obviously wrong answers**

- **Consider which of the remaining answers** is or are the **most likely** to be correct or best and select that option or (for multiple response questions) option(s)

*Step 5*     If you are still unsure, **continue to the next question**.

If you are nowhere near working out the correct option(s) after a couple of minutes, leave the question and come back to it later. Make a note of any questions for which you have submitted answers but you need to return to later.

*Step 6*     **Revisit questions** you are uncertain about. When you come back to a question after a break, you may find that you are able to answer it correctly straight away. If you are still unsure, have a guess. You are not penalised for incorrect answers, so **do not leave a question unanswered!**

chapter

1

# The financial services industry

## Chapter topic list

## CHAPTER LEARNING OUTCOMES

1.      **Understand the UK financial services industry in its European and global context**

   1.1    **Describe** the role, structure and context of the UK and international financial services markets.

   1.2    **Explain** the function and operation of financial services within the economy.

   1.3    **Describe** the role of government and the impact of the EU on UK regulation.


# 1 The role and structure of financial services

## 1.1 A monetary economy

**Money** is the main **medium of exchange** in our society. In a **barter economy**, goods and services are exchanged one for another. If someone works to harvest corn, and is given corn in payment for their labour, this is a barter exchange. The use of money as a medium of exchange creates much flexibility in economic transactions. If the harvester is paid in money instead of corn, he may be able to use that money to buy cooking pots and meat. He cannot subsist only on corn.

Most measures of 'money' include balances (e.g. at banks and building societies) as well as notes and coin. Money functions as a medium of exchange because:

- It is **divisible** into small units (pounds and pence, dollars and cents)
- There are **sufficient quantities of money** to use for transactions
- Money is **generally accepted** by all parties in transactions

The modern **monetary economy** involves a huge variety of types of transactions involving money. Because money is a recognised medium of exchange among people, it is accepted that debt relationships between people, and claims by one person or institution over another, can be expressed in monetary terms.

The **financial services industry** covers various activities within our monetary **economy**. At the national level, we have the economy of the United Kingdom, with its own currency, the pound sterling. The financial services industry also operates within an international framework, resulting from both the multinational nature of many financial services activities and from various international agreements and regulatory influences. As a member of the **European Union (EU),** although not of the common currency 'Euro zone', the United Kingdom is subject to EU legislation.

In this first chapter, we look at the place of the financial services industry within the economic system, and at the main institutions and markets within the industry. We examine also the roles of the national government and the EU.

## 1.2 The flow of funds in the economy

The **flow of funds** in an economy describes the movement of funds or money between one group of people or institutions in the economic system and other groups.

If we begin by ignoring the country's imports and exports of goods and services and foreign investments, we can start to build up a picture of the flow of funds by identifying three sectors in the economy.

   (a)    The **personal sector** – mainly individuals or households
   (b)    The **business sector** (or industrial and commercial sector) – i.e. companies and other businesses
   (c)    The **government sector** – i.e. central government, local government and public corporations

Within each of these three sectors, there are continual **movements of funds**.

    (a)    Individuals will give money or lend money to other individuals.

    (b)    Companies will buy goods and services from other companies, and may occasionally lend money direct to other companies.

    (c)    Central government will provide funds for local government authorities and loss-making nationalised industries.

As well as movements of funds within each sector, there are flows of funds between different sectors of the economy.

But reality is not quite so simple, and our analysis of the flow of funds in the UK should also take account of two other main factors.

    (a)    The **overseas sector** comprises businesses, individuals and governments in other countries. The UK economy is influenced by trade with the foreign sector and flows of capital both from and to it.

    (b)    **Financial intermediaries** – see below.

# 1.3 Financial intermediation

An intermediary is a go-between, and a financial intermediary is an institution which **links lenders with borrowers**, by obtaining deposits from lenders and then re-lending them to borrowers. Such institutions can, for example, provide a link between savers and investors.

The role of **financial intermediaries** such as banks and building societies in an economy is to provide means by which funds can be transferred from **surplus units** (for example, someone with savings to invest in the economy) to **deficit units** (for example, someone who wants to borrow money to buy a house). Financial intermediaries develop the facilities and **financial instruments** which make lending and borrowing possible.

If no financial intermediation takes place, lending and borrowing will be direct.

If financial intermediation does take place, the intermediary provides a service to both the surplus unit and the deficit unit.

For example, a person might deposit savings with a bank, and the bank might use its collective deposits of savings to provide a loan to a company.

A **financial intermediary** is a party bringing together providers and users of finance, either as a broker facilitating a transaction between two other parties, or in their own right, as principal.

**UK financial intermediaries** include the following sectors of the financial services industry:

    (a)    Banks
    (b)    Building societies
    (c)    Insurance companies, pension funds, unit trust companies and investment trust companies
    (d)    The Government's National Savings & Investments (NS&I)

Financial intermediaries might lend abroad or borrow from abroad.

In spite of competition from building societies, insurance companies and other financial institutions, banks arguably remain the major financial intermediaries in the UK.

The clearing banks are the biggest operators in the retail banking market, although competition from the major building societies has grown in the UK.

There is greater competition between different banks (overseas banks and the clearing banks especially) for business in the wholesale lending market.

**Financial intermediaries** can link lenders with borrowers, by obtaining deposits from lenders and then re-lending them to borrowers. But not all intermediation takes place between savers and investors. Some institutions act mainly as intermediaries between other institutions. Almost all place part of their funds with other institutions, and a number (including finance houses, leasing companies and factoring companies) obtain most of their funds by borrowing from other institutions.

## 1.4 Benefits of financial intermediation

Financial intermediaries perform the following functions.

(a) They provide obvious and **convenient** ways in which a **lender can save money** to spend in the future. Instead of having to find a suitable borrower for their money, lenders can deposit money. Financial intermediaries also provide a ready **source of funds for borrowers**.

(b) They can aggregate or 'package' the amounts lent by savers and lend on to borrowers in different amounts (a process called **aggregation**). By aggregating the deposits of hundreds of small savers, a bank or building society is able to package up the amounts and lend on to several borrowers in the form of larger mortgages.

(c) Financial intermediaries provide for **maturity transformation**; i.e. they bridge the gap between the wish of most lenders for liquidity and the desire of most borrowers for loans over longer periods. For example, while many depositors in a building society may want instant access to their funds, the building society can lend these funds to mortgage borrowers over much longer periods, by ensuring that it attracts sufficient funds from depositors over this longer term.

By pooling the funds of large numbers of people, some financial institutions are able to give small investors access to professionally managed **diversified portfolios** covering a varied range of different securities through collective investment products such as unit trusts and investment trusts.

**Risk** for individuals is reduced by **pooling**. Since financial intermediaries lend to a large number of individuals and organisations, losses suffered through default by borrowers or capital losses are pooled and borne as costs by the intermediary. Such losses are shared among lenders in general.

# 2 Markets and institutions

## 2.1 Capital markets and money markets

The capital markets and the money markets are types of market for dealing in capital.

(a) **Capital markets** are financial markets for raising and investing largely **long-term** capital.
(b) **Money markets** are financial markets for lending and borrowing largely **short-term** capital.

## 2.2 Long-term and short-term capital

What do we mean by **long-term** and **short-term** capital?

- By **short-term capital**, we mean capital that is lent or borrowed for a period which might range from as short as overnight up to about one year, and sometimes longer.

- By **long-term capital**, we mean capital invested or lent and borrowed for a period of about five years or more, but sometimes shorter.

- There is a **grey area** between long-term and short-term capital, which is lending and borrowing for a period from about one to two years up to about five years, which is not surprisingly referred to as **medium-term** capital.

## 2.3 Stock markets

The **London Stock Exchange** (LSE) is an organised **capital market** which plays an important role in the functioning of the UK economy. The LSE provides the main way for larger companies to raise funds through the issue of **shares** (equity) or through **corporate bonds**. It makes it easier for large firms and the government – through the gilt-edged market – to raise **long-term capital**, providing a market place for issuers seeking capital and investors to come together. The LSE also owns the equities and **derivatives** trading platform called **Turquoise**. Derivatives include options and futures and comprise instruments whose value is based on the value of an 'underlying' security or other asset, such as a share or a commodity.

The European Markets in Financial Instruments Directive (MiFID) has encouraged the development of many new cross-border trading and reporting systems that compete with the main exchanges. A new generation of platforms known as **Multilateral Trading Facilities (MTFs)** offers the prospect of firms making use of internal crossing networks – more often now called dark liquidity pools or 'non-displayed liquidity venues', whereby firms can buy and sell blocks of shares off-exchange, away from the public domain. Traders are able to stay anonymous, without prices being displayed on the public order book usually found on exchanges. MTFs are a challenge to the mainstream exchanges, and have taken a significant market share of transactions.

The **Alternative Investment Market** (AIM), which opened in 1995, is a second-tier London-based market where smaller companies which cannot meet the more stringent requirements needed to obtain a full listing on the LSE can raise new capital by issuing shares. It is cheaper for smaller company to be on the AIM than to meet the requirements for a full listing. Like the Stock Exchange main market, the AIM is also a market in which investors can trade in shares already issued. The AIM is regulated by the LSE.

**ISDX (ICAP Securities and Derivatives Exchange)** was created after the inter-dealer broker ICAP acquired PLUS Stock Exchange (PLUS-SX) in June 2012 and re-branded it. ISDX (formerly PLUS-SX) has been described as London's third stock market, after the LSE main market and AIM. The market is lightly regulated and was established (as PLUS-SX) to help smaller companies raise capital. The **ISDX Growth Market** aims to provide growing small- and medium-sized enterprises (SMEs) with a source of equity finance for companies coming to a public market for the first time, as well as being a venue for existing issuers to raise further funds. The **ISDX Main Board** is an EU Regulated Market which aims to provide companies and other issuers with lower-cost admission to trading through the UKLA's Official List, or other European Competent Authority.

ISDX faces the prospect of future competition as a listing venue for SMEs from NYSE Euronext's proposed Entrepreneurial Exchange, and from the LSE, which is believed to have been considering possibilities of improving opportunities for SMEs to raise equity.

## 2.4 Banks

Banks can be approached directly by individuals (**retail** business) and businesses for medium-term and long-term loans as well as short-term loans or overdrafts.

The major clearing banks, many investment banks and foreign banks operating in the UK are often willing to lend medium-term capital, especially to well established businesses.

## 2.5 The gilt-edged market

The **gilt-edged market** is a major capital market in the UK. The government borrows over the medium and longer term when the **Debt Management Office (DMO)** issues government stocks (called 'gilt-edged stock' or '**gilts**'). Trade in second-hand gilts will continue until the debt eventually matures and the government redeems the stock.

The **primary** gilts market is the market for the sale of new gilt issues. There is an active **secondary** market in second-hand gilts on the **LSE** with existing holders selling their holdings of gilts to other investors in the gilts market.

## 2.6 Providers of capital

Providers of capital include **private individuals** in the retail sector. This includes those who buy stocks and shares on the Stock Exchange, and those who deposit money with banks, building societies and National Savings & Investments (NS&I). NS&I is a government institution set up to borrow on behalf of the government, mainly from the non-banking private sector of the economy.

There are also important groups of **institutional investors** which specialise in providing capital and act as financial intermediaries between suppliers and demanders of funds. Many financial services organisations now have diversified operations covering a range of the following activities.

(a)   **Pension funds**. Pension funds invest the pension contributions of individuals who subscribe to a pension fund, and of organisations with a company pension fund.

(b)   **Insurance**. Insurance companies invest premiums paid on insurance policies by policy holders. Life assurance policies, including life-assurance based savings policies, account for substantial assets, which are invested in equities, bonds, property and other assets.

(c)   **Investment trusts**. The business of investment trust companies is investing in the stocks and shares of other companies and the government. In other words, they trade in investments.

(d)   **Unit trusts** and **Open-ended Investment Companies (OEICs)**. Unit trusts and OEICs are similar to investment trusts, in the sense that they invest in stocks and shares of other companies. A unit trust comprises a 'portfolio' – i.e. a holding of stocks or shares in a range of companies or gilts, perhaps with all the shares or stocks having a special characteristic, such as all shares in property companies or all shares in mining companies. The trust will then create a large number of small units of low nominal value, with each unit representing a stake in the total portfolio. These units are then sold to individual investors and investors will benefit from the income and capital gain on their units – i.e. their proportion of the portfolio.

(e)   **Hedge funds**. This type of fund is sold to more sophisticated or higher net worth investors. Various strategies are employed by hedge funds.

(f)   **Venture capital**. Venture capital providers are organisations that specialise in raising funds for new business ventures, such as 'management buy-outs' (i.e. purchases of firms by their management staff). These organisations are therefore providing capital for fairly risky ventures.

## 2.7 Overview of capital markets

The role of financial intermediaries in capital markets is illustrated in the following diagram.

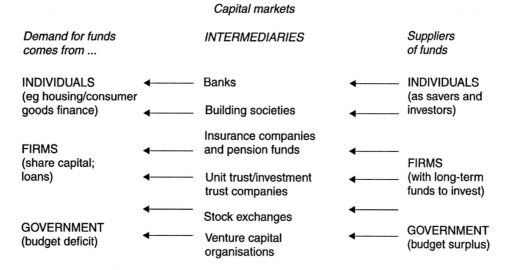

## 2.8 Competition

**Competition for business** between financial institutions for business is fiercer than it has ever been. Building societies have emerged as competitors to the banks, and foreign banks have competed successfully in the UK with the big clearing banks. Banks have changed too, with some shift towards more fee-based activities (such as selling advice and selling insurance products for commission) and away from the traditional transaction-based activities (holding deposits, making loans).

## 2.9 The money markets

The UK **money markets** are operated by the banks and other financial institutions. Although the money markets largely involve **wholesale borrowing and lending** by banks, some large companies and the government are also involved in money market operations. The money markets are essentially shorter term debt markets, with loans being made for a specified period at a specified rate of interest.

The money markets operate both as a **primary market**, in which new financial claims are issued and as a **secondary market**, where previously issued financial claims are traded.

Amounts dealt in are relatively large, generally being above £50,000 and often in millions of pounds. Loans are transacted on extremely 'fine' terms – i.e. with small margins between lending and borrowing rates – reflecting the **economies of scale** involved. The emphasis is on liquidity: the efficiency of the money markets can make the financial claims dealt in virtually the equivalent of cash.

## 2.10 Banks and the banking system

### 2.10.1 Introduction

There are different types of **banks** which operate within a banking system, and you will probably have come across a number of terms which describe them. **Commercial banks** make commercial banking transactions with customers. They are distinct from the country's **central bank**.

- **Clearing banks** are those that operate the clearing system for settling payments (e.g. payments by cheque by bank customers).

- The term **retail banks** is used to describe the traditional High Street banks. The term **wholesale banks** refers to banks which specialise in lending in large amounts to major customers. The clearing banks are involved in both retail and wholesale banking but are commonly regarded as the main retail banks.

- **Investment banks** offer services, often of a specialised nature, to corporate customers, including institutional investors such as pension schemes.

These categories are not mutually exclusive: a single bank may be a retail clearing bank, with wholesale and investment banking operations.

### 2.10.2 Banking reform

The **Vickers Report (2011)** of the **Independent Commission on Banking** considered the future of UK banking, in the wake of the late 2000s financial crisis. Stopping short of advocating a full-scale separation of 'High Street' banking from the banks' high-risk 'casino'-style investment banking activities, the Report recommended that the main UK banks be required to 'ring-fence' their retail banking operations within separate entities from their investment banking arms. The Financial Services (Banking Reform) Act 2013 (the **Banking Reform Act**) implements the Report's recommendations. The ring-fencing of retail and investment banking, which will be implemented along with stricter capital requirements for the banks, is intended to avoid financial losses in investment banking from de-stabilising a retail bank and thus possibly requiring a rescue at taxpayers' expense. The banks have until **2019** to complete the ring-fencing process.

## 2.11 Banks and building societies: indirect services

Retail banks and building societies offer various indirect services, including the following.

- **Stockbroking**. Many retail banks, and some building societies, have divisions which offer customers broking services for buying and selling securities including shares, gilts and bonds. ISAs are often offered as a wrapper for securities holdings.

- **Funds**. Some banks and building societies have subsidiaries that manage **unit trusts** and/or **open ended investment companies (OEICs)**, the two types of UK collective fund.

- **Portfolio management**. Most retail banks, although few building societies, offer a **discretionary portfolio management** service to manage portfolios on behalf of investors with substantial funds to invest in individual securities.

- **Pensions**. All the major retail banks and building societies offer pension products for customers' retirement savings.

- **Insurance**. Services available cover **life assurance** and also **general insurance** of various types, including car, household, travel and payment protection insurance.

## 2.12 Building societies

The **building societies** of the UK are **mutual** organisations whose main assets are mortgages of their members. Among their liabilities are the balances of the investor members who hold savings accounts with the society. The **Building Societies Act 1986** requires that at least **50%** of a building society's funds must be raised from share accounts held by individual members.

The distinction between building societies and banks has become increasingly blurred, as the societies have taken to providing a range of services formerly the province mainly of banks, and banks have themselves made inroads into the housing mortgage market. Some building societies now offer cheque book accounts, cash cards and many other facilities that compete directly with the banks.

The building society sector has shrunk in size over the last 20 years or so as a number of the major societies have either converted to public limited companies and therefore become banks or have been taken over by banks or other financial institutions.

## 2.13 The Bank of England

A **central bank** is a bank which acts on behalf of the government. The central bank for the UK is the **Bank of England ('BoE')**. The BoE is a nationalised corporation.

**Functions of the Bank of England**

(a)     The BoE acts as **banker to the central government** and holds the 'public deposits'. Public deposits include the National Loans Fund, the Consolidated Fund and the account of the Paymaster General, which in turn includes the Exchange Equalisation Account.

(b)     It is the **central note-issuing authority** in the UK – it is responsible for issuing bank notes in England.

(c)     It is the **manager of the National Debt** – i.e. it deals with long-term and short-term borrowing by the central government and the repayment of central government debt.

(d)     It is the manager of the Exchange Equalisation Account (i.e. the UK's **foreign currency reserves**).

(e)     It acts as adviser to the government on **monetary policy**.

(f)     The BoE's **Monetary Policy Committee (MPC)** acts as agent for the Government in carrying out its monetary policies. Since May 1997, the MPC has had operational responsibility for **setting short-term interest rates** at the level it considers appropriate in order to meet the Government's inflation target.

(g)     The BoE acts as a **lender to the banking system**. When the banking system is short of money, the BoE will provide the money the banks need – at a suitable rate of interest.

(h)     Under sweeping **regulatory reforms** instituted during **2013**, working with HM Treasury and other regulatory bodies, the BoE has a wide regulatory role, with responsibility to protect and enhance the stability of the UK financial system.

(i)     Under the 2013 regulatory reforms, the **Prudential Regulation Authority (PRA)** was created as a subsidiary of the BoE, with responsibility for prudential regulation of banks, building societies, insurers and larger investment firms. ('**Prudential regulation**' is concerned with overseeing whether financial institutions remain stable and with adequate liquidity of funds and capital.)

(j)     The **Financial Policy Committee (FPC)** of the Bank has been established under the regulatory reforms to monitor the stability and resilience of the financial system ('macro-prudential' regulation) and to make recommendations and directions to the regulatory bodies.

(k)     Following implementation of the Financial Services Act 2012, which re-structured the regulatory system creating the FCA, PRA, FPC and so on, the BoE gained new responsibilities as the **supervisor of financial market infrastructure providers** – these include recognised clearing houses (RCHs) central counterparties (CCPs), and settlement systems.

(l)     The BoE has the primary operational responsibility for **financial crisis management**. The Treasury has indicated that the Chancellor of the Exchequer would however retain the right to overrule the Bank of England Governor in a crisis.

## 2.14 The central bank as lender of last resort

In the UK, the **short-term money market** provides a link between the banking system and the government (Bank of England) whereby the Bank of England lends money to the banking system, when banks which need cash cannot get it from anywhere else.

(a)   The Bank will supply cash to the banking system on days when the banks have a cash shortage. It does this by buying eligible bills and other short-term financial investments from approved financial institutions in exchange for cash.

(b)   The Bank will remove excess cash from the banking system on days when the banks have a cash surplus. It does this by selling bills to institutions, so that the short-term money markets obtain interest-bearing bills in place of the cash that they do not want.

The process whereby this is done currently is known as **open market operations** by the Bank. This simply describes the buying and selling of short-term assets between the Bank and the short-term money market.

The Bank acted as lender of last resort to the bank Northern Rock, when the bank became unable to raise enough funds on the wholesale money markets during 2007.

## 2.15 Developments in the supply of financial products

As highlighted in the regulator's **Retail Conduct Risk Outlook** , financial firms have been affected by macroeconomic developments, market conditions and new regulation in various ways, as follows.

- **Banking** has been affected by the environment of low interest rates. This has especially affected those banks with a large back-book of tracker mortgages pegged close to the Bank Rate. Because of fierce competition for retail deposits and the withdrawal of traditional sources of income, banks are trying to develop alternative ways to generate profit, either by seeking to move customers into premium products or services, or by cutting costs aggressively.

- **Asset managers** are offering increasingly complex investment products and strategies to consumers searching for yield in the current low interest rate environment. Some of these products, the regulator argues, seek to address potentially incompatible consumer demands for both high yield and investment security.

- **Life insurers** are considering how to change their business models and product mix to alleviate pressures on their long-term prospects – for example, by targeting the changing needs of the pre-retirement market. They are also responding to a number of large-scale regulatory initiatives, which will have a significant effect on the way they do business, including the **Retail Distribution Review (RDR)**, which brought major changes for **retail financial advisers** from 31 December 2012.

- For **retail intermediaries**, recent economic conditions and pressures in the mortgage market have meant that many **mortgage intermediaries** have struggled to maintain income levels with many deciding to close their business. The number of firms whose primary business is home finance broking almost halved in the three years to December 2010. The number of **financial advisers** has also been falling.

The regulator's **Product Sales Data Trend Report** showed that total **sales of retail investment products** reached an annual low figure of 2.46 million in the year 2011/12. The most common products remained Personal Pensions (40.2%), followed by ISAs (17.5%), Decumulation Pensions (15.3%), Trusts and OEICs (9.1%), Bonds (7.4%), Occupational Pensions (6.9%), Endowments (2.6%), Structured Capital-At-Risk Products (SCARPs) (1%), and Long-term Care Insurance (well below 1%).

All firms are affected by various regulatory and public policy initiatives. In some cases (for example, the implementation of the Retail Distribution Review), **regulatory change** requires firms to radically change business models and strategy. This should bring benefits to most consumers, but it may also introduce new risks.

The regulator considers that one of the **major risks consumers face** is buying and being sold unsuitable products – everything from products that are too risky for them, to products they do not understand or that do not meet their individual circumstances.

Early intervention to try and stop issues escalating into mass consumer detriment is one of the main objectives of the regulator's conduct agenda, particularly as it developed the approach of the FSA's successor body, the **Financial**

**Conduct Authority (FCA)**, which was formally established as the UK's conduct regulator in the major 2013 restructuring of the UK financial regulatory system. Under the new regulatory structure, the FCA took over from the FSA its responsibility for **conduct regulation** – i.e. making rules to govern how financial firms conduct their business. The separation of **prudential regulation** (governing stability and capital strength, as defined earlier) and **conduct regulation** is often referred to as the 'twin peaks' model of regulation.

In its **Risk Outlook and Business Plan 2014/15**, the **FCA** identified the following seven forward-looking **areas of focus**, based on its assessment of underlying and environmental drivers of risk, and of cross-market pressures.

- **Technological developments may outstrip firms' investment, consumer capabilities, and the regulatory response**. Risks include over-reliance on outsourced functions, threats to consumer protection from the use of digital platforms, including financial crime risks.

- **Poor culture and controls continue to threaten market integrity**. The FCA is concerned about the effect that poor culture in wholesale markets may have on market integrity, and knock-on effects for retail markets.

- **Large back-books may lead firms to act against their existing customers' best interests**. Firms might over-rely existing back-book customers to bolster profitability, e.g. by cross-selling products to existing customers, taking advantage of inertia by offering existing customers worse terms, and by making it difficult to switch between products.

- **Retirement income products and distribution may deliver poor consumer outcomes**. The regulator considers it paramount that consumers understand the choices available to them at retirement.

- **The growth of consumer credit may lead to unaffordable debt**. Household debt remains relatively high and growing, and the FCA is concerned about the sustainability of debt for some borrowers, for example in areas of credit card debt, overdrafts, and short-term credit such as 'payday lending'.

- **Terms and conditions may be excessively complex**. The regulator will monitor: the understanding that consumers have of the degree of protection they have (e.g. on insured risks); barriers to exiting a product that may be unclear to consumers at the outset; complicated terms making product comparisons difficult; and the trade-off between the length of documents and the need to explain clearly complex terms and conditions.

- **Substantial and rapid house price growth may give rise to conduct issues**. The FCA is concerned that consumers may take on additional debt to buy property or to extract equity if, with house price growth, they believe that prices will keep on rising. The regulator will monitor affordability, standards of underwriting, prudential pressures on firms, the treatment of consumers in negative equity, increased demand for non-mainstream credit, and withdrawals from products.

The FCA published its **Business Plan 2015/16** in March 2015, and this Plan contained the following key elements.

- The FCA's new supervision and authorisations divisions operated under a new structure announced in December 2014, and the regulator has identified as priority areas continued work on understanding how well the pension and mortgage markets are working for consumers, and intervening where it identifies potential detriment.

- The FCA intends to make active use of its competition powers, and will conduct planned market studies into competition in wholesale and investment banking, the use of 'big data' in the insurance sector, and charges in asset management.

# 3 The international context

## 3.1 The UK's position in the world

The financial services industry is a key sector of the UK economy. The UK financial services industry employs over 1 million people and net overseas earnings from the industry amount to over 5% of national output or GDP.

With a long history going back to the time of merchant adventurers who sought finance for world-wide overseas trading, the 'Square Mile' of the **City of London** is the centre for the UK financial services industry. The City is the largest centre for many international financial markets, such as the currency markets. The UK has the world's largest share in the metals market (95%), Eurobond trade (70%), the foreign equity market (58%), derivatives markets (36%) and insurance (22%).

## 3.2 Banking

While there are over 300 **banking** groups and building societies operating in the UK, the ten largest UK-owned banking groups hold some 70% of UK households' deposits. Building societies hold over 20% of household deposits.

The UK has the greatest concentration of foreign banks, numbering around 500 compared with around 300 in the USA, in the world. London accounts for 19% of global cross-border bank lending, more than any other financial centre. The total assets of the UK banking system exceed £3,000 billion of which approximately 55% belongs to foreign banks. The assets of UK-owned banks, totalling around £1,300 billion, are dominated by around a dozen retail banks, with national branch networks serving domestic, personal and corporate customers.

The banks and building societies form a significant part of the market for financial services. A banking institution could maintain access to a full range of products and product providers by setting up an independent arm. However, few have maintained a wholly independent stance. Most have either formed tied links to life insurance companies ('life offices') or have acquired or set up their own insurance companies which mainly or wholly offer products to clients introduced through the bank or building society.

## 3.3 Insurance

UK **life insurance companies** sell various products within the UK retail market, including collective investment schemes such as unit trusts, OEICs and investment trusts, pension products and individual life insurance. The development of life assurance provision by **banks** is known as **bancassurance** or **all finanz**. The Association of British Insurers (ABI) defines **bancassurers** as 'insurance companies that are subsidiaries of banks and building societies and whose primary market is the customer base of the bank or building society'.

The UK has a major **general insurance** and **reinsurance** market ranging from personal motor insurance to insurance for space satellites. Reinsurance is a process by which a company – for example, a life office writing new business – can sell or pass on the risks on its policies to a third party **reinsurer**.

The UK insurance business generates premium income in the UK insurance market of over £170 billion annually. This makes the third largest such market in the world, exceeded only by the US and Japan. The London market – centred on **Lloyds** of London – is the global market leader in aviation and marine insurance, with market shares of 31% and 19% respectively.

**Lloyds** acts as a major reinsurer for life assurance. Lloyds is a long-established market in which **underwriting syndicates** operate independently. Syndicates are made up of companies and individuals (**Lloyds 'names'**) who provide capital and assume the risk of liabilities they insure or reinsure. Syndicates are run by **managing agents** who appoint **underwriters** to write (assess) risks on behalf of the syndicate.

## 3.4 Pensions

With a rapidly ageing population, there is a **pensions crisis** worldwide. Many countries are passing the pensions provision from the state sector to the private sector.

Domestically, the UK pensions market is of great importance, and a higher proportion of pension payments are provided by the private sector in the UK than in nearly any other country.

## 3.5 Fund and asset management

Collective funds such as unit trusts and investment trusts need to be managed. In the **fund management** sector, the value of assets under management exceeds £3 billion. Around one quarter of these funds were managed on behalf of overseas clients. The UK fund management sector offers liquid markets, with the opportunity to trade in large blocks of shares, and a relatively liberalised operating environment combined with protection against abuse. More funds are invested in the London than the ten top European centres combined. Edinburgh is the UK's second major fund management centre and is the sixth largest in Europe.

## 3.6 Securities and currency markets

As well as having a substantial domestic market in **equities** (company shares) and **bonds** (interest-bearing securities), the UK is a major international centre for trading in the Euromarket, which is the market for debt denominated in other currencies – not just the euro. Eurobonds account for the majority of all bonds issued and the UK issues 60% of them and has a 70% share of the secondary market.

More **foreign companies** are traded on the London Stock Exchange than on any other exchange. Turnover in these companies' shares in London represents approximately half of global turnover in foreign equities.

The UK has over around one-third of the global market in **currency trading**, making London the leading world centre for foreign exchange ('forex') trading.

## 3.7 International regulatory challenges

### 3.7.1 The financial markets crisis

The Financial Stability Forum (FSF) was a body made up of authorities from various major countries and international institutions. After the April 2009 G20 Summit in London, the FSF became the **Financial Stability Board (FSB)**. In April 2008, the FSF reported on the recent turmoil in financial markets.

The FSF's report noted that the turmoil that broke out in the summer of 2007 followed an exceptional boom in **credit growth** and **leverage** in the financial system. A long period of **benign economic and financial conditions** had increased the amount of risk that borrowers and investors were willing to take on. Institutions responded, expanding the market for securitisation of credit risk and aggressively developing the **'originate and distribute' model**: institutions originating loans then distributed them as packaged securities. The system became increasingly dependent on originators' underwriting standards and the performance of credit rating agencies.

By the summer of 2008, accumulating losses on securities linked with US **subprime mortgages** were triggering widespread disruption to the global financial system. Large losses were sustained on complex structured securities. Institutions reduced leverage and increased demand for liquid assets. Many credit markets became illiquid, hindering credit extension.

Eight months after the start of the market turmoil, many financial institutions' balance sheets were burdened by assets that have suffered major declines in value and vanishing market liquidity. Market participants were reluctant to transact in these instruments, adding to increased financial and macroeconomic uncertainty.

## 7.2 Steps to re-establish confidence

To re-establish confidence in the soundness of markets and financial institutions the FSF authorities began to take exceptional steps with a view to facilitating adjustment and **dampening the impact on the real economy**. These steps have included **monetary and fiscal stimulus**, **central bank liquidity operations**, policies to **promote asset market liquidity** and actions to **resolve problems at specific institutions**. Financial institutions have taken steps to rebuild capital and liquidity cushions.

Even with these measures in place, the financial system and world economies remained under great stress. While national authorities may continue to consider short-term policy responses should conditions warrant it, the FSF has proposed the following **further steps** to restore confidence in the soundness of markets and institutions:

- Strengthened prudential oversight of capital, liquidity and risk management
- Enhancing transparency and valuation of financial instruments
- Changes in the role and uses of credit ratings
- Strengthening the authorities' responsiveness to risks
- More robust arrangements for dealing with stress in the financial system

Some would argue that the financial crisis of the late 2000s has revealed various shortcomings in the **oversight of financial markets and institutions**. There are likely to be changes at national and international levels along the lines proposed by the FSF to seek to address these issues.

## 3.7.3 Regulatory consequences in Europe

The turmoil in markets heightened focus on the debate about how European regulatory initiatives were organised, through the **Lamfalussy** four-step process. Some believe that too much was entrusted to its 'Level Three' committees which bring together regulators from each country to agree on the details of implementing directives and to coordinate wider efforts, such as the supervision of cross-border institutions such as investment banks. Changes under the **Financial Services Action Plan (FSAP)** meant that the three committees, for banking, insurance and securities regulators, have wielded substantial power in how rules are applied.

Recent changes the EU has agreed to the structure of regulatory and supervisory cooperation include the new **European Systemic Risk Board (ESRB)** that was set up in January 2011.

Operating at arm's length from the European Central Bank (ECB), the **ESRB** has powers to issue warnings and recommendations on threats to economies and financial systems. The ESRB has 37 voting members, including the 27 EU countries' central bank governors, the ECB President and ECB Vice-President, and the chairmen of the following three new **pan-European Supervisory Authorities (ESAs)** covering banking, insurance and securities markets, which replace the earlier Lamfalussy Level 3 committees.

- **European Banking Authority (EBA)** – based in London
- **European Securities and Markets Authority (ESMA)** – based in Paris
- **European Insurance and Occupational Pensions Authority (EIOPA)** – based in Frankfurt

# 4 The role of the UK Government

## 4.1 Introduction

There are various ways in which Government actions impinge on people's lives and on the activities of businesses. Legislation introduced by Parliament often gives authority for Government departments to introduce secondary legislation in the form of additional regulations. Government agencies and local authorities affect our lives in many aspects, whether for example, through taxation or in the services they provide to us.

The extent to which the Government influences what we do reflects the type of economic system we have. The economic system of the UK and of the wider European Union to which the UK belongs can be described as a **mixed economy**. A mixed economy involves some degree of State intervention in economic activity, while mostly markets are allowed to operate as freely as possible so long as intervention is not needed in the public interest. This type of economy stands between the two extremes of a *laissez-faire* **free market economy** in which market forces are allowed to reign, with minimal State intervention, and of a centrally planned **command economy**, such as that of the former Soviet Union and other Communist-ruled States, in which the government controls most industries and regulates many prices and wages, possibly with a rationing system to distribute scarce goods and services.

There are various laws or pieces of legislation that affect the provision of financial services in the UK, and the regulation of the industry is of key importance. In this section, we also outline the Government's role in taxation, economic policy-making and the promotion of welfare and the provision of benefits.

## 4.2 Regulation of the financial services industry

Consumer protection in the financial services industry and other consumer markets became an increasingly important aspect of UK Governments' policy from the 1970s onwards. The Financial Services Act 1986 (FSA 1986) was brought in to replace the system of **self-regulation** which had previously prevailed in the UK financial sector.

The FSA 1986 brought a new system of **self-regulation within a statutory framework**, with financial services firms authorised by Self-Regulatory Organisations (SROs).

When the Labour Party gained power in 1997, it wanted to make changes to the regulation of financial services. A series of **financial scandals**, including those involving the Maxwell Group, Barings Bank, BCCI and pensions mis-selling, had added weight to the political impetus for change, leading to the establishment of the Financial Services Authority (FSA).

## 4.3 FSA, and its successors: FCA and PRA

The **FSA** was set up as the single statutory regulator of the financial services industry, under the **Financial Services and Markets Act 2000 (FSMA 2000)**. This Act brought together the regulation of investment, insurance and banking. Giving **financial advice on investments** became a regulated activity under the new statutory regime from 1 December 2001 (a date known as 'N2').

The FSA was not set up as a government agency, but it carried out the work of statutory regulation. **HM Treasury** has overseen the activities of the FSA, and so the **Chancellor of the Exchequer**, the Cabinet Minister responsible for all economic and financial matters, was ultimately responsible for the system of regulation for the financial services industry.

The Financial Services Act 2012 has made substantial amendments to FSMA 2000, putting into effect a major re-structuring of the regulation of the UK financial sector. As part of the re-structuring, on 1 April 2013, the FSA was replaced by the new **Financial Conduct Authority (FCA)** – which is accountable to HM Treasury – and the **Prudential Regulation Authority (PRA)** – as already mentioned, a subsidiary of the Bank of England.

## 4.4 Voluntary codes and statutory regulation

In some areas, financial services providers are subject to **voluntary codes**, which an industry sector develops itself, rather than rules imposed through the law (statutory rules). The area of banking can be taken as an example. The PRA regulates banks' status as authorised deposit-taking institutions, and supervises the banks' liquidity and capital adequacy. The FCA regulates the conduct of business of the banks, for example in respect of retail banking accounts. However, many banks and building societies also follow a voluntary code (the **Lending Code**), which sets standards of good lending practice.

Clearly, statutory regulation can be extended by the Government to areas previously governed by voluntary codes. For example, **mortgage advice and selling**, previously governed by the voluntary Mortgage Code, came under regulation in October 2004. **General insurance** regulation followed in January 2005.

## 4.5 Fiscal policy

A government's **fiscal policy** concerns its plans for **spending, taxation and borrowing**.

These aspects of fiscal policy reflect the three elements in public finance.

(a) **Expenditure**. The government, at a national and local level, spends money to provide goods and services, such as a health service, public education, a police force, roads, public buildings and so on, and to pay its administrative work force. It may also, perhaps, provide finance to encourage investment by private industry, for example by means of grants.

(b) **Income**. Expenditure must be financed, and the government must have income. Most government income comes from taxation, but some income is obtained from direct charges to users of government services such as National Health Service charges.

(c) **Borrowing**. To the extent that a government's expenditure exceeds its income, it must borrow to make up the difference. The amount that the government must borrow each year is known as the **Public Sector Net Cash Requirement (PSNCR)** in the UK.

Government **spending is an injection** into the economy, adding to the level of overall demand for goods and services, whereas **taxes are a withdrawal**.

A government's **fiscal stance** may be **neutral, expansionary** or **contractionary**, according to its overall effect on national income.

(a) **Spending more money** and financing this expenditure by borrowing would indicate an expansionary fiscal stance. Expenditure in the economy will increase and so national income will rise, either in real terms, or partly in terms of price levels only: the increase in national income might be real, or simply inflationary.

(b) **Collecting more in taxes** without increasing spending would indicate a contractionary fiscal stance. A government might deliberately raise taxation to take inflationary pressures out of the economy

The impact of changes in fiscal policy is not always certain, and fiscal policy to pursue one aim (e.g. lower inflation) might for a while create barriers to the pursuit of other aims (e.g. employment).

Government planners need to consider how fiscal policy can affect savers, investors and companies.

(a) The tax regime as it affects different savings instruments will affect **investors'** decisions.

(b) **Companies** will be affected by tax rules on dividends and profits, and they may take these rules into account when deciding on dividend policy or on whether to raise finance through **debt** (loans) or **equities** (by issuing shares).

The formal planning of fiscal policy usually follows an annual cycle. In the UK, the most important statement is **the Budget**, which takes place in the Spring of each year. The Chancellor of the Exchequer also delivers a Pre-Budget Report each Autumn. The Pre-Budget Report formally makes available for scrutiny the Government's overall spending plans.

# 4.6 Monetary policy

## 4.6.1 Overview

**Monetary policy** is the area of government economic policy making that is concerned with changes in the **amount of money** in circulation – the **money supply** – and with changes in the **price of money** – **interest rates**. These variables are linked with **inflation** in prices generally, and also with **exchange rates** – the price of the domestic currency in terms of other currencies.

## 4.6.2 Setting interest rates

Since 1997, the most important aspect of monetary policy in the UK has been the influence over interest rates exerted by the **Bank of England**, the **central bank** of the UK. The **Monetary Policy Committee (MPC)** of the Bank of England was charged with the responsibility of setting interest rates with the aim of meeting the government's inflation target of **2%, plus or minus 1%** as measured by the **Consumer Prices Index (CPI)**. Inflation below the target of 2% is judged by the Bank of England to be unsatisfactory, as is inflation above the target.

The **UK inflation objective** was originally formalised in the **Bank of England Act 1998**. That Act states that the Bank of England is expected 'to maintain price stability, and, subject to that, to support the economic policy of HM Government including its objectives for growth and employment'.

The MPC decides the short-term **benchmark 'repo' rate** at which the Bank of England deals in the money markets. This will tend to be followed by financial institutions generally in setting interest rates for different financial instruments. However, a government does not have an unlimited ability to have interest rates set how it wishes. It must take into account what rates the overall market will bear, so that the benchmark rate it chooses can be maintained. The Bank must be careful about the signals it gives to the markets, since the effect of expectations can be significant.

The monthly minutes of the MPC are published. This arrangement is intended to remove the possibility of direct political influence over the interest rate decision.

The Bank of England **reducing** interest rates is an **easing** of monetary policy.

(a)     Loans will be cheaper, and so consumers may increase levels of debt and spend more. Demand will tend to rise and companies may have improved levels of sales. Companies will find it cheaper to borrow: their lower interest costs will boost bottom-line profits.

(b)     Mortgage loans will be cheaper and so there will be upward pressure on property prices.

(c)     Values of other assets will also tend to rise. Investors will be willing to pay higher prices for gilts (government stock) because they do not require such a high yield from them as before the interest rate reduction.

(d)     Interest rates on cash deposits will fall. Those who are dependant on income from cash deposits will be worse off than before.

The Bank of England **increasing** interest rates is a **tightening** of monetary policy.

(a)     Loans will cost more, and demand from consumers, especially for less essential 'cyclical' goods and services, may fall. Companies will find it more expensive to borrow money and this could eat into profits, on top of any effect from reducing demand.

(b)     Mortgage loans will cost more and so there will be a dampening effect on property prices.

(c)     Asset prices generally will tend to fall. Investors will require a higher return than before and so they will pay less for fixed interest stocks such as gilts.

(d)     Interest rates on cash deposits will rise, and those reliant on cash deposits for income will be better off.

### 4.6.3 Money market operations

The central bank puts monetary policy into effect by controlling interest rates and the supply of money through **open market operations**. The bank will satisfy the market's demand for liquid **'base' money** at its target interest rate by buying and selling government securities (in the UK, 'gilts'). For example, if there is an increase in demand for base money, the central bank may act to maintain short term interest rates by buying government securities. New base money will be credited to the sellers' bank accounts, thus increasing the total amount of base money in the economy. When the central bank, conversely, sells government securities, it mops up money from the buyers' bank accounts and base money is withdrawn from the economy.

**Quantitative easing (QE)** is a term given to the method by which the central bank (in the UK, the Bank of England) manipulates liquidity in the financial system. This allows adjustments to the **money supply** when the interbank interest rate is at or close to zero, and interest rates can therefore no longer be lowered.

Although this process is sometimes characterised as 'printing money', it actually involves the central bank purchasing mostly short-term financial assets using money it has created *ex nihilo* ('out of nothing') and has shown as a credit in the central bank's books. The new money is intended to increase the overall money supply through deposit multiplication, as the institutions receiving the money will be encouraged to lend and the cost of borrowing will be reduced.

The effect of QE can be direct and indirect. The direct effect is to raise the price and lower the yield of the assets purchased. The indirect effects are to raise the price and lower the yield of all other competing assets, thereby lowering the cost of capital to companies. Also, through the banking multiplier, banks are able to increase their lending by a multiple of their increased cash balances at the Bank of England. However, if the markets fear an upsurge in inflation, any beneficial effects may be short-lived.

### 4.6.4 Quantitative easing and investment strategy

There are differing interpretations of the **implications of QE for investment strategy**. The immediate impact may be favourable to gilts and other bonds purchased, raising their prices and lowering yields. If there is a flow through to other asset classes, it may also produce gains to equities and property (the process referred to as 'portfolio balance'), particularly if there is a macro-economic stimulus produced by increased bank lending. The diversification effect is also seen as an outflow into emerging markets, accompanied by a fall in the home currency.

An alternative scenario is that the effect is minimal, producing a small but temporary basis point cut in interest rates but negligible increase in demand because the problem in bank lending was a demand constraint, or because banks were still unwillingly to lend due to increased risk aversion. This interpretation was applied to Japan in the early 2000s.

## 4.7 Exchange rate policy

The **exchange rate** of the national currency (pounds sterling) against other major currencies (such as the US dollar, the euro and the Japanese yen) is another possible focus of economic policy.

The Government could try to influence exchange rates by buying or selling currencies through its central bank reserves. However, Government currency reserves are now relatively small and so such a policy might have to be limited in scope.

Another way the Government might wish to influence exchange rates is through changes in **interest rates**: if UK interest rates are raised, this makes sterling a relatively more attractive currency to hold and so the change should exert upward pressure on the value of sterling. As we have seen, interest rate policy is now determined by the MPC. Interest rate policy is decided in the light of various matters apart from exchange rates, including the inflation rate and the level of house prices.

If the UK joined the **single European currency**, the **euro**, interest rates would be largely determined at the European level, instead of at the national level as now. Currently, the Government has no plan to initiate a new assessment on

whether the UK should join the euro. In 2009, investors became concerned about rising government debt levels across the globe and a wave of downgrading of government debt downgrades in a number of eurozone countries. The problems led to speculation that the common currency could collapse, even though sovereign (government) debt increases have been most significant in only a few eurozone countries. In mid-2010, European finance ministers approved the European Financial Stability Facility (EFSF), a rescue package worth €750 billion. More measures followed to try to restore confidence and prevent a collapse of national economies.

# 4.8 Industrial policy

## 4.8.1 Overview

While macroeconomic policy-making is concerned with the economy as a while, industrial policy is focused on particular sectors of the economy. The UK government current's approach to industrial policy aims to create an institutional framework that allows businesses to prosper, and individuals and households to improve steadily their living standards.

The institutional framework has the following aims:

- Promoting effective competition.
- Flexibility in labour and capital markets.
- Maintaining a legal system which gives confidence and trust to market participants.
- Providing a stable macroeconomic framework.

Other aspects of UK policy concentrate on the advance and commercial application of scientific knowledge, and investment in physical infrastructure, education and health. **Innovation policies** seek to balance the benefits of intellectual property protection with facilitating the widespread exploitation of new knowledge through, among other things, easing barriers to the widespread dissemination and adoption of ideas.

Underpinning this approach is a presumption that, as a whole, the effective operations of markets are a better way of bringing about improvements to business efficiency and the most economically beneficial allocation of capital, knowledge and employment. Government is however seen to have a role where **market failures** arise, for example, in the provision of 'merit goods' such as education and healthcare services, and overcoming externalities through policies on science, skills, innovation and regulation.

Responsibility for the various themes of industrial policy is spread across difference central Government departments, although the **Department for Business, Innovation and Skills** plays a key role.

## 4.8.2 Industry policy and the European Union

The UK works with the European Commission and other EU Member States to address from the European perspective issues that are confronting all industrialised countries – the challenges laid down by globalisation, including for example the intense competition from growing economies like China and India, the greater fragmentation and wider dispersion of supply chains and increased pressures on industrial and local adjustment in relation to our international competitiveness, and energy and climate change.

**Actions under the EU Policy agenda**

- A commitment to focus on economic growth and employment.

- Shaping policies to allow businesses to create more and better jobs implemented in a way that balances and mutually reinforce economic, environmental and social objectives.

- An integrated approach aimed at improving the coherence between different policy dimensions and increasing their relevance to business.

- Bringing business directly into the process through the establishment of 'High Level Groups'.

These High Level groups bring together members of the various European Commission Directorates General, Member State Governments and relevant stakeholders from industry, consumers/civil society, trade unions, Non-Governmental Organisations and regulators and are mandated to provide advice to policy makers at Community and national levels, industry and civil society organisations on issues effecting European industrial competitiveness.

## 4.9 State aid and State ownership

**State aid** in the form of governmental subsidies may be used to protect particular industries or vulnerable companies. An example is the subsidies benefiting farmers in many First world countries. The United States currently pays around $20 billion annually to farmers in direct subsidies as 'farm income stabilization'. Agricultural subsidies to European farmers make up more than 40% of the EU's budget. Many would argue that the Common Agricultural Policy of the European Union distorts trade.

The UK Government is limited in what State aid it can provide because favouring particular companies or industries could fall foul of European competition law. State aid can be regarded as a type of protectionism or trade barrier as it makes domestic goods and services artificially competitive against imports.

**State ownership** in various industries was once a major aspect of the UK economy. However, most of the former nationalised industries were 'privatised' under the Governments of Margaret Thatcher in the 1980s and earlier 1990s. The rationale behind the privatisations was that industries would be better run under private ownership, and the privatisation programme also provided an opportunity to widen share ownership by encouraging individuals to take up share offers in the newly privatised companies.

Although UK Labour Governments in power from 1997 to 2010 did not pursue a policy of encouraging State ownership, the Government did use State ownership and State aid as part of its measures to deal with the credit and banking crisis of the late 2000s. The crisis resulted in the nationalisation of the banks Northern Rock and Bradford & Bingley, and the launching of a £37 billion banking support initiative for three other major banking groups in the UK. On the other side of the Atlantic, the US Government also launched 'bail-out' initiatives in an effort to stabilise the crisis-hit financial sector and, in spite of a political climate that is generally hostile to nationalisation, took a majority ownership in the major car manufacturer General Motors, which had filed for bankruptcy.

## 4.10 Welfare and State benefits

Maximising the **welfare** of its citizens is, on the face of it, a potentially positive objective for a Government to have. But how is this to be achieved? Is it desirable to have policies which attempt to equalise welfare levels among the population, or should market forces be allowed to operate freely even if this results in a relatively unequal distribution of wealth between people?

We have outlined the **mixed economy model** of countries like the UK. In such a system, should the State provide a **'safety net'** to protect those who are least advantaged? If so, how can the Government provide **benefits** in such a way that people's incentive to work or to save is not removed by the benefit system of benefits? All of these questions are the subject of political debate in democratic countries.

The UK underwent great change with the introduction of the so-called **Welfare State** after World War II. Health care for all was provided through the National Health Service. Benefits have been provided for the jobless, for example **Jobseeker's allowance**.

**Child benefit** was, for many years, paid irrespective of the recipient's income or wealth. However, 'means-testing' of this benefit, with a phase-out of the benefit for couples one of whom earns more than £50,000, was introduced in 2013. Other benefits include **incapacity benefit** and **disability benefits**.

**Income Support** exists as a top-up of the income of those under 60 whose income from all sources is below a minimum threshold level set by Parliament. **Working tax credit** and **child tax credit** are also available.

The **Welfare Reform Act 2012** makes major changes to the benefits system. A new single-payment **Universal Credit (UC)** is being introduced across the UK over the period from **October 2013 to the end of 2017**. When fully introduced, the **UC** will replace various existing benefits, as explained in Chapter 2.

A basic **State pension** is paid to those who have paid sufficient National Insurance contributions and is supplemented by **pension credit** for those with limited means.

The **State Second Pension (S2P)** is aimed at providing improved pensions, particularly for the lower paid, compared with the **State Earnings Related Pensions Scheme (SERPS)** which S2P has replaced. Employees have been able to opt out or '**contract out**' of S2P through low-charging stakeholder pensions: however, contracting-out was abolished on 6 April 2012, except for salary-related work-based pension schemes. The S2P benefit is becoming a flat rate benefit over a period of time. **Self-employed** individuals do not accrue S2P benefits.

In spite of the Government's wish for people to make their own retirement provision and not to rely wholly on State provision, there are still many who have not made any private pension arrangement. **Auto-enrolment**, which is being phased in over the period 2012-2017, means that employees will be automatically enrolled into a qualifying pension by their employer, unless the worker opts out. However, pension plans are only one way of saving for retirement: ISAs, for example, are an alternative.

Financial advisers need to be aware of the availability of State benefits as part of the overall financial circumstances of clients, and Chapter 2 of this Study Text explains more about many of the various benefits available.

# 5 The European Union

## 5.1 Introduction

The **European Union (EU)**, formerly called the EEC or the European Community (EC), is one of several international economic associations. Its immediate aim is the integration of the economies of the member states. A more long-term aim is political integration. The association dates back to 1957 (the Treaty of Rome) and the EU has grown to 28 member States, including the UK.

## 5.2 UK sovereignty and EU membership

UK Statute law is made by Parliament (or in exercise of law-making powers delegated by Parliament). Until the United Kingdom entered the European Community in 1973, the UK Parliament was completely **sovereign**.

Membership of the EU has restricted the previously unfettered power of Parliament. There is an **obligation**, imposed by the Treaty of Rome on which the EU is founded, to bring UK law into line with the Treaty itself and with EU Directives. Regulations, having the force of law in every member state, may be made under provisions of the Treaty of Rome.

## 5.3 The Single European Market

Under the Single European Act 1986, the EC heads of government committed themselves to the progressive setting-up of a **Single European Market**. The Act defines a single market as 'an area without internal frontiers in which the free movement of goods, persons, services and capital is ensured in accordance with the provisions of this Treaty'.

The process of establishing a single market in financial services was advanced in November 2007 with the introduction of the **Markets in Financial Instruments Directive (MiFID)**. However, it is debatable whether the Single European Market project has been successful overall.

**Problems in creating a full Single European Market**

- Failure of some member States to implement some Directives fully and on time
- Lack of enforcement action against member States that do not comply
- Unwillingness of customers to deal with foreign service providers
- Failure to integrate cross-border settlement and clearing processes
- Legal and cultural differences between member States
- Protectionist measures by some member States

## 5.4 EU law

**EU legislation** takes the following three forms.

- **Regulations** have the force of law in every EU state without need of national legislation. Their objective is to obtain uniformity of law throughout the EU. They are formulated by the Commission but must be authorised by the Council of Ministers.

- **Directives** are issued to the governments of the EU member states requiring them within a specified period (usually two years) to alter the national laws of the state so that they conform to the directive. Until a Directive is given effect by a UK statute it does not usually affect legal rights and obligations of individuals.

- **Decisions** of an administrative nature are made by the European Commission in Brussels. A decision may be addressed to a state, person or a company and is immediately binding, but only on the recipient.

The Council and the Commission may also make recommendations and deliver opinions, although these are only persuasive in authority.

# Key chapter points

- In this chapter, we have looked at the place of the UK financial services industry in the national economy, and at wider influences on the industry exerted by government.

- Financial intermediaries such as banks and building societies take deposits from savers and re-lend to borrowers. Financial intermediation brings benefits from aggregation and maturity transformation.

- Financial services products can offer access to diversified portfolios of assets at relatively low cost.

- Capital markets, such as the Stock Exchange, are markets for long-term capital. Money markets are shorter term debt markets in which banks and other financial institutions deal mainly with each other, on a wholesale basis.

- The UK financial services industry employs over 1 million people in the UK and accounts for around 5% of national output. Key areas are banking, life insurance, general insurance, pensions, fund and asset management, currency markets and securities markets.

- In 2001, the UK Government established the Financial Services Authority as the overall regulator of the financial services industry. The successor bodies to the FSA under 2013 regulatory reforms are the Prudential Regulation Authority (PRA) and the Financial Conduct Authority (FCA).

- The financial crisis of the late 2000s highlighted severe strains in the global financial system. Policy steps taken in different countries included monetary and fiscal stimulus, central bank liquidity operations, policies to promote asset market liquidity, and actions to resolve problems at specific institutions.

- The Government plays a role in economic and industrial policy, regulation, taxation and social welfare. Regulatory interventions seek to avoid or provide remedies for cases of market failure, thus protecting consumers and providing free and fair markets. Economic policy encompasses monetary policy (particularly through interest rates), fiscal policy (public spending and taxation) and exchange rate policy (occasional intervention ion currency markets).

- European Union legislation has an increasing importance, and takes precedence over UK law.

## Chapter Quiz

1   Identify the three main sectors of the domestic economy. ........................................................ (see para 1.2)

2   Outline the benefits of financial intermediation. ................................................................................(1.4)

3   Distinguish between capital markets and money markets. ....................................................................(2.1)

4   State four functions of the Bank of England. .................................................................................... (2.13)

5   Under what Act of Parliament is the UK system of financial regulation established? ........................................(4.3)

6   What is fiscal policy? .........................................................................................................................(4.5)

7   Describe the mechanism whereby short-term UK interest rates are set in line with Government policy. .......(4.6.2)

8   What are the three types of provision in EU law? ...............................................................................(5.4)

chapter

# 2

## Financial services and the retail consumer

## CHAPTER LEARNING OUTCOMES

2.  **Understand how the retail consumer is served by the financial services industry**

    2.1   **Explain** the obligations that the financial services industry has towards consumers.

    2.2   **Explain** consumers' main financial needs and how these may be prioritised and met.

# 1 Serving retail customers

## 1.1 Overview

Authorised **firms** have an obligation to abide by the regulators' **Principles for Businesses** and **detailed rules**, as set out in the FCA and PRA Handbooks, in their dealings with consumers. Over-arching principles include the requirement to treat customers fairly, while detailed rules cover many areas, including disclosures to be made to customers.

Beyond these requirements, firms will clearly serve themselves best if they work hard to maintain and enhance the **reputation** of the firm and of the financial services industry among consumers.

The **Retail Distribution Review (RDR)**, which we describe later in this chapter, is an initiative which has brought – since its implementation on **31 December 2012** – major changes to arrangements for retail financial advice giving that are intended to enhance **consumers' confidence** in using financial services.

## 1.2 Consumers' ethical perceptions

In DP 18 *An Ethical Framework for Financial Services* (2002), the regulator (the FSA, at that time) recognised that consumers are increasingly understanding an ethical stance.

- Professional conduct and ethical behaviour could **strengthen the level of confidence** enjoyed by the industry.

- On the other hand, if consumers have **diminishing trust** in the sector and in individual firms, they will hesitate to use the products and services available.

Furthermore, there is increasing pressure from consumers and Government to 'put something back'. An example of this is the growing interest in policies to combat **social exclusion**, particularly from a financial standpoint.

**Financial exclusion** has been defined as: 'the inability, difficulty or reluctance of particular groups to access mainstream financial services' (McKillop and Wilson, 'Financial Exclusion', *Public Money and Management*, 2007). Access to financial services may be limited, for example, by firms closing branches, by strict credit history or identity requirements, or by lower-income people being priced out of services. Because financial exclusion can lead to social exclusion, reducing financial exclusion has been a priority of government.

Higher business and individual standards of behaviour promoting the integrity and the general probity of all working in financial services will, the regulator believes, enhance public perceptions and trust in the firms and individuals concerned.

## 1.3 Customer trust and confidentiality

The consumer must have every reason to **trust** a financial adviser. Trust is gained through respect, and an adviser will be able to project the attitudes needed by professional presentation at all times, and through the way the adviser deals with customers.

Acting as a professional means that it should be clear in the way business is conducted that all relevant regulations are being adhered to. Regulations exist to **protect the consumer**, and a client will be reassured if there is no suggestion that regulatory rules might be breached.

If the adviser is trusted, the client will be more open about his or her circumstances, and a more satisfactory basis for giving financial advice will be created. The adviser must always treat personal information with the utmost **confidentiality**.

Regarding confidentiality, all professional people need to be aware of the provisions of the **Proceeds of Crime Act 2002**. This Act requires a professional to disclose to the relevant authorities any information regarding possible crimes having been committed. These provisions mean that, by law, there are some circumstances – for example, if an adviser became aware of tax evasion having been committed – in which the professional requirement of confidentiality is overridden by the statutory requirement to breach that confidentiality by informing the authorities.

## 1.4 The adviser's fiduciary duty

The regulatory system codifies many obligations and many of the expectations that apply to professional investment advisers. Even if the various obligations had not been codified through written regulations and regulator's principles, the adviser may still owe a fiduciary duty to his or her client.

A decision in the Federal Court of Australia – *Australian Securities and Investment Commission v Citigroup Global Markets (2007)* – could be persuasive in UK courts. In that decision, the court held that the parties' rights and liabilities could be excluded or modified by the terms of the contract between the parties (although **unfair terms regulations** discussed below would affect exclusions in consumer contracts). Citigroup's letter of engagement with a company it was advising had excluded any fiduciary relationship, and that exclusion was found to be effective by the court. The court stressed that, where there were **no explicit contractual exclusion or alteration**, a court would be likely to find that **a financial adviser has a fiduciary duty** towards its client.

An **adviser's fiduciary responsibility** implies that the adviser ought not to take advantage of a client's trust in him or her. The adviser (or firm) agrees to act in the sole interests of the client, to the exclusion of his or her own interests.

- The adviser's fiduciary duty implies that the adviser should act so as to avoid an influence being exerted by any conflict of interest the adviser may have.

- The adviser must make a full and fair disclosure of material facts, particularly where there may be a conflict of interest.

- In fulfilling his or her fiduciary duty, the adviser must always act in the client's best interests. This is codified in the regulators' **client's best interests rule**.

The **client's best interests rule** (in the COBS Sourcebook within the regulatory Handbooks) states:

'Firms must act honestly, fairly and professionally in accordance with the **best interests of the client**.'

The adviser's fiduciary duty runs through all of his or her work and his or her relationships with clients. The adviser must do more than merely stick to the letter of the regulations. Under its **principles-based regulation** approach, the regulator expects the industry to pay due attention to the **higher level Principles for Businesses** it has formulated, rather than only to slavishly tick checklists of detailed regulations and codes.

## 1.5 Fair treatment of customers

The regulators aim to maintain efficient, orderly and clean markets and to help retail customers achieve a fair deal. A number of years ago, the financial services regulator examined what a fair deal for retail customers actually means and this has led to much discussion of the concept of **TCF** – 'treating customers fairly'.

The regulator does not define **treating customers fairly (TCF)** in a way that applies in all circumstances. The regulator's **Principle for Businesses 6** states that a firm must pay due regard to its customers and treat them fairly. By adopting a 'principles-based approach' to TCF through Principle 6, the regulators put the onus on firms to determine what is fair in each particular set of circumstances. Firms therefore need to make their own assessment of what TCF means for them, taking into account the nature of their business.

The emphasis of the regulators' philosophy is not so much on the principles themselves. It is on the actual consequences of what firms do. Increasingly, the term used for the current approach has been **outcomes-focused regulation**.

TCF is treated as a part of the **FCA's core supervisory work**. Firms – meaning senior management, including the Board – are expected to be able to demonstrate to themselves and to the regulator that they deliver **fair outcomes to their customers** across the full range of its activities.

With regard to **TCF**, the regulator specifically expects firms to focus on delivering the following six **consumer outcomes**, to the extent that each is relevant to the particular firm's activities.

**TCF consumer outcomes**

- **Corporate culture**: consumers can be confident that they are dealing with firms where the fair treatment of customers is central to the corporate culture.

- **Marketing**: products and services marketed and sold in the retail market are designed to meet the needs of identified consumer groups and are targeted accordingly.

- **Clear information**: consumers are provided with clear information and are kept appropriately informed before, during and after the point of sale.

- **Suitability of advice**: where consumers receive advice, the advice is suitable and takes account of their circumstances.

- **Fair product expectations**: consumers are provided with products that perform as firms have led them to expect, and the associated service is both of an acceptable standard and also as they have been led to expect.

- **Absence of post-sale barriers**: consumers do not face unreasonable post-sale barriers imposed by firms to change product, switch provider, submit a claim or make a complaint.

## 1.6 Requirements for fair agreements

In communications relating to **designated investment business**, a firm must not seek to **exclude or restrict any duty or liability** it may have under the **regulatory system**. (**Designated investment business** includes regulated activities generally, but not deposits, mortgages nor non-savings insurance contracts.) If the client is a retail client, any other exclusion or restriction of duties or liabilities must meet the 'clients' best interests rule' test.

The general law, in particular the **Unfair Terms in Consumer Contracts Regulations 1999 ('the Regulations')**, also limits a firm's scope for excluding or restricting duties or liabilities to a consumer. As a qualifying body, the FCA has an agreement with the Office of Fair Trading – the lead enforcer of these Regulations – that the Authority will apply the Regulations to financial services contracts issued by regulated firms and appointed representatives for carrying out regulated activities.

- As well as its principles and rules which require firms to treat their customers fairly, the FCA has powers under the Regulations to challenge firms that use unfair terms in their standard consumer contracts.

- The Authority may consider the fairness of consumer contracts, make recommendations to firms, and apply for injunctions against them to prevent the use of such terms.

- The FCA also has a statutory duty to consider all complaints made to it about unfair contract terms.

The regulator has made clear that it considers fairness in consumer contracts to be an important visible factor in firms treating their customers fairly.

The Regulations state that an unfair term is not binding on the consumer but that the contract will continue to bind the parties if it is capable of continuing in existence without the unfair term. Therefore, if the court finds that the term in question is unfair, the firm would have to stop relying on the unfair term in existing contracts governed by the Regulations.

The regulator may consider the fairness of a contract following a complaint from a consumer or another person.

Under the Regulations, the FCA has the power to request, for certain purposes:

- A copy of any document which that person has used or recommended for use as a pre-formulated standard contract in dealings with consumers.

- Information about the use, or recommendation for use, by that person of that document or any other such document in dealings with consumers.

**Terms** are regarded as **unfair** if, contrary to the requirement of good faith, they cause a significant imbalance in the parties' rights and obligations **to the detriment of the consumer**.

Unless the case is urgent, the regulator will generally first write to a firm to express our concern about the potential unfairness of a term or terms (within the meaning of the Regulations) and will invite the firm to comment on those concerns. If we still believe that the term is unfair, we will normally ask the firm to stop including the term in new contracts and to stop relying on it in any concluded contracts. If the firm either declines to give an undertaking, or gives an undertaking but fails to follow it, the regulator will consider the need to apply to the courts for an injunction.

# 2 Adviser status and charging

## 2.1 Background to the Retail Distribution Review (RDR)

The **Retail Distribution Review (RDR)** is a key component of the regulators' overall retail market strategy, complementing initiatives on Treating Customers Fairly (TCF) and financial capability.

The RDR aimed to enable more consumers to have sufficient confidence in the market to want to use its products and services more often. To achieve this objective, it was argued, the financial services industry needs more clearly to act in the best interests of its customers and to treat them fairly.

Changes introduced by the RDR – which took effect from **31 December 2012** – brought to an end the previous commission-based system of adviser remuneration. The rules ban product providers from offering amounts of commission to secure sales from adviser firms. Consumers can still have their adviser charges deducted from their investments if they wish, but these charges are no longer determined by the product providers they are recommended.

The changes have impacted all regulated firms involved in producing or distributing retail investment products and services, including banks, building societies, insurers, wealth managers and financial advisers. The RDR rules represent a fundamental change and will necessitate many firms re-thinking their business models. However, the regulators consider that removing the potential for commission to bias product recommendations means that consumers can be more confident that they are being sold the product that best fits their needs.

The rules affect advised sales of investments to retail clients, and include a new independence standard, new charging rules designed to remove influence by providers by banning commission, and disclosure requirements to give customers a clearer picture of the charges for advice.

In summary, the RDR rules:

- Have introduced a new definition of **independent advice**, relating to a wider range of products than packaged products, with other services being described as **restricted advice**: firms offering independent advice must demonstrate that their recommendations are based on a comprehensive and unbiased analysis of the market, and that any product selection is made in their clients' best interests.

- Tackle the potential for adviser remuneration to bias advice by removing provider influence and introducing **adviser charging**, consisting of charges for advice set by the adviser / intermediary instead of commission set by the provider.

- Require **disclosure** of the adviser firm's status and charges.

There are provisions for product providers to facilitate collection of adviser charges through the product, if desired.

There are also requirements for advisers to obtain a **RDR-compliant qualification**, such as the CII's Diploma in Regulated Financial Planning, and for advisers to provide their firm with a **Statement of Professional Standing (SPS)** issued by an accredited body. We return to these **RDR professionalism requirements** later in this Study Text.

## 2.2 Independent advice and restricted advice

### 2.2.1 Introduction

In making the distinction between **independent advice** and **restricted advice**, the regulator has wanted to set a new standard for independent investment advice and to improve clarity for consumers about the different types of advice on offer. All advisers must inform their clients before providing advice, whether they provide 'independent or 'restricted' advice.

- If an adviser declares themselves to offer **independent advice**, they will need to consider a broader range of products beyond the existing definition of 'packaged products'.

- Advice which is not independent must be labelled as **restricted advice**, for example as advice on a limited range of products or providers. Advisers offering restricted advice must still meet the requirement to assess the suitability of products for the client.

'**Packaged products**' are products that can be bought 'off-the-shelf', with the terms and conditions and price identical for all potential investors. This category existed before the RDR, and a **packaged product** is defined as one of the following:

- A unit in a regulated collective investment scheme
- A life policy
- An interest in an investment trust savings scheme
- A personal pension scheme
- A stakeholder pension scheme

### 2.2.2 The standard for independent advice

The standard for **independent advice** is intended to ensure that such advice is genuinely free from bias towards particular solutions or any restrictions that would limit the range of solutions that firms can recommend to their clients. In providing independent advice, a firm should not be restricted by product provider, and should also be able to objectively consider all types of retail investment products which are capable of meeting the investment needs and objectives of a retail client.

**Restricted advice** is advice that does not meet the standard for independent advice (and see also the Handbook Glossary definition given a little later below). Restricted advice will come in many different forms. While a firm needs to describe the nature of its restricted advice service to clients, it is free to choose the words that are appropriate for its service.

**Independent advice** is defined in the Handbook as 'a personal recommendation to a retail client in relation to a **retail investment product [RIP]** where the personal recommendation provided meets the requirements of the **rule on independent advice** ('the **standard for independent advice**'), which requires that the personal recommendation is:

- Based on a comprehensive and fair analysis of the relevant market, and
- Unbiased and unrestricted.

**Retail investment products (RIPs)** is defined in the Handbook Glossary as a product that is one of the following, whether or not held within an ISA or Child Trust Fund:

- Life policy

- Unit in an authorised unit trust or Open Ended Investment Company (OEIC)

- Personal or stakeholder pension scheme (including group schemes)

- Investment trust savings scheme

- Investment trust shares

- Investments which offer exposure to underlying financial assets, in a packaged form which modifies that exposure when compared with a direct holding in a financial asset

- Structured capital-at-risk product (SCARP)

The definition of a RIP is intentionally broad to ensure that all comparable investment products sold to retail clients on an advised basis, including those developed in the future, are subject to the same relevant selling standards, for example the requirement to be remunerated by adviser charges.

Examples of financial instruments that are **not** RIPs would include a share in an individual company which is not an investment company / trust, an individual fixed interest security (i.e. Government gilts and other 'bonds'), and individual derivatives (such as options and futures), where the exposure to the relevant asset is not modified in any way.

Note the use of the term 'relevant market' in the standard for independent advice above. A **relevant market** should 'comprise all retail investment products which are capable of meeting the investment needs and objectives of a retail client'.

- For example, if a client indicates that they are only interested in ethical and socially responsible investments (SRI), it is clear that there is a range of products that would never be suitable for them, namely non-ethical investments. Their relevant market would exclude non-ethical investments, and an adviser would not need to consider these products when forming independent advice for such a client.

- So, a relevant market in the context of the standard for independent advice is defined by a client's investment needs and objectives and not, for example, by product or service types.

**Advisers specialising in a relatively narrow field** must explain the nature of this relevant market as part of its written disclosure to the client and should not hold itself out as acting independently in a broader sense. The firm would need to be able to market itself in a way that attracted only the intended type of clients, and only take on such clients. Examples of such limited markets could include:

- SRI and ethical investments
- Islamic financial products
- Specialist advice for trusts and charities
- Advice limited to pension income drawdown and annuities

Firms specialising in a relevant market must have systems in place to ensure that it does not make a recommendation where there is a **suitable product outside the relevant market** . In such a case, the regulator expects the firm to **refer the client to another adviser** who can meet the client's needs.

What are the implications of the terms '**comprehensive and fair analysis**' and '**unbiased and unrestricted**' as used in the standard? The regulator gives the following guidance.

- If a firm cannot or will not advise on a particular type of retail investment product, and that product could potentially meet the investment needs and objectives of its new and existing clients, then its advice will not meet the standard for independent advice.

- In other words, the justification for a firm excluding types of retail investment products from its range needs to be **centred on the client**. As an example, the fact that a firm's professional indemnity insurance policy specifically excludes certain products would not be a valid reason for never advising on such products. However, firms may consider **Unregulated Collective Investment Schemes (UCIS)** too risky for the clients they usually deal with, and the regulator would not expect a firm to recommend these just to prove they are offering independent advice.

The regulator expects that UCIS will be suitable for very few retail clients, if any. Where the regulator has identified high-risk products and recommended that they should not reach UK retail investors in the UK, a firm does not need to consider them for its clients to meet the standard for independent advice.

Since the beginning of 2014, a category of investments called **non-mainstream pooled investments (NMPIs)**, which includes UCISs as well as special purpose vehicles that invest in anything other than shares or bonds, generally must not be marketed to retail investors. Promotion of NMPIs must be limited to **high net worth and sophisticated investors**.

Providing unbiased and unrestricted advice might include considering **financial products that are not RIPs**, such as National Savings & Investments products or cash ISAs, if they could meet the client's needs and objectives.

**Ownership or financing of an advisory firm by a product provider** will not contravene the requirement for unbiased or unrestricted advice, provided the advice remains genuinely unbiased and unrestricted.

### 2.2.3 Restricted advice

**Restricted advice** is defined (in the regulators' Handbook Glossary) as:

- A personal recommendation to a retail client in relation to a retail investment product which is not independent advice, or
- Basic advice (on stakeholder products, using pre-scripted questions)

In other words, if a personal recommendation on a retail investment product does not meet the standard for independent advice, then it is restricted advice. For example, advice limited to the products of one or more particular companies will be restricted advice.

Restricted advice must meet the same suitability, inducement, adviser charging and professionalism standards as independent advice. The key difference in the requirements is in **disclosure**.

- In its **written disclosure**, a firm that provides restricted advice must explain the nature of the restriction.
- A firm must also provide **oral disclosure** if it engages in spoken interaction with a retail client.

### 2.3 Communicating the nature of a firm's advice services

How may a firm hold itself out as providing independent advice?

A firm will '**hold itself out**' through a variety of means, some of which are untargeted, an obvious example being a firm's trading name. If a firm includes '**independent**' in its **trading name**, it is likely to be holding itself out as providing independent advice to all clients that approach the firm.

If a firm provides **both** independent advice and restricted advice on retail investment products, there are a number of ways in which it could make it clear to clients that it offers both. For example, a firm may have a name that does not include 'independent' and offer clients who approach it a choice of independent or restricted advice, or it may have two or more trading names to clearly separate its independent advice and restricted advice business arms.

A **directly authorised firm** (or '**principal firm**') that has one or more **appointed representatives (ARs)** is responsible for ensuring that those ARs are meeting the relevant selling standards, including the independent advice rules.

# 2.4 Advice tools and investment strategies

## 2.4.1 Introduction

A firm may adopt a number of **tools and strategies** to help it to advise clients and manage their Investments, for example the use of **panels**, **platforms**, **model portfolios** and **referrals to discretionary investment services**.

## 2.4.2 Panels

A firm might use a **third party** (such as a 'panel') to conduct a fair and comprehensive analysis of its relevant market. The firm must make sure that the third party is using fair criteria, for example that it is **not** selecting product providers on the basis of payment of a **fee** while excluding those not paying a fee.

A firm that provides independent advice needs to be able to advise **off-panel** if that would be in the best interests of a particular client.

## 2.4.3 Platforms

A similar rationale applies to the use of **platforms** – as well as **discount brokers and other channels** for buying investments – as for panels. Firms can use platforms in providing independent advice, but need to remain aware of the limitations of its chosen platform and advise '**off-platform**', or through another platform, where this is best for a client.

The current market is frequently changing and platforms do not generally offer products from the whole of the retail investment product market. So, in the current market, the regulator expects it to be rare, if possible at all, that a firm could use a single platform for all of the investment business of all of its clients and still meet the standard for independent advice.

## 2.4.4 Model portfolios

The regulator uses the term '**model portfolio**' to mean a **pre-constructed collection** of designated investments, including some retail investment products, that meets a specific risk profile, sometimes offered with a periodic **re-balancing** of investments to maintain a consistent asset allocation. Model portfolios allow a firm to pre-determine what will generally be its advised asset allocation for certain investment objectives or attitudes to risk, and to distil its product research in line with these asset allocations.

Some individual retail investment products have similar characteristics to model portfolios, such as **funds of funds**, and a firm may use the term model portfolio, or similar, to describe them.

If any aspect of the model portfolio is not suitable or consistent with the client's investment needs and objectives, then either:

- The model portfolio should not be recommended, or
- The model portfolio should be tailored so that it is suitable (which would make it a '**bespoke portfolio**')

A firm should be able to recommend other investment solutions and advise on **retail investment products not held in the model portfolios**, if these could meet the investment needs and objectives of its clients. Advisers should maintain a good understanding of the make-up of any model portfolios their firm uses.

## 2.4.5 Discretionary investment managers

If a firm is providing independent advice, it should objectively consider a wide range of investment solutions in the market before recommending a client use a **discretionary investment manager (DIM) service**. Recommending a DIM service should not be a default investment solution.

## 2.5 Recognised specialist activities

There are two specialist activities related to advising on investments that require specialist qualifications, and these are:

- Advising on occupational pension transfers and pension opt-outs, and
- Advising on long-term care insurance (LTCI) contracts.

A firm must have a separate permission to provide advice on pension transfers and opt-outs. Without this permission, a firm can still give independent advice, since occupational pension schemes are not classified as RIPs.

LTCI contracts are RIPs. Advising on LTCI requires a specialist qualification, but not a separate permission. As with pension transfers, all competent retail investment advisers who give independent advice should be able to identify clients for whom a LTCI should be considered and be in a position to refer these clients on to someone who can provide advice on these products. A firm giving independent advice might not have its own specialist in the 'niche' market of LTCI.

## 2.6 Other adviser roles

A firm providing independent advice should ensure that appropriate **systems and controls** are in place so that all personal recommendations in relation to retail investment products meet the standard for independent advice, including from **inexperienced** advisers or advisers who may wish to **specialise** in a particular area of investment advice, such as pensions.

## 2.7 Multiple advisers and teams

**More than one adviser** may be involved in developing independent advice for a client. An adviser may, for example, wish to consult an experienced colleague on a particular subject before delivering personal recommendations. Similarly, a number of people could be involved in **product research and investment monitoring**. A **team approach** could be adopted. Mechanisms to ensure that any resulting personal recommendation meets the standard for independent advice could include a particular adviser having oversight of all personal recommendations given to a particular retail client.

## 2.8 Simplified advice

The regulator has recognised that there could be benefits from a well-designed, low-cost method of meeting consumers' straightforward investment advice needs.

**Simplified advice** is not a defined term in the regulatory Handbooks, but the term has been adopted to describe **streamlined advice** processes which aim to address **straightforward needs of consumers**. It is used to mean a **limited form of advice**, in that it is focused on one or more **specific needs** and does not involve analysis of the consumer's circumstances that are not directly relevant to those needs. The outcome of a simplified advice process may be a **specific product recommendation**.

**Simplified advice models** are typically **automated**, **process-driven** advice services, which could be delivered over the internet, face-to-face or over the telephone.

From a regulatory perspective, simplified advice is a form of **restricted advice** because it does not consider all retail investment products that may be suitable for consumers.

Any firm that provides simplified advice should not hold itself out as acting independently for its business as a whole, and must comply with the disclosure rules for restricted advice – thus, disclosing in writing to a retail client, in good time before the provision of its services, that its advice will be restricted, and the nature of that restriction. (To meet disclosure obligations, a firm could use a **services and costs disclosure document (SCDD)** – as described later in this Study Text – or a **combined initial disclosure document (CIDD)**.)

A **simplified advice process may be appropriate** for consumers who:

- Have their priority needs met, that is, they do not need to reduce existing debt, they have adequate access to liquid cash (i.e. savings), and have any core protection needs met

- Have some disposable income or capital that they wish to invest, and

- Do not want a holistic assessment of their financial situation, but rather advice on a specific investment need

Simplified advice has some similar characteristics to **'focused advice'**. Focused advice is also not defined in the Handbook, but is a term commonly used to describe a situation where the client requests that a firm only gives personal recommendations relating to a specific need, designated investment or certain assets. The key difference between focused advice and simplified advice is that the former involves the client stipulating the boundaries of the service they wish to receive.

The product suite for simplified advice will need to correspond to the needs of each firm's target market, and be appropriate for its specific advice process.

# 2.9 Non-advised (execution-only) services

The RDR rules applying the end of 2012 do not affect **non-advised** sales, alternatively termed **execution-only sales**. Firms are still able to earn commission on such sales, in the same way as applied before the RDR was implemented. The regulator will however keep this under review, looking for evidence that firms are exploiting the situation, for example by providing advice and then referring the client to a related company to complete a 'non-advised' sale, or by mis-labelling services as non-advised.

# 2.10 Adviser charging under RDR rules

## 2.10.1 Overview

A key element of the new RDR rules on **adviser charging** is a **ban on firms receiving or paying commission** in relation to personal recommendations to retail customers on retail investment products (RIPs) or providing related services. As with other RDR rules, these rules have applied to advice given since the end of 2012.

**'Related services'** in this context cover arranging or administering recommended transactions, and managing the relationship between the client and a discretionary investment manager (DIM).

So, since the end of 2012, a firm making a personal recommendation to a retail client to **invest in a retail investment product**, or providing **related services** does not receive commission from the product provider. The firm will instead receive an **adviser charge** that has been agreed with the client in advance.

- The **adviser** must not solicit or accept commission, remuneration or benefit of any other kind, even if the intention is to pass it on to the client.

- The **product provider** must not offer or pay commission, remuneration or benefits of any kind in connection with advice or related services. However, product providers may facilitate the payment of adviser charges from the client's investment and is not barred from paying administrative or other charges to third parties, such as fund supermarkets.

This charging regime applies for both independent advice and restricted advice, but not for basic advice on stakeholder products (a form of advice using pre-scripted questions). (For this kind of basic advice, advisers can still earn commission on individual sales, post-RDR.)

## 2.10.2 Charging structure

Adviser charges can be tailored for the particular client or may be structured as a standardised **price list**. The **charging structure** is a matter for the firm, and could be based on fixed fees, hourly rates or on a percentage of funds invested, for example, subject to the requirement to act in the client's best interests.

The charging structure must be **disclosed to the client** in writing and in clear and plain language, 'in good time' before any advice or related services are provided. This disclosure could be made in the **SCDD** or in a **CIDD**. Material **discrepancies** between actual charges and the disclosed charging structure must be disclosed to the client as soon as practicable.

There should only be **ongoing charges** if the firm is providing an ongoing value-added service and if this is disclosed to the client. The regulator has stated that:

- The service must be a genuine service for the provision of **personal recommendations or related services** and not just, for example, a vague statement (even if agreed with the client) that the adviser is 'available on the end of a phone at any time'.

- It is however acceptable, where a recommendation is for a **regular payment product**, that the adviser charge can be **payable over time**, without further ongoing advice.

The total adviser charge payable by the client, in cash or cash-equivalents, and in what amounts and at what times, must be agreed with and disclosed to the client as soon as is practicable in a durable medium or via a website. Consequences of **cancellation** must be stated where payments are to be made over time, for example in instalments.

## 2.10.3 Records

Firms must keep **records** of:

- The charging structure
- The total adviser charge payable for each client
- Reasons for any material difference between the adviser charge and the charging structure

## 2.10.4 Product providers

The RDR adviser charging regime also applies to **product providers** who advise clients directly on their own products, based on the following rules.

- Product providers' adviser charges must be 'at least reasonably representative' of adviser services provided and should thus not include costs of creating and administering the product. Amounts charged should be such as would be appropriate if the services were offered by an unconnected firm.

- Product costs should not be structured so that they mislead or conceal the distinction between product costs and adviser charges. (The regulator is seeking to end product providers' past practice of offering to allocate over 100% of a client's investment without indicating clearly that higher charges will apply.)

The rules allow a client to pay adviser charges direct to an adviser or to agree that the provider should pay them from the investment. An adviser charge can be deducted from the investment as a lump sum or, if an ongoing service is provided or the product is a regular payment one, as a series of regular payments. **Facilitation** is said to take place where the customer, instead of paying the adviser charge direct to the adviser, pays a single amount to the product provider, who then pays the adviser charge to the adviser on behalf of the customer.

### 2.10.5 Assets held pre-RDR: 'legacy' assets

Guidance from the regulator states that a firm may continue to accept commission after 30 December 2012 if there is a clear link between the commission payment and an investment in a retail investment product that was made by the retail client following a personal recommendation made, or a transaction executed, on or before 30 December 2012.

Thus, **trail commission** on advice given before the RDR rules come into effect can continue until the product matures or is terminated.

---

**Trail commission** (or 'renewal commission') comprises annual payments to a financial adviser, normally by deduction from the value of investments, over the years after an investment contract has been commenced.

---

Trail commission can be transferred to another firm, for example where the original adviser retires or sells his business.

Trail commission can also be re-registered where a retail client chooses to move to a new adviser, in which case:

- The new adviser must **disclose** the actual amount of commission to the client 'as soon as reasonably practicable'.

- The new adviser will have to provide the client with an **ongoing service** in return for the trail commission.

For these purposes, there is not deemed to be an additional investment into the product, and so trail commission can continue, when there is:

- No change to the product
- A reduction in the investment amount or the level of regular payments
- A change from accumulation units to income units or *vice versa*, or
- A fund switch within a life policy

## 2.11 Post-implementation review of the RDR

In December 2014, two years after the introduction of new rules under the Retail Distribution Review, the FCA published a post-implementation review commissioned from an independent economics consultancy. The review pointed to early indications of reductions in product bias and an increased number of advisers in the sector obtaining further qualifications.

In December 2014, the FCA also published a report setting out the findings of a thematic review on adviser charging and services. This reported significant progress on how advisers are reporting costs, the scope of service, and the nature of services to clients. The report also indicates areas where improvement is required, especially in how the cost of ongoing services are explained to customers.

# 3 Budgeting

## 3.1 What is a budget?

**Budgeting** is an organised way of managing one's money. It can be described as setting out and totalling all of the various items of **income** and **expenditure** one has, using weekly, monthly or yearly figures.

Constructing a simple **spreadsheet** on a computer is an easy way to set out such a budget.

A financial adviser will often collect information on the client's monthly income and expenditure through a **fact-find** interview about the client's circumstances.

## 3.2 Categories for a budget

### Exercise: Budgeting

Set out the categories of income to include in a standard budget sheet that would apply to individuals with different circumstances.

(The regulator's Consumer Help web pages suggest ten categories of income. The first category is:

Earnings from your job or self-employment)

Then, compare your listing to the Consumer Help listing given below.

The regulator's **Consumer Help** section, on its website, suggests the following categories for a personal budget.

**Your income**

- Earnings from your job or self-employment
- Less tax and other deductions
- Pensions from former employers or your own plans
- State pension
- Child benefit and tax credits
- Other state benefits
- Interest from savings accounts
- Income from shares, unit trusts etc
- Other income from investments
- Miscellaneous

**Your spending**

- Mortgage, rent, home maintenance
- Council tax and water rates
- Fuel and power bills
- Food and non-alcoholic drinks
- Alcohol
- Tobacco
- Clothing and footwear
- Household goods
- Home insurance, telephone, other household services
- Medicines, toiletries, hairdressing, other personal items
- Motoring, fares, other travel
- Going out, holidays, other leisure
- Life insurance, medical insurance
- Regular savings
- Loan repayments (other than mortgage)
- Miscellaneous

In practice, the categories chosen can be tailored to suit the particular circumstances, whether they are those of a student, a family with children or a retired professional, for example.

## 3.3 Taking action

What **action** should be taken as a result of the budgeting exercise?

The regulator has put it in these simple terms, in advice aimed directly at the consumer:

- If spending exceeds income, there is an income shortfall: cut back on spending to keep it within income.
- If income exceeds spending, you could put your surplus income towards achieving your financial goals.

Certainly, you will have many clients who have not systematically set out a budget of their personal circumstances. Those clients that do know how they spend their money will generally have better control over their personal finances than those who do not budget.

Preparing such a budget may suggest to a **client** their own ideas about how they would like to change how they spend their money.

An **adviser** may also be able to point out ways in which expenditure might be reduced, particularly where financial planning aspects are involved. For example, if there are borrowings, there may be ways of re-arranging these so that the overall interest burden is lower. A further advance might be sought on a mortgage, at relatively low cost, to replace higher-cost credit card, personal loan or other borrowings. In this type of case, the costs of re-arranging loans should be considered.

Clients who rely heavily on **investment income** should find a budgeting exercise a useful way of indicating whether, given their current income needs, they will be able to maintain the real value of their income in the future.

In budgeting incomes and expenditures, it can be useful to check what the outcome will be if current incomes and expenditures continue.

Budgeting can also be an excellent aid to planning possible **changes in an individual's circumstances or lifestyle**.

For example:

- What will the impact be on a family's finances if a daughter is sent to a fee-paying school for her two final years of schooling? A budget covering the years concerned will help to show whether this can be financed from income, or whether loans may be required or investments may need be sold.

- What will be the effect of a salary earner switching to part-time working? Expenditure may be affected as well as income: travel-to-work costs may be lower, although there could be additional costs if the person is planning to take up new interests as part of the change in lifestyle.

# 4 Borrowing

## 4.1 Introduction

We saw in Chapter 1 of this Study Text how the financial system plays a role in channelling funds from those who have a **surplus** to invest to those who wish or need to **borrow**.

## 4.2 Advising on borrowings

Individuals commonly take on a high level of borrowings at the time when they buy a house, and so decisions about mortgages – loans secured on property – are significant. A buy-to-let investor may be borrowing money to buy several properties.

Financial advisers may be involved in helping clients with **mortgage choices** and, if an interest only option is being considered, the choice of an appropriate **repayment vehicle** for the mortgage will be a part of this. However, as explained later in this Section of the Chapter, with the implementation of the Mortgage Market Review (MMR), the requirement on intermediaries to assess affordability has been removed, with this responsibility now falling on lenders.

**Re-mortgaging** – the process of switching a mortgage to a new lender without moving home – has become increasingly popular. As the mortgage market has become more competitive, lenders have been keen to encourage mortgage borrowers to switch borrowings away from other lenders to them. Incentives such as free legal and survey fees are sometimes offered to re-mortgaging customers.

- Re-mortgage business can be attractive to the lender because the borrower will already have a track record with the previous lender, and the average loan-to-value ratio on re-mortgages will generally be lower than for new loans, since the value of the house will probably have risen since the borrower first bought the property.

- For borrowers, re-mortgaging is an opportunity to 'shop around' for the best deal, and may also be treated as an opportunity to take out a larger loan than before, perhaps to finance other spending such as purchase of a car. (This is the process of **equity withdrawal**.)

Advice on borrowing is however more than just a matter of advising on the selection of mortgage and loan products. The borrowings that a client has, or potentially could have, is a matter that can be reviewed in the light of the client's overall financial circumstances.

For example:

- Is there scope for re-organising or re-scheduling borrowings, to reduce their overall cost? (Consider: interest rates, arrangement and other costs arising from changing loans.)

- If the client has savings as well as a mortgage, should some of the savings be applied to make a part-repayment of the mortgage? (Mortgage providers often now allow part-repayments to be made easily, without penalty. If savings will earn a lower after-tax return than is being paid on the loan, a repayment will save money. An offset mortgage, where the mortgage balance on which interest is payable is offset by a positive savings balance, could be the answer. The client's need or desire to keep some savings available, for example in an emergency, is an aspect to consider here.)

**Loan consolidation** (or **debt consolidation**) is a service that involves negotiating a new loan to replace existing loans, typically over a longer period so that repayments can be kept down. This may be available to those with an acceptable credit history, although overall costs may be high. Although many borrowers focus on the level of periodic (e.g., monthly) repayments, and these must be kept within an affordable range to be manageable, the true cost of borrowing is reflected in the annual percentage rate (APR).

## 4.3 Mortgage Market Review

Proposals for major reforms of the mortgage market were issued in 2009 and 2010, as part of the regulator's **Mortgage Market Review (MMR)**. Final rule changes were issued in October 2012, and most of the changes came into effect on **26 April 2014**. The changes reflect the regulator's move to a more intrusive style of supervision and seek to reform a market whose weaknesses underlay the financial crisis of the late 2000s.

The MMR set out the case for reforming the mortgage market to ensure it is sustainable and works better for consumers.

The FCA stated: 'It had become clear by the height of the market in 2007 that, while the mortgage market had worked well for many people, it had been a cause of severe hardship for others. The regulatory framework in place at the time had proved to be ineffective in constraining particularly high-risk lending and borrowing. The MMR package of reforms is aimed at ensuring the continued access to mortgages for the great majority of customers who can afford it, while preventing a return to the poor practices of the past.'

Lenders had already been responding to the problems arising from the financial crisis by applying more stringent checks in the mortgage application process. Because of this, the MMR changes are not likely to result in major changes to lenders' practices.

**Changes for intermediaries**

- The removal of the requirement on intermediaries to assess **affordability**.

- The removal of the non-advised sales process.

- For most interactive sales (e.g. **face-to-face or telephone**), intermediaries must provide **advice**. For borrowers who opt out of receiving advice, there is however an **'execution only'** sales process for **non-interactive sales (internet and postal)**, and also for certain other exceptions such as sales to mortgage professionals, for business loans, and for sales to **high net worth** borrowers (who have an annual income of over £300,000 or net assets of over £3 million).

- Every seller is required to hold a **relevant mortgage qualification** (with a transitional timetable for this requirement).

- It is no longer compulsory to provide customers with an **Initial Disclosure Document**, but firms can continue to do this if they want to. Instead, certain key messages about a firm's service must be given to customers.

- A **Key Facts Illustration (KFI)** does not have to be given every time the firm provides the customer with information about a product that is specific to them. Instead, it is only required where a firm recommends a product or products, where the customer asks for a KFI, or where the customer has indicated what product they want in an execution-only sale.

**Changes for lenders**

- Lenders are **fully responsible for verifying the income of a mortgage applicant**, and for scrutinising their finances, in order to assess whether the customer will be able to afford the repayments over the first five years of the loan. They can still choose to use intermediaries in this process, but lenders remain responsible. Less stringent affordability checks apply to high net worth borrowers.

- New affordability guidelines include **'stress testing'**, which checks **how mortgage applicants would manage with a rise in interest rates**. Lenders have flexibility in deciding the interest rate to apply for the test. Many lenders are already using 7% as a yardstick in this test.

- Lenders are still allowed to grant **interest-only loans**, but only where there is a **'credible strategy' for repaying the capital**. Placing reliance on anticipated house price rises will not be sufficient.

- There are transitional provisions in the MMR that allow lenders to provide a new mortgage or deal to customers with existing loans who may not meet the new MMR requirements for the loan. The borrowing is not able to exceed the amount of their current loan, unless funding is required for essential repairs. The decision on whether or not to lend in these cases remains with the lender.

## 4.4 Mortgage Credit Directive

This EU Directive on credit agreements relating to residential property came into force on 20 March 2014. Member States have two years to implement this Directive into national law. Although the Directive accords fairly closely with the MMR rules, some changes may result from the implementation of the Directive.

## 4.5 Second charge mortgages

The Government decided that the responsibility for regulating second charge mortgages should transfer to the FCA alongside the wider transfer of consumer credit regulation in April 2014.

# 5 Investment and saving

## 5.1 Introduction

Access to a varied range of different forms of **investment** is wider than it has ever been. Equally, along with the great variety of client circumstances you may encounter, people have different attitudes to risk and they have different levels of interest and available time in managing their financial affairs.

The variety of client circumstances will include people at different stages of their lives. Some will have outgoings and commitments that preclude them from making significant regular **savings** from their income. Others may have disposable income that they wish to save and invest, possibly to meet some future need or savings target.

## 5.2 Advising on investment and saving

To be able to give sound financial advice on investment and saving, the adviser's knowledge of financial products, assets and markets needs to be put to work along with his or her knowledge of the client's circumstances.

There are various ways of building up the information about a client's circumstances that is necessary for the necessary financial advice to be given. The most comprehensive way of obtaining this information is through a formal **fact find interview** with the client. This will record information in a questionnaire format, which may be compiled on a laptop computer. The purpose is to collect sufficient facts about the client or prospective client for a properly considered and comprehensive recommendation to be made.

## 5.3 Client needs and plans

Savings and investment needs can be divided into **short- and long-term needs**.

- The **short-term need** could be for a car or a holiday, for which an obvious type of investment will a deposit account, such as a bank or building society account.

- **Longer-term needs** could include savings for retirement and school fees or providing capital for children as they reach adulthood. Those with longer to save might possibly choose an equity backed investment, such as an Individual Savings Account (ISA) or a unit trust savings plan. Those with a shorter period until they will require the funds may select safer deposit type schemes to reduce the risk of capital losses.

A client's investments may originate from existing funds, which might have come from a recent inheritance or other lump sum, or from savings from income.

**How much can the clients afford to save?** A budget will analyse income and expenditure. Having established the amount of disposable income, a financial adviser can discuss how much the client wishes to spend and how much to save. The adviser should not recommend a course of action in which the client becomes over-committed to a long term contract which carries penalties for cancellation or for reducing the level or saving.

The financial adviser should look to the **client's future**. He or she should ask: Do the client's circumstances look likely to change? Are there clear signs that the client's earnings may increase, say from a promotion at work or income from another source? If this is the case, a savings plan where contributions either increase automatically or by selection may be appropriate.

The client's own **aims and ambitions** for the future are very important, but they need to be realistic in line with the amount the client has available to save.

An important consideration is **ease of access**. This will influence the choice of type of savings or investment and is particularly relevant for any savings into an emergency fund. As its name implies, this is money which may be needed at very short notice, so it should not be tied up in accounts that do not permit easy withdrawals.

## 5.4 Attitudes and risk

In advising on savings and investments, the attitude of the client to **risk** is very important. The client must have risks properly explained, or his awareness must be checked. If the client's assets and the amount available to save are small, then the recommendation is most likely to be for a low-risk deposit-type schemes.

Risky investments have the potential to produce possibly high **rewards**, but also the potential to produce significant losses. The **risks** faced by an investor can be categorised as follows.

- **Capital risk** is the risk of losing part or all of the capital invested.

- **Shortfall risk** applies when there is a financial target, and this is the risk that the chosen investments will fail to meet the target amount.

- **Interest risk** is a term we can apply to interest-bearing investments and describes the risk that interest received will be lower than it might have been. For example, if a saver makes a long-term investment that locks into a fixed rate of interest, this may turn out to be relatively unfavourable if variable interest rates generally rise.

- **Inflation risk** describes the risk that rising prices will reduce the purchasing power of what is invested.

## 5.5 Clients' ethical preferences

A client may have **ethical preferences** that influence their savings and investment requirements. Clients have various opportunities to match their preferences with a range of collective investments.

- A client may want to avoid investments in certain industries or companies, for example those connected with armaments or tobacco. There are **ethical funds** that screen investments on ethical, social or environmental criteria and the adviser's task will be to present the relevant information on such funds being considered to the client, so that the client can decide if the investment is consistent with their preferences.

- While '**dark green**' funds adopt negative screening criteria, '**lighter green**' funds adopt positive criteria, choosing companies that adopt a positive approach to ethically sensitive issues.

- Some funds focus on a particular **theme**, such as renewable energy or public transport.

- A further approach for a fund is to choose the '**best of class**' companies that surpass other companies in their sector in respect of ethical, social or environmental issues.

## 5.6 Diversifying investments

If the client has a relatively large amount of money to invest, then a diversified **spread of types and terms of investment** may be recommended. If the amount were only small, it may not be economical or practicable to diversify widely.

Consider investments that are:

- Low risk
- Higher risk
- Easy access
- Fixed term

A **portfolio** made up of different **asset classes** may be constructed if there are sufficient funds, mixing lower-risk **deposits** or **bond** investments with higher-risk **property** and **equity** investments.

**Existing investments and savings plans** must be taken into account when giving advice for a new savings scheme. Any new recommendations should fit in, giving a good spread of type and risk.

## 5.7 Pound cost averaging

If a client is saving in an equity-backed investment, such as a unit trust or investment trust savings plan, the client should be made aware of the effects of **pound cost averaging**.

The following Example explains the concept.

---

### Example: Pound cost averaging

The client is investing a regular premium each month in, say, a managed fund. Each month his premium will buy units in this fund. However, the price of the units will vary from month to month depending on the performance of the fund. The fund units purchased by a monthly contribution of £30 over a period of six months are as follows (prices in pence).

| Month | Bid price | Units purchased* |
|---|---|---|
| August | 208.40 | 14.395 |
| September | 201.20 | 14.911 |
| October | 210.50 | 14.252 |
| November | 201.40 | 14.896 |
| December | 181.40 | 16.538 |
| January | 182.30 | 16.456 |

*Contribution/Bid price

The price inevitably fluctuates through time. The number of units purchased by the same monthly premium will vary from month to month. Over the long-term, the client will benefit from shorter-term fluctuations in the market by buying more units when the price is low and buying fewer units when the price is high.

Now try the **Exercise** below.

---

### Exercise: Pound cost averaging

Alana invests £30 per month in a unit trust savings plan. The prices (in pence) at monthly dates were as follows.

| Month | Offer price |
|---|---|
| August | 257.60 |
| September | 263.00 |
| October | 272.90 |
| November | 280.00 |
| December | 278.90 |
| January | 291.00 |

Calculate the number of units purchased on each occasion. Compare the total amount of units with the amount Alana would have purchased if she had invested a lump sum of £180 in November.

### Solution

| Month | Offer price | Number of units purchased |
|---|---|---|
| August | 257.60 | 11.646 |
| September | 263.00 | 11.407 |
| October | 272.90 | 10.993 |
| November | 280.00 | 10.714 |
| December | 278.90 | 10.757 |
| January | 291.00 | 10.309 |

Total units purchased during the period are 65.826. If £180 had been invested in November, 64.285 units would have been purchased.

## 5.8 ISAs

Whatever the level of **tax** paid by the client, the income tax and capital gains implications of all investments must be considered so that advantage can be taken of any tax incentives or reliefs available.

Savings for investment can be protected from income tax and capital gains tax in an ISA (**Individual Savings Account**) tax 'wrapper'. It is not possible to hold an ISA jointly or as a trustee for someone else. **Income** and **capital gains** within ISAs are **tax-free**.

To be eligible for an ISA, the planholder must be aged 18 or over and resident in the UK for tax purposes, except for a cash ISA, which is open to investors aged 16 or over. (The different rules for a **Junior ISA** are explained separately below.)

For subscriptions in a particular tax year, an investor may have one (but only one) manager for a cash ISA and another manager (but only one) for a stocks and shares ISA, or may have the same manager for both. If the investor has two managers, it is the investor's responsibility to make sure that contributions do not exceed the annual limits.

There are two types of ISA:

- **Cash**, including all the kinds of bank and building society accounts as well as NS&I products and similar, and

- **Stocks and shares**

**Stocks and shares** ISAs can include:

- Shares and corporate bonds issued by companies officially listed on a recognised stock exchange anywhere in the world (including shares on the AIM)

- UK gilt-edged securities, similar securities issued by governments of other countries in the EEA, and 'strips' of all these securities

- Units or shares in FCA-authorised funds (unit trusts or OEIC) and similar UCITS European funds

- Units or shares in non-UCITS retail schemes authorised by the FCA for sale to UK retail investors

- Shares and securities in investment trusts

- Shares which have been transferred from an HMRC-approved SAYE share option scheme or share incentive plan (The shares must be transferred at market value within 90 days of the individual receiving them.)

- Life insurance policies

- Stakeholder medium-term products

Investments producing a 'cash-like' return (capital not at risk or at minimum risk) are restricted to the **cash component**. The cash component can include bank and building society deposits, units in authorised unit trust money market funds ('cash funds') and 'funds of funds' unit trusts investing in money market funds and **stakeholder products** passing the '5% test', ie guaranteeing a return of at least 95% of the capital invested. Cash ISAs can include alternative finance arrangements, such as Sharia-compliant products. There is also a National Savings & Investments (NS&I) product which has been designated as a cash ISA.

In 2014, the Government made changes to how ISAs work. Arrangements for the **'New ISA' (NISA)** increased the overall tax year 2014/15 contribution limit for ISAs to £15,000 from 1 July 2014.

The **maximum ISA contribution** for the tax year **2015/16** is **£15,240**.

Under the new rules:

- There is no separate limit for Cash ISAs: the investor can allocate money between cash and stocks & shares however they want

- The individual can open only one cash NISA and one stocks and shares NISA in a tax year

- From 1 July 2014, all existing ISAs became 'New ISAs', although in practice the term 'ISA' is still the one generally used

Once the maximum amount has been subscribed in any type of ISA for a year, it is not possible to make further investments, even if funds have previously been withdrawn.

ISA savers are able to **transfer** money saved in a cash ISA to their stocks & shares ISA without this counting as a new subscription. Under the 'New ISA' rules, a transfer is also possible from a stocks & shares ISA into a cash ISA.

**ISA managers**, who must have HMRC approval, must follow the detailed rules set by HMRC. They are required to allow **transfers between managers**, although a manager is not required to accept a transfer in.

- The investor may transfer an ISA to a different manager in the year of subscription, in which case the entire ISA subscription for that year must be transferred. After the first year, partial (or full) transfers between ISA managers are permitted.

- Securities within the ISA can be re-registered in the new manager's name. They do not have to be sold and re-purchased.

- If a manager returns ISA proceeds to the investor, this will be treated as a **withdrawal**.

## 5.9 Junior ISAs

**Junior ISAs** are long-term tax-free savings accounts for children. Like the normal adult ISAs, JISAs are available from a range of banks, building societies, credit unions, friendly societies and stockbrokers.

The Junior ISA has replaced the Child Trust Fund (CTF). The Junior ISA is available for UK-resident children who are under 18 and were born after 2 January 2011 and therefore were not eligible for a CTF. (Since April 2015, it has been possible to transfer money held in a CTF to a JISA.)

There are cash JISAs, and stocks and shares JISAs, with a single **overall limit** for each child of **£4,080** in the **tax year 2015/16**.

A child may hold up to one cash JISA and one stocks & shares JISA at one time. As with adult ISAs, the overall limit can be allocated between cash and stocks and shares in any combination.

The qualifying investments for JISAs are the same as for adult ISAs. As with adult ISAs, all income and gains within the JISA are tax-free.

For under 16s, a JISA can be opened, on the child's behalf, only by someone with parental responsibility for the child. Children aged 16 or over can open a JISA for themselves. The person with personal responsibility can alternatively open a JISA for a child aged 16 or 17.

Anybody can put money into a JISA – not only parents or other relatives. The JISA will be in the child's name, but the person who opens the account is the 'registered contact' who is responsible for managing it. The child can choose to become the registered contact from age 16 and can withdraw money from age 18, when the JISA converts to a normal adult ISA.

Someone who holds a JISA account is also able to open an adult cash ISA from age 16, as well as a JISA. JISA contributions do not affect the maximum subscription permitted in the adult cash ISA.

# 6 Protection

## 6.1 Risk and protection

Life always involves **risk** of various kinds. There are many risks that we are prepared to take, and life could become dull if everything was certain. For example, someone may embark on a training course, bearing the risk that there may not be a job available to them when they qualify. If there is not, they may have borne considerable training costs, for no eventual return. An investor may take on the risk of investing in the stock market quite deliberately, preferring the chance of a better return from equities to a much safer deposit-based investment.

These examples illustrate how we may actively choose risks. There are other risks that are with us whether we like it or not: for example, risks of death, injury or loss of possessions.

Most of us want to be sure that the contents of our house, and our valuable possessions including our car, are **protected against loss** by theft, fire or flood. We can protect ourselves against this financial loss by means of insurance. We pay a premium into a pool with others. In the event of the unexpected happening, such as our car being stolen or our carpet being burnt by a log from the fire, then a claim is paid. Because the insurer anticipates that only a proportion of those insured will need to make a claim, he can meet that risk and hopes to still make a profit. **Insurance** offers **protection** to those who are insured.

However, insurance against risks we cannot avoid is not the only option. A person can choose to 'self-insure' some risks. This means that the person knowingly takes on the risk themselves, and is prepared to take on the consequences. The benefit for the person is that they do not then have to pay for insurance. For example, owners of older cars often take out insurance for 'third party, fire and theft' risks only – a cheaper option than comprehensive insurance. Third party cover meets legal requirements, but if the owner is at fault in an accident which damages the car, the owner must bear the loss themselves. Thus, the owner has self-insured this risk.

Many of us take out insurance for our physical possessions, but we should also consider whether we need to **protect our income** and that of our **clients** from adverse situations. What will happen to our families if our income ceases through **death, sickness** or **redundancy**?

**When a person dies** or is taken **seriously ill**, some sort of **financial problem** will usually result. On death, for example, the costs of a funeral will have to be met. If the person who dies is a person with a young family, the rest of the family will still have the problem of finding the money for all of the normal living expenses, such as food, clothes and energy, in changed circumstances. On top of that, if the husband and wife were buying a house with the help of a mortgage, the widow or widower will be faced with an outstanding loan.

Sometimes the financial difficulties which follow **long-term disability** are even worse as someone can lose their job if they are too ill to carry on working. The State may give some help, but it may well not be enough.

**Index-linking** of protection policies means keeping the amounts insured updated in line with price inflation. Premiums are likely to rise in line with the index-linking. Index-linking protects the policyholder from the additional risk of inflation.

## 6.2 Financial protection on death

There are three main potential **financial consequences** of a death.

- Loss of income
- What to do about debts (liabilities)?
- Tax liabilities created by death

These potential consequences create a need for two different types of life cover: one providing a **replacement income**, the other a **lump sum to repay debts, pay taxes or meet one-off expenses** such as funeral costs.

In the case of the death of someone who does not have earnings – and the most common example of this will be a non-working parent with young children – a working co-parent will still be faced with financial problems: who will care for the children while the parent is at work, and how will they be paid? If the widowed parent wishes to give up work, their income will need to be replaced, to the extent that outgoing expenditures cannot be reduced.

We are therefore looking for a method that will provide financial help at the time when it is needed in order to replace income, repay debts (e.g. mortgage), pay taxes and at least live without financial worry. **Life assurance** fulfils this function.

## 6.3 Business protection

Many businesses fail to protect themselves from the financial consequences of the loss of one or more of their most important assets, namely the **key people** that they employ. For many businesses, the untimely **death or disablement** (either temporarily or permanently) **of a director or a key member of staff** could be at best inconvenient or at worst financially disastrous.

These are events that can be insured against, for businesses of different legal forms (for example, limited companies or partnerships). A business would suffer a financial loss following the death or disablement of a key person and so there is no question of the existence of one of the fundamentals of any contract of insurance – namely an **insurable interest**.

## 6.4 Life assurance

Which term should be used: **life assurance** or **life insurance**? The activity started hundreds of years ago as 'life assurance', but in recent years the term 'life insurance' has also been in widespread common usage. For all practical purposes there is no longer any significant difference.

- In exchange for taking on the liability to make payments following a death, someone with a life assurance policy must pay **premiums** to the insurance company (or 'life office').

- The sum that is payable on a claim under a life assurance policy may be called either the **sum assured** or the **sum insured**.

- The person whose death triggers off a payment under the policy is the **life assured** or the **life insured**.

- The person who is initially the legal owner of the policy is referred to by one of the following terms: **policyholder, assured, insured, grantee, policy owner**.

- When a person is applying for a life policy, they are known as either the **proposer** or the **applicant**.

- If you were applying for a policy on your own life, then you would initially be the **proposer** and then, when the policy came into existence, you would become both the **policyholder** and the **life assured**.

Because the information on a life assurance contract application form is the basis of the assurance contract, it is very important to ensure that all information entered on the form is accurate.

The proceeds of a life policy will often be paid to the legal **personal representatives** of a person who has died. They will be either the **executors** or the **administrators** depending upon whether or not a will has been left by the deceased. If a policy has been temporarily transferred (**assigned**) to someone else (the **assignee**) then the assignee will receive the proceeds.

## 6.5 Term assurance

**Term assurance**, as the name implies, provides life assurance for a fixed term. The sum assured is payable only if the life assured dies within that period. There is no benefit payable on maturity or on cancellation. Premiums are payable throughout the term of the contract. The major advantage of term assurances is that they can provide high amounts of life cover for relatively low premiums.

Some term assurances are **renewable**, which means that on expiry there is an option to cover a further term.

A **renewable increasable term assurance** policy has all the features and benefits outlined above for a renewable policy *plus* the ability to **increase the sum assured** either by a fixed percentage or the RPI.

A **convertible term assurance** policy is a level term assurance with an option enabling the assured to convert the policy to a permanent **whole of life** or **endowment** assurance **without further evidence of health**.

With **decreasing term assurance**, the sum assured reduces each year (or each month) by a specified amount, falling to nil by the end of the term. Such a policy could be used to cover a reducing debt, such as the capital outstanding on a house purchased using a repayment mortgage or the inheritance tax liability on a potentially exempt transfer.

## 6.6 Family income benefit policies

Instead of a term assurance paying out a lump sum on death, it is possible to have a policy that pays out an income over a specific term. A **family income benefit** policy is so-called because it is intended to replace the income which the life assured would earn for his or her family if alive.

Technically, rather than paying an income, these policies are written to provide a **capital sum payable by instalments** for the selected period: this ensures that the 'income' is tax-free.

In order to overcome the effect of inflation, it is possible to effect an **increasing family income benefit policy**.

- The **benefit increases each year by a set percentage**, say 5%, or the RPI (in which case premiums also increase).
- The **benefit remains constant**. When a claim arises, the benefit increases by an agreed amount.

## 6.7 Whole of life policies

A **whole of life policy** for which regular premiums are payable provides for the payment of a lump sum on death. There are three different ways for deciding how much that lump sum will be.

- The sum assured may be fixed at the same level throughout: a **non-profit policy**.
- The sum assured may be increased at regular intervals: a **with profits policy**.
- The sum assured is linked to the value of investments: a **unit linked contract**.

**Non-profit policies** are sometimes called **without profit** or **non participating policies**. The sum assured **is fixed** at the same level for the entire duration of the contract. There is a little demand for or take-up of such contracts now.

A **with profits policy** is sometimes referred to as a **participating policy**: it is a policy which shares in the profits of the insurance company.

## 6.8 Disability protection

If someone is disabled and consequently unable to work, there is a loss in potential **earnings**. A disabled person could also be facing additional expenses such as structural alteration of their house in order to convert a downstairs room into a bedroom (if they cannot get upstairs), or to widen doorways to take wheelchairs.

There may be some help from the State in the form of **income** but, rather like the State payments made on death, this may be little more than a minor solution to a major problem.

There are various forms of **disability protection** that can help to solve these problems (see below).

## 6.9 Accident and sickness insurance

**Accident and sickness insurance** is designed to provide benefits in the event of the death of or injury to the life insured resulting from an accident. The policy pays a lump sum on death or for serious disability, such as loss of a limb or one or both eyes. This type of policy also pays an income in the event of less serious disability, including temporary and partial disablement. It may be considered particularly important to provide such cover for those with significant commitments linked to a mortgage.

**Income payments** may be paid for a defined number of weeks, possibly up to 52 or 104 weeks. There may be a deferment period from the date of injury or commencement of illness during which no income will be payable. This period is typically between one and seven days.

Unlike income protection insurance (IPI) (see below), which is a long-term type of contract, accident and sickness insurance policies are shorter term, and may be renewable after a term of one year only. At the end of each year both the insured and the insurer can choose not to renew the contract. This contrasts with IPI where, under most circumstances, the insurer cannot refuse to renew the policy.

## 6.10 Income protection insurance

The objective of **income protection insurance (IPI)** (also sometimes called by its older name, **permanent health insurance (PHI)**) is to replace earnings lost through long-term illness or disability. This means that the benefit is not a capital sum but an **income**.

The level of IPI benefit is typically restricted to 50% or 60% of earnings, to avoid the **'moral hazard'** that claimants might lack an incentive to return to work.

The principal factors to take into account in assessing clients' need for IPI are:

- Their level of earnings
- Any other benefits receivable

The main source of other benefits is the **state incapacity benefit** and (for employees) initially **statutory sick pay**. For employees, any continuing benefits from an employer must be taken into account.

An income will be payable during disability which aims to **replace at least some of the consequent loss of earnings**. The basis for the level of benefit is loss of earnings. If a person has no earnings, e.g. through unemployment or because he has sufficient investment income to live on, there cannot *normally* be payment under an IPI policy.

In the case of an employee who receives full salary for, say, six months from the time disability begins, there will be no payment under an IPI contract during that period of time. The reason is that an IPI income is intended to replace lost earnings and, in such a situation, no earnings have been lost.

The existence of IPI cover can ensure that clients do not have to take retirement benefits early in the event of disability. This would cause them to receive a lower pension than they would receive by delaying the pension's starting date.

IPI is usually more expensive for **women** than for **men**: this is because statistics and claims experience shows that females suffer more ill health than males.

## 6.11 Critical illness insurance

**Serious illness** can cause **financial problems** which arise for a number of reasons.

- The cost of primary health care
- A person giving up work to care for a spouse
- The cost of home help
- The cost of a holiday needed for recovery or convalescence
- The cost of home alterations, including installing a chair lift

- The cost of equipment for treating kidney failure at home
- The cost of transport for the disabled, e.g. adapting a car
- Cash needed to supplement an early retirement pension

The cause of the problems lie in the possibility of an illness or disability that may be serious enough **to alter a person's lifestyle**. The solution is a policy that pays a **lump sum** on the diagnosis of an illness specified in the policy – that is, **critical illness cover (CIC)**.

Possible uses are to:

- Repay a mortgage
- Provide specialist care and equipment
- Modify a home or car
- Meet responsibilities of dependants
- Provide aid for older people (widows or widowers with no family to support them)

A **wide variety of conditions** may be insured through critical illness policies, including: Alzheimer's disease, major organ transplant, blindness, multiple sclerosis, cancer, paralysis, coronary artery disease, stroke, heart attack, total permanent disability and kidney failure.

AIDS (Acquired Immune Deficiency Syndrome) is generally a specific **exclusion**.

**Reviewable critical illness policies** are increasingly becoming available. The policy will be reviewed, typically every two, five or ten years, and premiums adjusted in the light of inflation but also general advances in medical science at the time, rather than on the individual's health circumstances. Reviewable premiums will generally be less expensive than policies with guaranteed premiums. With a **guaranteed premium**, the insurance company guarantees that premiums will not be raised during the life of the policy.

## 6.12 Unemployment insurance

The level of protection in the event of **redundancy** (involuntary unemployment) is limited. Insurers will typically only cover mortgage repayments for up to a maximum of two years. The Government is keen for insurance companies to expand this market. They wish to reduce the individual's reliance on the State to help meet mortgage payments.

The State benefit **contributions-based Jobseekers' Allowance** is only paid for the first 26 weeks. The longer-term unemployed will need to live on their redundancy payments, if any, then their savings and, when these are sufficiently depleted, the **income-based Jobseekers' Allowance**. The changes in the **Welfare Reform Act 2012** include the phased introduction of a single streamlined **Universal Credit**, which is intended to ensure that 'work always pays'.

## 6.13 Private medical insurance

**Private medical insurance (PMI)** generally covers the cost of **hospital care in a private hospital,** outside the National Health Service (NHS).

Premiums could be payable monthly or annually. Various levels of cover may be provided, and premiums may differ according to the range of hospitals covered.

PMI is often provided as a benefit to employees, and many employers consider that it is of benefit to them for employees who need hospital treatment to be treated as quickly as possible so that they can soon work as normal again.

PMI is also worth considering for a self-employed person. PMI cover could help in providing treatment more quickly than under the NHS, thereby minimising time spent off work and the resulting loss of income.

## 6.14 Financing long-term care

Many elderly people need long-term care towards the end of their lives, and the costs of care can be substantial. **Long-term care insurance (LTCI)** was introduced into the UK in 1991.

Policies may be **protection-based** or **investment-based**.

- **Protection-based** LTCI may be available as an option on a **whole of life policy**: the benefit is provided as an acceleration of the sum that would have been payable on death. With protection-based policies, there will be no surrender value.

- **Investment-based** policies are based on the principle of building up a sum to cover potential long-term care costs.

An **immediate needs annuity** is an LTCI product, purchased using a lump sum, that is individually underwritten. The annuity provides an income for life and is usually purchased after an elderly person has been admitted to a care home. Payments from the provider are free of tax if paid directly to a recognised care provider.

# 7 Retirement planning

## 7.1 Introduction

Longer life expectancies and lower birth rates than in the past have all contributed to the relative ageing of our population. There are more people who are over retirement age than in the past. With the population growing older and on average living longer, planning for retirement, when people need money to meet expenses, but no longer have their full working income, is an important issue at the level of national policy as well as for the individual.

The working population will be unable to contribute enough through national insurance contributions and taxation to maintain the growing numbers of elderly people by means of State benefits. Individuals and their advisers must include retirement planning as a key element of their overall financial planning.

## 7.2 How much income?

A starting point for a retirement planning evaluation is the **amount of income the client requires to live on in retirement**.

The first answer that the client gives may be unachievable. She may think that she would like an income of two-thirds of her original earnings. The cost of this, particularly if the client is trying to achieve it himself without any help from an employer, may be prohibitive.

With a personal or stakeholder pension plan, the income will be provided from the pension funds either by drawing down income from the fund, or by using the fund to buy from an insurance company an **annuity** which can provide an income for life.

The client must be asked to sit down and work out her **expected income needs** in retirement. In many cases, a mortgage will have been paid off. Perhaps the client will move to a smaller house which will involve lower outgoings. Will there still be dependant children from a second or third marriage?

## 7.3 Influencing factors

Having established how much income the client would like to achieve, the adviser can move on to establish, with the help of a **full fact find**, whether this is possible and **the means of achieving the client's aims**. It is sensible to plan towards a target pension of a percentage of final earnings and to review the situation each year to ascertain the proximity to the target. In making his recommendations, the adviser will take into account a number of factors.

## 7.4 Previous and current pension arrangements

It may be that the benefits from existing and previous pension schemes, together with the State benefits, will be sufficient and therefore there is no need for additional pension planning.

- Checking on the client's **existing pension arrangements** and his entitlement to the State pension is the first stage in the assessment process.

- The next step is to ascertain details of all previous pension schemes of the client, whether company schemes, retirement annuities or personal pensions.

- If it is difficult to ascertain the information from the client, then the adviser must obtain his authority to write to the insurance companies concerned and the trustees of previous pension schemes, or even to trace old schemes through the Registrar of Pension Schemes.

- When all the information is received, it needs to be analysed to ascertain the total values of the schemes, in particular if there are any benefits on death or if the pensions increase up to retirement age and/or in retirement.

- A client's current pension scheme needs to be thoroughly researched. This can usually be done by means of the scheme booklet and the up-to date report and accounts.

## 7.5 Pension schemes eligibility

Pension schemes recognised by HMRC are known as **registered** schemes.

Tax relief on member contributions to registered pension schemes is only available to 'relevant UK individuals'.

A relevant UK individual is someone who:

- Is chargeable to UK tax, or

- Is **resident** in the UK, or

- Was resident in the UK during one of the previous **five tax years** and joined the scheme while he was a UK-resident, or

- Is a **Crown servant** subject to UK tax or is the spouse or civil partner of a Crown servant

## 7.6 Lifetime allowance and annual allowance

A new UK pension regime was introduced on 6 April 2006, a date known as 'A-day'. The rules cover all types of registered pension arrangement, including occupational as well as personal and stakeholder schemes. The regime is based on allowances rather than absolute limits.

- The **lifetime allowance** puts a limit on the total amount of benefit that can be accumulated under tax-advantaged pension schemes by a single individual. The lifetime allowance is tested as benefits crystallise (for example, on retirement), and is set at £1,250,000 for 2015/16 (reducing to £1,000,000 in 2016/17). If the lifetime allowance is exceeded, a lifetime allowance tax charge will apply to the excess fund at the time benefits crystallise (at 25% on income and 55% on a lump sum).

- The **annual allowance** puts overall limits on the amount of contributions, or the increase in benefits in the case of defined benefit schemes, which can receive tax advantages for a single individual. The allowance is £40,000 (subject to a maximum of 100% of the individual's income) for 2015/16. If the amount of contributions for an individual exceeds this annual allowance there is an income tax charge, set at the individual's marginal tax rate.

- However, if the new form of income drawdown known as **flexi-access drawdown** (see below) is taken (allowing income withdrawals form the fund with no upper limit), then a money purchase annual allowance (MPAA) of £10,000 applies for contributions to money purchase pension plans.

For those who have taken them up, **transitional protection** arrangements may remain significant, generally for many years after registration deadlines have passed. These arrangements served to protect funds in existence when the lifetime allowance was introduced.

## 7.7 Pension scheme tax reliefs

Individuals can contribute to, and build up benefits in, as many registered schemes as they want. Registration of a pension scheme with HMRC means that tax reliefs will apply to contributions made **before age 75**, within certain limits.

- **For those with UK earnings of £3,600 or less, or no earnings:** tax relief up to £3,600 (gross contributions) is available.

- **For those with earnings of £3,600 or more:** full tax relief at the individual's marginal tax rate is given on gross member contributions up to the lower of: 100% of earnings, or: £40,000 (2015/16 annual allowance).

- **Employers' contributions** will be deducted from the business profits for tax purposes, and will count towards the annual allowance.

- If contributions are made in excess of the annual allowance in a tax year, an **annual allowance tax charge** (determined by adding the amount subject to the charge to the individual's net income) applies to the excess amount. However, a member of a registered pension scheme can **carry forward** unused annual allowances from the **three previous tax years**. No claim needs to be made to HMRC to use the carry forward rules.

- **Investment returns** in the pension fund are free of tax on income and gains, although dividend tax credits cannot be reclaimed.

- Part of the retirement benefits can be taken as a **tax-free lump sum** (25% of the fund for a defined contribution scheme, or an equivalent amount based on a commutation factor for a defined benefit scheme).

Considering that, excepting the 25% tax-free lump sum that can be taken when commencing benefits, income from a pension scheme is taxable, the tax relief on contributions and investment returns should be viewed largely as a **tax deferral**. The effect of this on the individual will depend partly on the individual's marginal tax rates when making contributions and when taking benefits, respectively.

## 7.8 Occupational pension schemes (OPSs)

### 7.8.1 Overview

There are two main types of occupational (work-based) pension scheme:

- **Defined benefit** (also known as **final salary**) schemes
- **Defined contribution** (also known as **money purchase**) schemes

### 7.8.2 Defined benefit – final salary

Typically the maximum occupational pension for most people in a defined scheme will be two-thirds of final salary after 40 years of service. With final salary (defined benefit) schemes, the pension paid on retirement is related to the service

of the individual with the company, e.g. 1/60<sup>th</sup> of the final pay. Tax relief is available for both the employer and employee on contributions into occupational schemes.

The benefit that is paid on retirement is guaranteed and thus is attractive to the employee. It is possible to increase the benefit paid on retirement by contributing into an Additional Voluntary Contribution (AVC) scheme provided through the employer ('in-house') or by an external provider.

In recent years, many final salary schemes have been closed to a new employees of a firm, leaving them with a choice between money purchase schemes or having all contributions paid into a type of personal pension plan. The cost of meeting the funding requirements of defined salary schemes has become high in recent years, hence the increasing unwillingness of employers to continue providing them.

### 7.8.3 Defined contribution – money purchase

Money purchase schemes are also provided by employers but the pension provided on retirement is not normally linked to final remuneration. The employer pays a set amount of money into the fund (i.e., a defined contribution), with the value of the fund at retirement being used to purchase an annuity. The level of pension that will be provided therefore is linked not only to the value of the fund but the annuity rate at retirement. The risk of such a scheme is with the employee as there is **no link with final remuneration**.

## 7.9 Personal and stakeholder pension plans

### 7.9.1 Personal pension plans (PPs)

**Personal Pension Plans (PPs)** are individual arrangements to provide for a pension on retirement, although **group** personal pensions may be offered by an employer who does not have an occupational scheme. PPs are generally **money purchase schemes**.

As with other registered pension schemes, the normal minimum age for taking benefits is 55 years. Income, within given limits, can be drawn down from the fund after this age.

A tax-free cash lump sum of 25% of the funds can be taken when income benefits start. If the tax-free cash lump sum is taken, there will of course be less money in the fund to pay for income 'drawdown' or to buy an annuity and thus the pension will be lower than it would be otherwise.

### 7.9.2 Self-invested personal pension (SIPP)

With a **Self Invested Personal Pension (SIPP)**, as its name implies, the individual can decide which investments to buy.

### 7.9.3 Small self-administered schemes

**Small Self Administered Schemes (SSASs)** are OPSs used by small companies (often family owned) and can have no more than 11 members, one of whom must be a controlling director.

The fund can borrow money, i.e. gear up, and often buy property then rent it to the company at prevailing market rates.

Members benefit by buying annuities or drawing income from the fund.

### 7.9.4 Stakeholder pensions

**Stakeholder pension plans (SHPs)** were introduced in April 2001 and follow similar rules to personal pension plans, except that the following rules or '**CAT** standards' apply to SHPs.

- Charges. For new plans, charges are limited to 1.5% of the fund value p.a. for the first ten years and 1% p.a. thereafter. For plans started before April 2005, a limit of 1% applies in all years.

- Access. The minimum contribution level must not exceed £20.

- Terms. Contributions can be raised or stopped without penalty. Transfers in or out attract no exit penalty.

## 7.10 Income drawdown

There have been various ways of drawing an income from money purchase pension plans over the years. As an alternative to buying an annual **annuity** from an annuity provider, it has been possible to **draw down** regular withdrawals from the fund.

From 6 April 2015, it became possible to make unlimited withdrawals using '**flexi-access drawdown**'. From this date, all new drawdown arrangements follow the flexi-access drawdown rules. Funds in flexible drawdown automatically converted to flexi-access drawdown on 6 April 2015.

**Flexi-access drawdown rules**

- Pension benefits can be taken at age 55, except where there is a lower protected pension age or in cases of ill-health

- A tax-free lump sum can be taken amounting to 25% of the individual's funds

- Income withdrawals of any amount can be taken at any time from the drawdown fund

- The income taken will be taxed at the individual's marginal tax rate

- When the individual receives their first flexi-access drawdown income payment, this triggers a money-purchase annual allowance (MPAA) of £10,000. If the individual takes a tax-free lump sum but no income, then the MPAA is not triggered.

- Flexi-access drawdown is available to beneficiaries, including dependants, nominees and successors.

    - If the individual dies before age 75 with remaining flexi-access drawdown funds, any lump sum, or income payments to beneficiaries, are paid tax-free.

    - If the individual dies on or after age 75 with remaining flexi-access drawdown funds, any lump sum is taxed at 45% (or, for payments made on or after 6 April 2016, at the recipient's marginal tax rate). Any income payments made to beneficiaries are taxed at the recipient's marginal rate.

## 7.11 NEST and auto-enrolment

### 7.11.1 National Employment Savings Trust (NEST)

A 2006 White Paper outlined the Government's workplace pension reforms, including proposals for **NEST** – the **National Employment Savings Trust**, previously referred to as Personal Accounts. This led to the provisions set out in the Pensions Act 2008. The reforms aim to increase individuals' savings for retirement and include the introduction of NEST, a new, simple, low-cost pension scheme to encourage people to save enough for their retirement.

There is an **annual contribution limit** of £4,700 (2015/16, reviewed annually) into NEST.

**Transfers** in and out of NEST are not allowed except in specific limited circumstances.

### 7.11.2 Auto-enrolment overview

**Auto-enrolment** means workers being automatically enrolled into their employer's **qualifying pension scheme** without any active decision on their part. Employers can choose the qualifying scheme they use, which could include **NEST**.

Previously, many workers have failed to take up pension benefits because they do not make an application to join their employer's scheme: auto-enrolment is meant to overcome this.

Each qualifying scheme must meet minimum standards in respect of the benefits it provides or the amount of contributions paid to it. Qualifying schemes may be **money purchase schemes** or **defined benefit schemes**: each type of scheme has its own requirements.

### 7.11.3 Auto-enrolment requirements

There are a number of **staging dates**, from **2012 up to 2018** depending on the number of employees an employer has, by which employers must meet requirements to auto-enrol their employees. Smaller employers are being given more time to comply.

**Requirements** that employers must meet are as follows.

- Enrol **eligible jobholders** who are not already active members of a qualifying scheme into an automatic enrolment scheme, and maintain that membership while the jobholder works for the employer and chooses to be in the scheme. Eligible jobholders are at least 22 years old but under the State pension age, and earning an income of at least £10,000 (2015/16).

- Make relevant employer and employee **contributions**. Minimum contribution rates, for money purchase schemes, are expressed as a percentage of qualifying earnings (between specified limits). The **full rate of 8%**, of which **employers must pay at least 3%**, will be **phased in** over a transitional period.

- **Register** with the Pensions Regulator, keep specified **records** and provide certain **information** to employees.

Under the **Pensions Act 2011**, employers will have the **option of deferring up to three months** the auto-enrolment of some or all eligible jobholders, subject to giving the jobholders notice within one month from the date they should have been enrolled and allowing them to opt-in during the waiting period.

### 7.11.4 Opting out by employees

Jobholders will be able to **opt out** of auto-enrolment, subject to time limits. However, they will only be able to opt out and receive a **refund of contributions** after achieving active membership. The purpose of this requirement is that jobholders should see the effect of pension saving on their monthly pay before they are able to opt out.

To minimise the risk of encouraging members to opt out, opt-out forms will be available only from the scheme and not from the employer.

## 7.12 Non-pension assets

The extent of a client's **non-pension assets** should be ascertained, as these are also relevant to retirement planning.

These assets might include company shares or property, for example. A client may wish to use such assets to provide for living expenses in retirement, and this may reduce the extent to which pension arrangements are required by the client.

## 7.13 Non-pension investment and saving

Retirement planning is more than just pensions planning. Pensions schemes provide a range of options for providing for retirement, but these vehicles are not the only method of providing for retirement years.

Some people who are owner-occupiers of a house may plan to 'trade down' to a smaller house with a lower value, and realise a capital gain on their previous house in the process. This capital, which would be tax-free, could form a part of provision for retirement years.

With pension arrangements, a **tax-free pension commencement lump sum** equivalent to 25% of funds can generally be taken when benefits are initiated, along with an income based on the remaining portion. Savings and investment vehicles other than pension plans can alternatively be used for saving for retirement. **ISAs** offer tax-free capital gains, with greater flexibility than many pension arrangements in how and when proceeds can be used.

## 7.14 State pension

The State scheme was previously the major source of pension for most individuals, but in recent years the Government has been encouraging individuals to move towards providing their own pension arrangements.

State pension provision comprises the basic **State pension** and the additional **State Second Pension (S2P),** which replaced the State Earnings Related Pension Scheme (SERPS) from 6 April 2002. The level of S2P is linked to the earnings of the individual while they were at work. It is only paid in respect of employment, not self-employment.

Most clients will be entitled to a **basic State pension**. However, the amount will depend on the amount of national insurance contributions paid. Those reaching the State Pension Age from 6 April 2010 onwards receive the full level of the basic State pension if they have 30 qualifying years, generally through their national insurance contributions record. Those with fewer qualifying years will receive one-thirtieth of the full amount for each qualifying year. A couple receives a higher rate of basic State pension than a single person.

A Pensions Green Paper (April 2011) has proposed to introduce a much **higher universal basic pension** in 2016. More qualifying years would then be required to qualify for a full basic State pension. This would be partly financed by scrapping the S2P.

The **State Pension Age** is 65 for men. Equalisation of the State Pension Age for women from age 60 to age 65 is set to be phased in gradually by November 2018. As laid down in the **Pensions Act 2011**, the State Pension Age for both men and women will then increase to age 66 between December 2018 and October 2020. The **Pensions Act 2014** provides for a further increase to 67 between 2026 and 2028,with a new framework calling for a regular review of the State Pension age in the future.

Both the basic State pension and pensions paid under S2P are paid gross but, like other pensions, are taxable. However, pensions are not subject to national insurance contributions.

## 7.15 Additional State pension

### 7.15.1 State Earnings Related Pension Scheme (SERPS)

The **State Earnings Related Pension Scheme**, or **SERPS**, is in addition to the basic pension and is linked to an individual's pensionable earnings. It was only available to employees, not to self-employed people. It was previously based on 25% of average revalued pensionable earnings for the best 20 years prior to retirement.

However, under the terms of the Social Security Act 1986, this was amended to be a lower percentage (20%) of the **average lifetime** revalued pensionable earnings (sometimes called **middle band earnings**), with effect from April 2000. Benefits already earned under SERPS are preserved, but SERPS was replaced by the State Second Pension (S2P) from April 2002.

### 7.15.2 State Second Pension (S2P)

The **State Second Pension (S2P)**, introduced in April 2002, was designed to provide higher benefits than SERPS for the lower paid, for those looking after young children, and the disabled. S2P benefits are based on average lifetime earnings between a lower and upper earnings limit.

Contracting out of SERPS/S2P means transferring the pension liability to a private arrangement. This will reduce the individual's entitlement to the State pension, since the individual will not be entitled to SERPS/S2P in relation to the years in which he or she contracted out. However, it means that the individual will effectively pay lower national insurance contributions along with other incentives.

**Contracting out through defined contribution schemes** (i.e. money purchase, personal pension and stakeholder arrangements) was **abolished** from **6 April 2012**. This change does not affect **salary-related occupational pension schemes**, which may be contracted-out schemes.

The State pension scheme benefits are **complex** and it would be very difficult for anyone to calculate correctly a client's benefit without help. It is a worthwhile exercise for the adviser or the client to write to the Department for Work and Pensions for a forecast of state pension entitlement, as this will include basic, graduated and S2P/SERPS benefits.

## 7.16 Age

The **age at which the client wishes to retire** is important. The adviser should ascertain the age at which the client wishes to retire – is it 65, 60, or some other age? Retirement planning should be considered in the context of the normal retirement age under the client's contract of employment, if the client is in a long-term job.

The adviser should discover if the client wishes to **retire early** at say 50 or 55. Is this likely to be a reality or just a dream? The adviser will need to stress the expense of planning for early retirement. Advisers need to be aware that the reverse can happen. Many directors of family companies have **no intention of retiring,** certainly not before the age of 70.

It is important to take into account the age of the **client's spouse or partner**. It is unlikely that one will wish to retire without the other, so the retirement planning must be dovetailed if possible. If the client is older than the spouse, there may be a greater requirement to provide for adequate pensions for a widow or widower.

The **current age of the client** is also significant. If he or she is young he has many years to achieve his objectives. The older the client, the fewer the years and the more expensive the exercise becomes. Many insurance companies provide leaflets emphasising the effect of 'delay' in pension planning.

## 7.17 Income

Current income and outgoings should be analysed to ascertain the income available for investment into pensions or other retirement planning investments. If income is likely to increase on a regular basis, some form of indexing of premiums should be considered.

In looking at the **client's outgoings**, it may be discovered that, because of current commitments, such as school fees, she is unable to fund sufficient pension at the present time. It would then be useful to advise the client of how many years she can afford to delay if she wishes to achieve her aim – also, the increased amounts which would then be involved to provide an adequate pension benefit.

A client may typically have limited spare income to commit to her financial needs. **Identified needs** should generally be accompanied by **stated priorities**, such as the following.

- Cover for dependants
- Protection of income in the event of sickness
- Mortgage requirements
- Pension
- Savings

- Investment

If the client is a director of his or her own company, then the discussion will centre around the amount which the **company can contribute** on his or her behalf, and also on the ability of the company to afford this from a cashflow point of view and to maintain the contribution level in the future. Often an adviser is called in when the company has had a good trading year. Before deciding on a level of contribution, it is important to ascertain whether this can be maintained in future, perhaps less profitable, years.

## 7.18 Dependants

The **costs of dependants**, particularly children, can limit the amounts available to contribute to pension. It is also important to stress to clients that they should consider the consequences if they will be **dependent on others for their pension provision**. In the past, women in particular have often taken the view that they did not have to fund a pension in their own right because their spouse had made adequate provision. Yet, changes in circumstances, such as a divorce or death of the spouse, can leave the client with no provision at all. The situation on divorce is changing. Pension benefits are now being taken into account in the settlement including splitting the fund.

The client should ensure that in the event of **death prior to retirement**, his or her spouse, partner or dependants are sufficiently covered. If life policies are not already in force this can be covered by pension life assurance and the return of the fund from the pension arrangement.

In designing the pension arrangements for a particular client care must be taken to ensure that any **dependants in retirement** will be properly covered, e.g. the spouse, partner or dependent children.

# 8 Estate planning

## 8.1 What is estate planning?

Someone's **estate** is the wealth they leave when they die. **Estate planning** is therefore concerned with how that wealth is passed on to beneficiaries, who may typically be children or grandchildren.

## 8.2 Inheritance tax

Some people will wish to find ways of passing wealth on during their lifetime, in ways that reduce the liability to **inheritance tax**. Careful planning can make this possible. It may be possible to make maximum use of the nil rate band, gifts and other exemptions.

Steps taken to reduce tax liabilities should not dominate planning for a client so much that the steps taken prevent the client from achieving the outcomes he or she wants.

Whatever the client's plans and wishes are, a client should have a properly drafted **will**.

## 8.3 Financial products

Another aspect of estate planning is to consider financial products that can meet **inheritance tax liabilities** that will fall due.

**Life assurance products** can be very useful for this purpose. A **whole of life policy** will pay out on death, just when the funds are needed to meet the liability.

If a life assurance policy is **written under trust**, this will ensure that:

- Proceeds will normally be free from inheritance tax

- Premiums are usually exempt as gifts
- Proceeds will be paid without delays in obtaining probate

For a married couple, inheritance tax is likely to have most impact on the death of the second person (the surviving spouse). A whole of life assurance on a joint life second death basis written under trust for the beneficiaries would then be appropriate.

If the client dies within seven years of making a gift, the value will be included in the estate for inheritance tax purposes, with tapering relief applying. To mitigate any inheritance tax liability in these circumstances, a gift *inter vivos* seven-year decreasing term assurance can be used to protect the recipient against the potential inheritance tax liability if the donor of the gift dies within the seven-year period.

Some **investment products** make use of a **trust** in order to reduce inheritance tax liability. Lifetime gifts may be made into a trust for the benefit of children or grandchildren, and the trust assets may be invested.

Some people may choose to pass on wealth by making regular lifetime gifts to children or grandchildren. **Savings products** could be used, either in the name of the beneficiary or under trust.

**Long-term care insurance (LTCI)**, designed to meet some or all of the costs of nursing care if required, could be used as a way of preserving wealth that would otherwise be quickly depleted if such care were needed. Given the relatively high care costs involved and the proportion of people requiring it, such insurance can involve significant outlay.

# 9 Tax planning

## 9.1 Introduction

In the previous section of this Chapter – on estate planning – we have been looking broadly at some of the ways in which inheritance tax effects may be reduced or mitigated. Inheritance tax planning is, of course, one aspect of tax planning.

## 9.2 Tax planning points

In giving financial advice on various matters, there are of course tax considerations to be borne in mind, particularly for a client with substantial assets.

- Is the client a non-taxpayer, savings income starting rate (10%), basic rate (20%), higher rate (40%), or additional rate (45%) taxpayer?
- Are all personal allowances for income tax purposes being used?
- What is the likely capital gains tax (CGT) position, and is there a way for the client to make use of annual CGT exemptions, or any brought forward capital losses that can be set against capital gains?
- What is the tax position of financial products being considered? Are proceeds exempt from tax? Are there planning steps that can ensure that tax effects are mitigated?
- At the **end of a tax year**, key issues are whether an individual wishes to top up **pension plans** or **ISAs,** for which there are limits on contributions within a tax year (subject to carry forward rules, in the case of pension plans).

## 9.3 'Tax-free'?

Note that just because a product has no tax to pay on maturity does not mean that it is truly 'tax-free'. An **endowment policy** will often carry no tax liability for the policyholder at the time of surrender or maturity, but the life company has already deducted tax at source.

On the other hand, when a qualifying endowment policy is sold to someone else (a '**traded endowment policy**'), the **purchaser** will be liable to capital gains tax on any subsequent gain made.

## 9.4 Tax planning in context

As with estate planning, it is important to consider tax planning in the light of all the client's circumstances and needs, and in the context of all of their plans and wishes.

Any **tax advantages** should not be sought at all costs, without considering other aspects. For example, there will be no benefit to a client if a particular financial product carries a tax advantage which is cancelled out by the effect of higher charges on that particular product, or by exposure to **investment risks** that the client would not otherwise wish to be exposed to.

# 10 Benefits

## 10.1 Overview and future changes

Individuals can claim State benefits for various reasons, and other benefits may arise from employment.

The **Department for Work and Pensions (DWP)** website **www.dwp.gov.uk** includes **information on benefits**.

In his 2012 Autumn Statement, the Chancellor of the Exchequer announced that most working-age benefits and tax credits would be uprated by just 1%, below inflation – in line with the 1% cap on public sector pay rises – for three years from 2013/14. Benefits have historically risen in line with inflation and, without any change, would have been due to rise by 2.2% in April 2013. In the 2015 Summer Budget, the Government announced that most working age benefits would be frozen for four years from 2016.

The **Welfare Reform Act 2012** legislated for major changes to the welfare system. A new single-payment **Universal Credit (UC)** is being introduced, starting with a pilot introduction in areas of North-West England followed by a progressive roll-out nationally across the UK **between 2013 and the end of 2017**.

The benefits changes will affect hundreds of thousands of households. The Government estimates that 3.1 million households will be entitled to more benefits as a result of UC. Approximately 2.8 million households will be entitled to less, but will receive a top-up payment to protect them from a drop in income. However, new claimants will receive the lower payment.

When fully introduced, the **UC** will replace all of the following:

- Income support
- Income-based jobseeker's allowance
- Income-related employment and support allowance
- Housing benefit
- Child tax credit
- Working tax credit

## 10.2 Benefit cap

The **benefit cap** is a limit on the total amount of various benefits that most people aged 16 to 64 can receive.

The level of the benefit cap is:

- £500 a week for couples (with or without children living with them)
- £500 a week for single parents whose children live with them, and
- £350 a week for single adults who do not have children, or whose children do not live with them

## 10.3 Disability living allowance for children under 16 years

**Disability living allowance (DLA)** is a tax-free benefit which helps with the extra costs of looking after a child who needs help to look after themselves or move around because of a disability or health condition. It is paid to a child's parent or a person who looks after the child as if they are a parent (e.g., step-parents, guardians, grandparents, foster parents and older brothers and sisters over 18 years).

Someone only qualifies for DLA if the child concerned needs much more day-to-day help than other children of the same age who do not have a disability. The child must have needed help for three months and be expected to need help for at least a further six months.

DLA is made up of a 'care component' which is paid at either the low / medium / high rate and a 'mobility component' which has a lower and higher rate. Claimants can be paid either or both of these components.

## 10.4 Benefits for working age people (16 – 64 years)

### 10.4.1 Personal independence payment (PIP)

**Personal independence payment (PIP)** is gradually replacing DLA for people aged 16 to 64. PIP has already replaced DLA for **new claimants** over the age of 16.

PIP helps with the extra costs arising from a long term condition (ill-health or disability expected to last 12 months or longer). There are two components to PIP: a Daily living component and a mobility component. Each component has two rates: standard and enhanced.

PIP is based on how a person's condition affects them, not the condition itself. It is not affected by income or savings, it is not taxable, and people can get it whether they are in or out of work.

To qualify for PIP, unless they are terminally ill, someone must have needed help with extra costs caused by a health condition or disability for three months or more and be reasonably likely to need help for the next nine months, although someone can submit a claim for PIP during the first three months of having a condition.

### 10.4.2 Employment and support allowance (ESA)

**Employment and support allowance (ESA)** offers financial support to ill or disabled people who are unable to work, or personalised help so that someone can work if they are able to.

Everyone currently receiving **incapacity benefit** will be assessed for ESA, since 2014.

### 10.4.3 Income support

**Income support** is an income-related benefit that can be paid to some people who are on a low income but not able to work, including:

- Carers
- Lone parents with children under 5 years
- Pregnant women
- Sick and disabled people who need money to top up their Statutory Sick Pay

Savings of more than **£16,000** usually mean that there is no entitlement.

### 10.4.4 Jobseeker's allowance (JSA)

**Jobseeker's allowance (JSA)** is a taxable benefit paid to unemployed people who are available and actively looking for work. Claimants must attend regular work-focused interviews at a Jobcentre and provide proof that they are looking for work.

People can claim one of two types of JSA:

- **Contribution-based** – paid for up to 182 days to people who have paid enough National Insurance contributions in the previous two tax years.

- **Income-based** – paid to people who do not qualify for Contribution-based JSA, if their income and capital (and/or their partner's income or capital) is low enough.

A family should ideally have **emergency funds**, equal to perhaps four to six months of income, to cope with unexpected contingencies such as unemployment. Having such an emergency fund would not affect **contributions-based jobseekers' allowance**, which is based on national insurance contributions having been made, but **income-based jobseekers' allowance** will not usually be payable to someone with savings of over **£16,000**. The **risk of unemployment** may make it desirable to improve pension provision or long-term savings while there are earnings.

### 10.4.5 Redundancy payments

**Redundancy payments**. An employee who has worked for a firm for two years or more will be entitled to receive a lump sum if made redundant, payable by the employer and determined by three factors: age, length of continuous employment with the employer and weekly gross pay. **Additional voluntary payments** may be made by an employer. A sum up to £30,000, including the statutory payments, will be **tax-free**.

## 10.5 Attendance allowance: for people aged 65 years and over

**Attendance allowance** supports people over 65 who have a disability and so need extra help with personal care. Payment is not affected by income or whether a person works. To qualify, the person must have needed help for six months and be over 65.

Attendance allowance has two levels – lower and higher.

## 10.6 Carer's allowance and Carer's credit

**Carer's allowance** is payable to people aged 16 or over if they spend at least 35 hours a week caring for a person who is receiving:

- DLA care component at the middle or highest rate, or
- PIP daily living component at either rate, or
- Attendance allowance / Constant attendance allowance, or
- Armed Forces independence payment

Those who spend at least 20 hours a week as a carer may also be entitled to **carer's credit** – a National Insurance credit that can build entitlement to the basic State Pension and additional State Pension by helping to ensure there are no gaps in the carer's National Insurance record.

## 10.7 Child benefit

**Child benefit** is a benefit paid to people bringing up children. A weekly amount is payable in respect of each qualifying child.

Child benefit is now means-tested: there is an **income tax charge** that reduces the effect of the benefit above an adjusted net income for either parent or carer of £50,000, eliminating the benefit entirely at an income level of £60,000.

## 10.8 Benefits available following a death

**Bereavement payment** is a one-off **tax-free** lump sum payment of **£2,000,** available to a surviving partner where the spouse or civil partner made sufficient national insurance contributions (NICs), if one of the couple is below State pension age.

**Widowed parent's allowance** is a weekly taxable benefit available to widow and widower parents with at least one dependant child, where the late spouse or civil partner made sufficient NICs.

**Bereavement allowance** is a taxable weekly benefit paid for 52 weeks after the death of the claimant's spouse or civil partner, based on their NICs record.

## 10.9 Statutory sick pay (SSP)

**Statutory sick pay (SSP)** is payable for up to a maximum of 28 weeks to employees who have been continuously sick for four or more successive days. SSP is a flat-rate taxable benefit, irrespective of the income of the recipient, provided the employee earns at least the NI lower earnings limit. If this requirement is not met then income support may be claimed.

## 10.10 Maternity and paternity

**Statutory Maternity Pay (SMP)** is paid to mothers earning above the NI lower earnings limit who have been employed by the same employer continuously for at least 26 weeks up to the 15th week before the baby is due. It will be paid at 90% of average earnings for the first six weeks with no upper limit, and for a further 33 weeks at 90% of earnings subject to a ceiling.

Mothers who are **self-employed**, or **employed but not entitled to SMP**, may be eligible for **Maternity Allowance**.

**Statutory Paternity Pay (SPP)** may be available for up to two weeks at 90% of average earnings, subject to a ceiling.

SMP and SPP are **subject to tax** and **national insurance contributions**.

## 10.11 Benefits available on retirement

### 10.11.1 State pension

If sufficient Class 1 or Class 2 NICs have been paid, then a full basic State **national insurance retirement pension (NIRP)** will become payable at State Pension age.

**State Second Pension (S2P)** – outlined earlier – will be earned by those Class 1 NIC contributors who satisfy the entitlement conditions by having a sufficiency of such contributions paid at the contracted-in rate. Those who pay Class 2 NICs only, that is the **self-employed**, accrue no S2P benefit. A **widow or widower or surviving civil partner** may inherit S2P from their late spouse / civil partner.

Both the **NIRP** and **S2P** are **taxable**.

### 10.11.2 Pension credit

The **Pension Credit** is a **means tested** benefit, intended to ensure that pensioners are in receipt of at least a **minimum income level**, set by the Government. Pension credit is not taxable.

Pension credit has two elements:

- **Guarantee credit** (currently available at a qualifying age in line with the State Pension Age)
- **Savings credit** (available if one of a couple is at least 65)

The **Guarantee credit** is intended to ensure that those aged 60 and over an income of at least:

- £151.20 a week (2015/16) for a single person, or
- £230.85 a week (2015/16) for a couple

Income from most sources is taken into account, but **income from savings** is dealt with **on a notional basis**. This assumes that each £500 of savings in excess of a threshold of £10,000 generates income of £1 per week. This means that **savings in all forms are taken into account** even if the actual income generated is very small, or is tax-advantaged, for example, under the ISA rules.

The **Savings credit** is intended to go some way towards compensating for how the Guarantee Credit could penalise savings by providing an additional benefit to those with an income equal to or more than the state basic pension up to where income equals the appropriate Guarantee credit amount.

Although this is a useful benefit, it could create **difficulties for advisers** when dealing with low income clients (for whom saving is arguably most important). The adviser could face criticism if his advice resulted in a client providing out of his own resources for benefits which otherwise the State would have provided.

## 10.12 Working tax credit

The **working tax credit (WTC)** is for people who are employed or self-employed who usually work for at least a certain number of hours per week and who have a **relatively low income**. WTC is **not taxable**.

A **childcare element** of WTC is paid to the main carer (not necessarily the main earner).

## 10.13 Child tax credit

The **child tax credit (CTC)** can apply to those with children. It is payable to the **main carer** of a child who is under 16, or under 20 and in approved education or training. CTC is **not taxable**.

# Key chapter points

- Given consumers' experience and the benefits of fostering a positive perception of financial services, firms will do well to treat customers fairly, as the regulator requires, and to ensure that ethical practices prevail in their business.

- Under the RDR (Retail Distribution Review) changes that took effect from the end of 2012, firms that give investment advice must set their own charges in agreement with their clients, and have to meet standards regarding how they determine and operate these charges. The proposals bring to an end the previous commission-based system of adviser remuneration.

- The standard for independent advice governs personal recommendations to retail clients in relation to retail investment products (RIPs) that are based on a comprehensive and fair analysis of the relevant market, and are unbiased and unrestricted. Advice that is not independent advice is termed restricted advice.

- Budgeting involves a detailed examination of income and expenditure. This is a great help in financial planning.

- The fact find is a way of building up as full a picture as possible of the client's circumstances.

- Borrowing can take various forms and can be for various reasons, but borrowing for house purchase is often the most significant borrowing that an individual takes on.

- In investment and saving, client needs must be researched. Recommendations should be for products and investments appropriate to the client's attitudes.

- Protection against various risks is possible. There are various kinds of life assurance, and other forms of protection include ASU (accident, sickness and unemployment insurance), income protection insurance, critical illness insurance and private medical insurance.

- Financial advisers are involved in many clients' retirement planning. Pensions schemes or other investment products may be used in retirement planning.

- Estate planning is concerned with passing on wealth, and tax efficiency is often a consideration. Financial products of different kinds may be used to fund an anticipated inheritance tax liability.

- An adviser should always be alert to possible tax implications of a client's financial decisions, so that the adviser's recommendations take account of possible tax savings, within the context of the client's overall needs and plans.

- Various state benefits may be available on death, illness, disability, unemployment and retirement. State benefits are also be available to those with children and those who look after the disabled. By 2017, a new Universal Credit will have replaced many existing benefits in stages.

- Pension credit is paid to people aged 60 or over to give them a guaranteed minimum income.

## Chapter Quiz

1    List the seven financial advice areas we have considered in this Chapter.  ...........................(see Chapter topic list)

2    What does it mean to say that the adviser owes a fiduciary duty to the client? ............................... (see para 1.4)

3    How is 'independent advice' defined? ...........................................................................................(2.2.2)

4    What is meant by 'budgeting' in the context of an individual's circumstances? ...............................(3.1)

5    How would you explain to a client what is meant by re-mortgaging? ...........................................(4.2)

6    Who is responsible for assessing customer affordability for a mortgage loan? ...............................(4.3)

7    What is pound cost averaging? ...................................................................................................(5.7)

8    What are generally the most significant financial implications of a death occurring?  ...................... (6.2)

9    What does IPI aim to do? .........................................................................................................(6.10)

10   'Retirement planning is pensions planning.' Do you agree? ........................................................(7.13)

11   What is estate planning?  ..........................................................................................................(8.1)

12   What are the different levels of UK income tax? ......................................................................... (9.2)

## Chapter topic list

# Legal concepts

## CHAPTER LEARNING OUTCOMES

3    **Understand legal concepts and considerations relevant to financial advice**

   3.1    **Explain** the concepts of legal persons, powers of attorney, law of contract and agency, and ownership of property.

   3.2    **Explain** relevant laws governing insolvency and bankruptcy.

   3.3    **Explain** relevant laws governing wills, intestacy and trusts.

# 1 Legal identity

## 1.1 Legal personality

A legal person possesses legal rights and is subject to legal obligations. In law, the term **person** is used to denote two categories of legal person.

- An individual human being is a **natural person**.
- The law also recognises **artificial persons** in the form of corporations.

A corporation, such as a limited company, is distinguished from an unincorporated association. An **unincorporated association** (for example, a partnership) is not a separate legal entity; it does not have a legal identity separate from that of its members.

## 1.2 Artificial persons

A corporation is a **legal entity** separate from the natural persons connected with it, for example as members. Corporations are classified in one of the following categories.

| Categories | Description |
|---|---|
| **Corporations sole** | A corporation sole is an **official position** which is filled by one person who is replaced from time to time. The Public Trustee and the Treasury Solicitor are corporations sole. |
| **Chartered corporations** | These may be **charities**, or professional bodies such as the Institute of Chartered Accountants in England and Wales or the Chartered Insurance Institute. |
| **Statutory corporations** | Statutory corporations are formed by special Acts of Parliament. This method is little used now, as it is slow and expensive. It was used in the nineteenth century to form railway and canal companies. |
| **Registered companies** | Registration under the Companies Act is the normal method of incorporating a commercial concern. Any body of this type is properly called a company. |

## 1.3 Companies and limited liability

The most important consequence of registration of an enterprise as a company is that a company becomes a **legal person distinct from its owners**. The owners of a company are its members, or shareholders.

A significant consequence of the fact that the company is distinct from its members is that its members therefore have **limited liability**.

The **company** itself is **liable without limit for its own debts**. If the company buys plastic from another company, for example, it owes the other company money.

The members (shareholders) own the business, so they might be the people who the creditors logically asked to pay the debts of the company if the company is unable to pay them itself. Limited liability prevents this by stipulating the creditors of the company cannot demand the company's debts from members of the company, for example if the company fails.

Although the creditors of the company cannot ask the members of the company to pay the debts of the company, there are some amounts that members are required to pay, in the event of a winding-up.

| Type of company | Amount owed by member at winding-up |
|---|---|
| **Company limited by shares** | Any outstanding amount from when they originally purchased their shares. If the member's shares are fully paid, they do not have to contribute anything in the event of a winding-up. |
| **Company limited by guarantee** | The amount they guaranteed to pay in the event of a winding-up. |

Liability is usually limited by **shares**. Companies limited by guarantee are appropriate to **non-commercial activities**, such as a charity or a trade association which aims to keep income and expenditure in balance but also have the members' guarantee as a form of reserve capital if it becomes insolvent.

A company, as a separate legal entity, may also have liabilities in tort (e.g. to pay damages for negligent acts) and crime.

It is difficult to prosecute a company on criminal charges, as it is necessary to show a '*mens rea*', or controlling mind. Unless a company is very small, it is problematic to show that the mind controlling the company was connected with the criminal act.

However, the Law Commission has issued proposals which include a charge of killing by gross carelessness, which it would be easier to charge companies with. There is, at present, no such criminal offence in the UK.

## 1.4 Unlimited liability companies

A company may also be formed with unlimited liability: its memorandum makes **no reference** to **members' liability**. If the company goes into insolvent liquidation, the liquidator can then require members to contribute as much as may be required to enable the company to pay its debts in full. An unlimited company can only be a private company since a public company is by definition always limited.

An unlimited company has two main advantages.

(a)     It need not **file** a copy of its **annual accounts** and reports. There are some exceptions, the most notable of which being if the unlimited company is a subsidiary of a limited company.

(b)     An unlimited company **may without formality purchase its shares** from its own members.

The unlimited company certainly has its uses. It provides a corporate body (a separate legal entity) which can conveniently hold assets to which liabilities do not attach.

## 1.5 Public companies and private companies

A **public company** is a company registered as such under the Companies Acts with the Registrar of Companies. Any company not registered as public is a private company: s1(3). A public company may never be unlimited.

- A **public company (plc)** is limited by share or by guarantee, with a minimum issued share capital of £50,000 in sterling or alternatively 57,100 euros, on which all the share premium and at least 25% of the nominal value have been paid up.

- A **private company (Limited or 'Ltd')** is a company which has not been registered as a public company under the Companies Act. The major practical distinction between a private and public company is that the former may not offer its securities to the public.

**Private companies** are generally small enterprises in which some if not all shareholders are also directors and *vice versa*. Ownership and management are often combined in the same individuals. In that situation, it is unnecessary to impose on the directors complicated restrictions to safeguard the interests of members and thus a number of rules that apply to public companies are reduced for private companies.

Only a **public company** can obtain a **Stock Exchange listing** for its shares. This option is not open to private companies. Listed companies are sometimes referred to as **quoted companies** (because their shares are quoted publicly).

The following rules also apply to public companies.

(a) A **public** company must have at least **two directors**: a **private** company need only have **one director**.

(b) The rules on **loans to directors** are much **more stringent** in their application to **public companies** and their subsidiaries than to private companies.

(c) A **public company**, except by ordinary resolution with special notice, may **not appoint a director aged over 70**.

## 1.6 Sole traders

Many small businesses start with someone becoming **self-employed**, as a **sole trader**.

In a sole tradership, there is no legal distinction between the individual and the business. The trader is **personally liable** for any **debts of the business**.

## 1.7 Partnerships (Partnership Act 1890)

**Partnership** was traditionally the normal organisation in the professions as most professions prohibit their members from carrying on practice through limited companies, and the **Partnership Act 1890 (PA 1890)** set out law governing this form of business organisation.

In a partnership governed by the PA 1890, a partner is **personally liable** for all the debts of the firm (incurred while he is a partner and sometimes even after he has ceased to be a partner).

'**Partnership** is the relation which subsists between persons carrying on a business in common with a view of profit' (Section 1, PA 1890).

'Person' includes a corporation such as a registered company as well as an individual living person.

## 1.8 A partner's authority as agent of the firm

Each partner is an **agent** of the firm when he acts in carrying on in the usual way business of the kind carried on by the firm, although his authority may be restricted by the other partners. (We discuss the concept of agency further later in this Chapter.)

The PA 1890 defines the apparent authority of a partner to make contracts as follows.

*'Every partner is an agent of the firm and his other partners for the purpose of the business of the partnership; and the acts of every partner who does any act for carrying on in the **usual way business** of **the kind carried on** by the firm of which he is a member bind the firm and his partners, unless the partner so acting has in fact no authority to act for the firm in the particular matter, and the person with whom he is dealing either knows that he has no authority, or does not know or believe him to be a partner' (s5).*

### 1.9 Limited liability partnerships

Under the **Limited Liability Partnership Act 2000**, it is possible to register a **Limited Liability Partnership** (an **LLP**). A limited liability partnership combines the features of a partnership with the limited liability and creation of a legal personality more usually associated with limited companies. Many of the larger accountancy firms, for example, have taken advantage of this structure.

Every member of an LLP is an **agent** of the LLP. As such, where the member has authority, the LLP will be bound by the acts of the member.

# 2 Power of attorney

## 2.1 What is a power of attorney?

A **power of attorney** is a document made by a person ('the donor') which appoints another person ('the attorney' or 'the donee') or persons, to act for the donor in legal matters. An example of the use of a power of attorney is where the donee is given power to sign documents on behalf of the donor.

The power of attorney may be a **general** power, to allow the donee to act for the donor in all matters, or restricted to a **specific** act, for example to execute a specific document. In either case, the donor can still act himself. The donor is liable for the acts of the donee, for example, the donor would be bound by a document signed by the donee, provided that the donee has acted within the terms of the power of attorney.

## 2.2 Making a power of attorney

A general power of attorney may be set out in the form set out in s10 of the Powers of Attorney Act 1971. This shows the names of the donor and donee and states that the donee is appointed as attorney for the donor. The document must be executed as a deed. In general, this form cannot be used by trustees to delegate trustee powers. However, under s1 of the Trustee Delegation Act 1999, it can be so used in the case where the trustee is a co-owner of land and also has a beneficial interest in the land e.g. where land is held in joint ownership, whether as tenants in common or joint tenants.

A limited form of power of attorney should be drawn up by a lawyer and specify exactly the powers being given to the donee. It should be formally executed (as a deed).

A **trustee** may delegate his powers by executing a power of attorney under the terms of the Trustee Act 1925 (as amended). The delegation can be for a period up to twelve months in length. Notice of the execution of the power of attorney must be given within seven days to any person who has power to appoint trustees and to the other trustees.

## 2.3 Length of a power of attorney

An ordinary power of attorney (whether given as an individual or as a trustee) is only valid while the donor is capable of giving instructions. It can be revoked by the donor and is automatically revoked if the donor or attorney become bankrupt or die. The power will also cease at the end of a time specified in it or when a specific act has been carried out.

## 2.4 Mental Capacity Act 2005

The **Mental Capacity Act 2005** sets out a single **'decision-specific' test** for assessing whether a person lacks capacity to take a particular decision at a particular time. A lack of capacity cannot be established merely by reference to a person's age, appearance, or any aspect of a person's behaviour. Carers and family members have a right to be consulted.

The Act deals with two situations where a designated decision-maker can act on behalf of someone who lacks capacity.

- **Lasting powers of attorney (LPAs).**This is similar to the previous Enduring Power of Attorney (EPA), except that the Act also allows people to let an attorney make health and welfare decisions.

- **Court appointed deputies.** The Act provides for a system of court appointed deputies to replace the previous system of receivership in the Court of Protection.

## 2.5 Lasting power of attorney (LPA)

Lasting powers of attorney were established under the **Mental Capacity Act 2005.**

An LPA is a legal document that the Donor makes using a special form available from the **Office of the Public Guardian (OPG).** It allows the Donor to choose someone now (the Attorney) that he or she trust to make decisions on the Donor's behalf about things such as the Donor's property and affairs or personal welfare at a time in the future when the Donor no longer wishes to make those decisions or may lack the mental capacity to make those decisions for himself or herself.

An LPA **can only be used** after it is registered with the **Office of the Public Guardian (OPG).**

Where there is no power of attorney, the Court of Protection may make orders concerning the person's property and may appoint a **receiver** with specified powers to manage the person's affairs with the authority of the court.

Anyone aged 18 or over, with the capacity to do so, can make an LPA appointing one or more Attorneys to make decisions on their behalf. Someone cannot make an LPA jointly with another person; each person must make his or her own LPA.

If no lasting power of attorney is made before a person becomes incapable, it may be necessary to apply to the **Court of Protection** – a more cumbersome and possibly expensive procedure. The Court of Protection is intended to protect the finances of people who are no longer able to manage their own affairs.

If there are no other attorneys or replacements available to act, an LPA will automatically be cancelled:

- When the attorney dies, refuses to act or ceases to have capacity to act.
- If the attorney and donor are spouses and they become divorced.
- For a Property and Affairs LPA (see below), when the attorney or donor become bankrupt.

There are two different types of LPA:

- **Personal Welfare LPA**
- **Property and Affairs LPA**

## 2.6 Personal Welfare LPA

A **Personal Welfare Lasting Power of Attorney (LPA)** allows a person to plan ahead by choosing one or more people to make decisions on their behalf regarding personal healthcare and welfare.

These personal welfare decisions can only be taken by somebody else when the person lacks the capacity to make them for himself or herself – for example, if the person is unconscious or because of the onset of a condition such as dementia.

The **Personal Welfare Attorney(s)** will only be able to use their power once the LPA has been registered and provided that the person cannot make the required decision for himself or herself.

A person can decide to give the Attorney the power to make decisions about any or all of their personal welfare matters, including healthcare matters. This could involve some significant decisions, such as:

- Giving or refusing consent to particular types of health care, including medical treatment decisions, or

- Whether the person continues to live in their own home, perhaps with help and support from social services, or whether residential care would be more appropriate.

There is provision on the LPA form to give the Attorney(s) the power to make decisions about 'life-sustaining treatment', but this power must expressly be given.

The person can also give the Attorney(s) the power to make decisions about day-to-day aspects of their personal welfare, such as diet, dress or daily routine.

## 2.7 Property and Affairs LPA

A **Property and Affairs Lasting Power of Attorney (LPA)** allows someone to plan ahead by choosing one or more people to make decisions on their behalf regarding their property and financial affairs.

Someone can appoint a **Property and Affairs Attorney** to manage their finances and property while they still have capacity as well as when they lack capacity. For example, it may be easier to give someone the power to carry out tasks such as paying bills or collecting benefits or other income.

This might be easier for lots of reasons: someone might find it difficult to get about or to talk on the telephone, or they might be out of the country for long periods of time.

The Property and Affairs LPA does not allow the Attorney to make decisions about the person's personal welfare: this requires a **Personal Welfare LPA**.

## 2.8 Pre-existing Enduring Power of Attorney (EPA)

The Mental Capacity Act 2005 replaced the former Enduring Powers of Attorney (EPA). It is not possible to make any changes to an **existing EPA** or make a new one. However, an unregistered EPA can still be used and the Attorney will still need to register it with the OPG if they have reason to believe the person is, or is becoming, mentally incapable in the future.

Someone can also make an LPA to run alongside an EPA if they wish. For example, someone may have an existing EPA that makes provision for decisions about their property and affairs, and decide to make a Personal Welfare LPA to run alongside that, to provide for decisions concerning their healthcare and welfare.

Someone may also consider replacing your an unregistered EPA with a Property and Affairs LPA. An unregistered EPA can be revoked at any time while the person has the mental capacity to do so. However, if the EPA has been registered, it cannot be revoked except by permission of the Court of Protection.

The best way to revoke an unregistered EPA is to sign a formal document (called a 'Deed of Revocation').

## 2.9 Registering a LPA

A LPA can be registered at any time after it is made, with OPG. The Donor can register their own LPA providing they are able to make these sorts of decisions for themselves. Alternatively, the Attorney can register the LPA if they believe that the Donor is no longer able to make these decisions themselves.

To register the LPA, the applicant must complete a form to notify the people the Donor has said they want to be informed (the named persons) of the registration. If any of the named persons have concerns about the registration of the LPA – for example, if they feel that the Donor was put under pressure to make it – then they can object to the LPA being registered.

The OPG will check the LPA and the application form. If there are no problems, the OPG will set a registration due date. This date will be six weeks from the date that the OPG gives notice of the application to register to either the Donor or the Attorney(s), depending on who has made the application (for example, if the Donor applies to register the OPG will give notice of the application to the Attorneys). This is because everyone who is entitled to notice is also entitled to object to the application for registration. If there are any objections, it may not be possible to register the LPA until these have been resolved.

If there are no objections or problems with the application, the registered copy of the LPA will be sent within five working days of the end of the six-week waiting period.

The **Public Guardian** is responsible for establishing and maintaining a **register of LPAs**, as well as a **register of EPAs**.

# 3 The law of contract

## 3.1 Elements of a valid contract

A contract is a legally binding agreement between mutually consenting two parties who intend to enter into a legal relationship.

There are **three essential elements** to look for in the formation of a valid contract: **agreement, consideration** and **intention**.

The first essential element of a binding contract is **agreement**. To determine whether or not an agreement has been reached, the courts will consider whether one party has made a firm **offer** which the other party has **accepted**.

In most contracts, offer and acceptance may be made **orally** or in **writing**, or they may be implied by the conduct of the parties. The person making an offer is the offeror and the person to whom an offer is made is the offeree.

In life assurance, the **proposal form** makes up the offer which the life assurance company can either accept at standard rates or on special terms, or reject. If the assurance company accepts on special terms, it is effectively rejecting the proposal and making a **counteroffer**, which the proposer then either accepts or rejects.

The second of the three essential elements of a contract is **consideration**. The promise which a claimant seeks to enforce must be shown to be part of a bargain to which the claimant has himself contributed.

Third, an agreement is not a binding contract unless the parties **intend to create legal relations**. What matters is not what the parties have in their minds, but the inferences that reasonable people would draw from their words or conduct.

The requirements of standardisation in business have led to the **standard form contract**. The **standard form contract** is a document prepared by many large organisations setting out the terms on which they contract with their customers. The individual must usually take it or leave it.

## 3.2 Contract law and consumer protection

Many contracts are made between experts and ordinary consumers. The law will intervene only where the former takes unfair advantage of his position. The law seeks to protect the idea of **'freedom of contract'**, although **contractual terms** may be regulated by **statute**, particularly where the parties are of unequal bargaining strength.

In the second half of the twentieth century, there was a surge of interest in consumer matters. The development of a mass market for often complex goods has meant that the consumer can no longer rely on his own judgement when buying sophisticated goods or services. Consumer interests are now served by two main areas.

- **Consumer protection agencies**, which include government departments (the Office of Fair Trading) and independent bodies (the Consumers' Association)

- **Legislation**, for example, Consumer Credit Act 1974 and Unfair Contract Terms Act 1977

BPP
LEARNING MEDIA

## 3.3 Form of a contract

As a general rule, **a contract may be made in any form**. It may be written, or oral, or inferred from the conduct of the parties.

For example, a customer in a self-service shop may take his selected goods to the cash desk, pay for them and walk out without saying a word.

However, certain contracts must be in **writing**, such as for the purchase of land and property.

## 3.4 Capacity to contract

**Capacity to contract** is the legal ability to enter into a contract.

Someone who is insane (mentally disordered) or drunken may have their capacity to contract limited by law, if they were unable to understand the agreement and the other party knew this.

**Minors** – that is, those aged under 18 – do not have unrestricted capacity to enter into contracts.

## 3.5 Legality of object

If you enter into an agreement with an accomplice to steal property, such a contract would be **illegal** and the contract would **not be valid**.

## 3.6 Utmost good faith

If you buy a used car from a private seller and find that it falls apart soon after you bought it, that usually is your problem. Provided that the seller answered honestly any questions that you asked, they were not obliged to volunteer information that you did not seek. The general principle here is: *caveat emptor* – the buyer beware.

However, if you make a proposal for insurance, including life insurance, you are expected to give to the insurance company **all relevant information** which will enable the company to assess the risk, e.g. if you are seriously ill or in a dangerous occupation or have a risky lifestyle, or whether you are a normal risk for which the company would issue a contract on standard terms.

This requirement to **disclose all relevant information** is fundamental to an insurance contract. If the rule is not observed the policy can be treated by the insurer as **voidable**. The requirement is termed **'utmost good faith'** or *uberrimae fidei.*

## 3.7 Insurable interest

For **contracts of insurance**, **insurable interest** is normally a required element.

In the late 18th century, it was decided that insuring the lives of people simply because you wanted to make a profit was unacceptable. The Life Assurance Act 1774 introduced a rule that there must be **the risk of losing money** if you were to have the right to insure somebody else's life, and that rule has been unchanged ever since.

But there is a difference from the law on general insurance. If, for example, you own a house, you can insure it only for as long as you have an **insurable interest**. That means that insurable interest must exist when you first effect an insurance, it must continue to exist throughout the time that the contract exists, and if damage occurs to the house you must still have insurable interest at the time the damage occurs.

With life assurance, insurable interest need exist only at the time that the policy is effected. This means, for example, that if a married person insures the life of their spouse and they become divorced, the person can continue the insurance after the divorce, even if they no longer have an insurable interest in the death of the other. However, someone could not effect a **new** contract after a divorce has taken place unless they can show that the ex-spouse's death would result in their suffering some kind of financial loss. A further implication is that policies with an investment value – generally, endowment policies – can be sold in the secondhand market. The buyer will continue to pay the premiums.

You can insure **your own life** and the life of your **spouse** or **same-sex civil partner** for any amount: the insurable interest is deemed to be **unlimited** in these cases. In other cases, the amount of insurable interest must, in principle, be **measurable** and the amount of the cover must match the amount of that interest.

Specific examples of **insurable interest** include:

- One spouse/civil partner in the life of the other
- A partner in a partnership in the lives of the other partners
- An employer in the lives of employees for the value of services to be rendered or on a **key person** basis
- A creditor on the life of a debtor

Specific circumstances where **no insurable interest** exist include:

- A parent in the life of a child
- A child in the life of a parent

# 4 Agency

## 4.1 The agency relationship

'Agents' are engaged by 'principals' generally in order to perform tasks which the principals cannot or do not wish to perform themselves, because the principal does not have the time or expertise to carry out the task. In normal circumstances, the agent discloses to the other party that he (the agent) is acting for a principal whose identity is also disclosed.

**Agency** is a relationship which exists between two legal persons (the **principal** and the **agent**) in which the function of the agent is to form a contract between his principal and a third party.

The relationship of principal and agent is usually created by mutual consent. The consent need not generally be formal nor expressed in a written document. **It is usually an 'express' agreement**, even if it is created in an informal manner.

When an agent agrees to perform services for his principal for reward there is a contract between them.

## 4.2 Examples of agency relationships

There are many examples of agency relationships which you are probably accustomed to, although you may not be aware that they are examples of the laws of agency. Some examples are as follows.

(a) **Partnerships.** A feature of partnerships is that the partners are agents of each other.

(b) **Brokers.** Any broker is essentially a middleman or intermediary who arranges contracts in return for commission or brokerage. For example, an **insurance broker** is an agent of an insurer who arranges contracts of insurance with the other party who wishes to be insured. However, in some contexts (for example, when the broker assists a car owner to complete a proposal form) he is also treated as the agent of the insured. Insurance, especially marine insurance, has complicated rules applicable to the relationship (insurer-broker-insured).

(c) **Appointed representatives of product providers.** A financial adviser who works as an appointed representative (tied adviser) for a product provider firm (such as a life office) is an **agent of the product provider firm**, while the firm is principal. The firm, as principal, is responsible for the acts and omissions of its appointed representatives (its agents) and must ensure that its agents comply with the financial regulators' rules.

(d)    A **retail investment adviser (RIA)**, who offers independent advice on products from a full range of providers, is the **agent of his client** in respect of the advice or recommendations offered to the client. This is the case whether or not the adviser is a member or appointed representative. The insurer or other product provider is not liable for the acts or omissions of the adviser, and the adviser owes no duty to the product provider. The adviser owes a **duty of care** to his or her client.

## 4.3 Obligations of an agent

Even if the agent undertakes his duties without reward, the agent has obligations to his principal.

(a)    **Performance and obedience.** The agent must **perform** his obligations, following his principal's instructions with **obedience**, unless to do so would involve an illegal act.

(b)    **Skill and accountability.** The agent must act with the standard of **skill and care** to be expected of a person in his profession and to be **accountable** to his principal to provide full information on the agency transactions and to account for all moneys arising from them.

(c)    **No conflict of interest.** The agent owes to his principal a duty not to put himself in a in a situation where his own interests conflict with those of the principal; for example, he must not sell his own property to the principal (even if the sale is at a fair price).

(d)    **Confidence.** The agent must keep in **confidence** what he knows of his principal's affairs even after the agency relationship has ceased.

(e)    **Any benefit** must be handed over to the principal unless he agrees that the agent may retain it. Although an agent is entitled to his agreed remuneration, he must account to the principal for any other benefits. If he accepts from the other party any commission or reward as an inducement to make the contract with him, it is considered to be a bribe and the contract is fraudulent.

## 4.4 Authority of the agent

The **contract** made by the agent is **binding** on the principal and the other party **only if** the **agent was acting within the limits of his authority** from his principal.

# 5 Property ownership

## 5.1 Real property

In legal terminology, **land** includes buildings and anything else which is permanently attached to the land.

**Real property** (also called 'realty') is land owned in perpetuity – in other words, **freehold property.** The mediaeval common law courts granted special remedies: the right of the dispossessed owner to have the land returned to him. For that historical reason, land in freehold ownership is in a category (real property) of its own.

Freehold property is distinguished from **leasehold property.** With leasehold property (in legal terminology, 'chattels real'), the right of a tenant (or lessee) will come to an end either by expiry of a fixed period (which may be as much as 999 years) or by termination by notice (and in other more unlikely events). When it terminates the landlord (or lessor) resumes possession from the tenant. The landlord is therefore said to have a 'reversion' which becomes possession when the lease terminates. While the lease continues, the tenant has possession but is usually required to pay a rent to the landlord.

A **lease** is a form of **contract**. If granted for a term of more than three years it must generally be in the form of a **deed**.

## 5.2 Personal property

**Personal property** – or **'personalty'** – is anything that is not **realty**, i.e. **real property** (freehold land). It is so called because the owner's claim could be satisfied by payment of the value instead of returning the property – his claim was against the wrongdoer personally and he could not automatically recover the property or thing.

Personal property comprises:

- **Leasehold land**, and
- Pure **personalty** (including chattels and things in action)

Banknotes and coins are 'things in action'.

These technical legal terms can be significant. For example, someone (the **testator**) may by his **will** give his 'real estate' to A and his 'chattels' to B and his remaining personalty to C.

Moveable tangible property – generally called **chattels** – are literally those items of property of which ownership and possession can be transferred simply by delivery, such as furniture, books and jewellery.

## 5.3 Forms of co-ownership of land

It is possible for more than one person to own land. If land is purchased or transferred to two or more persons, these persons become either **joint tenants** or **tenants in common**. (Note that this applies to owning freehold land outright, even though the word 'tenant' is used.)

- **Joint tenancy** is where two or more people acquire land but no words of 'severance' are used. This means that the transfer does not state what share in the land each person has. The land is merely 'held by X and Y'. It is both legal and equitable co-ownership. **Joint tenancy** is a convenient and commonly used way for a husband and wife to own the matrimonial home.

- **Tenants in common** have shares in the land. For instance, a conveyance may state that the land should go to 'P, Q and R equally' – each then owns one-third part of the interest. It is equitable ownership.

## 5.4 Significance of the type of ownership

The importance of the distinction is that if a **joint tenant** dies his interest lapses and the land is owned wholly by the survivor(s). He may not pass his interest on by **will**. The advantage is that only a limited number of interests can exist. The disadvantage is the fact that survival decides ownership. With tenants in common, each tenant can bequeath his interest which means that a house owned by tenants in common (A, B and C equally) will, if C dies and leaves his interest to D, E, F and G, be owned by A, B, (one-third part each) D, E, F and G (one-twelfth part each). While perhaps being fairer, this can be cumbersome!

The Law of Property Act 1925 achieved a compromise by providing that, where land is owned by two or more persons, no more than four of those persons hold the **legal estate** as joint tenants and trustees, for the benefit or **equitable interest** of themselves and other co-owners. Thus transfers can be effected by four signatures but the sale proceeds are subject to trusts so that all the owners get fair shares.

## 5.5 Leasehold land

A freehold owner may grant a **leasehold estate** (in England, Wales and Northern Ireland) which gives the right to occupy the land for the period of the lease in exchange for a ground rent which may be relatively nominal in amount.

With leasehold property (in legal terminology, 'chattels real'), the right of a tenant (or lessee) will come to an end either by expiry of a fixed period (which may be as much as 999 years) or by termination by notice (and in other more unlikely events). When it terminates, the landlord (or lessor) resumes possession from the tenant. The landlord is therefore said

BPP
LEARNING MEDIA

to have a '**reversion**' which becomes possession when the lease terminates. While the lease continues, the tenant has possession but is usually required to pay a rent to the landlord.

A **lease** is a form of **contract**. If granted for a term of more than three years, it must generally be in the form of a **deed**.

If the expiry date of the lease is some way into the future, the leasehold estate can be treated as being virtually as good as a freehold estate. A lease cannot be perpetual: it must have an expiry date.

As the expiry date of a lease approaches, the market value of the lease reduces. For this reason, **lenders** may require there to be at least 30 years or 40 years remaining on a lease beyond the end of the term of a mortgage.

## 5.6 Leasehold reform

The **Leasehold Reform Act 1967** gave to non-commercial leaseholders the **right to buy the freehold** of their property and to extend lease periods by up to 50 years.

The **Leasehold Reform, Housing and Urban Development Act 1993** allowed extension of the term of leases of 21 years or more by 90 years, for qualifying tenants. To qualify, tenants must have been resident for two years or more and at least 50% of the qualifying tenants must agree to buy the freehold.

The value of the freehold of land on which there are long leases will mainly be determined by the capital value of ground rents, plus any 'marriage value' resulting from bringing the leasehold and freehold together. For leases that are closer to expiry, the freehold will have a higher value.

The **Commonhold and Leasehold Reform Act 2002 (CLRA 2002)** created commonhold as a further form of tenure, although it remains fairly unusual. Owners of flats ('units') in an apartment building or complex can form a Commonhold Association. This Association owns the land, building and common areas, and has responsibility for repairs, maintenance and servicing of the building. The unit-owners, unlike leaseholders, have perpetual rights. They can play a part in running the Commonhold Association.

Under the CLRA 2002, long leaseholders have the '**right to manage**' by establishing a company to manage an apartment building, provided that the original lease terms were **more than 21 years** and no more than 25% of the internal floor area is for non-residential use.

CLRA 2002 has simplified the procedure for buying freeholds and extending leases. There is no longer a requirement to prove residence of the flat.

## 5.7 Shared ownership, 'Help to Buy' and 'NewBuy'

**Shared ownership** schemes are operated by **Housing Associations**. Shared ownership properties are always leasehold.

The homebuyer purchases a share of the property – typically 25%, 50% or 75% – and the rest is owned by the Housing Association. The homebuyer pays rent on the share owned by the Housing Association.

The shared ownership property can be sold on to a new purchaser, with the new purchaser taking on the same owned/rented split.

'**Staircasing**' refers to the option often offered by the Housing Association for the purchaser to increase their percentage share in the property.

In England, the **Help to Buy** scheme offers equity loans to both first-time buyers and home movers on new-build homes worth up to £600,000. The homebuyer must contribute at least 5% of the purchase price. The government will provide a loan for up to 20% of the price of the house. The home buyer must obtain a mortgage of up to 75% to cover the remainder of the price. There are no loan fees to pay to the government for the first five years. In the sixth year, the home owner is charged a fee of 1.75% of the value of the loan, rising by the Retail Prices Index plus 1% each year. Any gain on selling the home accrues to the home owner, but the equity loan must be repaid when the home is sold or at the end of the mortgage period.

**NewBuy** enables qualifying homebuyers to buy a newly built or newly converted house or flat priced at £500,000 or less as their main home with a deposit of only 5% of the purchase price, while obtaining a loan for the remainder from an approved lender.

There are different schemes in Wales and Scotland.

# 6 Bankruptcy

## 6.1 Introduction

From time to time, a client of a financial adviser might run into financial difficulties, and face **bankruptcy** or, in the case of a corporate client, **insolvency** proceedings. It is important for the financial adviser to have a broad understanding of the legal and financial implications for the client in these circumstances.

## 6.2 Bankruptcy

**Bankruptcy** occurs when an individual's financial affairs are taken over by a court. The individual's assets are transferred into a **trust** which is used to repay as much debt as possible.

The term 'bankruptcy' applies to individuals, not to companies. A sole trader or partner who owes money (a debtor) and is unable to pay the debt could be faced with bankruptcy proceedings.

Inability to pay a debt will occur when the individual cannot find the money. Inadequate cash flow, rather than a loss-making business, may be the problem. Typically, the business will have insufficient cash coming in to meet its various payment obligations, and will be unable to borrow more money. In this situation, the individual's business will have more current liabilities than liquid assets.

The current legislation dealing with bankruptcy is the **Insolvency Act 1986**, as amended by the **Insolvency Act 2000** and the **Enterprise Act 2002**.

## 6.3 Creditors' petition for a bankruptcy order

Bankruptcy proceedings against an individual begin with the presentation of a petition for a bankruptcy order to the court. (This could be the High Court or a County Court with power to deal with such proceedings.)

The petitioner is usually a creditor, or several creditors acting jointly. (However, a debtor may petition to have himself/herself declared bankrupt.) The court will not entertain a petition from a creditor unless the creditor is owed at least £750 (currently) on an unsecured debt.

A creditor's petition must allege that the debtor is unable to pay the debt or has very little prospect of being able to pay it. This inability to pay must be demonstrated in court by showing one of the following:

(a) That a **'statutory demand'** (in the prescribed form) has been served on the debtor, requiring him or her to pay, and this demand has not been satisfied within three weeks.

(b) That a **judgement debt** (i.e. a payment ordered by a court or judge) has been returned unsatisfied, in whole or in part.

In the time between the presenting of a petition for a bankruptcy order and the court's decision, the debtor may be tempted to dispose of some of his or her property, in order to put it outside the reach of the creditors. Under the Insolvency Act 1986, however, any disposal of property or payment of money after a petition has been presented will be **void** if the debtor is subsequently judged to be bankrupt, **unless** the court approves the disposal or payment.

## 6.4 Bankruptcy order

When a petition for a bankruptcy order has been presented, the court may decide to make a bankruptcy order, i.e. declare the individual bankrupt. The bankruptcy of the individual begins on the day this order is made.

When a bankruptcy order has been made, the Official Receiver takes control of the debtor's assets, as **receiver and manager**. The Official Receiver is an official of the Department of Business, Innovation and Skills and an officer of the court.

The duty of the receiver and manager is to protect the bankrupt's property until a **trustee in bankruptcy** has been appointed.

## 6.5 Trustee in bankruptcy

The function of the **trustee in bankruptcy** is to get possession of and realise the value of the bankrupt's assets, and distribute them to the creditors, in accordance with the Insolvency Act.

Every bankruptcy is under the general control of the court, which has wide powers to control the trustee.

All property owned by the debtor on the date of the bankruptcy order, and any property acquired subsequently, passes to the trustee. The only items of property the debtor is allowed to retain are:

(a)     The tools of his/her trade
(b)     A vehicle, if one is needed for his/her trade or employment
(c)     Clothing, bedding and furniture belonging to the debtor and his/her family

## 6.6 Income payments order

As regards the income of a bankrupt person, the trustee is entitled only to the excess income above what is needed to support the bankrupt and his/her family. Income includes income from employment or holding office and profits from carrying on a business. The trustee can apply to the court, claiming for all such excess income to belong to the bankrupt's estate.

The court may then make an **income payments order**, permitting the debtor to receive an income from his/her trade or employment. However, the trustee may take any income in excess of what is considered reasonable.

## 6.7 Disposal of matrimonial homes

If the debtor owns his/her own **home**, and lives alone, lives with a co-habitee and/ or lives with adult children, the debtor's interest in the home passes to the trustee. The trustee will immediately obtain a court order for sale of the property.

If the **matrimonial home** is owned by the bankrupt's spouse or former spouse, the trustee should not normally have an interest in the property for the bankrupt's estate. However, if the property has been transferred by the bankrupt to the spouse under suspicious circumstances, the trustee can apply to the court to have a claim on the property for the bankrupt's estate.

After one year from the date of the bankruptcy order, it is presumed that the needs of the creditors outweigh all other considerations, unless there are exceptional circumstances. As a consequence, after that time a court order can probably be obtained for the eviction of the debtor and his/her family, and for the sale of the home.

Under the Enterprise Act 2002, there is a limit of three years during which the trustee in bankruptcy can deal with the bankrupt's interest in the home. After this period it will revert back to the bankrupt.

Banks and other **lenders of mortgage finance** to buy a matrimonial home need to be aware of the potential problems in the event of the borrower's bankruptcy. Before granting a mortgage, the lender will ask about any potential legal or beneficial interest in the property of a person other than the borrower. The lender might insist that the mortgage should be in joint names. If one person is declared bankrupt, the other person remains subject to the mortgage, and is responsible for the mortgage payments in full.

## 6.8 Distribution of assets following a bankruptcy order

The job of the trustee is to dispose of the bankrupt's assets, and distribute the proceeds to the creditors.

The debts of the bankrupt person must be paid by the trustee in the following order of priority:

(a) The costs of the bankruptcy (including the professional fees of the trustee)

(b) Preferential debts. Preferential debts include:

    (i) Accrued holiday pay owed to employees

    (ii) Wages and salaries of employees due in the last four months before the bankruptcy order, subject to a maximum amount of £800 per employee

(c) Ordinary unsecured creditors. These can only be paid once the other categories of debt have been paid in full. If the proceeds from selling the bankrupt's assets are insufficient, these creditors are treated equally. For example, if there is £50,000 left over from the disposal of assets to pay ordinary unsecured creditors of £100,000, each unsecured creditor will receive 50p in the £1 on their unpaid debt.

---

### Example: Creditors

A bankruptcy order was made against Peter Wilton. The trustee eventually disposed of his home, which was subject to a £170,000 mortgage, for £250,000. His other assets realised £200,000. Preferential debts were £25,000, the costs of bankruptcy were £15,000 and unsecured creditors totalled £500,000.

How much did unsecured creditors receive?

### Solution

Realisation of:

|  | £ |
|---|---|
| Home | 80,000 |
| Other assets | 200,000 |
|  | 280,000 |
| Bankruptcy costs | (15,000) |
| Preferential debts | (25,000) |
|  | 240,000 |

Unsecured creditors will receive £240,000/£500,000 = 48p in the pound.

---

## 6.9 Voidable transactions by the bankrupt

A trustee in bankruptcy has a duty to obtain the most money possible in order to pay the bankrupt's creditors. If the bankrupt undertakes certain transactions that harm the interests of the creditors (or harm some creditors at the expense of others), the trustee can apply to the court for the transactions to be declared void.

## 6.10 Automatic discharge of bankruptcy order

Following the enactment of the Enterprise Act 2002, a bankruptcy order is normally discharged automatically **one year** after the date of the order. This means that the individual is no longer a bankrupt, and is free of debts, even if these have not been paid in full. Once the bankruptcy order has been discharged, any property subsequently obtained by the ex-bankrupt belongs to him/her, and does not vest in the trustee.

## 6.11 Bankruptcy Restriction Orders

**Bankruptcy Restriction Orders (BROs)** are designed to protect the public from a bankrupt whose conduct has been irresponsible or reckless. A BRO imposes restrictions that apply after a bankrupt has been discharged. The restrictions can apply for between two and fifteen years.

# 7 Insolvency

## 7.1 Introduction

The law on **corporate insolvency** in the UK is similar in many respects to the law on bankruptcy. The courts responsible for administering corporate insolvency law are the High Court (Chancery Division) and the county courts. (This chapter deals with the law in England and Wales. The law in Scotland differs in some respects but the syllabus is tested on the basis of English law and practice.) The **Insolvency Act 2000** and the **Enterprise Act 2002 (EA 2002)** introduced major changes to corporate insolvency laws.

## 7.2 Aims of insolvency law

The purpose of insolvency law is to govern what should happen to the property of a company that is insolvent. The basic aims of the law are to:

- (a) **Protect** the creditors of the company
- (b) **Balance** the interests of competing groups
- (c) **Control or punish** directors responsible for the company's financial collapse
- (d) **Encourage** 'rescue' operations

## 7.3 Tests of corporate insolvency

There are two tests of corporate insolvency as follows.

- (a) **Inability to pay debts when they fall due.** A company can be the subject of a winding-up petition if it fails to pay an undisputed debt, currently of more than £750.

- (b) A **'balance sheet test'.** A company can be deemed insolvent if its liabilities exceed its assets.

It is important to be able to establish whether a company is solvent or insolvent.

- (a) It is often a requirement for a company to be deemed insolvent for insolvency proceedings to be started.

- (b) In the case of a voluntary liquidation, the liquidation cannot be initiated by the members (company shareholders) if the company is insolvent.

## 7.4 Types of insolvency proceeding

There are three types of **corporate insolvency** 'officials', depending on whether a company goes into **administration, receivership** or **liquidation**.

(a) **Administration. Administrators** are officers of the court. They may be appointed under an administration order or may be appointed by companies and directors without a court order. The purpose of an administration is to provide a better way of realising the company's assets than could be achieved by a liquidation or receivership (see below), when the company is in financial difficulties.

(b) **Receivership**. In most cases, **a receiver is appointed out of court by a debenture holder (usually a bank)** in pursuance of powers to do so contained in the debenture. A receiver is concerned principally with the interests of the secured creditors who appointed him and will try to take control of the charged assets. If the receiver is appointed under a debenture giving a general floating charge over the company's assets, he will be an **administrative receiver** and take over the management of the company's property. **EA 2002** has largely abolished administrative receivership, in favour of a more streamlined procedure than there used to be for appointing an administrator.

(c) **Liquidation**. A **liquidator** acts mainly in the interests of **unsecured creditors** and **members** (shareholders) of the company. Liquidators of insolvent companies might be appointed either:

(i) Under a voluntary liquidation arrangement, or
(ii) Following an unsecured creditor's petition to the court for liquidation of the company

Liquidation means that the company must be dissolved and its affairs 'wound up', or brought to an end. The assets are realised, debts are paid out of the proceeds, and any surplus amounts are returned to members. Liquidation leads on to dissolution of the company.

## 7.5 Fraudulent and wrongful trading

If, when a company is wound up, it appears that its business has been carried on with **intent** to **defraud creditors** or others, the court may decide that the persons (usually the directors) who were knowingly parties to the fraud shall be **personally responsible** for debts and other liabilities of the company: s213 Insolvency Act 1986.

# 8 Wills and intestacy

## 8.1 The will

A **will** is a legal document which gives effect to the wishes of an individual (the testator, if male, the testatrix if female) as to how their estate should be distributed after their death. It appoints the persons who will have the responsibility for dealing with the estate (the executors) and gives instructions as to how the estate should be distributed.

A will must be signed in the presence of two witnesses. A **witness** or the **spouse of a witness** cannot benefit from a will. If a witness or the spouse of a witness is named as a beneficiary, the will is not made invalid, but that person will not be able to inherit under the will.

## 8.2 Administration of the estate

The **executors** (also called **personal representatives**) need to obtain a **Grant of Probate** from the Probate Registry to show they are entitled to **administer the estate**. Probate is a certificate provided by the court, giving evidence that the will has been registered and administration has been granted to the executor.

Then they can collect the assets of the estate. The executors are responsible for settling all liabilities of the estate before paying out the money to the beneficiaries. The liabilities include funeral expenses, inheritance tax (in respect of which the executors must submit an account and pay any IHT due before obtaining the **Grant of Probate**), liabilities incurred while the testator was alive and expenses incurred during the period of administration (i.e. while the estate is under the control of the executors). The estate cannot be paid out to the beneficiaries until all liabilities have been settled and the executors are satisfied that no claims will be made against the estate.

Where a personal representative is **appointed by the court**, he or she is referred to as an **administrator** rather than an executor.

The assets comprising the estate are held by the executors on trust for the beneficiaries until they are distributed to them. Usually this will only last as long as it takes to administer the estate. However, longer term trusts are frequently created by wills. The trustees of these can be separate individuals to the executors and the trust terms can be the same as those of lifetime (*inter vivos*) trusts. Trusts are typically created to cater for minors. Another common use is the creation of a discretionary trust to use the inheritance tax nil rate band of the first of a married couple to die.

An important reason to effect a will is for a parent to indicate whom they would like as **guardians** to care for minor children. If this is not done (or if there are objections to the parent's choice), the guardians will be appointed by a court.

A will is made **invalid** if the testator **marries**, unless the testator expressly stated that the will was made in contemplation of marriage. If the testator **divorces**, bequests in favour of the **ex-spouse** no longer have effect.

## 8.3 Letters of administration

Where an executor has not been appointed in the will or an individual dies intestate (i.e. without leaving a will), the principal beneficiary of the will may apply to court to be appointed as administrator. The appointment is made by means of letters of administration.

If there is no dispute about representation for an estate or whether a will is valid, the application for grant of representation is referred to as **non-contentious** or **common form**. Where there is a dispute, it is referred to as **contentious** or **solemn form**.

An application for grant of representation in common form must contain a representative's oath. This is a document where the applicant swears as to the date of death and the fact that he is best entitled to act as administrator or is named as executor. In addition, the applicant must produce an account of the deceased's estate for inheritance tax purposes, certified by the HMRC, and the will, if applicable.

## 8.4 Mirror and mutual wills

A husband and wife or an unmarried couple may make wills in similar terms. For example, the husband may make a will which leaves his estate to his spouse, if she survives him, failing that to their children. The wife's will leaves her estate to her husband, if he survives her, failing that to their children. Such wills are called **mirror or reciprocal wills**.

Under general legal principles, a will may be revoked at any time. This also applies to mirror/reciprocal wills. In particular, after one of the spouses has died, the other may alter his or her will, for example in favour of a new spouse.

Under the doctrine of **mutual wills**, two persons (often husband and wife) **make an agreement** that their property is to devolve in a certain way. For example, the agreement may specify that on the first of them to die the deceased's property passes to the survivor, and after his or her death, the property of both of them passes to nominated beneficiaries, such as their children. The agreement must amount to a contract, not merely an understanding.

Clearly, this is very similar to the creation of mirror wills and it will be important to show that there was indeed an agreement to create mutual wills (which are effectively irrevocable dispositions), not merely mirror wills.

If it is decided that mutual wills have been made, the law will allow the ultimate beneficiaries to enforce the agreement.

## 8.5 Reasons for making a will

There are the following reasons for making a will.

- To arrange for beneficiaries other than those appointed under the intestacy rules to benefit. Unmarried partners and stepchildren cannot benefit other than by a will. Children of a previous marriage might also lose out if the testator remarries.
- To use tax reliefs and allowances.
- To create trusts to cater for the long-term needs of the beneficiaries or to enable capital to skip generations.
- To choose executors and trustees and to extend their statutory powers.
- To specify funeral arrangements.

## 8.6 Intestacy

An individual who dies without a will is known as an **intestate**. The estate of an intestate individual is dealt with under the intestacy rules.

Under the **Inheritance and Trustees' Powers Act 2014**, for deaths on or after 1 October 2014:

- If an individual is survived by a spouse or civil partner but no children or remoter issue, the entire estate goes to the surviving spouse or civil partner. (Under previous law, the spouse or civil partner would only receive the first £450,000 and half of the excess over £450,000; the other half of the excess passed to parents or siblings.)
- If the deceased person is survived by spouse or civil partner and children or remoter issue, the surviving spouse or civil partner will receive the first £250,000 and half of the excess over £250,000. The children will receive the other half of the excess equally between them.

Although the recent changes help a surviving spouse or civil partner, such persons would be in a much better position if the deceased had left a properly drawn-up will. The changes make no difference to **cohabitees**, who still have no rights to the assets of their deceased partner.

# 9 Trusts

## 9.1 What is a trust?

A **trust** is an equitable obligation (see below for an explanation of 'equitable') in which certain persons (the **trustees**) are bound to deal with property over which they have control (the **trust property**) for the benefit of certain individuals (the **beneficiaries**).

The trustees may also be beneficiaries of the trust. An individual who transfers assets into a trust during his lifetime is known as a **settlor** and such trusts are known as **settlements**. A settlor may also be a trustee and/or a beneficiary. A trust may also be set up in a **will** and is then usually called a **will trust**. Where the trust is set down in writing, this document is called the '**trust instrument**'.

A trust may be created during the **lifetime of the settlor**, in which case the terms of the trust will be documented in the **trust deed**. Alternatively, a trust may arise on the **death of the settlor**, in which case the terms of the trust will be laid down in the will, or by the statutory provisions which apply on an intestacy.

The first trustee will normally be specified in the trust deed or will. Trustees may retire and new trustees may be appointed, but for tax purposes they are regarded as a single continuing body of persons. The beneficiaries will also be specified in the trust deed or will. They may be separately named, 'my daughter Ann', or may be members of a particular class of persons, 'my children'. The trust property will comprise the original property settled (or property replacing it), plus any property added to the trust, plus income accumulated as an addition to capital, less any amounts advanced to beneficiaries.

Trusts will often be **express** trusts, in that they are expressly and explicitly set up by a settlor identifying the **trustee** and the **beneficiary**. Alternatively, they may be set up only by accident or implication, in which case they are referred to as **resulting** or **constructive** trusts.

## 9.2 Trustees and beneficiaries: equitable interest

The word **'equity'** derives from the Latin word meaning justice or fairness.

Trusts are an invention of the law of equity. Originally the law of England was made up primarily of ancient customs which varied from one region to another. This was eventually compiled into a law which was uniform throughout England and known as the **common law**.

Over time, common law attained a definite shape but it did not tend to evolve sufficiently fast to cater for the changing needs of society. In particular, it tended to look at the form of a transaction (e.g. in a land purchase whose name appeared on the title deeds) rather than the substance (e.g. who provided the purchase money). It therefore became customary for individuals to appeal to the King's Chancellor in circumstances where the enforcement of common law would have been unduly harsh. The King's Chancellor was empowered by the King to give redress and relief from the full effects of common law where conscience indicated that this was appropriate.

Eventually definite principles were evolved and these were compiled into a system of rules. These rules became known as **Equity**. For example, equity would recognise the interest of the provider of purchase monies whether or not that person's name appeared on the title deeds.

Equity and common law frequently conflicted and in 1873 the Judicature Act provided that equity should override common law. The Act also provided that all courts could administer both types of law. The two types of law, however, still remain distinct. Legal rights (those derived under common law) and equitable rights (those derived under equity) therefore need to be distinguished from each other.

Trusts encompass both types of interest. The **legal title** (i.e. legal ownership) to the property in a trust will be held by the **trustees** whereas the **equitable (or beneficial) interest** will belong to the **beneficiaries**. For example, land could be transferred to the trustees and the legal title would be in their names. Equity would recognise that the land was not transferred to the trustees for their own benefit but to be held for the benefit of the beneficiaries in accordance with the terms of the trust. If the trustees do not act in accordance with the terms of the trust, the beneficiaries may apply to the Court to enforce the trust.

## 9.3 Participants in a trust

### 9.3.1 Settlor

The **settlor** is the original owner of the property in question, who creates a trust by transferring legal ownership of the property to one or more trustees. The settlor will have to state expressly that the property is to be held in trust for one or more beneficiaries for there to be a legal trust. The act of transferring the property in this way is referred to as 'constituting' the trust.

It is possible for almost anyone to be a settlor so long as they have legal title to the property in question. However, if someone is deemed to be incapable of making decisions due to a mental disorder then he will not be able to settle property.

### 9.3.2 Beneficiary

The beneficiary (also known as the *'cestui que trust'*) is the individual for whose benefit the property is being held. There may be more than one beneficiary and it is possible for both the settlor and a trustee to be a beneficiary.

Beneficiaries do not have control over the property held in the trust. However, they can ensure through the courts that the trust is administered correctly and can obtain information on the trust and inspect trust documents. If all the **beneficiaries are aged 18 or over** and absolutely entitled under the trust, they can, by unanimous agreement, **bring a trust to an end** or **vary its provisions**.

### 9.3.3 Trustee

The trustee is the legal owner of the property and has control over the property settled in the trust. Although the legal owner, the trustee is obliged to manage the settled property for the beneficiaries, in accordance with the terms of the **trust deed**. The trust deed sets out the terms of the trust and the rights and duties of each of the participants in the trust. It is not essential for there to be a written trust deed, except in the case of a trust for land (it is a legal requirement that transfers of land are evidenced in writing). However, it is recommended to issue a written trust deed to avoid subsequent legal problems in interpreting the objects and beneficiaries of the trust.

It is possible for there to be more than one trustee and for a trustee also to be the settlor, a beneficiary or both. In the case of trusts over land, there must be a minimum of two and a maximum of four trustees. The maximum of four trustees is prescribed by law. Two trustees are needed to give a valid receipt on the sale of land owned by the trust. In the case of trusts set up under a will, there must be a maximum of four trustees. In any other case, there are no restrictions on the number of trustees.

A trustee must be able to hold legal title. Trustees will often be solicitors, banks or trust corporations specifically set up for the purpose. Children under the age of 18, however, are not allowed to be trustees.

The case of **Speight v Gaunt (1883)** concerns the **duty of care** owed by trustees. In this case, the standard of care expected of the trustee was stated to be that of a prudent businessman acting on his own behalf. Beyond that, there was no liability or obligation on the trustee

## 9.4 Types of trust

A trust may be a **bare trust**, also known as a **simple trust** or an **absolute trust**, where there is a sole beneficiary. In such a trust, the trustee has no discretion over payment of income or capital to the beneficiary, who has an immediate and absolute right to both capital and income. Administration of this type of trust is relatively simple. The beneficiary of the trust can instruct the trustee how to manage the trust property, and has the right to take actual possession of the trust property at any time.

An **interest in possession trust** arises where a beneficiary, known as an 'income beneficiary' or a 'life interest', has a legal right to the income or other benefit derived from the trust property as it arises. For example, the **life interest** may have the right to occupy a house during his or her lifetime, or an **income beneficiary** the right to receive income from the trust property for a specified period or until death. On the death of the life interest/income beneficiary, the assets of the trust will be held for the benefit of the second class of beneficiary, known as the **remainderman** or the reversionary interest. A trustee of an interest in possession trust has the duty to safeguard the interests of both classes of beneficiary.

A trust may be a **discretionary trust**, where the trustees exercise their discretion as to which beneficiaries will be entitled to receive income or capital from the trust. The exact rights of each beneficiary are not determined in advance. This can be of use in family situations. First of all, it may enable the settlor to control the conduct of the beneficiaries by the trustee's use of discretionary powers. Second, it keeps the trust flexible. For example, the settlor can constitute a discretionary trust for the benefit of a class of people, such as his grandchildren. If a new grandchild is born after the trust is set up, the grandchild will automatically rank as a beneficiary.

## 9.5 Charitable trusts

**Charitable trusts** are those set up for the purpose of charitable works. Such trusts enable the settlor to give some degree of individuality to a gift, specifying how it may be used and, as **charities**, are basically free from tax.

Wealthy persons with perhaps £10 million or more to devote to philanthropy may consider setting up a private **charitable foundation** in order to manage the distribution of funds to the charitable causes they wish to support. This gives the individual donor more control over the way funds are used.

A major **benefit of charitable status** is that charities are exempt from all forms of taxation on income and capital. In addition, charities may claim back income tax at the basic rate on donations made under deed of covenant. This tax exemption may be restricted, however, if some of its income is used for non-charitable purposes.

Charities may invest in a pooled vehicle known as a **common investment fund** under the Charities Act. This must be specified as a special range investment in the trust deed as it is not an investment permitted under the **Trustee Act 2000** (see below) and thus not bound by its terms.

Whatever their size or purpose, the essential **requirement** and **limitation** of all charities is that they operate for the public benefit and independently of government or commercial interests. In the **Charities Act 2006**, Parliament passed new legislation for charities which, among other provisions, gave new emphasis to the requirement for all charities' aims to be, demonstrably, **for the public benefit**.

## 9.6 Discretionary trusts

A **discretionary trust** for a family could have the following provisions.

- Settlor: James Brown
- Trustees: John Brown (son) and Jean White (daughter)
- Beneficiaries: the children and remoter issue of the settlor, and their spouses/civil partners
- Trust property: £100,000 originally settled and any property deriving therefrom
- Income is to be distributed to the beneficiaries at the trustees' discretion. (For trusts created **before 6 April 2010**, income may be accumulated by the trustees for only up to 21 years from the date of the settlement.)
- Capital may be advanced to beneficiaries at the trustees' discretion. Any capital remaining undistributed on the 80th anniversary of the date of settlement is to be distributed to the settlor's grandchildren then living, failing which to Oxfam. (There is a maximum term of **125 years for trusts created after 5 April 2010** under the **Perpetuities and Accumulations Act 2009**; 80 years for earlier trusts.)

## 9.7 Interest in possession trusts

An **interest in possession trust** could have the following provisions.

- Settlor: Alice Rawlings
- Trustees: Alice Rawlings and Crispin Armitage (solicitor)
- Trust property: 10,000 Tesco plc shares, £5,000 cash
- Beneficiaries: Ruth Bishop (daughter), Lawrence Bishop (grandson)
- Income: payable to Ruth Bishop during her lifetime
- Capital: distributed to Lawrence Bishop on the death of Ruth Bishop

In this trust, the trustees have no discretion over the payment of either income or capital: both must be dealt with in accordance with the terms of the trust. Ruth Bishop has an **interest in possession** in the trust because she is entitled to the income of the trust now. She might also be called the life tenant of the trust because her right to income lasts for her lifetime. Lawrence Bishop has **reversionary interest** in the trust because he is only entitled to the capital after Ruth's interest has come to an end. He may be called the **remainderman**.

## 9.8 Trustee Act 2000

The **Trustee Act 2000** (TA 2000) widened the investment powers and powers of delegation for trusts that do not have wide investment powers provided for in the trust deed. Trustees and their advisers need to follow the Act unless the trust deed overrules the Act.

Under the Trustee Act 2000, trustees can make any investment of any kind that they could as if the funds were their own, except for investment in overseas land. Trustees are however, subject to a fundamental duty to act in the best interests of all the beneficiaries, and are also be subject to a **statutory duty of care** in exercising new investment powers.

TA 2000 imposes the following duties on trustees.

- The need to be aware of the need for diversification and suitability of the investments of the trust.
- A duty to obtain and consider 'proper advice' when making or reviewing investments.
- To keep investments under review.

## 9.9 Reasons to use trusts

### 9.9.1 Introduction

**Trusts are useful vehicles for non-tax reasons** such as to preserve family wealth, to provide for those who are deemed to be incapable (minors, and the disabled) or unsuitable (due to youth or poor business sense) to hold assets directly.

### 9.9.2 Will trusts

A discretionary trust may be set up by will. The rate of inheritance tax on principal charges and exit charges within the trust will then depend on the settlor's cumulative transfers in the seven years before his death and the value of the trust property. The discretionary trust allows the transferee flexibility about who is to benefit from the trust and to what extent. This can be useful if there are beneficiaries of differing ages and whose financial circumstances may differ.

### 9.9.3 Lifetime trusts

Although gifts to trusts during lifetime can lead to an inheritance tax charge, there can be tax benefits from setting up trusts during the settlor's lifetime. As long as the cumulative total of chargeable lifetime transfers in any seven-year period does not exceed the nil rate band, there will be no lifetime IHT to pay on creation of the trust. The trust will be subject to IHT at 0% on the ten-year anniversary and later advances, unless the value of the trust property grows faster than the nil rate band.

If a discretionary trust is used, the settlor can preserve the maximum flexibility in the class of beneficiaries and how income and capital should be dealt with.

If the settlor is included as a beneficiary of the trust the gift will be treated as a gift with reservation.

### 9.9.4 Family settlements

As mentioned above, the purpose of many trusts is to enable the wealthy to retain their wealth. Trusts will tie up wealth within the family and will often be constructed to minimise tax liabilities. They may be created through a will but will often be set up when the settlor is alive, to make tax planning easier.

**Key benefits to the family**

- Controlling who owns and receives benefit from the property.
- Potential reduction of tax liabilities.
- Giving someone the benefit of property while preventing them from wasting it through careless actions.

For example, a house may be left on trust so that one member of the family can use it during their lifetime (i.e. have a **life interest in possession**), while another member can receive the house when the person with the life interest dies (i.e. the **remainderman**).

## 9.9.5 Those who cannot hold property on their own behalf

Unincorporated associations (for example, some charities, trade unions or clubs) are unable to own property, since they are not legally recognised as persons. In such a case, the property can be held on behalf of the association by a trustee.

Children under the age of 18 are not allowed to have legal ownership of land. In order to give land to a child, a trust will need to be set up for the benefit of the child, who can receive legal ownership of the land on reaching his or her majority.

## 9.9.6 Marriage

Whereas most of the trusts mentioned above will be expressly made, a trust in the context of marriage or cohabitation will often be a **resulting trust**. An example would be a situation where a house is held in the name of one of the two partners (X) but the other partner (Y) has contributed money to purchase the house. Since the house is intended to be occupied jointly, X may have legal ownership of the house but is holding part of the interest on trust for Y, even if this were not stated explicitly.

## 9.9.7 Confidentiality

Leaving property through a trust can protect the identity of the beneficial owner, who will only be known to the trustee. Such a trust will be referred to as a '**secret trust**'.

# Key chapter points

- The law attaches rights to a person and imposes legal obligations on him. Legal persons include natural persons (individual human beings) and artificial legal persons (for example, corporate bodies and local authorities).

- In a sole tradership, there is no legal distinction between the individual and the business.

- Partnership is defined as 'the relation which subsists between persons carrying on a business in common with a view of profit'. A partnership is *not* a separate legal person distinct from its members, it is merely a 'relation' between persons.

- A company has a separate legal personality from its members, while a traditional partnership does not. The liability of company shareholders is limited. They may lose their investment, but will not normally be expected to pay more to creditors, if the company goes bust.

- Powers of attorney are a form of agency. They allow a person to act in place of another person. They are particularly useful for older people who may not be able to manage their own affairs.

- Three essential elements in any contract are: agreement (made by offer and acceptance); consideration (there must be a bargain by which obligations assumed by one party are supported by value given by the other); intention (the parties must have an intention to create legal relations).

- Agency is a relationship which exists between two legal persons (the principal and the agent) in which the function of the agent is to form a contract between his principal and a third party.

- Freehold land is termed real property. Co-ownership of land may be as joint tenants or tenants in common. With a tenancy in common, the shares of the property that each owns are specified. If a joint tenant dies, the property becomes wholly owned by the survivor.

- An insolvent individual can be declared bankrupt. Every bankruptcy is under the general control of the court, which has wide powers to control the trustee.

- Insolvency signals that a company cannot pay all of its debts. Insolvency law is designed to protect the creditors of the company, to balance the interests of competing groups, to control or punish directors responsible for the company's financial collapse, and to encourage 'rescue' operations.

- A will is a legal document which gives effect to the wishes of an individual as to how their estate should be distributed after their death. It appoints the personal representatives who will have the responsibility for dealing with the estate (the executors) and gives instructions as to how the estate should be distributed.

- A trust is an equitable obligation in which certain individuals (the trustees) are bound to deal with property over which they have control (the trust property) for the benefit of other individuals (the beneficiaries).

- There are several reasons for creating trusts, including controlling ownership and benefits of assets, potential tax reductions or gifting assets while preventing careless use of the asset.

# Chapter Quiz

1   What are the two types of legal person? ........................................................................ (see para 1.1)

2   What is meant by the 'limited liability' of a company? .................................................................. (1.3)

3   What distinguishes public and private companies? ...................................................................... (1.5)

4   What is an 'LLP'? ................................................................................................................ (1.9)

5   What is a power of attorney and a lasting power of attorney? ................................................ (2.1, 2.5)

6   What are the three essential elements in a valid contract? .......................................................... (3.1)

7   Define the agency relationship. ................................................................................................ (4.1)

8   Distinguish real property and personal property. .................................................................. (5.1, 5.2)

9   What types of joint ownership are possible for two people who want to buy a house together? ...................... (5.3)

10  What reasons are there for making a will? .................................................................................. (8.1)

11  Define a trust. ...................................................................................................................... (9.1)

# The regulatory framework

4 **Understand the regulation of financial services**

    4.1   **Examine** the role of the PRA, FCA, HM Treasury and the Bank of England in regulating the market.

    4.2   **Examine** the role of other regulatory bodies and sources of additional oversight.

    4.3   **Examine** the statutory framework of regulation, including the role of EU regulation and key directives.

# 1 Development of the UK regulatory system

## 1.1 Creation of the FSA as the single regulator

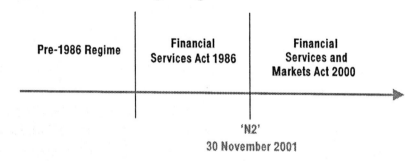

Before the advent of the **Financial Services Act 1986**, the UK financial services industry was self-regulating. Standards were maintained by an assurance that those in the financial services industry had a common set of values and were able, and willing, to ostracise those who violated them.

The 1986 Act moved the UK to a system which became known as '**self-regulation within a statutory framework**'. Once **authorised**, firms and individuals would be regulated by self-regulating organisations (SROs) each covering a different sector of the industry. The Financial Services Act 1986 only covered investment activities. Retail banking, general insurance, Lloyd's of London and mortgages were all covered by separate Acts and Codes.

When the Labour Party gained power in 1997, it wanted to make changes to the regulation of financial services. The late 1990s saw a more radical reform of the financial services system with the unification of most aspects of financial services regulation under a **single statutory regulator**, the **Financial Services Authority (FSA)**. The process took place in two phases.

## 1.2 Phases of the reforms

**First,** the **Bank of England's** responsibility for banking supervision was transferred to the **FSA** as part of the **Bank of England Act 1998**. Despite losing responsibility for banking supervision, the Bank of England (BoE) gained the role in 1998 of **setting official UK interest rates**.

The BoE is also responsible for maintaining stability in the financial system by analysing and promoting initiatives to strengthen the financial system. As we have seen, the BoE is also the financial system's '**lender of last resort**', being ready to provide funds in exceptional circumstances.

The **second phase** of reforms consisted of a new Act covering financial services which would repeal the main provisions of the Financial Services Act 1986 and some other legislation. The earlier 'patchwork quilt' of regulation would be swept away and the FSA would regulate investment business, insurance business, banking, building societies, Friendly Societies, mortgages and Lloyd's.

On 30 November 2001, the new Act – the **Financial Services and Markets Act 2000** (FSMA 2000, often referred to just as FSMA) – came into force, to create a system of **statutory regulation.**

The creation of the FSA as the UK's main **statutory regulator** for the industry brought together regulation of investment, insurance and banking.

With the implementation of FSMA 2000 at date 'N2' in 2001, the FSA took over responsibility for:

- **Prudential regulation** and **supervision** of all firms, which involves monitoring the adequacy of their management, financial resources and internal systems and controls, and

- **Conduct of business** regulations of those firms doing investment business. This involves overseeing firms' dealings with investors including **financial advice** given to any individual to ensure, for example, that information provided is clear and not misleading.

Arguably, the FSA's role as **legislator** diminished over the years following various EU Directives – in particular, the far-reaching **Markets in Financial Instruments Directive (MiFID)**, implemented in November 2007 – as the FSA increasingly needed to apply rules which have been formulated at the **European level.**

## 1.3 Responding to regulatory failures

The FSA-based regulatory regime sought to learn from many of the **regulatory failures** that occurred during the 1980s and 1990s.

- A widespread problem was that of of **pensions mis-selling**. Salespeople encouraged some 2.2 million people to move out of their employers' schemes into personal pension plans. These transfers were often unsuitable. It is partly this which has led to an increased emphasis in the new regime on educating investors to ensure that they understand the risks of transactions they undertake.

- The Bank of Credit and Commerce International (**BCCI**), an important international bank with many UK offices and customers, was the subject of an £8 billion fraud. This led to the FSA taking on regulatory responsibility for banks and increased regulation in the field of money laundering.

- The **Barings Bank** crisis was caused by the actions of a single rogue trader, Nick Leeson, whose unauthorised trading, coupled with the inadequacy of controls, led to the collapse of the bank. This has led to a big drive towards ensuring that senior management take their responsibilities seriously and ensure that systems and controls are adequate.

- In a further instance, world copper prices were manipulated by the unauthorised trading of Mr Hamanaka of **Sumitomo**, with much of his trading taking place on the London Metal Exchange. As a result, the new regime introduces more stringent rules to deal with market abuse.

Regulators need to keep aware of potential types of failure that occur. For example, a more recent mis-selling problem in retail financial services has concerned the mis-selling of PPI (payment protection insurance).

A recent and substantial case of regulatory failure in the USA was the case of **Bernard Madoff**, who was responsible for running a 'Ponzi' scheme in which billions of dollars of funds that investors thought they had in their accounts was illusory. Following Madoff's arrest in 2008, it transpired that his advisory fund, which repeatedly reported successful results, was paying 'profits' to existing investors out of funds provided by new investors. This Ponzi scheme appeared to have been in existence since the 1990s. Economic downturns are likely to lead to such Ponzi schemes coming to light, as indeed was found in the downturn of the late 2000s, since investors are then more likely to wish to make withdrawals.

The regulation of the UK financial services industry continues to evolve and react to new circumstances as they develop. There was criticism of the FSA for failing to be aware of the weakness of banks such as **Northern Rock**, which required emergency assistance and had to be nationalised. The **financial turmoil of the late 2000s (2007 to 2009)** stemmed in large part from excessive lending by banks, particularly to sub-prime borrowers, and from the 'securitisation' or packaging of mortgages by lenders for selling on to investors who were insufficiently aware of the risks attached to the securities, This period of turmoil in the late 2000s has highlighted the need for continuing review and reform of regulatory arrangement and, in the early 2010s, a major re-structuring was planned, for implementation in 2013.

In mid-2010, with a Conservative-Liberal Democratic coalition Government in power, it was announced that **the FSA in its existing form would be abolished**. The idea of abolishing the FSA and re-transferring core regulatory functions to the Bank of England was referred to by the Chancellor of the Exchequer in his Mansion House address in June 2010.

- Under the reforms, there would be a sweeping increase in the powers of the **Bank of England**, which would have a new remit of preventing a build-up of risk in the financial system. At the top of the regulatory structure, a new subsidiary of the Bank based on the FSA's Prudential Business Unit (which was formed in April 2011), the **Prudential Regulation Authority (PRA)** would become the prudential regulator responsible for ensuring the safe operation of over 1,000 deposit-taking institutions, as well as insurers, investment banks and some other institutions.

- The FSA legal entity would become the **Financial Conduct Authority (FCA)**, which would become responsible for consumer protection in financial services, the regulation of conduct of business (including in firms regulated by the new PRA) and market conduct. The European Supervisory Authorities (ESAs) have the task of drawing up European standards including rules for consumer protection and financial innovation. The FCA has become the lead UK authority in the European Securities and Markets Authority (ESMA) and is also active with the other ESAs, the European Banking Authority (EBA) and the European Insurance and Occupational Pensions Authority (EIOPA), in consumer protection activity.

# 2 The current regulatory structure

## 2.1 Bank of England

### 2.1.1 Core purposes

The Bank of England ('the Bank') – the central bank of the United Kingdom – plays an important role in the regulatory system. The Bank has two core purposes: to **ensure monetary stability** and to **contribute to financial stability**.

- **Monetary stability** means stable prices and confidence in the currency. Stable prices are defined by the Government's inflation target, which the Bank seeks to meet through the decisions delegated to the Monetary Policy Committee (which sets benchmark interest rates), explaining those decisions transparently and implementing them effectively in the money markets.

- **Financial stability** entails detecting and reducing threats to the financial system as a whole. This is pursued through the Bank's financial and other operations, including lender of last resort, oversight of key infrastructure and the surveillance and policy roles delegated to the Financial Policy Committee (FPC).

The Bank's **FPC** plays a key regulatory role, and the **PRA** is a subsidiary of the Bank.

### 2.1.2 Systemic financial crisis management

Under the new regulatory framework, the Bank of England has primary operational responsibility for **financial crisis management**.

When it is clear that **public funds may be put at risk**, the Governor of the BoE will have a statutory duty to notify the Chancellor.

Underpinning the process is a crisis management **memorandum of understanding (MoU)** which addresses:

- The responsibilities of the Bank and HM Treasury in a crisis
- The duty of the BoE to notify the Treasury of a risk to public funds
- The Chancellor's exercise of a power of direction over the Bank in a crisis

This process will now be backed up by a **statutory duty** to coordinate the exercise of these functions in a crisis.

As a power of last resort, the **Treasury** can direct the Bank:

- To provide **liquidity support** during a crisis, and
- To exercise its powers over the banking system under the **special resolution regime (SRR).**

This power is exercisable only where there is a real risk to financial stability, or public funds have already been used, and that the BoE retains operational autonomy when managing threats to stability in which public funds are not at risk.

## 2.1.3 Financial Policy Committee (FPC)

The creation of the **Financial Policy Committee** was motivated by the perception that the absence of any effective macro-prudential agency was a major failing in the UK, EU and US before the recent financial crisis. This lack was highlighted with the inability of the authorities to deal with asset price bubbles, especially in the property market, and the accumulation of debt and leverage across the financial system.

The would-be functions of the Council for Financial Stability and the Bank of England's Financial Stability Committee have been merged into the FPC of the Bank. The FPC includes the FCA Chief Executive and representatives from HM Treasury. The FPC will also have some external representation. The FPC meets four times annually and at times of crisis. The committee publishes a record of its formal meetings.

S9C Bank of England (BoE) Act 1998 (as amended by FSA 2012) provides that the FPC is to exercise its functions with a view to:

- Contributing to the achievement by the Bank of England of the **Financial Stability Objective**, and
- Subject to that, supporting the economic policy of the Government, including its objectives for growth and employment.

The Bank's **Financial Stability Objective** is stated in s2A Bank of England Act 1998 (as amended by FSA 2012), which states that an objective of the Bank shall be: **To protect and enhance the stability of the financial system of the UK**.

The responsibility of the Committee in relation to the achievement by the Bank of the Financial Stability Objective relates primarily to the identification of, monitoring of, and taking of action to remove or reduce, **systemic risks** with a view to protecting and enhancing the resilience of the UK financial system (s9C(2) BoE Act 1998).

Those systemic risks include, in particular:

- Systemic risks attributable to structural features of financial markets, such as connections between financial institutions
- Systemic risks attributable to the distribution of risk within the financial sector, and
- Unsustainable levels of leverage, debt or credit growth (s9C(3) BoE Act 1998)

The legislation does not require or authorise the FPC to exercise its functions in a way that would in its opinion be likely to have a significant adverse effect on the capacity of the financial sector to contribute to the growth of the UK economy in the medium or long term.

**Systemic risk** here means a risk to the stability of the UK financial system as a whole or of a significant part of that system, whether the risk arises in the UK or elsewhere.

The **FPC** has the following **tools** at its disposal:

- Setting system-wide cyclical capital requirements, reducing capital buffers required in a crisis while toughening them in more favourable economic times.

- Altering risk weights, enabling the Bank to force banks to hold more capital against specific classes of assets in apparently frothy markets.

- Setting limits on leverage as a backstop against excessive lending where changing risk weights might not be effective.

- Requiring forward-looking loss provisioning to prepare for future losses when lending growth is strong.

- Setting limits on borrowing, e.g. with maximum loan-to-value ratios for mortgages.

- Setting limits on lending through regulation.

The FPC publishes two **Financial Stability Reports (FSRs)** a year, including a summary of its activities and an assessment of the effectiveness of its actions in the period since the last report. (The FPC will be able to exclude confidential or market-sensitive information from what it publishes.)

## 2.2 Prudential Regulation Authority (PRA)

The new PRA is responsible for the prudential regulation of banks, insurance companies and large investment firms. Only these firms will be subject to '**dual regulation**' (see the diagram *New UK regulatory architecture*).

The PRA will focus on the stability of the system overall, albeit through the mechanism of the supervision of individual firms. This will require close coordination with the new **Financial Policy Committee (FPC)** (see below), whose role it will be to manage the risks in the system as a whole. The PRA will be a key contributor to the information and analysis on which the FPC will base its judgements.

The PRA's supervisory efforts relating to financial stability will focus particularly on **large international banks**. In the case of UK subsidiaries of overseas banks, links of the UK entity with the group as a whole as well as the group's viability need to be an integral part of the PRA's supervisory assessment.

The PRA will take a forward-looking and **judgment-based approach to supervision**. Baseline monitoring will be undertaken for all firms, including those that can be resolved with minimal disruption to the financial system (e.g. credit unions and small deposit-takers). This monitoring will include a review of a firm's resolvability (at least) once a year, analysis of a firm's financial position, discussions with senior management and ensuring compliance with minimum prudential standards for capital, liquidity and large exposures, as well as early interventions (where necessary) driven by a new **Proactive Intervention Framework (PIF)** (explained in Chapter 5).

## 2.3 Financial Conduct Authority (FCA)

As the successor body to the FSA and the UK's chief regulator of the conduct of financial services firms, the new **Financial Conduct Authority (FCA)** will not of course be starting from scratch. But the FCA will be more interventionist than the FSA was. It will build upon earlier initiatives such as the FSA's **Consumer Protection Strategy**.

**Smaller investment firms** will continue to be supervised by a **single regulator** under the new regulatory structure, but this will be the **FCA**, rather than the FSA as in the past. Thus, the FCA will be responsible for both prudential and conduct regulation for these firms, as illustrated in the diagram showing the *New UK regulatory architecture*.

The FCA's **supervisory model** has the following elements.

- A revised **risk assessment process** (replacing the FSA's 'ARROW' framework) that can be communicated to senior executives and boards of firms, thus enabling good business practice to be aligned with good regulatory practice.

- In response to the regulatory problems that have arisen since 1990, a **lower risk tolerance** than under the previous regulatory regime: this may mean (using new powers under FSMA 2000, as amended by FSA 2012) banning products before they reach the market, or banning a firm from selling a widely accepted product if its sales processes are unacceptable.

As an 'integrated conduct' regulator, the FCA will look across the whole financial services sector, not only in **investment and capital markets** but also in **banking and wholesale insurance markets**. Under its consumer protection remit, the Authority will define 'consumer' as including even the largest wholesale firms. This will enable the FCA to exercise wide discretion over the interpretation of its objectives and to ensure high standards across the financial services industry in the service of its strategic objective.

## New UK regulatory architecture

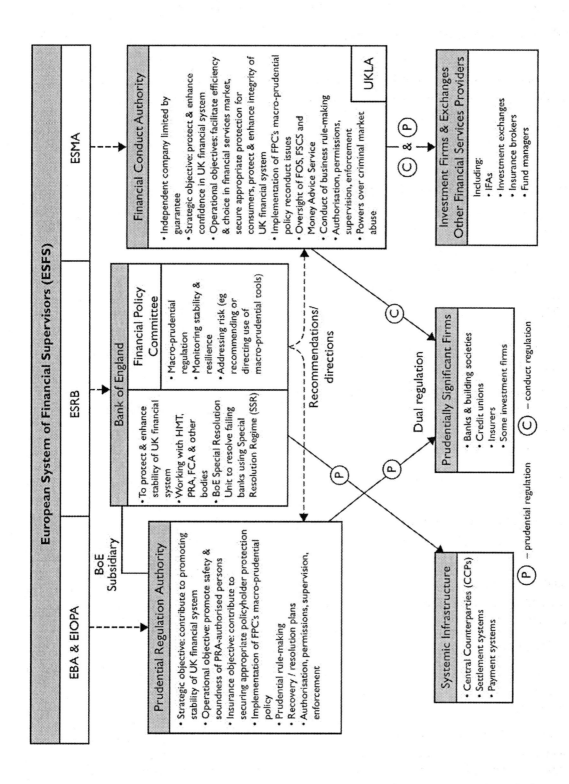

The FCA will set out to recognise that wholesale activities can have a direct impact on retail markets. It will need to consider the interactions and linkages across the financial value chain where risks are transmitted between wholesale and retail customers. In particular, the FCA will look at intervention further up the value chain, targeted at **product governance**. Where activity in wholesale markets may lead to mis-conceived, overly complicated or confusing products, aimed at the mass market, the FCA would plan to intervene.

Clearly the intention of FCA senior management is to develop a new culture, given the perceived regulatory failures of recent years. Speech-making to launch the FCA has spoken of a **pro-active 'can do' approach**, and of the regulator being **bold** in the use of its powers.

## 2.4 FCA and PRA, and dual regulation

Firms that are '**dual regulated**' – by both the FCA and the PRA – such as banks, insurers and major investment firms, will be supervised by two independent groups within the regulators for **prudential** and **conduct** regulation. These groups will work to different objectives and act separately with firms, but will coordinate internally to share information and data.

All other firms will be supervised by one supervision area for both conduct and prudential issues.

## 2.5 HM Treasury and the FCA

The minister with overall responsibility for the Treasury, the Chancellor of the Exchequer, is ultimately responsible for the regulatory system for financial services under FSMA 2000.

HM Treasury, to which the **FCA is accountable**, will judge the regulator against the requirements laid down in FSMA 2000 which includes a requirement to ensure that the burdens imposed on the regulated community are proportionate to the benefits it will provide.

**Accountability of the FCA to HM Treasury**

- HM Treasury has the power to appoint or to dismiss the Board and Chairman of the FCA.

- HM Treasury requires that the FCA submit an annual report covering such matters as the discharge of its functions and the extent to which the regulatory objectives have been met.

- HM Treasury also has powers to commission and publish an independent review of the economy, efficiency and effectiveness of the FCA's use of resources and to commission official enquiries into serious regulatory failures.

The **responsibilities of the BoE and HM Treasury** in the event of a **financial crisis** are underpinned by a **Memorandum of Understanding (MoU)** that we mentioned earlier.

## 2.6 Evaluating the re-structuring of the regulatory framework

Arguments raised about the re-structuring have concerned breaking-up an apparently less effective monolithic authority (while at the same as creating an even larger one), separating prudential from consumer protection and market oversight, promoting the Bank's expertise in economic monitoring and integrating market oversight with market support (traditionally referred to as the role of lender of last resort).

- **Advantages** of the new regime include more focused and dedicated supervision, tailored regulation, separate agency mandates, additional powers and possible prioritisation of action and function.

- **Disadvantages** include the inconsistent treatment of consumer protection and market oversight, the potentially systemic effect of market failure, the need to promote consumer and market confidence, the split enforcement function, the institutional separation arising from creating the PRA as a subsidiary rather than division of the Bank, possible over-centralisation of the macro-prudential function and

decision-taking, linkage created between monetary and financial stability policy, substantial cost and significant regulatory obligations imposed and consequent market and competitive disruption created.

The most important justification for the new regime is the establishment of a strong **macro-prudential function** within the UK regulatory system. While this will be carried out by the FPC, this was previously dealt with by the internal Financial Stability Committee (FSC) set up within the Bank of England under the Banking Act 2009 and the external Council for Financial Stability (CFS) which replaced the earlier Tripartite Committee.

While the need for a strong macro-prudential function is generally accepted, it is less clear whether a separate twin peaks division of prudential and conduct regulation was necessary or whether this could have been more effectively dealt with within a larger, better funded FSA divided into two separate prudential and conduct divisions. This could arguably more clearly reflect the integrated and interconnected nature of modern financial markets.

## 2.7 Complaints against the regulators

Under the new 2013 regulatory structure, there is a single independent **Complaints Commissioner** who will assess complaints whether they are against the FCA, the PRA, or the Bank of England (who are 'the regulators' for this purpose).

Complaints are first be investigated by the regulators themselves. If the complainant remains unsatisfied, they can refer their complaint to the Complaints Commissioner.

The Complaints Commissioner and his staff must not be employees of the regulators and they are required to act independently of, and without favouring, the regulators.

The FCA is responsible for recording details of the complaint and for allocating it to the relevant regulator to investigate.

Complaints against the regulators that will be considered include complaints alleging mistakes and lack of care, unreasonable delay, unprofessional behaviour, bias and lack of integrity.

## 2.8 Competition scrutiny

The regulators' rules and practices are subject to competition vetting by the **Competition and Markets Authority (CMA)**. The regulators therefore need to be careful to ensure that they do not draft rules that are, or act in a way that is, anti-competitive.

## 2.9 Judicial review

The regulators are performing a public function and is empowered to do so by statute. Therefore, the regulators will be subject to administrative law – in particular, **judicial review**. This is a process by which public bodies' actions can be scrutinised in court if they have acted outside the scope of their powers or been procedurally unfair. However, many provisions in FSMA 2000, such as the regulatory objectives, give the regulator broad discretion on how they use their powers and the effect of this may be to limit the practical availability of judicial review.

## 2.10 Consumer and practitioner groups

The regulators' accountability is further advanced by statutory panels – the FCA and PRA **Practitioner Panels**, the FCA **Markets Practitioner Panel** and the FCA's **Consumer Panel** which, under s1M-1R FSMA 2000, must be consulted on general policies and practices. FSMA 2000 requires that the respective regulators have regard to representations made by these panels. The membership of panels is determined by the respective regulators, although HM Treasury's approval is required for the appointment and dismissal of the Chairmen.

- The Practitioner Panels are designed to advise the regulator on the interests and concerns of regulated businesses.

- The FCA Consumer Panel is designed to advise on the interests and concerns of consumers.

The FCA also takes account of the opinions of its **Smaller Business Practitioner Panel**, which represents the interests of small regulated firms. This Panel provides input and views on the impact of regulation on small firms and monitors the regulator's treatment of small firms more generally.

## 2.11 The Upper Tribunal

A further significant check on the accountability of the regulators is the **Tax and Chancery Chamber of the Upper Tribunal (the 'Upper Tribunal')**, which took over the role of the former Financial Services and Markets Tribunal (FSMT) in April 2010, when the FSMT was abolished. The Upper Tribunal is an independent tribunal that will provide for a complete rehearing of enforcement and authorisation cases where the firm or individual and the regulators have not been able to agree the outcome.

FSMA 2000 made provision for an independent body accountable to the Ministry of Justice. This body (the FSMT) was established under the Financial Services and Markets Tribunal Rules 2001. The Upper Tribunal took over from FSMT when there was a major reorganisation of the UK tribunal system.

The **Upper Tribunal** has a wider role than just regulatory decision cases. It is a Superior Court of Record with UK-wide jurisdiction in tax cases and references as well as against decisions of the financial services regulators. For charity cases, the Tribunal has jurisdiction within England and Wales. The Tribunal also has jurisdiction against decisions of the **Pensions Regulator**, in England, Wales and Scotland, and it has the power of judicial review in certain instances.

The Tribunal hears references or appeals against decisions of the financial services regulators, as provided for under FSMA 2000. This will, for example, include the issue of decision and final notices (ss388 and 390) and supervisory notices under the regulators' Supervision Manual. This is distinct from an appeal on a point of law to the courts under s137, which is available from any decision of the Tribunal disposing of a reference to the Tribunal.

The Upper Tribunal can provide for a rehearing of enforcement and authorisation cases where the firm or individual and the regulator have not been able to agree the outcome. Thus, if a firm or individual receives a decision notice or supervisory notice or is refused authorisation or approval, it may refer this to the Tribunal. The Tribunal will determine what appropriate action the regulator should take and, in doing so, can consider any new evidence which has come to light since the original decision was made.

## 2.12 The Financial Ombudsman Service (FOS)

The **Financial Ombudsman Service (FOS)** was set up by Parliament to help settle individual disputes between businesses providing financial services and their customers. The FCA is responsible for oversight of the FOS.

Additionally, the **Consumer Credit Act 2006** amended FSMA 2000, giving the FOS power to make rules to resolve certain disputes against credit providers.

FSMA 2000 sets out the roles and responsibilities of the FCA and the FOS. Both organisations are concerned with protecting consumers, but within this overall objective they have distinct and separate responsibilities.

The FCA's rules require firms to deal with complaints properly. It has power to take disciplinary action against firms and prosecute them under FSMA 2000.

The FOS investigates individual disputes between consumers and regulated firms. The regulations governing complaints are covered in more detail in Chapter 6 of this Study Text.

## 2.13 Regulation of consumer credit

Most businesses that offer goods or services on credit, lend money to consumers or provide debt solutions and advice to consumers will be carrying out consumer credit activities. This includes firms providing personal loans, credit card

issuers, credit brokers, payday loan companies, pawnbrokers, businesses offering hire purchase agreements, log book lenders, peer to peer lenders, and debt management and collection firms.

In 2014, the FCA took over the **regulation of consumer credit**. The FCA operates a **Consumer Credit Register** of firms that were previously licensed by the OFT and have interim permission to continue carrying out consumer credit activities.

Firms carrying out regulated consumer credit activities must follow certain rules about how they manage their businesses and treat their customers. These include rules made by the FCA, which are in the FCA Handbook, and the requirements of the Consumer Credit Act (CCA) and secondary legislation.

A firm that has interim permission will ultimately have to apply for full authorisation to continue carrying out consumer credit activities. If this is approved, the FCA's updated record for the firm will move to the Financial Services Register.

As part of its campaign of taking action in the consumer credit market, the FCA has imposed a **price cap on high-cost short-term credit**, which took effect on **2 January 2015**. There is a cap on initial costs set at 0.8% per day, a cap on fixed default fees of £15, and a 100% cap on total costs. The new rules aim to lower the cost of credit for most borrowers and to protect borrowers with repayment difficulties from rising costs. The rules do this by making sure that total costs do not exceed £24 per £100 borrowed and that no borrower will be required to repay more than double the amount borrowed.

# 3 Other regulators and oversight

## 3.1 The Competition and Markets Authority

The **Competition and Markets Authority (CMA** is an independent non-ministerial department of government based in London, with representatives in Scotland, Wales and Northern Ireland. The CMA was established under the **Enterprise and Regulatory Reform Act 2013**.

The CMA works to promote competition for the benefit of consumers, both within and outside the UK. Its aim is to make markets work well for consumers, businesses and the economy.

The Authority acquired its powers on 1 April 2014 when it took over many of the functions of the Competition Commission (CC) and the Office of Fair Trading (OFT), both of which were abolished at the same date.

The CMA is responsible for:

- Investigating mergers which are significant enough to restrict competition
- Conducting market studies and investigations in markets where there may be competition and consumer problems
- Investigating where there may be breaches of UK or EU prohibitions against anti-competitive agreements and abuses of dominant positions
- Bringing criminal proceedings against individuals who commit the cartel offence
- Enforcing consumer protection legislation to tackle practices and market conditions that make it difficult for consumers to exercise choice
- Co-operating with sector regulators and encouraging them to use their competition powers

There is a voluntary regime of notifying the CMA of a proposed merger.

The CMA combines the **merger control** responsibilities that were previously within the scope of the OFT and the CC. These responsibilities are structured as initial **'Phase I' merger reviews** and, if the CMA believes that the merger will lead to a 'substantial lessening of competition', in-depth **'Phase II' investigations**.

There are separate Phase I and Phase II review periods and procedures.

- **Phase I** decisions are the responsibility of the CMA Board. There is a statutory time limit of 40 working days for Phase I decisions, and there is a time-limited process in which parties may offer undertakings following Phase I.

- **Phase II** decisions are taken by independent panels of experts. There is a statutory time limit of 12 weeks following the Phase II decision for remedies to be implemented.

The main statutory rules on competition are within the **Enterprise Act 2002**. The following scenarios will qualify for investigation by the CMA.

- The combined enterprise controls **at least 25%** of the goods or services in the sector in the UK (the **share of supply test**), or

- The UK turnover of the entity being acquired **exceeds £70 million** (the **turnover test**)

The CMA is empowered to impose **fines** of up to 5% of the combined worldwide turnover of merging companies for breach of an order preventing or reversing integration. The Authority can also impose fines for failure to provide information it has requested.

While the CMA has the power to investigate practices across markets, the Secretary of State for Business, Innovation and Skills has wider powers to intervene in investigations of markets on the grounds of the **public interest**. **National security** is the only public interest consideration that is currently defined.

## 3.2 The Payment Systems Regulator

Launched on 1 April 2015, the Payment Systems Regulator (PSR) is the economic regulator of the UK payment systems industry. The PSR is a subsidiary of the Financial Conduct Authority, but has its own objectives and governance arrangements.

The **purpose** of the PSR is to make payment systems work well for those that use them.

The PSR's **vision** is that payment systems are accessible, reliable, secure, and value for money.

The PSR's **statutory objectives** under the FSMA 2000 are, in summary:

- To ensure that payment systems are operated and developed in a way that considers and promotes the interests of all the businesses and consumers that use them

- To promote effective competition in the markets for payment systems and services – between operators, payment service providers (PSPs), and infrastructure providers

- To promote development of and innovation in payment systems, in particular the infrastructure used to operate those systems

The PSR has regulatory and competition powers to:

- Give directions to take action and set standards
- Impose requirements regarding system rules
- Require operators to provide direct access to payment systems
- Require PSPs to provide indirect access to smaller PSPs
- Amend agreements relating to payment systems, including fees and charges
- Investigate behaviour which isn't consistent with our directions
- Act where the PSR sees anti-competitive behaviour, alongside the Competition & Markets Authority

## 3.3 The Information Commissioner

Under the **Data Protection Act 1998 (DPA 1998)**, where persons process personal data, whether electronically or manually, they must (unless exempt) be registered with the **Information Commissioner** (who maintains a **public**

**registry of data controllers**) and must comply with the DPA 1998 provisions. The requirements apply to most organisations and cover all personal data whether it relates to clients, employees, suppliers or any other person.

If the Information Commissioner considers that a data controller is in contravention of any of the data protection principles, the Commissioner can serve an **enforcement notice**. If the data controller fails to comply with the enforcement notice, he is committing an offence and could be subject to a **fine** of **£500,000**.

## 3.4 Pensions Act 2004 and the Pensions Regulator

The **Pensions Regulator** is the regulatory body for work-based pension schemes in the UK, set up under the Pensions Act 2004. A work-based pension scheme is any scheme that an employer makes available to employees. This includes all occupational schemes, and any stakeholder and personal pension schemes where employees have direct payment arrangements.

The Pensions Regulator has a defined set of statutory objectives, wider **powers** to investigate schemes and take action where necessary and takes a proactive, risk-focused approach to regulation.

The Pensions Act 2004 gave the Pensions Regulator the following specific objectives.

- To protect the benefits of members of work-based pension schemes.
- To promote good administration of work-based pension schemes.
- To reduce the risk of situations arising that may lead to claims for compensation from the Pension Protection Fund (PPF).

The **Pensions Act 2004** introduced a **PPF** to protect employees in the event their company scheme is not able to meet its obligations. Where a sponsoring employer becomes insolvent and unable to pay its liabilities the PPF will provide compensation up to 100% of benefits to existing pensioners and up to 90% of benefits to those who have not yet retired. The PPF is funded by a levy on all benefit pension schemes. The greater the deficit of a company's pension fund between the present value of its future liabilities and the current fund size, the greater the amount that must be contributed into the scheme. This works as an incentive to firms to reduce their deficits.

The funding provisions of the scheme require the **trustees** to:

- Prepare a statement of funding principles specific to circumstances of each scheme, to be reviewed every three years and setting out how the statutory funding objective will be met.
- Obtain periodic actuarial valuations and actuarial reports.
- Prepare a schedule of contributions.
- Put in place a recovery plan where the statutory funding requirement is not met.

## 3.5 Additional oversight of firms' activities

### 3.5.1 Senior management

Oversight of business activities in the financial sector is not solely a responsibility of external agencies.

Rules are set out in the **Senior Management Arrangements, Systems and Controls Sourcebook (SYSC)** which forms part of the regulatory Handbooks. The main SYSC rules are known as the **common platform**. Almost all firms, including (since 1 April 2009) non-MiFID firms, come within the scope of the common platform. (The only firms outside the common platform are insurers, managing agents and the Society of Lloyd's.)

**PRIN 3** (Principle for Businesses 3) is as follows.

**Management and control**: 'A firm must take reasonable care to organise and control its affairs responsibly and effectively, with adequate risk management systems.'

The senior management of a firm is responsible for the corporate governance of the firm. Corporate governance can be summarised as the direction and management of the firm in order to achieve the firm's objectives: for a company, this will amount to maximising shareholder value.

Senior and executive management activities will typically include the following:

- Formulating and reviewing the firm's strategy.
- Setting management structures and lines of reporting.
- Addressing compliance issues, as required by the regulator.
- Delegating authority to competent employees and committees.
- Reviewing and acting on management information reports, and requiring further reports as needed.
- Monitoring risks and taking action as appropriate.
- Resolving problems arising with the activities of the business on an *ad hoc* basis.
- Addressing issues of key person risk, and carrying out succession planning as appropriate.
- Reviewing the performance of the firm and its divisions and employees.
- Setting policies on remuneration and approving periodic reviews of compensation.
- Reporting to shareholders and other stakeholder groups as appropriate.

**Senior Management Arrangements, Systems and Controls (SYSC)** in the regulatory Handbooks includes various requirements for senior management.

A significant requirement of SYSC is the need for the Chief Executive to apportion duties amongst senior management and to monitor their performance.

The rules regarding **apportionment of significant responsibilities** require firms to make clear who has particular responsibility and to ensure that the business of the firm can be adequately monitored and controlled by the directors, senior management and the firm's governing body.

Under **SYSC**, the firm has a general obligation to take reasonable care to establish and maintain systems and controls that are appropriate to its business. Firms should **monitor and regularly evaluate** the adequacy of its systems, internal control mechanisms and arrangements established to comply with the above.

Firms are required to have **robust governance arrangements** with a clear organisational structure, well-defined, transparent and consistent lines of responsibility.

**Senior personnel** and (where appropriate) the **supervisory function** are responsible for ensuring compliance with regulatory obligations and should receive frequent (at least annual) reports on remedial measures taken to address deficiencies.

Firms must employ **personnel with the skills, knowledge and expertise** necessary for the discharge of their responsibilities.

A larger firm may need to have a **separate risk assessment function**, to assess risks that the firm faces and to advise directors and senior managers on them. Risks of regulatory concern are those relating to the fair treatment of customers, the protection of consumers, confidence in the financial system and financial crime. An **internal audit function** may monitor compliance arrangements in a larger firm.

Firms should have arrangements to ensure **business continuity** in the event of unforeseen interruption (for example, a fire or a computer system failure).

**Small** and **large firms** are likely to have different kinds of systems and controls: the important point is that they should be 'fit for purpose'. With a sole practitioner, one person is responsible for all aspects of the firm's business, and in that case there should be adequate systems allowing that person to adequately monitor and manage the firm.

### 3.5.2 The compliance function

Some firms, particularly in the early days of UK regulation, sought to place responsibility for compliance with the **compliance function** alone. The compliance department in this model was acting as an imposed control function. Compliance Officers were sometimes uncharitably and unfairly referred to as 'business prevention officers'.

This approach has evolved to a new model in which compliance responsibility becomes borne by all the individuals within the business. The Compliance Officer and his team step back from day-to-day regulatory matters and instead focus on acting as consultants and on ensuring the infrastructure for firm-wide compliance is in place. In this role, the Compliance Officer is an integral part of the commercial functioning of the business – assisting business areas to develop business in profitable as well as ethical ways. Indeed, there has been a focus by the regulators on the need to instil a '**culture of compliance**' within authorised firms.

In accordance with SYSC, the **compliance function** should be designed for the purpose of complying with regulatory requirements and to counter the risk that the firm may be used to further **financial crime**.

The **compliance function** should have:

- The necessary authority, expertise and access to relevant information
- A compliance officer, responsible for the function and for reporting
- Remuneration policies not likely to compromise compliance officers' objectivity

The role fulfilled by the **Compliance Officer** in a particular financial services firm will depend upon its size, business profile, culture and, most crucially, on the approach adopted to compliance. The role of the Compliance Officer can be seen as that of co-ordinator of the firm's compliance approach, but with responsibility being carried by the individuals around the firm undertaking the actual tasks to which the rules relate.

With **principles-based regulation**, there is a need for financial services firms to adopt an intelligent approach to interpreting higher level regulatory principles, and to develop their own sets of rules, which fit their particular business circumstances, in order to implement these principles. There is clearly an important role for the Compliance Officer in developing suitable sets of internal rules in conjunction with senior management, as well as in seeing that they are implemented.

Where an authorised firm appoints an **external compliance support company**, the firm itself remains responsible for the compliance oversight function: the firm may not **delegate** its regulatory responsibilities.

### 3.5.3 Risk management

All firms confront the problem of balancing risk and reward. In an efficient market, if we take no risks, all we can expect is a risk-free reward. To make substantial profits requires significant risks to be taken.

Financial products, particularly if used in a leveraged way, can produce dramatic returns, but the opportunity of large rewards normally comes with commensurably high risks. It is vital for all investment businesses to have real-time access to their exposures so that risks can be accessed and, if necessary, reduced.

Even the smallest business will or should have a number of controls to ensure accuracy and prevent **fraud**. Simple requirements, such as the need to have two signatures on a company cheque, and an insistence on all staff taking a two-week holiday so that any manipulation of records can be uncovered, all help create a secure control environment.

The regulators' **Principle for Businesses 3** states that a firm must take reasonable care to organise and control its affairs responsibly and effectively, with adequate **risk management systems**.

It can be argued that **risk management** consists of three key elements:

- **Identification, approval and communication** of the risks appropriate to a firm's objectives, capital and skills
- **Operation of a control and reporting system** that checks whether the risks being run have been sanctioned by management

- **Assessment and communication of risks** as quickly as possible

There exists a potential friction between the design and operation of a control system and the needs of the market place. If the control system is too bureaucratic and slow moving, innovation can be stifled and competitive advantage lost.

As we explain later, SYSC includes provisions for firms to:

- Establish, implement and maintain adequate **risk management policies** and procedures which identify and set the tolerable level of risk relating to a firm's activities including employees' compliance with them, and

- Have a separate **risk control function**, where this is proportionate, depending on the nature, scale and complexity of its business

To meet the regulator's requirements, senior management must control risk in various areas, including:

- Insurance
- Financial resources (including market risk, credit risk and liquidity risk)
- Conflicts of interest
- Outsourcing
- Compliance
- Financial crime

### 3.5.4 The finance function

The **finance function** within a firm is responsible for various activities within the firm, and it may itself be split into a number of units.

- The **credit** department is responsible for setting up and operating credit policies in line with the firm's activities and its attitude to credit risk. Creditworthiness of counterparties will be assessed to determine the volume of credit business that will be accepted for each one and what credit limits will be imposed. Collateral may be required from counterparties. There should be appropriate controls over conflicts of interest, as those handling credit applications may have access to information on specific trades. Appropriate procedures should be in place to ensure compliance with the Data Protection Act 1998.

- The **accounts payable** department has the task of approving and processing payments made by the firm. Accounts payable staff should be trained with regard to what may be suspicious or unacceptable transactions, and liaison with the compliance function may be appropriate in order to prevent irregularities or fraud, including any evidence of inappropriate payments or inducements which may breach regulations.

- **Financial control** is the function of preparing statutory and management statements and reports, reporting to management, the regulator and government agencies (such as Companies House), and preparing, monitoring and reporting the firm's regulatory capital resources and capital resources requirements. This is a complex exercise that involves evaluating the firm's effective permanent capital against the value of the firm's risk positions, weighted in accordance with the regulations. The sum of the firm's risk-weighted positions must not exceed the total capital resources of the firm. The department should inform the compliance function immediately if there is a prospect that the firm may breach its capital resources requirements. The financial control department will need to liaise with the regulator regarding prudential rule interpretations, with the external auditors regarding the statutory audit, and with the tax authorities.

### 3.5.5 Outsourced functions

**SYSC** includes the following main requirements relating to outsourcing:

- The firm cannot contract out its regulatory obligations (as explained above regarding the compliance function).

- The firm must have appropriate management and must notify the regulator of any material outsourcing .

Before entering an outsourcing arrangement the following actions should be taken:

- Analyse the organisational fit regarding reporting, risk management, regulatory obligation and business strategy.

- Analyse how agreement allow monitoring and control of outsourced activity.

- Conduct appropriate due diligence.

- Consider transitional arrangements.

- Consider concentration risk if several firms are using a single provider.

The contract with the outsource provider should cover:

- Reporting and notification requirements
- Access by internal and external auditors
- Information ownership, confidentiality and Chinese walls
- Adequacy of guarantees and indemnities
- Compliance with internal policies
- Business continuity
- Arrangements for changes in the outsourcing agreements

The outsourcing arrangement should have service level agreements covering:

- Qualitative and quantitative performance targets
- Monitoring and evaluation of performance with regular reviews
- Escalation and resolution practice for inadequate performance

The firm should have independent business continuity plans to deal with unexpected disruption to the outsourcing arrangements.

## 3.5.6 Trustees

We looked at the position of the **trustee** in the previous Chapter of this Study Text.

Trustees are found in jurisdictions where trust law applies, that is English common law jurisdictions. Trustees are not found in funds on continental Europe. Different **types of investment vehicle**, for example unit trust funds and pension schemes, appoint trustees.

The trustee is the legal owner of the fund's assets and owes a fiduciary duty to the fund's investors, who are the beneficial owners of the assets of the fund. The trustee's role is similar to the control function assumed by a depositary: there is no depositary when there is a trustee, but there is a custodian.

**Roles of the trustee**

- Holding control over the asset of the fund that are entrusted to the trustee by investors.

- Ensuring that the investment policies provided in the trust deed and the laws governing the fund are observed by the investment manager.

- Ensuring that the fund assets are segregated from the manager's assets.

The **custodian** exercises a direct control over the assets of the scheme and has the main mission to hold, safeguard and operate them in accordance with the manager's investment decisions.

The respective roles of trustee and custodian are distinct. However, in some jurisdictions, a single entity can assume both roles, and will then be referred to as the **trustee/custodian**.

### 3.5.7 Auditors

An audit is an independent review of the functions, procedures and controls within an organisation.

- An **internal audit** is performed by an internal department solely for the purposes of senior management. The subject, depth and scope of the internal audit is chosen by the management. The audit findings are then reported to management.

- An **external audit** is performed by an external registered auditor. The scope and the methodology is in accordance with the Companies Act legislation and Auditing Standards. The aim is to report to the members (shareholders) on whether the financial statements give a 'true and fair' view and are in accordance with applicable accounting standards.

SYSC makes provisions for MiFID firms to have a separate and independent **internal audit function**, with responsibility for maintaining an **audit plan** to examine and evaluate the adequacy and effectiveness of systems and internal controls, and for issuing recommendations and verifying compliance with them.

The internal audit department of a firm has the task of providing independent assurance to the board and senior management regarding risks that the firm faces and in how the firm manages these risks.

To achieve this task, the internal audit function will:

- Review the risks to which the firm is exposed
- Prepare an annual audit plan
- Review activities of the firm in line with the annual plan
- Conduct *ad hoc* reviews of activities in response to a changing internal risk environment
- Recommend corrective action to remedy breaches of controls and weaknesses

As well as consulting on many issues with the compliance function, the internal audit department should liaise with the firm's external auditors.

Every regulated firm is required to have a suitable **external auditor** who will be granted access to the firm's records and who will charge the firm a fee for their audit services. Under Section 346 FSMA 2000, it is a criminal offence to give false or misleading information to the firm's auditor.

The auditor has the duty to make the following submissions to the regulator:

- An audit report, including information on the regulatory reporting activities of the firm during the period covered by the report

- An internal controls letter, either commenting on the firm's internal controls or reporting that the auditor has no such comments

- A report on the firm's compliance with the client assets rules

For a firm that is a registered company, the external auditor must also fulfil any statutory reporting obligations as appropriate.

## 3.6 Legal advisers

A financial services firm will make use of legal advisers – in the UK solicitors, who may instruct Counsel to act as advocate in Court – as required.

A larger firm will have its own legal department.

The legal function will typically cover:

- Interpretation of and advice relating to relevant legislation
- Negotiating and drafting legal agreements and contracts
- Review of customer communications and financial promotions
- Structuring of transactions
- Handling litigation, fraud cases and regulators' disciplinary actions against the firm

- Handling disciplinary action against an employee
- Handling more serious complaints against the firm

The legal function should consult with the compliance function on matters that may have regulatory implications.

# 4 European institutions and Directives

## 4.1 The European Central Bank

The **European Central Bank (ECB)** is the institution of the European Union (EU) that administers the monetary policy of the 17 EU member states that use the euro as their currency (the 'Eurozone').

The **primary objective** of the European Central Bank is to **maintain price stability** within the Eurozone: other objectives are subordinate to this primary objective. The Governing Council has defined price stability as inflation (as measured by the Harmonised Index of Consumer Prices, equivalent to the CPI) of around 2%.

From its objectives arise the following functions of the ECB.

- Issuing the European common currency (the euro)
- Conducting monetary policy on behalf of the central government authorities
- Acting as lender of last resort to European banks
- Managing the exchange rate for the common currency

The ECB also seeks to promote the smooth operation of the financial market infrastructure under the Target payments system and the platform being developed for securities settlement in Europe (TARGET2 Securities).

The ECB contributes to monitoring the banking sector and maintaining a stable financial system. The Bank's role in relation to financial stability was seen, for example, in its intervention during the 2007 credit crisis when it loaned billions of euros to banks in order to stabilise the financial system.

In May 2010, to address the European sovereign (government) debt crisis, the member states of the EU agreed to create the **European Financial Stability Facility (EFSF)**. The mandate of the EFSF is to safeguard European financial stability by providing financial assistance to Eurozone member States.

## 4.2 European Supervisory Authorities (ESAs)

Operating at arm's length from the European Central Bank (ECB), the **European Systemic Risk Board (ESRB)** has powers to issue warnings and recommendations on threats to economies and financial systems. The ESRB's voting members include the central bank governors of the EU member states, the ECB President and ECB Vice-President, and the chairmen of the **new pan-European supervisory authorities (ESAs)**.

The **ESAs**, as follows, cover banking, insurance and securities markets:

- **European Banking Authority (EBA)** – based in London
- **European Securities and Markets Authority (ESMA)** – based in Paris
- **European Insurance and Occupational Pensions Authority (EIOPA)** – based in Frankfurt

These authorities, replacing the previous Level 3 Committees of Supervisors, together make up the **European System of Financial Supervisors (ESFS)**. The ESAs work with the ESRB to ensure financial stability and to strengthen and enhance the EU supervisory framework. They aim to improve coordination between national supervisory authorities, and to raise standards of national supervision across the EU.

**Role of the ESAs**

- The ESAs aim to create a single EU rule book, by developing draft technical standards which will then be adopted by the European Commission as EU law. The ESAs will also issue guidance and recommendations with which national supervisors and firms must make every effort to comply.

- Where the ESAs believe that a national supervisory authority is failing to apply EU law, or is doing so in a way which appears to be in breach of EU law, they have the power to investigate. Their investigation may lead to the Authority issuing a recommendation to the national supervisor, followed by a formal opinion from the Commission if the recommendation is not acted upon. If the supervisor does not comply with the Commission's formal opinion, the ESA may then take decisions binding on firms or market participants to ensure they are complying with EU law.

- They can temporarily ban certain financial activities. Legislation will set out what they can ban and in what circumstances. Where an emergency has been called by the Council, they have wider-ranging powers to ban financial activities.

- In a crisis, the ESAs will provide EU-wide coordination. If an emergency is declared, the ESAs may make decisions that are binding on national supervisors and on firms. However, these would be subject to certain conditions and would be limited to ensuring compliance with EU law.

- The ESAs will mediate in certain situations where national supervisory authorities disagree. If necessary, they will be able to resolve disputes by making a decision that is binding on both parties to ensure compliance with EU law.

- ESAs have a role in EU supervisory colleges to ensure that they function efficiently and that consistent approaches and practices are followed.

- The ESAs will conduct regular peer reviews of national supervisory authorities to improve the consistency of supervision across the EU.

- ESAs will be able to collect information from national supervisors to allow them to fulfil their role. This information will be used for analysing market developments, coordinating EU-wide stress tests and for the macro-prudential analysis undertaken by the ESRB.

- The ESAs also have a remit to consider consumer protection issues.

## 4.3 MiFID

### 4.3.1 Overview

The **Markets in Financial Instruments Directive (MiFID)** was adopted by the European Council in April 2004 and is part of the European **Financial Services Action Plan (FSAP)**. After delays, MiFID eventually became effective on **1 November 2007**.

MiFID replaced the previous Investment Services Directive (ISD), and it applies to all **investment firms**, e.g. investment and retail banks, brokers, assets managers, securities and futures firms, securities issuers and hedge funds.

Although MiFID has extended regulation beyond what was regulated under the ISD, a significant part of the **retail financial services sector** falls outside the scope of MiFID.

The following are also **excluded** from the scope of MiFID.

- **Insurance companies** including reinsurers

- **Pension funds** and **collective investment schemes**, and their depositories or managers, although UCITS managers who provide advice or discretionary management to clients who are not funds will generally be subject to MiFID requirements

- **Group treasury activities**

- **Persons administering their own assets**

- **Professional investors** investing only for themselves

- **Commodity producers and traders**

- Investment services relating to administration of **employee share schemes**

- **Incidental business in the course of professional activity** bound by legal, ethical or regulatory provisions

- **Firms not providing investment services** or involved in investment activities

MiFID applies to **EEA-domiciled firms** only. However, the regulators' rules extend MiFID requirements to '**MiFID equivalent activities of third country firms**'.

The scope of MiFID is expected to be extended by the further Directive, introducing **MiFID II**, with technical standards being drafted during 2015.

## 4.3.2 Scope of MiFID

MiFID applies to a specified range of 'core' **investment services and activities** in relation to specified categories of **financial instruments**, as summarised below.

- **Investment firms** are firms which provide such services or engage in such activities.

- Investment firms are also regulated in respect of various 'non-core' **ancillary services** they may provide (as also listed below).

- **Credit institutions** (which includes banks and building societies, in the UK) are regulated by the Banking Consolidation Directive. However, most MiFID provisions apply to these institutions when they engage in activities within MiFID's scope.

### Investment services and activities

- Receiving and transmitting orders
- Execution of orders on behalf of clients
- Dealing on own account
- Managing portfolios on a discretionary basis
- Investment advice
- Underwriting of financial instruments
- Placing of financial instruments
- Operating a Multilateral Trading Facility (MTF)

### Financial instruments covered by MiFID

- Transferable securities, e.g. shares and bonds

- Money market instruments

- Units in collective investment undertakings

- Derivatives relating to securities, currencies, interest rates and yields, financial indices and financial measures settled either physically or in cash, including: options, futures, swaps and forward rate agreements

- Commodity derivatives capable of being settled in cash, or capable of being physically settled on a regulated market or multilateral trading facility, and certain other commodity derivatives are not for commercial purposes

- Derivative instruments for transferring credit risk

- Financial contracts for differences (CFDs)
- Derivatives relating to climatic variables, freight rates, emission allowances, inflation rates or other official economic statistics capable of being settled in cash

**Ancillary services**

- Safekeeping, custodianship and administration of financial instruments
- Granting credit or loans to an investor for a transaction in which the firm is involved
- Advising undertakings on capital structure, industrial strategy
- Advising on mergers and acquisitions
- Foreign exchange services connected with providing investment services
- Investment research, financial analysis or other general recommendations

## 4.3.3 Passporting and Home State / Host State regulation

The idea of a '**passport**' enables firms to use their domestic authorisation to operate not only in their **Home State**, but also in other **Host States** within the **European Economic Area** (EEA) (EU plus Norway, Iceland and Liechtenstein).

An important aspect of MiFID is that, to make cross-border business easier, the home country principle has been extended. Under MiFID, investment firms are authorised by the Member State in which their registered office is located (the **Home State**).

Where a **branch** is set up, **Host State** rules will continue to apply. A **tied agent** established in the EEA will be able to act on behalf of a firm instead of the firm needing to set up a branch. (A '**tied agent**', similar to an **appointed representative** under FSMA 2000, acts on behalf of, and under the authority of, an investment firm and as a result does not require authorisation.)

Where a firm makes use of a passport:

- **Organisational matters** will be regulated by the **home state**: these include authorisation, fitness and propriety, capital adequacy, Principles for Businesses, senior management arrangements, systems and controls, client assets including client money, conflicts of interest, personal account dealing (as covered in the conduct of business rules, COBS), investment research (COBS), transaction reporting and transparency, and compensation arrangements.

- **Operational matters**, for example conduct of business rules which are not 'organisational matters' will be regulated by:
  - The **host state**, for activities of a branch 'within its territory'
  - The **home state**, for cross-border services

## 4.3.4 MiFID II

The European Commission has conducted a review of the operation of MiFID. This will lead to new regulations – being called 'MiFID II' - to remedy unintended effects of MiFID and changes in markets that have come about since the original Directive was introduced.

Member states are required to transpose MiFID II into national law by 3 July 2016. MiFID will take effect in member states on 3 January 2017.

The MiFID II framework contains two pieces of EU legislation:

- A revised Directive, re-stating and amending MiFID, and

- MiFIR: a new regulation, setting out requirements for trade transparency, the mandatory trading of derivatives on organised venues, and the provision of services by third-country firms without a branch.

Unlike a Directive, a Regulation is directly applicable in member states and does not require national enabling legislation.

## 4.4 UCITS: Collective investment schemes

### 4.4.1 UCITS Directives

The EU has enacted a number of directives relevant to collective investment schemes (CISs). These are known as the **UCITS Directives. UCITS** stands for **Undertakings for Collective Investment in Transferable Securities**.

The aim of UCITS was to create a type of passport throughout the EEA for collective investment schemes that meet the UCITS criteria. The idea was to promote the free movement of services in the same way as the ISD (and later, its replacement MiFID) allow investment firms to passport their services throughout the EEA.

The CIS must be authorised in its home State and receive confirmation from its home State regulator that the CIS complies with UCITS criteria. That confirmation is then provided to the host State regulator, who the fund manager notifies that they wish to market the fund in that EEA State. Although UCITS aims to make cross-border sales of CISs easier, the CIS must comply with the marketing rules of the host State and the documentation requirements of the Directive.

In the first **UCITS Directive**, the definition of **permitted investments** was very narrow. UCITS was updated in 2002 by the **UCITS III Product Directive**, which expanded the range of assets that UCITS funds are able to invest in. It also made provision for a single UCITS scheme to replace all of the previous categories of fund which had separate rules.

**UCITS IV**, implemented in mid-2011, enhances the UCITS regime with changes that include the following.

- **Passporting for management companies**, which no longer need to be established in the same member State of the fund that they operate

- **Key Investor Information Documents (KIIDs)** – a point-of-sale consumer disclosure document, limited to two A4 pages, which replaces the simplified prospectus and provides investors with clearer and more concise information to help their decision-making

- **Improvements to cross-border marketing of authorised funds**, enabling funds to access markets in other member States without a delay

- **Single framework for cross-border fund mergers**

- **Master-feeder structures**, which enable a fund to hold most of its assets as an investment in another fund

- **Enhanced supervision**, with improved co-operation between regulators of different member States

**UCITS V** took effect on 17 September 2014. New depositary rules in this Directive seek to extend the investor protections adopted for the 'alternative' hedge funds sector through the Alternative Investment Fund Managers Directive (AIFMD) to investors in retail funds. Weaknesses in these rules had been highlighted by the Madoff fraud case and the default of Lehman Brothers. (A depositary is the person or institution taking responsibility for the deposit, while a depository is the institution or place where the deposit is kept.)

Under the **UCITS V rules**:

- A UCITS fund must appoint single depositary who is located in the same member State as the fund

- Duties of the depositary include: safekeeping, harmonised oversight, cash flow monitoring, delegation, liability, and investors' rights of action against the depositaries

- Requirements for UCITS managers include: governance arrangements, identified staff, and remuneration structures, applied proportionately according to the nature of the firm

### 4.4.2 UCITS schemes

As a result of the **UCITS Product Directive**, UCITS schemes are now able to invest in the following types of **permitted investment**.

- Transferable securities (see below)
- Money market instruments
- Forward contracts and financial derivatives
- Deposits
- Units in other UCITS and regulated non-UCITS Collective Investment Schemes

**Transferable securities** comprise shares, instruments creating or acknowledging indebtedness (e.g. debentures, loan stock, bonds, government and public securities) and certificates representing certain securities.

Although **commodity derivatives** are excluded, it would appear that derivatives based on commodity indices could be eligible as financial derivatives.

## 4.5 The Prospectus Directive

The **Prospectus Directive** is an EU directive which came into force in December 2003. It was implemented in the UK by the Prospectus Regulations 2005, which amended FSMA 2000, and by the Prospectus Rules in the FCA Handbook.

The Directive requires that a prospectus is produced whenever there is a public offer of securities or where securities are admitted to trading on a regulated market. The Directive specifies the content of prospectuses and requires that they are approved by the relevant **competent authority** (in the UK, the FCA).

Under the Prospectus Directive, there is a **'single passport'** for issuers, with the result that a prospectus approved by one competent authority can be used across the EEA without any further approval or burdensome administrative procedures in other member states. If the competent authority in the relevant member state approves the prospectus, it will be accepted throughout the EEA.

## 4.6 The Capital Requirements Directive

### 4.6.1 CRD and Basel II

The overall aim of capital **requirements** rules is to ensure that firms remain solvent by having greater assets at their command than they will need to cover their positions. In general, a firm must maintain, at all times, financial resources in excess of its financial resources requirement.

The UK financial resources requirements are based on the Basel Capital Accord known as 'Basel II'. Basel II is implemented in the European Union via the **Capital Requirements Directive (CRD)** for credit institutions and investment firms. CRD amends the two existing directives: the **Capital Adequacy Directive (CAD)** and the **Banking Consolidation Directive (BCD)**.

The **Basel Committee on Banking Supervision** does not have legal powers but creates common standards and guidelines of best practice with the aim that individual States will implement these in their own law. The Committee has tried to reduce divergences in international supervisory standards. They seek to ensure that all foreign banking establishments are actually supervised by someone and that supervision is adequate.

The second Basel Capital Accord (referred to as 'Basel II', which has the full formal title *International convergence of capital measurement and capital standards – a revised framework*), is reflected in EU law via the **Capital Requirements Directive** – see later below.

## 4.6.2 Key aspects of Basel II

**Basel II** is a revision of the existing prudential framework and aims to make the framework more risk-sensitive and more representative of modern banks' risk management practices. The new framework aims to leave the overall level of capital held by banks collectively broadly unchanged.

The **capital adequacy framework** is intended to reduce the probability of consumer loss or market disruption as a result of prudential failure. It does so by seeking to ensure that the financial resources held by a firm are commensurate with the risks associated with the business profile and the control environment within the firm.

In the light of the **banking and financial crisis of 2008**, some consider the Basel II regime partly to have led to the problems because it is a rule-driven system based on 'letter rating' of risks and is arguably by its nature backward-looking. The BCBS has indicated that, in the light of the financial crisis in which US and European governments have injected capital into banks:

- It would encourage banks to boost capital reserves by making **provisions for bad debts** throughout the economic cycle.

- It might introduce rules to limit the **leverage ratio** – the absolute amount of a bank's debt relative to its capital base. The new rules would probably be worked out during 2009, but new measures would not be forced through before the crisis was over.

## 4.6.3 The three pillars

The framework consists of three '**pillars**'.

- **Pillar 1** sets out the minimum capital requirements firms will be required to meet for credit, market and operational risk. There is a two-stage process. The first stage involves assessing the category of the firm. The second stage is to establish the method for calculating the minimum capital requirement.

- **Pillar 2:** firms and regulatory supervisors have to take a view on whether a firm should hold additional capital against risks not covered in Pillar 1 and must take action accordingly.

- **Pillar 3** aims to improve market discipline by requiring firms to publish certain details of their risks, capital and risk management.

## 4.6.4 CRD 4 changes

The **Capital Requirements Directive** was followed up by revisions coded CRD2 and CRD3. These changes aimed to strengthen the European prudential regime in the CRD, addressing lessons learned from the credit market turmoil of the late 2000s and issues discussed in the Turner Review. These directives were in effect until 31 December 2013, with new provisions coming into force under the CRD4 package of measures

**CRD4** (or **CRD IV**) was announced by the European Commission in July 2011. This represents the Commission's plan for implementing the Basel III regulations (see below), which aim to make the global financial system more resilient in the event of a crisis such as that of the late 2000s, when losses at large and highly indebted banks led governments around the world to bail out many banks.

CRD4 includes two elements:

- The **Capital Requirements Regulation (CRR)** – directly applicable, and therefore not to be transposed via the PRA and FCA Handbooks

- The **Capital Requirements Directive (CRD)** – to be transposed into UK law via Treasury regulations and the regulators' Handbooks

CRD4 includes detailed prudential requirements for credit institutions and investment firms. The Directive restates many of the existing CRD provisions, including passporting and principles for prudential supervision. It also includes proposals relating to capital buffers as well as on matters outside the Basel III framework relating to corporate governance, sanctions, supervision and reliance on ratings provided by rating agencies.

The **position on implementation of CRD4** was explained in **2013 statements** by the UK regulators. Following the adoption of the Capital Requirements Directive and associated legislation by the European Parliament on 16 April 2013, the FCA has stated that it plans to implement the provisions in the UK by **1 January 2014**. The FCA will carry out a consultation process during the summer of 2013 on the new measures and rules that will be required.

## 4.7 Basel III

The **Basel III regulations** comprise an update to the Basel Accords which include:

- Tighter definitions of common equity, with a requirement for banks to hold 4.5% by January 2015 (compared with 2.0% currently), then a further capital conservation buffer of 2.5% to withstand future periods of stress, totalling 7%

- A framework for counter-cyclical capital buffers, with banks having a capital ratio below 2.5% facing restrictions on dividends, buybacks and bonuses

- Measures to limit counterparty credit risk

- Short- and medium-term quantitative liquidity ratios

- The introduction of an internationally harmonised leverage ratio, acting as a backstop to risk-based capital measures

At the Seoul Summit of November 2010, the G20 leaders endorsed the Basel III framework as well as the **Financial Stability Board's (FSB)** policy framework for reducing the moral hazard of **systemically important financial institutions (SIFIs)**. Basel III is expected to be implemented in stages over a transition period from **2013 to 2021**.

In his **Mansion House speech** (September 2010), Lord Turner (FSA Chairman) welcomed the Basel III package of capital and liquidity reforms. He argued that the recent financial crisis had many causes, including 'absurd bonuses for excessive risk taking' and 'an explosion of exotic socially useless product development', but that underlying these problems were **prudential rules** and an entire philosophy of market regulation which failed to identify and address the dangers of **excessive leverage**, and which too confidently relied on supposedly efficient and rational markets always to produce good results.

In January 2012, it was stated that banks would be required to hold easily sold assets as liquidity buffers from 2015, but would be allowed to dip into these buffers at times of stress. (These buffers are therefore unlike Basel capital standards, for which falling below thresholds puts a bank at immediate risk of being shut down or nationalised.) There were pleas from the industry for a delay or a substantial re-write of the liquidity coverage ratio (LCR) which had proved to be controversial. The LCR rules require banks to maintain buffers against a 30-day crisis.

In **January 2013**, the Group of Governors and Heads of Supervision (GHOS) agreed to **delay the LCR requirements** by a further **four years**. Additionally, banks will be permitted to select from a longer list of approved assets including some equities and securitised mortgage debt in building up liquidity buffers for use in a financial crisis. Banks will now have to meet 60% of the LCR obligations by 2015, with the full rule being phased in annually through to **2019**.

## 4.8 EU Directive on regulation of alternative fund managers

An **alternative investment fund (AIF)** is collective investment undertaking that is **not subject to the UCITS regime** – this includes hedge funds, private equity funds and real estate funds.

The EU Commission adopted a proposal for an **Alternative Investment Fund Managers Directive (AIFMD)** in 2009. The AIFMD is a EU-wide framework for monitoring and overseeing the risks posed by AIFs.

The Directive seeks to create a framework for the direct regulation and supervision of the alternative fund industry, particularly targeting hedge funds and private equity.

**AIFM Directive objectives**

- Authorisation and registration requirements for AIFM providing management services within the EU
- Monitoring of macro-prudential risks by enhancing EU-wide regulatory oversight
- Improved investor protection
- Robust risk management and organisational safeguards (e.g. limits to leverage)
- Better transparency (e.g. independent valuers and custodians for private equity funds)
- An EU passport for AIFM

The AIFM Directive was finally published in the EU's Official Journal on 1 July 2011. Working with HM Treasury, the FCA has implemented the Directive through the **Investment Funds Sourcebook (FUND)**, which became effective on 22 July 2013. Firms must be authorised with relevant Part 4A permissions before providing AIFMD services.

## 4.9 European Market Infrastructure Regulation (EMIR)

The **European Market Infrastructure Regulation (EMIR)** has the purpose of enhancing stability in the over-the-counter (OTC) derivatives markets of the EU.

EMIR implements a G20 commitment to have all EU **standardised OTC derivatives** cleared through a CCP.

EMIR comprises a set of standards for regulation of OTC derivatives, central counterparties (CCPs) and trade repositories.

**Aspects of EMIR**

- **Reporting obligations for OTC derivatives.** Counterparties to all derivatives contracts are required to report post-trade contract details to a registered trade repository. This requirement will capture all exchange and OTC derivative trades, intragroup trades, and trades with non-financial counterparties.

- **Clearing obligations for eligible OTC derivatives to be cleared through CCPs.** This will apply to contracts between any combination of financial counterparties or non-financial counterparties (NFCs) that are above specified clearing thresholds.

- Transactions designed to reduce risks to commercial activity or treasury financing activity are exempted from the clearing threshold. The European Securities and Markets Authority (ESMA) will determine the classes of OTC derivatives that must be cleared and ESMA will maintain a register showing which CCPs are permitted to clear derivatives of each class.

- **New risk mitigation requirements for all OTC derivative trades that are not centrally cleared.** These requirements are concerned with timely confirmation, dispute resolution, reconciliations and portfolio compression. (Portfolio compression replaces existing contracts so as to reduce the overall notional size and number of outstanding contracts without changing the risk profile or present value of portfolios.) For counterparties subject to the clearing obligation, there will be additional requirements concerning initial and variation margin and daily valuation for their uncleared trades.

- **Common rules for CCPs and for trade repositories.** All derivative contracts are to be reported, by both financial and non-financial counterparties, to a trade repository by the following working day. Trade repositories include TriOptima and DTCC.

- **Rules on the establishment of interoperability between CCPs.**

  The EMIR came into force in mid-2012, but full implementation is expected to occur over a series of dates into 2014. Under the new rules, all standardised OTC derivative contracts should be traded on exchanges or electronic trading platforms, where appropriate, and cleared through CCPs.

In the UK, EMIR has been implemented through the Financial Services and Markets Act 2000 (Over the Counter Derivatives, Central Counterparties and Trade Repositories) Regulations 2013.

# 5 The Remuneration Code

## 5.1 Timing

The late-2000s financial crisis prompted calls for curbs on remuneration in order to prevent excessive risk-taking. The first Remuneration Code had an implementation date of 1 January 2010. In December 2010, the regulator published an updated Remuneration Code to take into account changes required by the revised **Capital Requirements Directive (CRD3)**. CRD3 aims to align remuneration principles across the EU.

Firms already within the scope of the Remuneration Code have been required to comply in full with the revised Code since **1 January 2011**. For other firms that are coming within scope for the first time, there are transitional rules. These firms were required to comply as soon as reasonably possible, and by 1 July 2011 at the latest.

## 5.2 Scope: firms covered

The FSA's previous Code required firms to apply 'remuneration policies, practices and procedures that are consistent with and promote effective risk management'. It applied to the largest banks, building societies and broker dealers. The revised Code will not only apply to these firms but will encompass a much larger group of firms including all banks and building societies and CAD investment firms – some 2,700 in total.

## 5.3 Proportionate approach

A **proportionate** approach will be applied to implementation of the Code in line with the purpose of the previous Code to ensure remuneration policies promote effective risk management. The proportionate approach allows firms to comply 'in a way and to the extent that is appropriate to its size, internal organisation and the nature, the scope and the complexity of its activities'.

Accordingly, there will be four tiers of firms with differing minimum expectations of compliance for each group:

- **Tiers 1 and 2** contain credit institutions and broker dealers that engage in significant proprietary trading/investment banking activities

- **Tier 3** consists primarily of small banks and building societies and firms that may occasionally take overnight/short-term risk with their balance sheets

- **Tier 4** comprises firms that generate income from agency business without putting their balance sheets at risk

## 5.4 Disclosure of remuneration

The regulator has also published new rules implementing CRD3 requirements on **disclosure of remuneration**. Under these rules, firms will be required to disclose information on their remuneration policies and pay-outs.

## 5.5 Scope: staff covered

The Remuneration Code covers staff whose professional activities have a material impact on the firm's risk profile (**'material risk-takers'** or **MRTs**) and who fall into one of four categories:

- Senior management
- Risk takers
- Staff engaged in control functions, and
- Any employee whose total remuneration is within the same remuneration bracket as senior management and risk-takers

## 5.6 Remuneration definition

The regulator defines **remuneration** as being any aspect of compensation that can have a bearing on effective risk management. This definition covers signing-on and severance packages, pensions, options and long-term incentive plans, as well as salaries and bonuses.

## 5.7 The Code

The revised (1 January 2011) Code is based on a set of **principles**, underpinned by Principle 1.

**Principle 1** requires firms to put in place a remuneration policy that:

- Is consistent with and promotes sound and effective risk management, and
- Does not encourage risk-taking that exceeds the level of tolerated risk of the firm

**Other Principles** in the Code include:

- Avoidance of conflicts of interest

- Ensuring that a firm's remuneration practices do not endanger its capital base

- Basing assessments of financial performance on profit, and

- Ensuring that employees undertake not to use personal hedging strategies to offset the risk-based approach to their compensation

Controversially, **Principle 12** sets out the following new requirements for remuneration structures, which must be adhered to subject to the principle of **proportionality**:

- Remuneration must be structured so as to promote effective risk management

- Performance-related remuneration must take into account individual, business unit and firm-wide performance and must encompass non-financial performance metrics

- Guarantees should be exceptional, for new hires only and limited to a year

- Firms must set appropriate ratios between fixed and variable elements of total compensation

- Early termination payments should not reward failure

- At least 50% of both the deferred and non-deferred elements of variable remuneration should consist of shares, ownership interests, share-linked instruments and/or equivalent non-cash instruments that are subject to a retention policy to align incentives with the firm's long-term interests

- At least 40% of variable remuneration should be deferred over a minimum period of 3 to 5 years and deferred remuneration must vest no faster than on a pro-rata basis

- For staff whose remuneration has a variable component of over £500,000, 60% should be deferred

- Variable remuneration should be paid or vest only if justified by the performance of the firm, business unit and employee; the firm should adjust unvested elements of remuneration if warranted by subsequent circumstances

## 5.8 Changes to the Code

Certain changes to the Remuneration Code are proposed for implementation in **2015**, in order to address shortcomings in the alignment of risk and reward, following the recommendations of the Parliamentary Commission on Banking Standards (PCBS).

The **PCBS recommendations** include:

- Power for regulators to impose deferral of up to 10 years

- Development of regulatory requirements on risk-adjustment

- Enhanced disclosure of individual pay, remuneration by division, and the link between pay, performance and risk

- Power to cancel unvested deferred awards, unvested pension rights, and loss of office payments for banks receiving Government support

# Key chapter points

- The creation of the FSA as the UK's main statutory regulator for the industry brought together regulation of investment, insurance and banking.

- In 2010, the new Government announced its plan to abolish the Financial Services Authority. On 1 April 2013, much of the FSA's role transferred to the new Financial Conduct Authority, which is the regulator for smaller investment firms. The powers of the Bank of England have expanded, with a new remit to prevent a build-up of risk in the financial system.

- The Prudential Regulation Authority, a subsidiary of the Bank of England, is the prudential regulator, responsible for ensuring the safe operation of deposit-taking institutions as well as insurers, investment banks and some other institutions.

- The Chancellor of the Exchequer is ultimately responsible for the regulatory system for financial services under FSMA 2000.

- Other regulators whose activities you need to understand are the Competition and Markets Authority, the Payment Systems Regulator, the Information Commissioner and the Pensions Regulator. Also be aware of the roles of the Financial Ombudsman Scheme, the Financial Services Compensation Scheme and the Upper Tribunal.

- Internal and external mechanisms within firms that provide additional oversight in support of the regulatory framework include: senior management; trustees; internal and external auditors.

- The Markets in Financial Instruments Directive (MiFID) replaced the Investment Services Directive (ISD), with effect from 1 November 2007. MiFID applies to all investment firms, including investment banks, securities dealers and portfolio managers.

- Under MiFID, firms are authorised by the Member State in which their registered office is located. Where a branch is set up, Host State rules will continue to apply. 'Passporting' enables them to operate throughout the EEA.

- UCITS Directives enable passporting for collective investment schemes which meet UCITS criteria, in the interests of facilitating cross-border financial services within Europe. The scheme must be regulated or authorised in its Home State, and the home State regulator will confirm that the scheme complies with UCITS criteria.

- In the interests of investor protection, the Prospectus Directive imposes disclosure standards when there is an offer of securities. A Prospectus which is formally approved in one EEA member state can be used across the EEA without further approval: this is referred to as the 'single passport' for issuers.

- The UK financial resources requirements are based on the Basel accord, which is implemented in the EU through the Capital Requirements Directive (CRD) for credit institutions and investment firms.

- The Remuneration Code sets out principles designed to require specified types of financial institution to align remuneration with risk.

- The Alternative Investment Fund Managers Directive (AIFMD) seeks to create a framework for the direct regulation and supervision of the alternative fund industry, particularly targeting hedge funds and private equity.

- EMIR – European Market Infrastructure Regulation – comprises a set of standards for regulation of OTC derivatives, central counterparties (CCPs) and trade repositories.

## Chapter Quiz

1    What are the core purposes of the Bank of England? ........................................................... (see para 2.1)

2    What is the meaning of 'dual regulation'? ...........................................................................(2.4)

3    Who handles complaints against the FCA and PRA? ...........................................................(2.7)

4    Outline the statutory objectives of the Payment Systems Regulator. ...................................(3.2)

5    Outline the role of the Information Commissioner. ..............................................................(3.3)

6    What are the objectives of the Pensions Regulator, as defined in the Pensions Act 2004? ...........................(3.4)

7    Outline the main elements of the scope of MiFID. ..............................................................(4.3.2)

8    Outline how 'home State' and 'host State' rules apply under MiFID. ....................................(4.3.3)

9    What are the main elements of UCITS IV? ..........................................................................(4.4.1)

10   What is the overall aim of capital requirements rules? ........................................................(4.6.1)

# chapter

# 5

## The role of the regulators

### CHAPTER LEARNING OUTCOMES

5     **Understand the financial regulators' responsibilities and approach to regulation**

     5.1    **Explain** the financial regulators' statutory objectives and how they are structured to achieve these objectives.

     5.2    **Explain** the main principles and rules in the PRA and FCA Handbooks.

     5.3    **Explain** the approach to risk-based supervision, discipline and enforcement, and sanctions to deal with criminal activities.

# 1 The regulators' functions and objectives

## 1.1 Powers of the regulators

Important **powers** of the new regulators – the FCA and the PRA – are set out below. (Note that the term '**firm**' is used generally in the regulations to apply to an authorised person, whether the person is an individual, a partnership or a corporate body.)

- Granting **authorisation** and **permission** to firms (under **Part 4A** of FSMA 2000) to undertake regulated activities
- **Approving** individuals to perform controlled functions
- Issuing (under **Part 9A FSMA 2000**):
    - (In the case of the FCA) general **rules** for authorised firms which appear to be necessary or expedient to advance the FCA's operational objectives (such as the **Conduct of Business** rules, and rules on firms holding clients' money)
    - (In the case of the PRA) general **rules** for PRA-authorised firms which appear to be necessary or expedient to advance the PRA's objectives
- **Supervision** of authorised firms to ensure that they continue to meet the regulators' authorisation requirements and that they comply with the regulatory rules and other obligations
- Powers to take **enforcement** action against authorised firms and approved persons
- Powers to **discipline** authorised firms and approved persons

The **FCA** has powers to:

- Take action against any person for **insider dealing** or **market abuse**
- **Recognise** investment exchanges and clearing houses
- As the **UK Listing Authority**, approve companies for stock exchange listings in the UK

The FCA oversees the **Financial Ombudsman Service (FOS)** and the **Money Advice Service**.

The FCA and PRA jointly oversee the **Financial Services Compensation Scheme (FSCS)**.

# 1.2 The Financial Conduct Authority (FCA)

## 1.2.1 Overview

As we have seen, the **Financial Conduct Authority (FCA)** is the **conduct regulator** for the UK financial services industry. The FCA also has responsibility for the **prudential regulation** of investment exchanges, many investment firms and other financial services providers.

Although set up by statute, the FCA is not regarded as acting on behalf of the Crown. Its members, officers and staff are, therefore, not Crown or civil servants. Like its predecessor – the FSA – the FCA is structured as a **company limited by guarantee**, and is given its powers by FSMA 2000.

The FCA is **accountable to the Treasury** and, through the Treasury, to **Parliament**.

The FCA is governed by a **Board** that is appointed by the Treasury. The majority of the Board members are non-executive. One of the non-executive members is a senior non-executive.

The FCA's Board sets the policy of the Authority. Day-to-day decisions and staff management are the responsibility of the FCA's **Executive Committee**.

The Authority is operationally independent of Government and is funded entirely by the firms it regulates.

Under Schedule 1ZA and 1ZB FSMA 2000, the FCA, as well as the PRA, have **statutory immunity** from prosecution other than where it can be shown to be acting in bad faith, or in breach of human rights legislation.

An independent non-governmental body, the FCA is funded by levies on the financial services industry. How are the regulators' **fees** levied? There are a number of **'fee-blocks'** which group together firms carrying out similar regulated activities, reflecting the fact that they pose similar risks to regulatory objectives. A firm may fall into one or more fee-blocks, depending on the scope of its permission.

## 1.2.2 Strategic objective

The Financial Services Act 2012 (FSA 2012) gives the new **Financial Conduct Authority (FCA)** a single **strategic objective**:

> **'Ensuring that the relevant markets function well'** (s1B(2) FSMA 2000, as amended by FSA 2012)

The **relevant markets** referred to in the strategic objective comprise (s1F FSMA 2000):

- The financial markets

- Markets for regulated financial services (as defined in FSMA 2000), and

- The markets for services that are provided by non-authorised persons in carrying on regulated activities without contravening the general prohibition

## 1.2.3 Operational objectives

The strategic objective of the FCA is supported by three **operational objectives** (s1C-E FSMA 2000):

- **The consumer protection objective**: securing an appropriate degree of protection for consumers

- **The integrity objective:** protecting and enhancing the integrity of the UK financial system

- **The competition objective**: promoting effective competition in the interests of consumers in the market for regulated financial services and for services provided by a recognised investment exchange

The Authority also has duties to **promote competition** (which may involve analysing pricing) and to **address financial crime** (broadly, following the existing approach to tackling such crime).

In 2012, a spokesperson for the regulator explained that the FCA has been set up to work with firms with the aim of ensuring that they put consumers at the heart of their business.

Underlining this are three outcomes:

- Consumers get financial services and products that meet their needs from firms they can trust

- Firms compete effectively with the interests of their customers and the integrity of the market at the heart of how they run their business

- Markets and financial systems are sound, stable and resilient with transparent pricing information

### 1.2.4 Consumer protection objective

In considering what degree of protection for consumers may be appropriate, the FCA must have regard to (s1C FSMA 2000):

- The differing degrees of risk involved in different kinds of investment or other transaction

- The differing degrees of experience and expertise that different consumers may have

- The needs that consumers may have for the timely provision of information and advice that is accurate and fit for purpose

- The general principle that consumers should take responsibility for their decisions

- The general principle that those providing regulated financial services should be expected to provide consumers with a level of care that is appropriate having regard to the degree of risk involved in relation to the investment or other transaction and the capabilities of the consumers in question

- The differing expectations that consumers may have in relation to different kinds of investment or other transaction

- Any information which the consumer financial education body has provided to the FCA in the exercise of the consumer financial education function

- Any information which the scheme operator of the ombudsman scheme has provided to the FCA

### 1.2.5 Integrity objective

Regarding this objective, the integrity of the UK financial system includes (s1D FSMA 2000):

- Its soundness, stability and resilience
- Its not being used for a purpose connected with financial crime
- Its not being affected by behaviour that amounts to market abuse
- The orderly operation of the financial markets, and
- The transparency of the price formation process in those markets

### 1.2.6 Competition objective

The matters to which the FCA may have regard in considering the effectiveness of competition include:

- The needs of different consumers who use or may use those services, including their need for information that enables them to make informed choices

- The ease with which consumers who may wish to use those services, including consumers in areas affected by social or economic deprivation, can access them

- The ease with which consumers who obtain those services can change the person from whom they obtain them

- The ease with which new entrants can enter the market, and

- How far competition is encouraging innovation

## 1.2.7 Product intervention by the FCA

A fairly recent FSA initiative that will be taken forward by the FCA concerns identifying consumer detriment problems at an earlier stage through **product intervention**.

- Backed by a new senior-level business and market analysis team, the FCA has new **powers in product intervention** enabling it, for example, to direct firms to withdraw or amend misleading financial promotions with immediate effect.

- The FCA's product intervention power will give it the 'flexibility to intervene quickly and decisively' where it considers that a product or product feature is likely to result in significant consumer detriment. The FCA will seek to deal with the root of the problem, rather than reacting to the effects, when it is already too late.

## 1.2.8 Temporary product intervention rules (TPIRs)

The FCA gets its power to make product intervention rules under s137D FSMA 2000 (as amended by FSA 2012) aiming to tackle issues relating to specific products (or types of products), product features or marketing practices.

Normally, the FCA must **consult the public** before making any rules. However, s138L FSMA 2000 provides a general exemption from this requirement if the FCA considers that the delay involved in complying with the requirement would be prejudicial to the interests of consumers.

S138M makes a more specific exemption for making **temporary product intervention rules (TPIRs)**, where the FCA considers it necessary or expedient in order to advance its objectives. Such TPIRs, made **without consultation** (under s138M FSMA 2000), are limited to a maximum duration of 12 months. TPIRs will offer protection to consumers in the short term while allowing either the FCA or industry to develop a more permanent solution to address the source of detriment. They may also be made in response to competition or (if applicable) market integrity issues.

The extent and intrusiveness of the rules which are made will generally depend on the type of intervention deemed necessary to address effectively the problems identified, having regard to whether the intervention would be a proportionate response to the perceived risk to consumers, competition failings or market integrity. Rules may range from requiring certain product features to be included, excluded or changed, requiring amendments to promotional materials, to imposing restrictions on sales or marketing of the product or, in more serious cases, a ban on sales or marketing of a product in relation to all or some types of customer.

Following consultations in 2012, **Policy Statement PS13/03** (March 2013) confirmed the FCA's approach to exercising this power. The regulator gave examples of some of the types of situation in which it may choose to make temporary product intervention rules.

**Scenarios in which TPIRs might be used**

- Products where a **non-essential feature** causes a serious problem for consumers

- Products where there is a significant incentive **for inappropriate or indiscriminate targeting of consumers**

- Markets where firms **restrict their product range or access to it to increase profitability** by restricting consumer choice, reducing competition, or creating barriers to search, switching, or entry

- Products which may bring about significant detriment as a result of being **inappropriately targeted** – to the wrong customers (e.g. complex or niche products being sold to the mass market), or

- In particularly serious cases, a product considered to be **inherently flawed** – for example, a product that has such disadvantageous features that the majority of consumers, or specified types of consumer, are unlikely to benefit

In PS13/03, the FCA pointed out that **banning** flawed products is only one possible type of product intervention, and one which is likely to be reserved for the most serious cases. **Other types of intervention** may, for instance, focus on problematic product features, or inappropriate marketing or selling practices.

## 1.3 Prudential Regulation Authority (PRA)

The PRA – established with effect from 1 April 2013 as a subsidiary of the Bank of England – is responsible for the prudential regulation of banks, insurance companies and large investment firms. Only these firms are subject to '**dual regulation**' (see the diagram *New UK regulatory architecture*).

Under s2B FSMA 2000 (as amended by FSA 2012), the PRA has a statutory **general objective** that is fundamentally different from that of earlier regulatory regimes:

**Promoting the safety and soundness of PRA-authorised firms**

The new Authority will meet this objective primarily by seeking to minimise any adverse effects of firm failure on the UK financial system and by ensuring that firms carry on their business in a way that avoids adverse effects on the system (s2B FSMA 2000).

Regarding insurance, the PRA has a more specific **insurance objective** of contributing to the securing of an appropriate degree of protection for those who are or may become policyholders (s2C FSMA 2000).

In order to deliver its objective of stability of the financial system, the PRA will use a new framework to assess risks to financial stability.

**Key elements of PRA risk assessment framework** are the assessment of:

- Potential impact on the financial system of a firm coming under stress or failing

- Impact on the viability of a firm's business model of the macroeconomic and business risk context

- A firm's overall safety and soundness, which may act to mitigate the potential risk a firm poses to financial stability

**Key mitigants to be assessed by the PRA**

- Degree of resolvability of a firm (working closely with the Bank's Special Resolution Unit)

- The firm's financial strength (including its ability to generate capital through earnings, its capital held against future risks, the quality of its liquid assets and its liquidity management)

- The quality of a firm's risk management and governance (including the competence of its senior management)

**Risks to a firm will be identified** by the PRA **using**:

- Baseline monitoring
- Investigation and assurance
- The macroeconomic and business context

## 1.4 Principles of good regulation (Regulatory or supervisory principles)

Building on the regulators' objectives are a number of **regulatory principles** (or '**supervisory principles**') set out in **s3B FSMA 2000**, as amended by FSA 2012. These oblige the regulator to take into account a number of factors when discharging their general functions.

- **Efficiency and economy**: the need to use the resources of each regulator in the most efficient and economical way

- **Proportionality**: the principle that a burden or restriction which is imposed on a person, or on the carrying on of an activity, should be proportionate to the benefits, considered in general terms, which are expected to result from the imposition of that burden or restriction. To judge this, the regulators should take into account the costs to firms and consumers, for example by carrying out cost-benefit analyses of proposed regulations

- **Sustainable economic growth**: the desirability of sustainable growth in the economy of the UK In the medium or long term

- **Consumer responsibility**: the general principle that consumers should take responsibility for their decisions

- **Senior management responsibility**: the responsibilities of the senior management of regulated firms, including those affecting consumers, in relation to compliance with regulatory requirements. This secures an adequate but proportionate level of regulatory intervention by holding senior management responsible for the risk management and controls within firms. Firms must make it clear who has what responsibility and ensure that its business can be adequately monitored and controlled

- **Business diversity**: the desirability of each regulator recognising differences in the nature and objectives of regulated firms

- **Openness and disclosure**: the regulators should publish relevant market information about regulated firms, or require them to publish it – with appropriate safeguards

- **Transparency**: the regulators should exercise their functions as transparently as possible. The regulators should provide appropriate information on their regulatory decisions, and they should be open and accessible to the regulated community and the general public

## 1.5 Financial capability and the Money Advice Service (MAS)

A 2007 **National Audit Office** review of the UK regulator (the FSA, at that time) proposed that the regulator should try to quantify the costs to society and the financial services market of low levels of **financial capability** among consumers. It should also set measurable goals for improvements in consumer behaviour and outcomes against which success can be judged.

The regulator's policy in the area of financial capability has been to ensure that consumers are better able to manage their financial affairs and take informed decisions in their best interests.

Promoting public awareness ceased to be one of the statutory objectives of the FSA following the implementation of the **Financial Services Act 2010**, and the FSA's previous responsibilities in this area were passed to the Consumer Financial Education Body (CFEB), which became the **Money Advice Service (MAS)** in April 2011. As stated on its own web site, the CFEB took on a role of being 'responsible for helping consumers understand financial services in the UK and manage their finances better'. The MAS is overseen by the FCA.

Bearing in mind the objective of promoting public awareness, the task is to ensure that full information is made available in all cases (through transparency and disclosure) as well as provide consumers with the necessary tools and support to allow them to make informed decisions with regard to financial matters.

The regulator has viewed financial capability as comprising:

- Being able to manage money
- Keeping track of finances
- Planning ahead
- Making informed decisions about financial products, and
- Staying up-to-date about financial matters

Over recent years, the regulator has undertaken a number of initiatives in this area, including:

- Maintenance of a dedicated consumer website function
- Production of a number of 'Key Facts' documents and other factsheets and information packs
- Running road shows

Under the slogan of **Delivering Change**, the regulator has sought to improve the financial capability of UK consumers, with a target audience including schoolchildren, young adults, those Not in Education, Employment or Training (NEETs), university and further education students, workplace employees and new parents.

Through its financial capability initiatives, the regulator has worked with charities and the voluntary sector as part of the **National Strategy for Financial Capability**. The Money Advice Service now leads this strategy, in partnership with the Government, the financial services industry, the voluntary sector and consumer education groups. The Money Advice Service is funded by fees levied on authorised firms.

The National Strategy has involved developing partnerships to build financial capability, including:

- Through the social housing sector, to implement good practice in the work of social housing providers

- With the National Housing Federation, to train front line housing professionals to promote financial capability to their tenants

- With Association for Real Change and United Response to train support workers helping people with a learning disability move into independent living

- With the Royal College of Psychiatrists, to promote resources for social and health care professionals to support patients with debt problems

- In partnership with the National Offender Management Service (NOMS) to deliver financial capability services to offenders and prisoners, as well as prison and probation staff

- With autism support services

Another aspect of the strategy is the adoption of **Personal Finance Education** in the **National Curriculum** for England.

The **MAS** provides information for consumers on its website.


# 2 The FCA and PRA Handbooks

## 2.1 Overview

The principles, rules and regulations made by the regulators and to which a firm must adhere are found in the **FCA Handbook** and the **PRA Handbook**. Even where standards are imposed by FSMA 2000 itself, such as in the case of market abuse and financial promotions, the regulatory handbooks provide additional requirements and guidance.

The FCA and PRA Handbooks were initially created largely by splitting the FSA's Handbook between the new PRA Handbook and the FCA Handbook. Most provisions in the FSA Handbook have been incorporated into the **PRA Handbook**, the **FCA Handbook**, or both, in line with each new regulator's set of responsibilities and objectives. More recently, the PRA has been developing new Rulebooks within its Handbook, so that the PRA Handbook is in time becoming more distinctively different from the FCA Handbook.

The **FCA and PRA Handbooks** are organised in a number of **blocks**. Within each block are a number of **Sourcebooks**. The full texts of the Handbooks are available at each of the regulators' websites: **www.fca.org.uk** and **www.bankofengland.co.uk/PRA**.

You will recall that the FCA is both the **conduct regulator** for FCA-regulated firms and dual- (FCA/PRA) regulated firms, and the **prudential regulator** for FCA-regulated firms. The PRA is not a conduct regulator: its role is as **prudential regulator** of prudentially significant firms (i.e. those firms that are dual-regulated). Given these differences, it can be appreciated why the FCA Handbook is more extensive and accordingly contains more of the material that was previously in the FSA Handbook than is included in the PRA Handbook.

Here are some important points to bear in mind when reading the Table that follows.

- FCA & PRA indicates Sourcebooks that appear in both the FCA Handbook and the PRA Handbook.

- FCA indicates those Sourcebooks that appear only in the FCA Handbook. (All of the blocks and Sourcebooks shown in the Table are included in the FCA Handbook.)

- However, note that the Sourcebooks that appear with the same name in both of the Handbooks do not always have the same contents in each Handbook. **Sections** within each of these Sourcebooks may relate to one of the two regulators, or to both regulators. Within each of the Handbooks, individual sections are marked either **[FCA]** or **[PRA]** to indicate where they relate only to one regulator, and they are marked **[FCA] [PRA]** in cases where they relate to both regulators.

| High Level Standards | | |
|---|---|---|
| Principles for Businesses (PRIN) FCA | Threshold Conditions (COND) FCA | Training and Competence (TC) FCA |
| Senior Management Arrangements, Systems and Controls (SYSC) FCA & PRA | Fit and Proper Test for Approved Persons (FIT) FCA & PRA | General Provisions (GEN) FCA & PRA |
| Financial Stability and Market Confidence (FINMAR) FCA | Statements of Principle and Code of Practice for Approved Persons (APER) FCA & PRA | Fees Manual (FEES) FCA & PRA |

| Prudential Standards | | | |
|---|---|---|---|
| General Prudential Sourcebook (GENPRU) FCA & PRA | | | |
| Prudential Sourcebook for Banks, Building Societies and Investment Firms (BIPRU) FCA & PRA | Prudential Sourcebook for Insurers (INSPRU) FCA & PRA | Prudential Sourcebook for UCITS Firms (UPRU) FCA | Prudential Sourcebook for Mortgage and Home Finance Firms and Insurance Intermediaries (MIPRU) FCA & PRA |
| Interim Prudential Sourcebooks (IPRU) FCA & PRA: <br><br> • Friendly Societies <br> • Insurers <br> • Investment Businesses | | | |

| Business Standards | | |
|---|---|---|
| Conduct of Business (COBS) FCA & PRA | Banking Conduct of Business (BCOBS) FCA | Mortgages and Home Finance Conduct of Business (MCOB) FCA |
| Insurance: Conduct of Business (ICOBS) FCA | Client Assets (CASS) FCA | Market Conduct (MAR) FCA |

| Regulatory Processes | |
|---|---|
| Supervision Manual (SUP) FCA & PRA | Decision Procedure and Penalties Manual (DEPP) FCA |

| Redress | | |
|---|---|---|
| Dispute Resolution: Complaints (DISP) [FCA] | Compensation (COMP) [FCA] | Consumer Redress Schemes (CONRED) [FCA] |

| Specialist Sourcebooks | | |
|---|---|---|
| Collective Investment Schemes (COLL) [FCA] | Consumer Credit [FCA] | Regulated Covered Bonds (RCB) [FCA] |
| Professional Firms (PROF) [FCA] | | Credit Unions (CREDS) [FCA & PRA] |
| Investment Funds (FUND) [FCA] | | Recognised Investment Exchanges (REC) [FCA] |

| Listing Prospectus and Disclosure [FCA only] | | |
|---|---|---|
| Listing Rules (LR) [FCA] | Prospectus Rules (PR) [FCA] | Disclosure Rules and Transparency Rules (DTR) [FCA] |

The following blocks have additionally been created by the PRA since 2013 and are included only in the **PRA Handbook**.

- Rulebook CRR Firms (UK banks, building societies and UK designated investment firms) [PRA]

- Rulebook non-CRR Firms [PRA]

- Rulebook Solvency II (SII) Firms (although the Solvency II Directive covering insurance companies does not come into force until 1 January 2016) [PRA]

- Rulebook non-Solvency II (SII) Firms [PRA]

- Non-authorised persons [PRA]

- General Provisions (GP) [PRA]

## 2.2 Regulatory Guides

Within the FCA Handbook, there are the following **Regulatory Guides** giving guidance on specific areas.

- Collective Investment Scheme Information Guide (COLLG) [FCA]
- Enforcement Guide (EG) [FCA]
- Financial Crime: a guide for firms [FCA]
- Perimeter Guidance Manual (PERG) [FCA]
- Responsibilities of Providers and Distributors for the Fair Treatment of Customers Guide [FCA]
- Unfair Contract Terms Regulatory Guide (UNFCOG) [FCA]

## 2.3 Additional material related to the Handbooks

There are various publications supporting the Handbooks, including the following.

- **Glossary** [FCA & PRA]. Both the FCA Handbook and the PRA Handbook contain a Glossary. This is important, as it provides the **definitions of terms** highlighted as hyperlinks in the Handbook.

- **Handbook Guides**, which are provided in the FCA Handbook to highlight the relevant parts of the Handbook which apply to the following specific areas.

  - Energy Market Participants (EMPS) [FCA]
  - Oil Market Participants (OMPS) [FCA]
  - Service Companies (SERV) [FCA]
  - General Guidance on Benchmark Submission and Administration (BENCH) [FCA]

- **Consultation Papers**, **Handbook Notices** and final **Policy Statements** are the means of amending and updating the Handbooks.

- There is a **Readers' Guide**, explaining the status of different kinds of provisions contained in the Handbooks – particularly, **R**ules, **E**vidential provisions, **G**uidance, **C**onclusive provisions, and **D**irections (see below).

## 2.4 Types of provision in the Handbooks

The different kinds of provisions in the regulators' Handbooks are indicated by letters, as follows.

| | |
|---|---|
| **R** | This indicates a **rule** and means that it places a binding duty on a firm. |
| **E** | This indicates an **evidential provision**. If a firm complies with an evidential provision, this will tend to establish compliance with the linked rule. If a firm breaches an evidential provision, this will tend to establish that a breach of the linked rule has occurred. |
| **G** | This indicates **guidance**, which is not binding on a firm but is used to flesh out particular issues arising from rules. |
| **D** | The letter **D** indicates **directions** and **requirements** given under various powers conferred by FSMA 2000 and relevant statutory instruments. Directions and requirements are **binding** upon the persons or categories of person to whom they are addressed. |
| **UK** | The **UK** flag icon is used to indicate directly applicable UK legislative material, such as Acts of Parliament and statutory instruments, Government regulations and orders. Cross-references to this material will use the letters UK. |
| **EU** | An **EU** flag icon indicates EU legislative material, such as EU Directives and directly applicable EU Regulations. Cross-references to this material will use the letters **EU**. |
| **P** | The letter **P** is used to indicate the **Statements of Principle for approved persons** made under s64 of FSMA 2000. The Statements of Principle are **binding** on approved persons. |
| **C** | The letter **C** is used for paragraphs made under s119(2)(b) of FSMA 2000 which specify descriptions of behaviour that, in the opinion of the regulator, **do not amount to market abuse**. These descriptions are conclusive because such behaviour is to be taken, for the purposes of the Act, as not amounting to market abuse. |

## 2.5 Industry guidance

**Industry Guidance** includes Codes of Practice and similar Statements generated by **trade associations and professional bodies** to help their members understand and follow good practice in meeting regulatory requirements.

As well as not taking action against a person for behaviour that it considers to be in line with **guidance**, the regulator will similarly not take action that is in line with **other materials** published by the regulators in support of the Handbook or **regulator-confirmed Industry Guidance** which were current at the time of the behaviour in question.

However, as **Industry Guidance** is not mandatory (and is one way, but not the only way, to comply with requirements), the regulator does not presume that because firms are not complying with it they are not meeting its requirements.

## 2.6 High Level Standards

The **High Level Standards** address various issues linked with the **principles-based approach to regulation**. An element of the High Level Standards that we cover later in this Study Text is the **Training and Competence Sourcebook (TC)**.

The **Principles for Businesses (PRIN)** state authorised firms' fundamental obligations under the regulatory system. They are formulated to require honest, fair and professional conduct from firms. In addition to PRIN, there are Statements of Principle and Code of Practice for Approved Persons **(APER)**, which we examine in a later Chapter of this Study Text.

The Principles are drafted by the regulator and derive authority from the regulator's rulemaking powers under FSMA 2000 and from the regulators' **statutory objectives**, and they also include provisions which implement EU Directives.

The regulators have drafted a large amount of guidance on **PRIN 3** (Principle for Businesses 3), which states:

> **Management and control**: 'A firm must take reasonable care to organise and control its affairs responsibly and effectively, with adequate risk management systems.'

This emphasis came from a desire to avoid a repetition of the collapse of Barings Bank, where it was clear that management methods and the control environment were deficient. Note that it would not be a breach of this Principle if the firm failed to prevent **unforeseeable** risks.

The regulator suggests that, in order to comply with its obligation to maintain appropriate systems, a firm should carry out a regular review of the relevant factors.

The main purpose of the section of the regulatory Handbooks called **Senior Management Arrangements, Systems and Controls (SYSC)** is to encourage directors and senior managers of authorised firms to take appropriate responsibility for their firm's arrangements and to ensure they know what their obligations are. Firms must make **records** of arrangements for **apportioning senior management responsibilities** and must keep such records for six years.

## 2.7 Approval of individuals

Some **individuals** within a regulated firm will need **approval** from the relevant regulator because they carry out one or more specified **controlled functions**.

Thus, an **approved person** can be defined as 'someone who is approved to perform a controlled function for an authorised firm or an **appointed representative** firm'.

We explain what the controlled functions are later in this Study Text.

Note that the process of an **individual** obtaining **approved person** status is different from the process of a **firm** obtaining **authorisation**.

To obtain approval, a person must satisfy the regulator that they are **fit and proper** to carry out the controlled function. The suitability of a member of staff who performs a controlled function is covered in the **Fit and Proper Test for Approved Persons (FIT)** (as can be seen earlier in this Section of the Chapter, FIT is in the High Level Standards section of the FCA and PRA Handbooks).

## 2.8 Conduct of Business (COBS)

The regulator includes various rules governing firms' day-to-day dealings with customers in a large section of its Handbook called the **Conduct of Business Sourcebook (COBS)**. The Conduct of Business Rules have been extensively revised, and shortened, with the implementation of the Markets in Financial Instruments Directive (MiFID), with effect from November 2007.

## 2.9 Client assets (CASS)

### 2.9.1 Key rules

The rules in this section of the FCA Handbook link to Principle for Businesses 10 *Clients' Assets*. The rules aim to restrict the commingling of client's and firm's assets and to minimise the risk of client's investments being used by the firm without the client's agreement or contrary to the client's wishes, or being treated as the firm's assets in the event of its **insolvency**. The focus therefore is on two main issues, namely custody of investments, and client money.

The client assets rules have a broader coverage than the rules contained in COBS, the Conduct of Business Sourcebook, in that they afford protection not only to retail and professional clients, but also to **eligible counterparties**.

Under MiFID, client assets are regulated by the **Home State**. Therefore, for example, if a French firm is **passporting** into the UK, it will adhere to French client assets rules.

The implementation of MiFID has resulted in more onerous requirements on firms in respect of custody of client assets and client money. In January 2009 revisions to CASS, non-MiFID and MiFID rules were largely harmonised.

Firms must, in general, **segregate clients' assets** from the firm's own assets. By being held in a **designated client bank account**, client money is effectively **held on trust** for clients and is **not available to creditors** of the firm if the firm becomes insolvent.

- Except in the case of credit institutions, firms may not use client funds for their own account in any circumstances.

- Sub-custodians and depositaries must be selected in accordance with specified rules.

- There are rules specifying that client funds be held with a bank on which due diligence has been carried out, or (if the client does not object) certain money market funds meeting specified criteria. The funds must normally be paid into the client bank account by the end of the next business day.

- One of the most significant impacts of MiFID implementation on the existing client money regime is that MiFID firms may not allow professional clients to 'opt-out' of the client money rules, for MiFID business. For non-MiFID business, firms may opt professional clients or eligible counterparties out of the client money rules, on the basis of a two-way agreement.

**Client money** must be deposited with:

- A bank, building society, or central bank
- An EEA credit institution
- A bank regulated in the Channel Islands or the Isle of Man
- A bank authorised in a third country, or
- A qualifying money market fund

A firm should undertake adequate **due diligence** before placing any client assets or client money with third parties. The due diligence should amount to more than simply checking the credit rating of the institution. Appropriate due diligence might assess a bank's market reputation, assess legal requirements or market practices, and consider risk diversification as well as credit ratings on an ongoing basis, The due diligence review carried out should be documented.

If a firm leaves some of its own money in a client money account, this is referred to as a **pollution of trust** and, if the firm fails, the liquidator will be able to seize all the money held in the client account for the general creditors of the firm.

**Interest** on client money belongs to the client unless it is agreed otherwise. **Client money reconciliations** must be performed regularly: discrepancies must be investigated and corrected promptly.

**Retail investment advisers (RIAs)** who do not have authority to handle client money should ensure that payments for investments are paid **directly to the product provider**.

Under rules that came into effect in June 2015, firms may pay away **unclaimed client money and assets** to a registered charity, provided that the balances have been held for at least six years (for client money) or twelve years (for client assets) and provided that the firm has taken reasonable steps to trace the clients.

## 2.9.2 Client money and assets return (CMAR)

The following are requirements for all regulated firms holding client money and/or assets:

- The **CASS operational oversight approved person controlled function (CF10a)**, with effect from 1 October 2011

- A **client money and assets return (CMAR)**, with effect from 1 June 2011

Firms that hold client money and/or client assets are required to apportion responsibility for CASS operational oversight to an appropriate senior manager or director performing a SIF role within the firm.

The CMAR must be reviewed by the responsible person half-yearly in the case of smaller firms, and monthly in the case of larger firms (with firm size defined on the basis of client money and assets holdings).

## 2.9.3 Intra-group client money deposits

Following the collapse of Lehman Brothers, it transpired that 50% of Lehman Brothers International (Europe)'s had placed 50% of its client money with a group bank that became insolvent.

Since 1 June 2011, firms are subject to a **20% maximum limit on intra-group client money deposits** in client bank accounts. Firms which already exceed the 20% limit before that date must conduct suitable due diligence and diversify their client money deposits over the next few months.

## 2.9.4 Client money distribution

**Client money distribution rules** in **CASS** seek to facilitate the timely return of client money if a firm fails, which is termed a **primary pooling event**. In that event, client money in the firm's client money account is treated as pooled. The money must be distributed so that each client receives a sum that is rateable (proportional) to that client's net balance.

A **secondary pooling event** is the failure of a third party with which client money is held. The client money distribution rules seek to ensure that a client who has specified that they were not willing to accept that bank's risk should not suffer a loss. Any client losses must be distributed rateably.

## 2.9.5 CASS Resolution Pack

The regulator introduced rules taking effect on **1 October 2012** that require firms to which either or both of CASS 6 (custody rules) and CASS 7 (client money rules) applies to maintain and be able to retrieve a **CASS Resolution Pack (CASS RP)**. The CASS RP contains documents and records – as specified in CASS 10.2 and 10.3 – that would help an insolvency practitioner to return client assets more quickly following an investment firm failure.

Rules require firms to ensure that CASS RP documents can be retrieved within 48 hours and that material inaccuracies in the content of certain CASS RP documents are corrected within five business days of the inaccuracy arising.

Following the collapse of both Lehman Brothers International (Europe) (LBIE) and (in 2011) MF Global UK Limited, the introduction of the CASS RP is one step towards ensuring the speedier return of client assets.

### 2.9.6 Client Asset Unit

The regulator has established a **Client Asset Unit**, within its Markets Division of the Conduct Business Unit, to focus specialist resources on CASS issues.

The Unit was created to provide confidence in the ability of the UK regulatory regime to deliver adequate protection of client money and safe custody assets (client assets), which is a critical component for a successful financial services industry.

The regulator has stated that it relies on the quality of the protections afforded by the client assets regime because they help to ensure that clients' assets and money are safe in the event of firms failing and exiting the market. Weaknesses in firms' client asset systems and controls can cause serious financial detriment to customers and counterparties, as well as reputational damage to the regulator and UK markets.

The **Client Asset Unit's mission** is to help minimise the risk of financial loss from control failings and mitigate the damaging effects of such potential failures on consumers, firms and the regulators.

Relevant **desirable regulatory outcomes** are as follows.

- Clients to be confident that their assets are being held by firms with robust client asset controls as well as strong risk management

- Clients to be assured that their client assets are safe and will be returned within a reasonable timeframe in the event of firm failure

- The UK market to be regarded as a safe place to conduct business and encourage market entrants

## 2.10 Code of Market Conduct

While the law is set out in FSMA 2000, the regulators also have a duty to draft a **Code of Market Conduct**, which includes:

- Descriptions of behaviour that, in the opinion of the regulator, do or do not amount to **market abuse**. (Descriptions of behaviour which do not amount to market abuse are called '**safe harbours**'.)

- Descriptions of behaviour that are or are not **accepted market practices** in relation to one or more identified markets

- Factors that, in the opinion of the regulator, are to be taken into account in determining whether or not behaviour amounts to market abuse

The Code does not exhaustively describe all types of behaviour that may or may not amount to market abuse.

# 3 Prudential standards

## 3.1 Capital requirements

The financial regulation of **capital adequacy** seeks to enhance investor protection. The rules seek to ensure that a firm always has enough capital to operate. If a firm is forced to maintain significant capital resources to remain in business, it means that there should be enough money to close down the business and transfer positions in an orderly manner, should it go into liquidation. Associated with these rules are requirements on **reporting**, **notification** and **internal controls**.

As a result of the implementation of the **Capital Adequacy Directive (CAD)** – which was amended by the **Capital Requirements Directive (CRD)** – there were two distinct sets of rules relating to capital adequacy, found in the **Interim Prudential Sourcebook (IPRU)** of the regulatory Handbook.

Before 1 January 2007, the **Interim Prudential Sourcebook for Investment Businesses (IPRU (INV))** was the part of the Handbook that dealt with capital requirements for investment firms subject to the position risk requirements of the previous version of the Capital Adequacy Directive. Now, however, investment firms which are subject to the risk-based capital requirements of the Capital Adequacy Directive are subject to the **General Prudential sourcebook (GENPRU)** and the **Prudential Sourcebook for Banks, Building Societies and Investment Firms (BIPRU)**.

---

**BIPRU** includes **guidance for firms** in managing the following risks.

- **Credit and counterparty risk** – This is the risk exposure of the firm to default on loans. A firm must base credit-granting on sound and well-defined criteria and clearly establish the process for approving, amending, renewing and refinancing credits.

- **Market risk** – A firm must implement policies and processes for the identification, measurement and management of all material sources and effects of specific market risks relating to different positions taken in trading.

- **Liquidity risk** – This is the risk that a firm may not be able to meet its liabilities as they fall due without borrowing at excessive cost. A firm should consider its exposure to liquidity risk and assess its response should that risk materialise. When assessing liquidity risk, a firm should consider the extent to which there is a mismatch between assets and liabilities.

- **Operational risk** – A firm must implement policies and processes to evaluate and manage the exposure to operational risk, including risk from errors in internal models and to cover low-frequency high severity events.

- **Concentration risk** – A firm must address and control, by means which include written policies and procedures, the concentration risk arising from, for example, a large exposure to a single counterparty, or a large loan to a single borrower.

- **Residual risk** – This is the risk that credit risk mitigation techniques used by the firm prove less effective than expected.

- **Securitisation risk** – This includes the risk that the own funds held by a firm for assets which it has securitised are inadequate having regard to the economic substance of the transaction, including the degree of risk transfer achieved.

- **Business risk** – This means any risk for the firm arising from changes in the firm's business, or its remuneration policy.

- **Interest rate risk** – Including interest rate risk in the non-trading book.

- **Risk of excessive leverage** – Procedures must include a specified leverage ratio as an indicator of this risk, and mismatches between assets and obligations.

- **Pension obligation risk** – This is the risk to a firm caused by its contractual or other obligations to, or with respect to, a pension scheme.

- **Group risk** – This is the risk that the firm's financial position may be adversely affected by its relationships (financial or non-financial) with other entities in the same group or by risks which may affect the financial position of the whole group (e.g., reputational contagion).

---

The overall aim of capital requirements rules is to ensure that firms remain solvent by having greater assets at their command than they will need to cover their positions. In general, a firm must maintain, at all times, financial resources in excess of its financial resources requirement.

By the end of 2013, a **capital resources requirement** of holding a minimum of **three months of relevant annual expenditure** (the **expenditure-based requirement (EBR)**) with a **minimum capital resources** floor of £20,000 is to be extended to all personal investment firms.

The required capital resources must be held in realisable assets such as cash.

There are more specific requirements for the level of additional capital resources required for firms that have any exclusion in their professional indemnity insurance policy.

## 3.2 Liquidity requirements

### 3.2.1 Adequacy of financial resources

Adequate financial resources and adequate systems and controls are necessary for the effective management of **prudential risks** – that is, the risk that the firm becomes financially unsound.

The regulatory requirements amplify **Principle for Businesses 4**, under which a firm must maintain adequate financial resources. They are concerned with the adequacy of the financial resources that a firm needs to hold in order to be able to meet its liabilities as they fall due. These resources include both capital and liquidity resources.

### 3.2.2 The overall liquidity adequacy rule

The **overall liquidity adequacy rule** states that: 'A firm must at all times maintain **liquidity resources** which are adequate, both as to amount and quality, to ensure that there is no significant risk that its liabilities cannot be met as they fall due.'

The liquidity resources that can be made available **by other members of the firm's group** must not be counted. Resources made available through **emergency liquidity assistance from a central bank** must also be excluded.

Foreign firms with UK branches may only include liquidity resources which meet certain conditions: the resources must be unencumbered, under day-to-day control of the senior management of the UK branch, held in the sole name of the UK branch, and attributed to the balance sheet of the UK branch.

Changes have allowed firms following BIPRU to obtain a simple waiver under certain conditions. This **BIPRU waiver** applies where firms hope to rely on other group members when looking to meet the overall liquidity adequacy rule. In allowing the waiver, the regulator needs to ensure that it satisfies statutory tests under section 148 of FSMA 2000, which allows certain rules to be waived in particular circumstances.

### 3.2.3 Individual Liquidity Adequacy Assessments

Firms must carry out an **Individual Liquidity Adequacy Assessment (ILAA)**, based on **stress testing**, at least annually. The ILAA should be undertaken more frequently if changes in a firm's business strategy, balance sheet, the nature or scale of its activities, or its operational environment suggest that the **level of liquidity resources** is no longer adequate.

- A key function of the ILAA is to inform a firm's Board of the ongoing assessment and quantification of the firm's liquidity risks, how the firm intends to mitigate those risks, and how much current and future liquidity is required.

- The ILAA document is also how the firm demonstrates and explains to the regulator its internal liquidity adequacy assessment process.

The regulator will generally request to see the ILAA as part of the ongoing supervisory process.

The **stress testing** on which the ILAA is based must cover:

- Firstly, an unforeseen 'name-specific' stress in which market participants and depositors consider that the firm is likely to be unable to meet its liabilities in the short term, and counterparties reduce intra-day credit allowed to the firm

- Secondly, an unforeseen market-wide liquidity stress of three months duration in which there is risk aversion in markets from which the firm derives its funds, uncertainty about the valuation of assets of the firm and its counterparties, and inability to realise classes of assets or an ability to realise them only at excessive cost

### 3.2.4 Overarching liquidity systems and controls requirements

Firms must have in place '**robust strategies, policies, processes and systems**' that are comprehensive and proportionate to the nature, scale and complexity of the firm's activities. These strategies, policies, processes and systems must enable the firm to identify, measure, manage and monitor liquidity risk, as well as to enable it to assess and maintain on an ongoing basis the amounts, types and distribution of liquidity resources that it considers adequate to cover:

- The nature and level of the liquidity risk to which it is or might be exposed, and
- The risk that the firm cannot meet its liabilities as they fall due

For investment firms in general (but subject to certain exemptions, including firms dealing only on their own account), the systems should also assess the resources needed to cover the risk that its liquidity resources might in the future fall below the level, or differ from the quality and funding profile, of those resources advised as appropriate by the regulator in that firm's individual liquidity guidance or, for firms with a simpler business model, a simplified buffer requirement.

# 4 FCA and PRA supervision approaches

## 4.1 Introduction

The FCA supervises the conduct of both FCA-regulated and dual-regulated firms, and also has the task of prudential regulation of FCA-regulated firms. The PRA is responsible for prudential regulation of dual-regulated firms.

The supervision models are different for the PRA and FCA:

- Prudential supervision will continue to have dedicated resources supervising firms, and
- Conduct supervision will focus more on thematic work, and less on firm-specific work

The previous 'ARROW' risk mitigation programme has been replaced by two separate risk mitigations programmes, one for **prudential** and one for **conduct**. Firms will have two separate sets of mitigating actions, of equal importance, to address.

## 4.2 Supervisory tools

The supervisory tools available to the regulators are of four types:

- **Diagnostic** – designed to identify, assess and measure risk
- **Monitoring** – to track the development of risks
- **Preventative** – to reduce or limit identified risks and prevent risks from crystallising
- **Remedial** – to address risks that have crystallised

In the supervisory process, the regulators may use a broad range of **tools**, including the following.

- Desk-based reviews
- Liaison with other agencies or regulators
- Meetings with the management and representatives of the firm
- On-site inspections
- Reviews and analysis of periodic returns and notifications
- Reviews of past business
- Transaction monitoring
- Use of auditors
- Use of skilled persons reports*

* Under s166 FSMA 2000, the regulator can require a firm to appoint an independent skilled person who will review a specified aspect of the business of the firm.

## 4.3 The FCA's risk assessment process

The FCA is a risk-based regulator and has declared that its risk framework will be the 'engine room' of the business, providing support to the key activities, namely: supervision, policy, enforcement and authorisation.

- Given its broad remit, the FCA will need to consider **detriment** when carrying out its risk assessments.

- In quantifying detriment, the FCA will assess **probability** and **impact**.

- Impact will be further broken down into **incidence** (for example, the number of consumers affected or potentially affected) and **severity** (for example, the amount of welfare or detriment involved per consumer).

Such assessments will be based on current understanding of the risk or opportunity as well as reasonable expectations of how they will develop under a variety of scenarios. This type of analysis will help to support the FCA's aim of intervening earlier and more swiftly to prevent detriment, by evaluating the costs and benefits of the timing of any action.

## 4.4 The FCA's approach to supervision

### 4.4.1 Introduction

The statutory objectives of the FCA will drive what the Authority will do.

As we have seen, the FCA's single **strategic objective** is, in summary, **'Making markets work well'**. The FCA's three operational objectives are: ensuring consumer protection, market integrity, and competition in the interests of consumers. Of these, the newest for the FCA is the latter. As a primary statutory objective, we will be obliged to consider the role of competition (or lack of it) as a driver of poor outcomes in markets and work out how to address these problems.

The starting point for the FCA's supervision process is the **categorisation of firms** into four conduct supervision categories – C1, C2, C3 or C4 – according to their impact on consumers and the market, while recognising that there is not a one-size-fits-all approach.

### 4.4.2 FCA's conduct supervision categories

These conduct supervision categories are broadly as follows.

- **C1**: Universal banks or investment banks with very large trading operations and substantial client assets; banking and insurance groups with large numbers of retail customers

- **C2**: Large wholesale firms; firms from different sectors having a substantial number of retail customers

- **C3**: Firms across different sectors with a significant wholesale presence and/or retail customers

- **C4**: Smaller firms, including almost all intermediaries

Overall, the new categorisation means that the FCA will have supervisors allocated to firms with the greatest potential to cause risks to consumers or market integrity. Given limited resources, **supervisors will be deployed flexibly to deal with problems** that arise and specific issues and products that have potential to or are already causing consumer harm.

Broadly, C1 and C2 firms will experience the most intensive focus and shorter, two-year regulatory cycles. C3 and C4 firms will too have their business models evaluated, but this will be done on a four-year cycle. (See the box below for more detail.)

## 4.4.3 FCA's conduct supervision activities

---

**CONDUCT SUPERVISION ACTIVITY SUMMARY** *(Source: 'Our Approach to Supervision', FCA, March 2014)*

*C1 firms*

**Business model and strategy analysis (BMSA) every two years**, reviewed at the halfway stage. (See more detail below on the BMSA.)

**Regular meetings** between FCA supervisors, senior management, Board members, key control functions and external auditors, with further meetings as changes happen or risks emerge.

**Regular reviews of management information**, eg Board and Executive Committee packs, and performance information.

**Annual strategy meeting** between FCA senior management, CEO and executives.

**One or two 'deep dive' assessments** during each annual assessment cycle.

**Annual firm evaluation**, explained in a letter to the firm and presentation to the Board.

**Regular baseline monitoring** of regulatory returns.

**Routine and other activities** such as transfers, acquisitions and permission changes.

**Participation in thematic reviews and market studies.**

*C2 firms*

**Annual peer group business model and strategy analysis.**

**Regular meetings** between FCA supervisors, senior management and Board members, with further meetings as changes happen or risks emerge.

**Regular reviews of management information**, eg Board and Executive Committee packs, and performance information.

**Annual strategy meeting** between FCA senior management and the firm's executives.

**One or two 'deep dive' assessments** during each two-year assessment cycle.

**Firm evaluation every two years**, explained in a letter to the firm and presentation to the Board.

**Regular baseline monitoring** of regulatory returns.

**Routine and other activities** such as transfers, acquisitions and permission changes.

**Participation in thematic reviews and market studies.**

*C3 firms*

**Annual peer group business model and strategy analysis.**

Routine interaction with the FCA via the **Firm Contact Centre**, and other interaction via trade body events and roundtable discussions.

**Regular baseline monitoring** of regulatory returns.

**Occasional routine tasks**, such as transfers, acquisitions and permission changes.

**Participation in thematic reviews and market studies**, and possible inclusion in **in issues and products** work or **competition market studies**.

**Periodic assessment** at least once every four years, with additional assessments where necessary, eg as a follow-up to the main assessment, or where the firm's business model has changed significantly.

*C4 firms*

Ongoing supervision by **sectoral analysis and thematic reviews.**

---

**Regular baseline monitoring** of regulatory returns.

**Occasional routine tasks**, such as transfers, acquisitions and permission changes.

**Four-yearly assessment** via phone or face-to-face interview, online assessment, or a combination of these.

The FCA will do further firm-specific work where risks need to be addressed.

The FCA will follow up with a random sample of firms that have completed the online assessment, to verify information provided.

### 4.4.4 Business Model and Strategy Analysis (BMSA)

When carrying out analyses of business models and strategy (**Business Model and Strategy Analysis – BMSA**), the FCA will take account of a firm's competitive position in various markets then assess potential conduct risks arising from their strategies.

The **BMSA** has the chief purpose of forming a view on whether a firm's business model exposes it to an unacceptable level of **conduct risk**.

### 4.4.5 Three pillars of the FCA supervision model

Alongside this approach is the way in which firms will be supervised on a day-to-day basis. The **FCA supervision model** will be based on three key **pillars – FSF, Event Driven**, and **Issues & Products**.

The FCA's forward-looking assessment of a firm's conduct risks will be undertaken within the first pillar: the **Firm Systematic Framework (FSF).** This is designed to answer the key question of 'Are the interests of customers and market integrity at the heart of how the firm is run?'

The **FSF** involves:

- Analysing firms' business models and strategies so that the FCA can form a view of the sustainability of the business from a conduct perspective and where future risks might lie, and

- Assessment of how the fair treatment of customers and ensuring market integrity is embedded in the way in which the firm runs its business, from the 'tone from the top', through how culture is embedded across the firm, to how the firm manages and controls its risks.

As we saw above, the approach is differentiated depending on the categorisation of the firm.

The regulator's assessment is achieved through the following **four FSF modules**:

- **Governance and culture**, which assesses how effectively the firm identifies, manages and reduces conduct risk

- **Product design**, which looks at whether the firm's products or services meet customer needs and whether customers are targeted accordingly

- **Sales processes**, which are an assessment of the firm's systems and controls, and

- **Post-sales handling**, which looks into how effectively the firm ensures that its customers are treated fairly after the point of sale, service or transaction, including complaints handling.

The FCA will also carry out studies of markets where its intelligence gathering indicates that competition is not functioning well.

The **second pillar** is based on dealing with **issues that are emerging** or have happened and are unforeseen in their nature. This is termed '**event-driven work**' and will cover matters from mergers and acquisitions, to whistleblowing allegations, to spikes in reported complaints at a firm. The FCA will seek to secure customer redress, where applicable.

The **final pillar** is broadly termed '**issues and products**' and will be largely driven by the analysis made of each sector by the regulator's sector teams. These teams will produce Sector Risk Assessments of conduct risks across all sectors. This will determine whether there are cross-firm and/or product issues driving poor outcomes for consumers or endangering market integrity, the degree of potential detriment, and whether the regulator should be undertaking any thematic pieces of work to assess or mitigate these risks.

---

**CONDUCT RISK**

What is **conduct risk**? It is perhaps not surprising that '**conduct risk**' was a term adopted early in the life of the **Financial Conduct Authority** – the UK's '**conduct regulator**'. The concept has been related to 'a range of inherent factors [that] interact to produce poor choices and outcomes in financial markets.' *(FCA Risk Outlook 2013)*

The FCA has referred to conduct risk as the risk of 'consumer detriment arising from the wrong products ending up in the wrong hands, and the detriment to society of people not being able to get access to the right products.'

Note that this definition recognises the need for a balance between these two sources of potential detriment. On one hand, regulatory action may seek to stop the wrong products being made available to consumers, while on the other hand regulation should not stifle or inhibit the financial services industry from making suitable products available.

---

## 4.4.6 FCA's prudential categories

The FCA will adopt a differentiated approach depending on how it prudentially categorises a firm. Firms will, in addition to the C1 to C4 categorisation, also be allocated one of three **prudential categories**. **CP1** firms are those whose failure would have a significant impact on the market in which they operate, but where the FCA is not yet confident that orderly wind-down can be achieved. These will still be supervised on a going-concern basis with the aim of minimising the probability of failure. Firms that have a significant market impact but for which an orderly wind-down can be achieved, will be categorised as **CP2** and supervised on a proactive 'gone-concern' basis.

Those where failure, even if disorderly, is unlikely to have significant impact, will be categorised as **CP3** and supervised on a reactive gone-concern basis.

For the vast majority of firms, the focus will be on managing failure when it happens, rather than focusing on reducing its probability.

## 4.5 The PRA's approach to supervision

The PRA adopts a 'judgement-based', forward-looking approach to supervision. Various **supervisory tools** will be available to the regulator, including: analysis of public information or that provided by firms, meetings with firms, inspections, on-site testing and stress testing, liaison with firms' external auditors, and liaison with the FCA. The level of core supervisory activity the PRA will carry out with a firm will depend on the firm's category. The Authority will have discretion to carry out additional work beyond the core on areas of particular concern.

The PRA plans to classify the firms it supervises into five categories, from high impact (1) to low impact (5), based on their potential impact on the stability of the UK's financial system.

- Firms that are most significant, given their size, complexity, interconnectedness and business type, have the capacity to cause 'very significant disruption' to the UK financial system, and so are categorised as '**high impact**'.

- **Low impact** firms have no significant capacity on their own to cause disruption, even though there is the potential that they could contribute to disruption that is occurring across a sector of the financial system.

The PRA will take into account **how close a firm is to failing** when considering the actions it will take. The PRA's '**Proactive Intervention Framework (PIF)**' will characterise the PRA's judgement about a firm's **proximity to failure**.

The PIF is designed to ensure that the PRA puts into effect its aim to identify and respond to emerging risks at an early stage. There will be five clearly demarcated PIF stages, each denoting a different proximity to failure, and every firm will sit in a particular stage at each point in time.

**The five stages of the PIF**

- Stage 1 – Low risk to viability of firm
- Stage 2 – Moderate risk to viability of firm
- Stage 3 – Risk to viability absent action by the firm
- Stage 4 – Imminent risk to viability of firm
- Stage 5 – Firm in resolution or being actively wound up

As a firm moves to a higher PIF stage – that is, as the PRA judges that the firm's viability has deteriorated – the senior management of firms will be expected to ensure they take appropriate remedial action to reduce the likelihood of failure, and the authorities will ensure appropriate preparedness for resolution.

For example, at Stage 3, a firm may be formally required to draw on the menu of options set out in its recovery plan.

## 4.6 Consumer Protection Strategy

The regulator has given the name **Consumer Protection Strategy** to its recent, more pro-active approach to regulating firms' conduct towards their retail customers.

The strategy requires the regulator to make judgements on firms' decisions and actively to intervene earlier in the product life cycle. It implies a greater willingness to test outcomes using methods such as mystery shopping and on-site visits.

The regulator began to implement the **Consumer Protection Strategy** in 2010 and 2011, including through:

- A more intensive supervision of the conduct of large retail firms (i.e. their 'retail conduct', which could be to the detriment of consumers)

- An increased focus on product intervention (i.e. regulatory action aimed at specific products or product types), and

- Greater use of the range of enforcement and other regulatory tools for dealing with poor conduct

This work continues under the FCA. The regulator sees another key part of the strategy as being earlier **identification of retail conduct risks**. This requires an analysis of key market trends and of current and future possible responses from firms and consumers.

## 4.7 GABRIEL

**GABRIEL** stands for **GAthering Better Regulatory Information Electronically**. GABRIEL is the FCA's electronic data collection and reporting system. It collects and analyses information about authorised firms and their activities as part of the regulator's supervision strategy.

The FCA uses data collected in order to:

- Monitor individual firms
- Construct risk profiles
- Identify trends in the market, for thematic work

The reporting requirements will depend on the firm's category and the nature of its business. The format and content of the reporting requirements is set out in the FCA Handbook at SUP16. Administration fees are charged if information is not submitted according to the relevant time limit.

# 5 Enforcement and discipline

## 5.1 Overview

The regulators' powers on enforcement are extensive. FSMA 2000 Part XI and the Decision Procedures and Penalties manual (**DEPP**) set out the regulators' powers in this area.

## 5.2 Information gathering and investigatory powers

The regulators have wide powers under ss165–176 FSMA 2000.

- **Information and documents.** The regulators have the power to require an authorised firm (or any person connected with it), appointed representatives or certain other persons, e.g. Recognised Investment Exchanges, to provide it with information, reports or other documents it needs to carry out its duties. The regulator can require the information or documents to be provided within a specified reasonable timescale and at a specified place. The regulator may also require that the information provided is verified and documents are authenticated. The regulator can require a firm to appoint accountants, actuaries and other professionals to carry out a one-off investigation into the firm's activities and report back to the regulator. This is known as a skilled person's report, which the firm must pay for.

  Returns required of firms include the **Retail Mediation Activities Return (RMAR)**, which must include information on (for example) the firm's accounts, its financial resources, its product sales data, its professional indemnity insurance (PII) and its adviser charging structures.

- **Investigators.** The regulators may appoint investigators to investigate possible regulatory breaches. This power covers authorised firms, approved persons, appointed representatives and, indeed in some cases such as market abuse, all persons. In some cases, such as money laundering and insider dealing, the regulator may share investigatory powers with the Department for Business, Innovation and Skills (BIS) and other bodies. Under s169 FSMA 2000, the UK regulators may also launch an investigation in support of an overseas regulator.

  The regulator can require a person under investigation or a connected person to attend for questioning by an investigator and can require a person to produce documents and answer questions. This effectively removes the right to silence. In order to ensure that the regime is compliant with human rights legislation, such answers will not be admissible in criminal or market abuse proceedings.

- **Entry to premises.** A regulator may seek access to an authorised firm's premises on demand (**without giving notice**). Where this is refused, a court warrant may be obtained.

Under s177 FSMA 2000, it is a criminal offence to falsify, conceal, destroy or dispose of a document that the person knows or suspects would be relevant to the investigation, or knowingly or recklessly provide false or misleading information. The maximum penalty for breaching s177 is two years' imprisonment and an unlimited fine in the Crown Court.

S170 FSMA 2000 provides that the regulator must give written notice of an investigation and the reason for it to the person being investigated. Written notice of a change in scope of the investigation must be given if the regulator considers that not providing this notice would be likely to prejudice that person.

The regulator must use its powers in a way that is transparent, proportionate, consistent and fair. The regulator will not normally make public the fact that it is or is not investigating a particular matter unless it is in the interests of consumers. (However, there are proposals for the successor body, the FCA, to give earlier publicity to investigations.

## 5.3 Authorisation and the general prohibition

**Section 19** FSMA 2000 contains what is known as the '**general prohibition**'. This states that no person may carry on a regulated activity in or into the UK **by way of business** or purport to do so, unless they are either **authorised** or **exempt** from authorisation.

The sanctions for breaching s19 are severe, namely criminal sanctions and unenforceability of agreements, compensation and actions by the regulator or Department for Business, Innovation and Skills (BIS) to restrain such activity.

- **Criminal sanctions:** under s23(1) breach of the general prohibition is an offence punishable by two years in jail and/or an unlimited fine. Under s23(3) it is a defence if it can be shown that all reasonable precautions were taken and all due diligence exercised to avoid committing the offence.

- **Unenforceable agreements:** any agreement made by an unauthorised person will be unenforceable against the other party. However, s28 provides that where a court decides that it is just and equitable to do so, it may allow the innocent party to the agreement to enforce the agreement against the other party, notwithstanding that performance may be a criminal offence.

- **Compensation:** under s26 the innocent party will be entitled to recover compensation for any loss sustained if the agreement is made unenforceable.

- The regulator may seek **injunctions** and **restitution orders** to restrain the contravention of the general prohibition and seek to disgorge profits from perpetrators.

It is also a criminal offence under s24 for a person who is not authorised or exempt to hold themselves out as authorised or exempt.

Where a person is authorised this does not mean that they may automatically undertake all regulated activities regarding all investments. The scope of their authorisation will be limited to the permissions that they have applied for and have been granted. Under s20 it is not a criminal offence for a firm to go **beyond its permission**, but it may give rise to claims from consumers, and the regulator will be able to use the full range of disciplinary sanctions such as fines or cancelling or varying permissions.

The **Perimeter Guidance Manual (PERG)** in the FCA Handbook gives guidance about the circumstances in which authorisation is required, or exempt person status is available, including guidance on the activities which are regulated under FSMA 2000 and the exclusions which are available.

## 5.4 Varying or cancelling permission and withdrawing authorisation

Under s55H-J FSMA 2000 (as amended), the regulators have a general power to vary or cancel a firm's '**Part 4A' permission** to undertake a regulated activity or withdraw authorisation entirely. This will generally take place where:

- The regulator has serious concerns regarding the firm's business activities

- A firm fails to continue to satisfy the Threshold Conditions Sourcebook (set out in the High Level Standards block of the FCA and PRA Handbooks) on an ongoing basis

- The firm has not carried out a regulated activity for which it has a Part 4A Permission for at least 12 months

- It is desirable to protect consumers

More commonly, the regulator will vary a firm's permission by placing tailored requirements on the firm. For example, the regulator may use the power to stop the firm seeking a particular class of client or selling particular investments. Such action is normally taken to protect consumers, but the regulator may vary permission for other reasons, such as the fact that a firm has changed its controller or stops using its permission. The process requires referral to the Regulatory Decisions Committee (RDC). The firm must be able to refer the matter to the Upper Tribunal.

## 5.5 Varying or withdrawing approval of individuals

**Variation or withdrawal of approval** applies to certain individuals who work within an authorised firm and require approval. Approval to perform a **controlled function** may be removed if the individual is no longer fit and proper to conduct that controlled function. To withdraw approval, the FCA must refer the matter to the RDC who will give the individual (copied to their employer) a warning notice followed by a decision notice, which the regulator may **publish**. The individual must be able to refer the matter to the Upper Tribunal. (The regulator's proposed approach is to publish the decision notice only if the person refers the matter to the Tribunal, unless there is a compelling reason to publish before that.)

In deciding whether to withdraw approval, the regulator will take into account the controlled functions being performed and a variety of factors including: qualifications and training; the fit and proper criteria, e.g. honesty, integrity, reputation, competence, capability, financial soundness; and whether the approved person has breached a statement of principle or been involved in their firm breaching a rule. The regulator will also consider the severity of the risk posed to consumers and confidence in the financial system and look at the individual's disciplinary record. Final notices of withdrawal of approval are normally published, unless this would prejudice the interests of consumers.

## 5.6 Prohibition of individuals

Section 56 FSMA 2000 allows the regulator to prohibit individuals from carrying out specified functions in relation to regulated activities within the investment industry. A **Prohibition Order** may be issued in respect of anyone whether they are approved or not: such an order could be imposed on a trader, a director, an IT staff member or a secretary, for example.

An unapproved person breaching a prohibition order is a criminal offence, subject to a maximum fine of £5,000 in the Magistrates Court. Final notices of the issue of prohibition orders are normally published on the regulator's website.

As well as maintaining a **public register** of **approved persons**, the FCA maintains a **public register** of **prohibited individuals**, which is available on the regulator's website.

## 5.7 Restitution and redress

There are two types of **restitution powers** available to the regulators – those that require a court order, and those the regulators can impose themselves. These are set out at ss382–386 FSMA 2000.

The regulators will be able to apply to the court to require any person who has breached a rule or other requirement of FSMA 2000 to provide compensation or restitution to those who have suffered loss as a result. This will be particularly important where the regulator seeks to enforce rules such as market abuse against non-authorised persons.

In determining whether to exercise its powers, the regulator will have regard to the circumstances of the case and also other facts including other ways the consumer might get redress and whether it would be more effective or cost effective for the regulator to require redress. It should therefore be borne in mind that while the regulator has these powers, it will only exercise powers of redress for consumers in very limited circumstances. More commonly, a person who has suffered a loss will seek redress themselves directly from the firm and, if unsuccessful, from the Financial Ombudsman Service or the courts.

Where an authorised firm has breached a rule or other requirement of FSMA 2000, the regulator may require the firm to provide compensation or restitution without a court order.

Where there is evidence of industry-wide rule breaches (such as that seen in the pensions misselling scandal) the regulator may ask HM Treasury to make an order authorising an industry-wide review or enquiry.

## 5.8 Injunctions

The regulator may also (under s380 FSMA 2000) apply to a court for an injunction to restrain or prohibit persons from breaking a rule or other requirement of FSMA 2000.

## 5.9 Fines and censure

The regulators may discipline firms or approved persons for acts of misconduct. Traditional disciplinary measures available are private warnings, public statements of misconduct or censures and fines.

In certain cases, the regulator may determine that it is not appropriate to bring **formal disciplinary proceedings**, for example, if the conduct is minor or where full remedial action was taken by the firm or approved person themselves (although these facts are not necessarily conclusive that the regulator will not bring formal proceedings). If the regulator thinks it would be beneficial for the approved person or firm to know that they are close to being the subject of formal proceedings then the regulator can issue a private warning. A private warning will state that while the regulator has cause for concern, the regulator does not intend to take formal proceedings. This warning will form part of the firm or approved person's compliance history and may be relevant when determining future proceedings. The recipient of the private warning is asked to acknowledge receipt and may comment on the warning if they so wish.

For more serious breaches, a public statement of misconduct or censure will be appropriate, often combined with a fine. There is no limit on the monetary amount of the fine the regulator can award. Fines must be applied for the benefit of the regulated community.

## 5.10 Market abuse

The regulator may take sanctions against **any person** who has engaged in **market abuse** under s118 FSMA 2000 or by taking or refraining from action has required or encouraged another to engage in market abuse. This means that, while it covers authorised firms and approved persons, it also covers those who do not work in the industry, whether they are located in or outside the UK. The regulator may issue a public statement stating that someone has engaged in market abuse and/or issue an unlimited fine.

## 5.11 Financial crime

Under ss401-s402 FSMA 2000, the regulator may prosecute authorised firms for certain criminal offences such as money laundering.

## 5.12 Unfair contract terms regulations

As mentioned earlier, the regulator has powers as a qualifying body to consider the fairness of financial services contracts under UK **Unfair Contract Terms Regulations**. The Authority may consider the fairness of consumer contracts, make recommendations to firms, and apply for injunctions against them to prevent the use of such terms.

## 5.13 Additional powers under FSA 2010

### 5.13.1 Overview

The **Financial Services Act 2010 (FSA 2010)** gave the following additional powers to the regulators which took effect on **8 June 2010**, through amendments to FSMA 2000:

- The power to impose suspensions or restrictions on authorised persons, under s206A FSMA 2000, and on approved persons, under s66 FSMA 2000 (the '**suspension power**')

- The power to impose penalties on persons that perform controlled functions without approval, under s63A FSMA 2000 (the '**non-approved persons penalty power**')

### 5.13.2 The suspension power

Where an authorised person has breached regulatory rules or requirements, the **suspension power** enables the regulators to suspend any permissions the person has to carry on a regulated activity, or to impose restrictions on the carrying on of a regulated activity by the person. Similarly, for approved persons, the suspension power enables the regulator to suspend a person from performing one or more controlled functions for which they are approved, or restrict the performance by them of one or more controlled functions for which they are approved. The regulator can impose a suspension on an **authorised person** for a period of up to **12 months** and on an **approved person** for a period of up to **two years**.

The suspension power is an alternative sanction to a financial penalty. The regulator proposes to use the suspension power where it considers that the imposition of a suspension will be a more effective and persuasive deterrent than the imposition of a financial penalty alone. The Regulatory Decisions Committee (RDC) is to be the decision maker for giving warning notices and decision notices where the suspension power is used.

### 5.13.3 The non-approved persons penalty power

The **non-approved persons penalty power** enables the regulator to impose a penalty on a person, of an amount it considers appropriate, if the regulators satisfied that:

- The person has at any time performed a controlled function without approval, and

- At that time the person knew, or could reasonably be expected to have known, that they were performing a controlled function without approval

## 5.14 Enforcement criteria

### 5.14.1 Overview

The primary responsibility for ensuring compliance with regulatory obligations rests with the authorised firm. The regulators' focus will thus primarily be on the firm when considering disciplinary action. Firms can be disciplined for breaches of rules and principles. However, where an approved person is personally culpable (covering deliberate or negligent conduct) the regulator may also take disciplinary action against an approved person.

The focus for an approved person will be whether they have breached the Statements of Principle for Approved Persons or have knowingly been concerned in a rule breach by the firm.

If a breach involves one of the various regulators (such as the UK regulators, overseas regulators, exchanges, the Takeover Panel or another relevant body), then the UK regulators will consult with the most appropriate bodies to consider the matter. The UK regulators has Memoranda of Understanding with various other organisations.

In determining whether or not to take any disciplinary action, the regulator will consider the full circumstances of the case. Some of the factors they may consider are as follows.

- **The nature and seriousness of the breach**, which includes: whether the breach was deliberate or reckless; the duration/frequency of the breach; the amount of any benefit obtained by the firm; whether the breach reveals serious or systemic weaknesses of the firm's management systems or internal controls of a firm; the loss or risk of loss to consumers and market users; and the nature and extent of any financial crime facilitated.

- **The conduct of the firm or approved person after the breach**: how quickly, effectively and completely the firm or approved person brought the breach to the attention of the regulator; how co-operative they were during the investigation and any remedial steps the firm or approved person has taken since the breach, e.g. compensating consumers and any internal disciplinary action.

- **The previous regulatory record of the firm.**

## 5.14.2 Credible deterrence

Up to 2007, the FSA had talked positively of being 'not an enforcement-led regulator'. From the second half of 2007, the Authority sought to advance its **'credible deterrence' philosophy**. This involves pursuing market abuse and inadequate management responsibility more aggressively. The regulators have been stepping up their enforcement activities in pursuit of their 'pro-active' credible deterrence approach to enforcement.

The Chief Executive Hector Sants stated in a March 2009 speech: 'There is a view that people are not frightened of the FSA. I can assure you that this is a view I am determined to correct. People should be very frightened of the FSA.'

## 5.14.3 Penalty setting: the five-step process

From March 2010, the Authority adopted a new approach to calculating financial penalties to support its credible deterrence approach. The policy is intended to establish a consistent and more transparent framework, and could result in enforcement fines trebling in size.

The **penalty-setting framework** is based on the principles of **disgorgement, discipline and deterrence** and consists of the following **five steps**.

- **Step 1 – Disgorgement**: identifying and removing any profits made from the misconduct

- **Step 2 – Discipline**: setting a figure to reflect the seriousness of the breach, using the fine levels set out below

- **Step 3 – Mitigating or aggravating circumstance**: considering any aggravating and mitigating factors, the amount derived from Step 2 may be increased or decreased

- **Step 4 – Deterrence**: the amount arrived at from Step 3 may be increased to achieve the appropriate deterrent effect

- **Step 5 – Discount under the Executive Settlement Scheme**: applying any settlement discount at levels of 30%, 20%, 10% or 0%, if a settlement occurs within one of four prescribed 'stages' respectively

**Fines** calculated at **Step 2** above will be linked more closely to income and will be based on:

- A series of fixed levels set at percentages (0%, 5%, 10%, 15%, 20%) of a firm's revenue from the product or business area linked to the breach over the relevant period

- A series of fixed levels set at percentages (0%, 10%, 20%, 30%, 40%) of an individual's salary and benefits (including bonuses) from their job relating to the breach in non-market abuse cases, and

- A minimum starting point of £100,000 for individuals in serious market abuse cases

The regulator will consider reducing the penalty for **serious financial hardship** only if:

- Verifiable evidence is provided, and

- The person provides full, frank and timely disclosure of the evidence and co-operates fully with the regulator's questioning about his financial position

The regulator takes the view that an individual will only suffer serious financial hardship if his net annual income will fall below £14,000 or his capital will fall below £16,000 as a result of paying the penalty.

## 5.15 Regulator's record on enforcement

The **public's appetite for enforcement action** by the regulator has been enlarged by market conditions and by the bail-out of many major financial institutions by taxpayers. Under fire over its effectiveness in the period of the market turmoil of the late 2000s, the regulator has gradually been regaining its reputation by taking action against individuals and firms that are believed to have been responsible for the financial crisis. The year 2008/09 appeared to bring a step-change in the regulator's enforcement activity levels. The Authority imposed a record level of fines (£27.3m), a record 30 prohibitions, and the Authority's first criminal prosecution of insider dealing. Enforcement activity at significant levels has continued since then.

In early 2012, the regulator asserted that '**credible deterrence** is here to stay'. The regulator stated: 'Where we do not see improvements from our actions, we will be willing to take tougher action – just as we have done in prosecuting insider dealing, in increasingly using our powers to prohibit individuals from the industry and in our continuing focus on senior management responsibility.' The new FCA will carry forward the enforcement work of the FSA.

The regulator was involved during 2012 in some of the largest and most complex trials to have been brought, including in the priority areas of organised insider dealers and market professionals.

In November 2012, the regulator described its current work to tackle insider dealing as being 'a world away' from where it was five or six years ago. From 2009 up to November 2012 there had been 21 convictions, confiscation orders totalling more than £2.2m, and prison sentences of up to 40 months. On the civil side, the regulator imposed penalties of £24.5 million (£18.5 million of which was imposed on individuals) and prohibited 17 people for market abuse. Fines saw a large increase in 2012/13, which was largely attributable to the LIBOR rate rigging scandal.

*Global Enforcement Review 2014*, a study conducted by Kinetic Partners, found that **individuals** accounted for 44% percent of the enforcement cases in 2013, although **fines** on individuals only made up 1% of the total of FCA fines. The number of enforcement cases showed a decline since 2008, but the size of fines had increased.

## 5.16 Investigation process

The **Decision Procedure and Penalties Manual (DEPP)** of the FCA Handbook is designed to protect the interests of the general public by providing powers which the regulator may exercise swiftly and conclusively to remedy or prevent wrongs. However, these powers must be exercised appropriately. DEPP sets out procedures to ensure powers are used fairly and the regulator does not exercise its powers without any accountability.

The decision-making process has also been designed to ensure that it is compliant with human rights legislation. Therefore, while the regulator's staff will investigate the matter and decide whether they feel enforcement action is appropriate, they will not take the final decision unless they are simply issuing a private warning. Instead, they pass the case to the **Regulatory Decisions Committee (RDC)**, which will decide whether or not to take action.

The RDC is appointed by the FCA Board and is therefore answerable to the FCA Board for its decisions, but is deliberately set up outside of the regulator's management structure so that it can make decisions independently. Only the Chairman of the RDC is an FCA employee. The rest of the RDC's membership is drawn from current or recently retired practitioners within financial services and other suitable individuals, all representing the public interest. The RDC can meet as a committee or in panels, the size of which will depend on the nature of the case under investigation.

If the RDC decide to take action, a **Warning Notice** will be sent, containing details of the proposed action and if appropriate, it will inform the recipient of the right to mediation in respect of the dispute. The person or firm concerned then has access to the material that the regulator is relying on and may make oral or written representations to the RDC. The RDC will then issue a **Decision Notice** detailing the reasons for the decision, proposed sanction and a notice of the right to refer the matter to the **Upper Tribunal**, which may undertake a complete rehearing of the case. Once the outcome has been determined, the RDC will issue a **Final Notice**. **Final notices** are issued at the end of the process and set out the sanction and effective date.

Decisions made by the Tribunal are also usually published: indeed arguments raised in 2002 during a hearing of the Financial Services and Markets Tribunal (as it was then) by Eurolife Assurance Company that a public hearing would

cause irreparable damage to the company's reputation were rejected. Some commentators argue this may discourage some referrals to the Tribunal because of adverse negative publicity.

An alternative to these procedures is the issue of a **Supervisory Notice**. This is preventative and protective rather than remedial and is designed in circumstances where the regulator requires immediate action to protect consumers. A firm must, therefore, comply immediately with the contents of a supervisory notice (although, once it has complied, it is able to respond and present its case in the usual way).

The investigation process is summarised in the following Table.

| Enforcement Procedure: a typical investigation | |
| --- | --- |
| **Appointment of investigators** by regulator, if appropriate sending Notice of Appointment of Investigators to the firm or individual.<br><br>**Scoping discussion** with firm / individual provides an indication of scope of investigation, how the process will unfold, and individuals / documents to which the investigators will initially need access. | |
|  | |
| **Investigation work.** Appointed investigators carry out the investigation, which may include, e.g., requests for documents or information and interviews of witnesses and subjects. Following the investigation work, there is an **internal legal review** of the case by a lawyer who has not been part of investigation team. | |
|  | |
| **Preliminary Investigation Report (PIR).** If appropriate, the regulator sends a PIR to the firm / individual, who has 28 days to respond. They can apply for extra time to complete their response. | |
|  | |
| **Submission to Regulatory Decisions Committee (RDC).** If, following the investigation, the regulator's staff believe action is justified, they submit case papers to RDC, including an **Investigation Report**, which takes account of the firm / individual's response to PIR. RDC considers submission. | **Private warning.** Regulator may issue a private warning at any stage in the procedure and so close the investigation.<br><br>**Settlement discussions.** The parties can seek to resolve the issue by having settlement discussions with the regulator, possibly using a **mediation process**, at any stage. |
|  | |
| **Warning Notice.** If RDC decides it is appropriate, it will send out a Warning Notice informing the person concerned that the regulator intends to take further action. The firm / individual has right to access material relied on by RDC in taking its decision, together with secondary material which might undermine that decision. The firm / individual has 28 days to make oral or written representations to RDC and can apply for extra time. | **Closure.** If the regulator finds that there is no case to answer, it can **close the investigation at any stage** in the procedure.<br><br>If the RDC finds there is no case, either before or after representations, the regulator closes the investigation. If after representations, RDC finds there is no case, a Notice of Discontinuance may be issued. |
|  | |

| Enforcement Procedure: a typical investigation | |
|---|---|
| **Oral and written representations to RDC.** After it receives the Warning Notice, the firm / individual may make written or oral representations to RDC. The RDC will then meet again to consider the facts of the case, including these written or oral representations (made before the RDC) and any new information that may have come to light.<br><br>↓ | |
| **Decision Notice.** RDC makes its decision and, if appropriate, issues Decision Notice. The firm / individual has 28 days to make a referral to the **Upper Tribunal**<br><br>↓ | **Final Notice.** If no referral is made to the Tribunal following the Decision Notice, a Final Notice is issued to the firm / individual.<br><br>The regulator will **publish** such information about the matter to which the Decision or Final Notice relates as it considers appropriate. |
| **Upper Tribunal.** Following a Decision Notice, the firm or individual has the right to refer their case to the Tribunal. The Tribunal is entirely independent of the regulator and will consider the entire case afresh. A Tribunal hearing is normally held in public. | **Tribunal's determination.** The Tribunal decides what action the regulator should take in relation to the matter (including issuing a **Notice of Discontinuance** if the case is not made out). |

## 5.17 Settlement and mediation

After receiving a Warning Notice, the accused person can discuss the proposed action with the regulator's staff on an informal basis to try and reach **settlement**, as indicated in the Table above. These discussions will take place on a without prejudice basis, which means that neither party may subsequently rely on admissions or statements made in the context of the discussion.

Before the **Enforcement Process Review** (discussed further below), all proposed settlements had to be considered by the RDC, but there is now a more flexible settlement decision procedure. Settlement decisions are now made by two decision-makers of at least Director status (the Director of Enforcement will usually be one of the decision-makers). This means settlement decisions are made entirely separately from the RDC and so the integrity of the RDC can be maintained for contested cases.

To ensure that the regulator is consistent in its approach to penalties between RDC decisions in contested cases and settlement decisions, the regulator will have regular liaison at policy level to ensure consistency of approach and ensure the RDC is fully briefed on the factors the regulator considers important for penalty setting.

If it is not possible to reach agreement via informal settlement discussions, then a party can choose to have the dispute mediated. **Mediation** is a confidential without prejudice dispute resolution process in which a neutral mediator tries to assist the parties to settle their differences. The mediator, however, has no power to bind the parties or give a ruling.

Mediation will be available in all disciplinary matters and market abuse cases, except where there are allegations of serious misconduct, e.g. allegations of criminal offences, dishonesty or lack of integrity. The mediation scheme is administered by an independent body, the **Centre for Effective Dispute Resolution**.

## 5.18 Publicising enforcement action

The FCA has a **new power** under the Financial Services Act 2012 to **publish Warning Notices**, after consulting the person concerned – thus announcing that they have begun disciplinary action against a firm or an individual.

Under s391(1) FSMA 2000 as amended by FSA 2012, the FCA is permitted to publicise information about the matter to which a warning notice relates that it considers appropriate. The published statements will generally include sufficient information to identify the firm or individual concerned and to enable consumers, other firms and market users to understand why the FCA is concerned about the matter. Information provided will include the rules and principles that are considered to have been breached, concise details of how the breaches are alleged to have occurred, and of the financial products involved, where applicable.

This power will apply only for disciplinary outcomes, e.g. where the regulator is proposing to censure, fine or suspend an individual or firm. It does not apply to non-disciplinary outcomes, e.g. proposals to prohibit an individual, withdraw an individual's approval or cancel a firm's permission.

Guidelines for the publication procedure are covered in **Consultation Paper CP13/8** (March 2013).

- The FCA must consult those involved before publishing any information about a warning notice, and those involved would normally have seven days to respond. The regulator's Regulatory Decisions Committee (RDC) will decide whether or not publication is unfair. To avoid the publication of information, firms and individuals would need to prove that disproportionate levels of damage would be caused by the publication of the details.

- The FCA proposes that it will not normally decide against publication solely for the reason that it would have a negative impact on a firm's or an individual's reputation.

- Proposed factors that would lead to the FCA refraining from publication are: Material effect on physical or mental health of the recipient or a family member; disproportionate effect on livelihood or loss of income, such as likely insolvency (although loss of employment or damage to career prospects would not be sufficient to avoid publication); prejudice to criminal proceedings; or 'some other equal degree of harm'.

- If action is discontinued, the FCA would publish a discontinuation notice.

In December 2012, the Upper Tribunal rejected challenges pursued by Arch Financial Products LLP and others to the publication of Decision Notices alleging breaches by them, and it seems likely that the FCA will adopt a fairly uncompromising approach in other such cases.

This change came at a time when a string of allegations of misconduct have been made (in **2012**) against London-based banks.

- Barclays reached a settlement with UK and US regulators relating to **manipulation of LIBOR**, the benchmark interbank interest rate, while a number of other banks including UBS were put under investigation for similar alleged LIBOR abuses

- Four of the leading UK retail banks agreed with the regulator to compensate small businesses over **mis-selling of interest rate hedging products**

- The US Congress accused HSBC of **money laundering** relating to Mexican drug money

- A New York regulatory authority accused Standard Chartered of **violating sanctions** against Iran, and subsequently a number of other banks were facing investigation over transactions involving Iran

Many of these allegations have emanated from the US, where the Securities and Exchange Commission (SEC), for example, can publicise charges when it has filed them with a judge or administrative proceeding. The UK changes brings the UK system more into line with the US, but some in the City of London opposed the change. Some point out that allegations can harm reputations and be unduly disruptive: to take an example, the allegations on Iran sanctions-breaking against Standard Chartered led to a 16% fall in the bank's share price in a single day. On the other hand, in the view of the UK Government, the public arguably have a right to know if a regulator considers that wrongdoing has taken place, just as, in criminal law, murder charges against an individual are made public.

## 5.19 Rights of private persons

### 5.19.1 Section 138D FSMA 2000

As we have seen, the regulator has broad powers to discipline authorised firms, approved persons and in some cases (eg, market abuse) anyone at all. However, except where the FCA exercises its redress powers, discipline by the regulator does not compensate consumers against wrongdoing.

Consumers, whether individuals or business, are always able to use the general law to bring their claims, for example for breach of contract, negligence or misrepresentation. However, this can be time consuming and expensive. Accordingly, **Section 138D** FSMA 2000 (as amended by the Financial Services Act 2012) creates a right of action, in damages, for a **'private person'** who suffers loss as a result of a contravention of certain rules by an authorised firm. A 'private person' means individuals not carrying out a regulated activity, and businesses, in very limited circumstances (where the loss does not arise from their business activities, eg setting-up an occupational pension scheme for their employees).

This right exists in addition to common law actions, such as negligence or misrepresentation. However, s138D provides a privileged right of action since that is no need to prove negligence. It is sufficient that there has been a **rule breach** leading to a **loss**.

- **Example 1**. An individual client might claim that an investment recommended to them by a firm was not suitable for that individual. Can the individual sue the firm?

  If the individual can show that he suffered a loss from the firm's failure to follow suitability rules in the Conduct of Business Sourcebook, then he has a basis for suing the firm under s138D.

- **Example 2**. A journalist working for an investment magazine discovers that a financial services firm on which he is writing an article is in breach of the regulators' Conduct of Business rules. Can the journalist bring an action under s138D FSMA 2000?

  The journalist has not suffered a loss, and has no right of action under s138D.

### 5.19.2 Section 71 FSMA 2000

**Section 59** FSMA 2000 states that a person (i.e. a member of staff at an authorised firm) cannot carry out a **controlled function** in a firm unless that individual has been approved by the regulator. If a person is performing a controlled function and is not approved, this is known as a **breach of statutory duty** and a private person has the right to sue the firm for damages if they have suffered loss, using s71 FSMA 2000, just as they have for a breach of rules under s138D.

## 5.20 Part 7 Financial Services Act 2012

Under **Part 7 (ss89-95) Financial Services Act 2012 (FSA 2012)**, the FCA has the power to enforce the following offences **in the UK**. (These offences replace the repealed older section 397 FSMA 2000.) What counts as a 'relevant' agreement, investment or benchmark in the summary below is determined by Treasury order.

- **Misleading statements (s89)**. A person commits this offence if they make a false or misleading statement knowingly or recklessly, or conceal material facts, with the intention of inducing another person to enter (or refrain from entering) into a relevant agreement, or exercising (or refraining from exercising) rights conferred by a relevant investment.

- **Misleading impressions (s90)**. This offence is committed when a person intends to create a false or misleading impression of the market in or the price or value of any relevant investments, in order to induce another person to take actions of buying, selling, subscribing or underwriting (or to refrain from taking such actions) regarding the investments. It is also committed if a person knowingly or recklessly creates such a false or misleading impression in order to make gains for the person or for another person, or to create losses or the risk of loss for another person.

- **Misleading statements or impressions relating to benchmarks (s91).** An offence is committed if a person knowingly or recklessly makes a false or misleading statement to another person in the course of arrangements for setting a relevant benchmark. An offence is also committed if a person intentionally and knowingly or recklessly acts so as to create a false or misleading impression of the price or value of an investment or of an interest rate, if the impression affects the setting of a benchmark.

Misleading statements or impressions relating to benchmarks would include misleading other parties in relation to the setting of **LIBOR**, for example. Making this an offence is in line with the recommendation of the **Wheatley Commission** on the manipulation by traders of the LIBOR benchmark, which is used to set various interest rates, for example on mortgages.

The possible defences to a misleading statements and impressions charge are as follows.

- The person **reasonably believed** that their **conduct would not create a false or misleading impression**.

- The person was acting within the FCA's **price stabilising rules**. For example, under FSA rules an investment bank can support the price of a new securities issue for their clients if certain disclosures are made.

- The person was acting within the FCA **control of information rules** relating to statements, forecasts and actions that are made on the basis of limited information. Fuller information may be known to the firm, but it is contained behind 'Chinese walls' and for that reason is not known to the person.

- The person was acting in conformity with certain EU provisions with regards to stabilising financial instruments (**EU Buy-Back and Stabilisation Regulations**).

The **maximum penalties** for these offences under Part 7 FSA 2012 are a prison term of seven years and/or an unlimited fine if tried in a Crown Court, and six months' imprisonment and/or a fine or £5,000 in a Magistrates' Court (a 'summary conviction').

# Key chapter points

- The regulators have rule-making powers, and the power to determine policy and principles.

- The statutory objectives for each regulator that are stated in FSMA 2000 spell out the purpose of the regulatory framework under the FCA and PRA.

- The FCA has the single strategic objective of 'ensuring that the relevant markets function well'. This is supported by operational objectives relating to consumer protection, integrity of the UK financial system, and promoting competition. The PRA has the single general objective of promoting the safety and soundness of PRA-authorised firms.

- The National Strategy for Financial Capability is being taken forward by the Consumer Finance Education Body.

- The FCA and PRA have separate Handbooks, which have some common elements. The Handbooks are divided into blocks. Within each block there are various Sourcebooks.

- The general prohibition (S19 FSMA 2000) states that no person may carry on a regulated activity in or into the UK by way of business or purport to do so, unless they are authorised or exempt.

- Principles for Businesses govern the principles-based approach to regulation, and approved persons must follow Statements of Principle.

- Client assets rules aim to restrict the commingling of client's and firm's assets and to prevent misuse of client's investments by the firm without the client's agreement, or being treated as the firm's assets in the event of the firm's insolvency.

- Capital adequacy rules are designed to enhance investor protection by ensuring that a firm always has enough capital to operate.

- The UK regulatory approach to supervision is 'risk-based', meaning that supervisory effort is directed at higher risk areas. The regulators aim to strike a balance between principles and rules with various corrective mechanisms being adopted to try to prevent any problems creating unacceptable levels of difficulty.

- The FCA and PRA each have their own supervisory approaches. The FCA categorises firms according to their impact on consumers and the market. Pillars of its approach are: the Firm Systematic Framework (How is the firm run?); Event-Driven work; Issues and Products. The PRA classifies firms according to their potential impact on the stability of the financial system.

- The regulators have wide powers to visit firms' premises without notice and to require documents to be produced.

- Regulatory enforcement measures include public censure, unlimited fines, restitution orders and cancellation of authorisation or approval. Various Statutory Notices may be issued in cases involving the FCA's Regulatory Decisions Committee.

- The Upper Tribunal can re-hear regulatory enforcement and authorisation cases.

# Chapter Quiz

1    Outline the FCA's statutory objectives.  .................................................................... (see paras 1.2.2 – 1.2.6)

2    What is the PRA's general objective, as set out in FSMA 2000? .................................................................. (1.3)

3    Outline the 'principles of good regulation' (or 'supervisory principles').  ....................................................... (1.4)

4    Outline the main elements of financial capability. ..................................................................................... (1.5)

5    List the seven blocks of the regulatory Handbooks. .................................................................................. (2.1)

6    What is the nature of an evidential provision in the FCA or PRA Handbook? .................................................. (2.4)

7    What is the purpose of the client assets rules? ........................................................................................ (2.9)

8    What are the main provisions of the Code of Market Conduct?.................................................................. (2.10)

9    State the overall liquidity adequacy rule for firms.  ................................................................................ (3.2.2)

10   What are the three pillars of the FCA's approach to supervision? ............................................................... (4.4)

11   How much notice must regulators give before they enters firms' premises? ................................................. (5.2)

12   What is the non-approved persons penalty power? .............................................................................. (5.13.3)

13   Outline the types of statutory notice that may be issued.  ...................................................................... (5.16)

# chapter

# 6

# Regulatory principles and obligations

6 **Apply the principles and rules as set out in the regulatory framework**

6.1 **Apply** the FCA's and PRA's regulatory principles and rules.

6.2 **Apply** current anti-money laundering, proceeds of crime, and data protection obligations.

6.3 **Apply** the rules of relevant dispute resolution and compensation schemes.

# 1 Regulated activities

## 1.1 The range of regulated activities

What range of activities are **regulated activities**? The activities regulated by FSMA 2000 are set out in the **Regulated Activities Order** (as amended).

**Regulated activities**

- **Accepting deposits**. These must be accepted by way of business to be covered.

- **Issuing electronic money**. Some banks and building societies issue 'e-money' which is a form of electronic money that can be used (like notes and coins) to pay for goods and services.

- **Effecting or carrying out contracts of insurance as principal**. From November 2001, the FSA took responsibility for regulating all insurers for capital adequacy purposes and life insurance firms for Conduct of Business Rules. Since January 2005, the sales and administration of general insurance has been regulated, as well as life insurance.

- **Dealing in investments as principal or agent**. This covers buying, selling, subscribing for or underwriting investments.

- **Arranging deals in investments**. This covers making, offering or agreeing to make any arrangements with a view to another person buying, selling, subscribing for or underwriting investments.

- **Arranging home finance transactions: regulated mortgage contracts, home reversion plans or home purchase plans**. This covers most mortgages, but generally does not cover buy-to-let or second charge loans. Home reversion plans are one of two types of equity release product, the other being lifetime mortgages. A home purchase plan serves the same purpose as a normal mortgage, in that it provides consumers with finance to buying a home. But it is structured in a way that makes it acceptable under Islamic law. As interest is contrary to Islamic law, a home purchase plan is in essence a sale and lease arrangement. The plan provider buys the property, which is then sold to the home purchaser by instalments.

- **Operating a multilateral trading facility (MTF)**. An MTF is a system (crossing network or matching engine) which may be operated by an investment firm that enables parties, who might typically be retail investors or other investment firms, to buy and sell financial instruments.

MTFs are operated by investment firms or other market operators. Instruments traded on a MTF may include shares, bonds and derivatives. The implementation of the Markets in Financial Instruments Directive (MiFID) created a wave of competition in equities trading, as the new alternative equities trading platforms known as MTFs were created to challenge traditional stock exchanges. MTFs in Europe include platforms such as Turquoise, Chi-X and BATS Europe. MTFs may operate as so-called dark pools, where buyers and sellers are matched anonymously. Under MiFID rules, these dark pools are not required to post prices publicly before trades take place. MiFID also provides for the operators of MTFs to passport their services across borders.

- **Managing investments**. Managing investments belonging to another person where there is exercise of discretion by the manager.

- Assisting in the administration and performance of a contract of insurance (see above).

- **Safeguarding and administering investments** or arranging such activities.

- **Sending dematerialised instructions**. This relates to the use of computer-based systems for giving instructions for investments to be transferred.

- **Establishing a collective investment scheme.** This would include the roles of the trustee and the depository of schemes. Sections 235 and 236 FSMA 2000 define 'Collective Investment Schemes' to mean arrangements regarding property of any description where the participants and profits or income are pooled and the property in the scheme is managed by an operator.

- **Establishing, operating or winding-up a personal pension scheme or a stakeholder pension scheme**. Personal pension schemes include Self-Invested Personal Pensions (SIPPs), as their name implies. A stakeholder pension scheme follows similar rules to a personal pension plan, with caps on charges in addition.

- **Giving basic advice on stakeholder products**. Stakeholder products conform to certain criteria governing cost and access. This category of regulated activity is for those who provide a basic level of advice, only on stakeholder products.

- **Advising on investments**. This covers advice on securities and specified investments, but not deposits nor occupational pension schemes. Not covered are providing information that is not framed as a recommendation, nor general advice such as: 'Invest in emerging markets'.

- **Advising on home finance transactions: regulated mortgage contracts, home reversion plans, home purchase plans and sale and rent-back agreements**

- **Lloyd's market activities**. Lloyd's is the UK's largest insurance market.

- **Entering as provider into a funeral plan contract**.

- **Entering into and administering home finance transactions: regulated mortgage contracts, home reversion plans, home purchase plans and sale and rent-back agreements**. These activities covers the activities of lenders and providers of these types of product.

- **Bidding in emissions auctions**.

- **Agreeing to carry on most regulated activities**. This is itself a regulated activity and so a firm must get the appropriate authorisation before agreeing to undertake business such as dealing or arranging for clients.

- **Operating dormant accounts for meeting repayment claims and managing dormant accounts**.

- **Administering a specified benchmark** (such as LIBOR).

- **Credit broking**.

- **Debt adjusting, debt counselling, debt collecting**, and **debt administration**.

- **Operating an electronic system in relation to lending** – this refers to the facilitation of lending and borrowing through electronic platforms (P2P or 'peer-to-peer' platforms).

- **Entering into a regulated credit agreement as lender** – and exercising lender's rights and duties under such an agreement.

- **Entering into a regulated consumer hire agreement as owner** – and exercising the owner's rights and duties under such an agreement.

- **Providing credit information services.**

- **Providing credit references**, but only where the firm's primary business is as a credit reference provider.

As you can see from the above list, the activities regulated cover the investment industry, banking, insurance and mortgage lending industries, consumer credit, and Lloyd's.

Advising, dealing and arranging activities when in connection with a contract of insurance, along with assisting in the administration and performance of a contract of insurance, are collectively known as **insurance mediation activity** and are subject to the Insurance Mediation Directive.

## 1.2 Activities carried on 'by way of business'

Note that the regulated activity must be carried on '**by way of business**' for the regulations to apply. Whether something is carried on by way of business is, ultimately, a question of judgement: in general terms it will depend on the degree of continuity and profit. HM Treasury has also (via secondary legislation) made explicit provisions for certain activities, such as accepting deposits. This will not be regarded as carried on by way of business if a person does not hold himself out as doing so on a day-to-day basis, i.e. he only accepts deposits on particular occasions. An example of this would be a car salesman accepting a down payment on the purchase of a car.

Someone performing **insurance mediation activities** will only be treated as doing so by way of business if he pursues that activity for remuneration.

## 1.3 Territorial scope

Broadly speaking, a person will be covered by FSMA 2000 if they carry on the activity:

- In the UK, e.g. has an establishment in the UK

- Into the UK from overseas, e.g. providing cross-border dealing services (subject to certain limited exclusions for overseas persons)

- In another European Economic Area (EEA) state, if his registered office is in the UK and he is passporting services into that state under one of the single market directives

- In another EEA state, if his registered office is in the UK and the day-to-day management of the activity is the responsibility of that UK office

## 1.4 Excluded activities

The **Perimeter Guidance Manual (PERG)** in the FCA Handbook gives guidance about the activities which are regulated under FSMA 2000 and the exclusions which are available.

As set out in the Regulated Activities Order and reiterated in PERG, the following activities are **excluded** from the requirement for authorisation.

- **Dealing as principal** where the person is not holding themselves out to the market as willing to deal. The requirement to seek authorisation does not apply to the personal dealings of unauthorised individuals for their own account, i.e. as customers of an authorised firm. It would also exclude companies issuing their own shares.

- **Trustees, nominees and personal representatives**. These persons, so long as they do not hold themselves out to the general public as providing the service and are not separately remunerated for the regulated activity, are excluded from the requirement to seek authorisation.

- **Employee share schemes**. This exclusion applies to activities which further an employee share scheme.

- **Media**, e.g. television, radio and newspapers. Many newspapers and other media give investment advice. However, provided this is not the primary purpose of the newspaper, then under the exceptions granted within FSMA 2000, it need not seek formal authorisation. On the other hand, the publication of '**tip sheets**' (written recommendations of investments) will require authorisation.

- **Overseas persons**. Overseas persons are firms which do not carry on regulated activity from a permanent place within the UK. This exception covers two broad categories: first, where the activity requires the direct involvement of an authorised or exempt firm and, second, where the activity is carried on as a result of an unsolicited approach by a UK individual. Thus, if a UK individual asks a fund manager in Tokyo to buy a portfolio of Asian equities for them, the Japanese firm does not need to be authorised under FSMA 2000.

---

The word **DEMOTE** can help you to learn the five excluded activities.

**D**ealing as principal, where the person is not holding themselves out to the market as willing to deal
**E**mployee share schemes
**M**edia
**O**verseas persons
**T**rustees
Nomin**E**es and personal representatives

---

## 1.5 Specified investments

Only activities relating to **specified investments** are covered by FSMA 2000. Specified investments are also defined in the **Regulated Activities Order** (as amended).

**Specified investments**

- **Deposits**. Simply defined, this is a sum of money paid by one person to another under the terms that it will be repaid on a specified event (e.g. on demand).

- **Electronic money**. This is defined as monetary value, as represented by a claim on the issuer, which is stored on an electronic device, is issued on receipt of funds and is accepted as a means of payment by persons other than the issuer.

- **Rights under a contract of insurance**. Included in this category are general insurance contracts (such as motor insurance, accident or sickness), long-term insurance contracts (such as life and annuity) and other insurance contracts (such as funeral expense contracts).

- **Shares** or stock in the capital of a company wherever the company is based.

- **Debentures, loan stock and similar instruments**, e.g. certificate of deposit, Treasury bills of exchange, floating rate notes, bulldog bonds and unsecured loan stock (but not cheques or other bills of exchange, banker's drafts, letters of credit, trade bills or Premium Bonds).

- **Government and public securities**, e.g. gilts, US Treasury bonds (not National Savings & Investments products, such as Premium Bonds and Savings Certificates).

- **Warrants**. A warrant gives the right to buy a new share in a company.

- **Certificates representing certain securities**, e.g. American Depository Receipts.

- **Units in a Collective Investment Scheme** including shares in, or securities of, an Open-ended Investment Company (OEIC). A collective investment scheme is a specified investment whatever underlying property the scheme invests in.

- **Rights under a personal pension scheme or a stakeholder pension scheme**. These are pension plans which are not employment-based (occupational) schemes. As indicated above, a SIPP is a personal pension scheme.

- **Greenhouse gas emissions allowances.** This specified investment comprises emissions allowances that are auctioned as financial instruments, or two-day emissions spots (together, **emissions auction products**).

- **Options** to acquire or dispose of any specified investment or currencies, gold, silver, platinum or palladium.

- **Futures** on anything for investment purposes. This differs from the treatment of options as it will cover all futures regardless of the underlying investment, provided it is for investment purposes.

  The definition of 'investment purposes' is complex. In general terms, any futures contract traded either on an exchange, or in an over-the-counter market or form similar to that traded on an exchange, will constitute an investment. The type of future, in effect, excluded by this definition would be a short-term contract between a producer and a consumer of a good to purchase that good in the future, e.g. a wheat buyer buying from a farmer. This can sometimes be referred to as a 'commercial purpose future'.

> As a rule of thumb, unless the examiner indicates otherwise, you should assume that a future *is* for investment purposes.

- **Contracts for differences (CfDs)**. A CfD is a contract whose price tracks the price of an underlying asset, while the CfD holder does not take ownership of the asset. The underlying asset might be a company's shares, a bond, a currency, a commodity or an index. Investors can use CfDs to take a short position – and thus gain from price declines, but lose if the price rises.

- **Lloyd's syndicate capacity and syndicate membership**. Lloyd's is an insurance institution specialising in risks such as aviation and marine insurance. Insurance is provided by members and syndicates.

- **Rights under a funeral plan contract**. These are contracts whereby someone pays for their funeral before their death.

- **Rights under home finance transactions:**

  - **Regulated mortgage contracts**. Note that not all mortgages are covered, only regulated mortgages. In a regulated mortgage the loan is secured by a first legal mortgage or property located in the UK, which will be occupied (at least 40% of the time) by the borrower or their family. Lifetime mortgages – a form of equity release transaction – are also included.

  - **Home reversion plans, home purchase plans**, and **regulated sale and rent-back agreements**. A home reversion plan is a type of equity release transaction where a customer sells part or all of their home to the plan provider in return for a lump sum or a series of payments. The customer keeps the right to stay in his home until death or a move into residential care. A home purchase plan is an alternative to a mortgage, designed to comply with Islamic principles. With a regulated sale and rent-back agreement, a person sells all or part of a qualifying interest in property but continues to occupy at least 40% of the property.

- **Emissions allowances**

- **Credit agreements**

- **Rights to or interests in anything that is a specified investment listed** (excluding 'Rights under regulated mortgage contracts'). 'Repos' (sale and repurchase agreements) in relation to specified investments (e.g. a government bond) are specified investments.

Spot currency ('forex') trades, general loans (e.g. car loans), property deals and National Savings & Investments products are *not* specified investments.

When applying for authorisation to carry out a regulated activity regarding a specified investment, the firm will specify on the application form which regulated activities relating to which specified investments it wishes to conduct.

# 2 Authorisation of firms

## 2.1 The requirement for authorisation

As the **general prohibition** directs, no person may carry on a regulated activity in the UK, nor purport to do so, unless they are either authorised or exempt.

Authorisation is provided under Part 4A of FSMA and is referred to as a Part 4A permission. A firm will apply to either the **Financial Conduct Authority (FCA)** or the **Prudential Regulation Authority (PRA)**, depending on the type of firm.

- **Dual-regulated firms** comprise banks and building societies, credit unions, insurers and some investment firms). Such firms are **authorised by the PRA but only with FCA approval**.

- **FCA-only regulated firms** include retail investment advisory firms, investment exchanges, insurance brokers and fund managers. Such firms are **authorised by the FCA**.

The following decision chart indicates the questions to be asked in establishing **whether a firm needs to be authorised**.

### Does My Firm Need Authorisation?

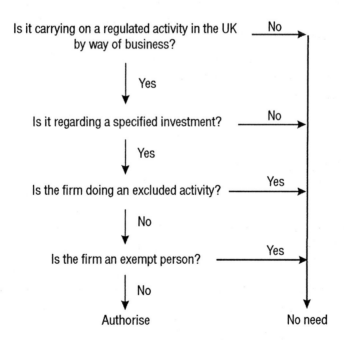

## 2.2 Exempt persons

The following are the types of person that are **exempt** from the requirement to seek authorisation under FSMA 2000.

- **Appointed representative.** In markets such as life assurance, the bulk of sales takes place through self-employed individuals who act on behalf of the companies. As the companies do not employ them, if this exemption were not in place, such persons would need separate authorisation. The exemption removes them from the scope of authorisation so long as they act solely on behalf of one firm and that firm takes complete responsibility for their actions.

- **Members of professions.** Solicitors, accountants and actuaries have been giving investment advice for many years. As long as giving such advice does not constitute a major proportion of their business (i.e. is incidental) and they are not separately paid for those activities, they are exempt from the requirement to seek authorisation. However, they will still be governed by their professional bodies (e.g. the Law Society, for solicitors). These professional bodies are known as **Designated Professional Bodies (DPBs)** and are subject to scrutiny by the regulators.

- **Certain persons listed in the Financial Services and Markets Act (Exemption) Order 2001**, including supranational bodies, municipal banks, local authorities, housing associations, the national grid, trade unions, the Treasury Taskforce, the English Tourist Board, government organisations (such as Bank of England, other central banks, and the International Monetary Fund and the UK's National Savings & Investments), enterprise schemes (i.e. bodies with the objective of promoting or disseminating information about enterprise). Charities and the Student Loans Company are also exempt in respect of deposit-taking activities. The Financial Services and Markets Act (Exemption) Order 2001 is written by HM Treasury under powers set out in s38 FSMA 2000.

- **Members of Lloyd's.** The requirement to seek authorisation is disapplied for members of Lloyd's writing insurance contracts. The Society of Lloyd's, however, is required to be authorised. This exemption covers **being** a Lloyd's member but does not cover the activities of **advising** on Lloyd's syndicate participation or **managing** underwriting activities.

- **Recognised Investment Exchanges (RIEs), Recognised Overseas Investment Exchanges (ROIEs)** and **Recognised Clearing Houses (RCHs).** FSMA 2000 gives to the FCA the role of recognising, regulating and supervising investment exchanges (such as the London Stock Exchange, NYSE Liffe and the London Metal Exchange) and clearing houses (such as Euroclear UK & Ireland). Under the reformed 2013 regulatory system, RCHs are, however, supervised by the Bank of England.

The word **APRIL** can be used to help learn the five types of exempt persons.

**A**ppointed representatives
**P**rofessional people, e.g. solicitors, accountants and actuaries
**R**IE, ROIEs and RCHs
**I**nstitutions who are exempt, e.g. the Bank of England
**L**loyd's members

## 2.3 Routes to authorisation

FSMA 2000 created a single authorisation regime for the regulated activities within its scope. This contrasts with the previous financial services regulation arrangements, which contained a variety of separate regulatory regimes.

A firm may be authorised by one of two main routes:

- Authorisation by the relevant regulator (FCA or PRA)('Part 4A permission' to carry on one or more regulated activities)

- Passporting under MiFID

### 2.3.1 Passporting within the EEA

As we have seen, the concept of a **passport** enables firms to use their domestic authorisation to operate not only in their **Home State**, but also in other **Host States** within the **EEA**.

### 2.3.2 Authorisation by the regulator

The main route to authorisation is to obtain permission from the FCA or PRA to carry out one or more regulated activities.

The permission that a firm receives will play a crucial role in defining the firm's business scope. This permission is sometimes referred to as **Part 4A permission** as it is set out in Part 4A of FSMA 2000 (as amended).

Where a firm obtains permission to do one or more regulated activities, it is then authorised to do those activities. In the application, the applicant must set out which regulated activities and specified investments it requires permission for. The permission will set out what activities and investments are covered and any limitations and requirements that the regulator wishes to impose.

It is not a criminal offence for a firm to go beyond its permission but doing so may give rise to claims from consumers. Furthermore, the regulator will be able to use the full range of disciplinary sanctions, such as cancelling or varying permission.

## 2.4 Threshold conditions

### 2.4.1 Introduction

Before it grants permission, the relevant regulator must be satisfied that the firm meets the '**threshold conditions**' for the activity concerned in order to be deemed fit and proper. The regulator must ensure that a firm meets the threshold conditions when agreeing an application by the firm to vary a permission, or when varying or imposing requirements on a firm.

The FCA and the PRA each have their own set of **threshold conditions**, but some of the conditions are common to both regulators. regulators – as clarified in the Summary Table in this section. Each regulator must ensure that a firm meets that regulator's threshold conditions when agreeing an application by the firm to vary permission, or when varying or imposing requirements on a firm.

The FCA will refuse applications at an earlier stage if it does not think that the proposed offering of products or services is in the interests of consumers or, more broadly, if it poses a significant risk to regulatory objectives.

### 2.4.2 Threshold Conditions Summary

The following table shows which Threshold Conditions apply to which type of firm (whether FCA-regulated, or dual-regulated) and, in the case of dual-regulated firms, the regulator responsible.

| Threshold condition | FCA firms | Dual-regulated firms | Regulator (dual-regulated firms) |
|---|---|---|---|
| Legal status | | • | PRA |
| Location of offices | • | • | PRA |
| Effective supervision | • | • | FCA & PRA |
| Appropriate resources | • | | |
| Appropriate non-financial resources | | • | FCA |
| Suitability | • | • | FCA & PRA |
| Business model | • | • | FCA |
| Business to be conducted in a prudent manner | | • | PRA |
| Appointment of claims representatives | | • | FCA |

## 2.4.3 The threshold conditions

The threshold conditions under the FCA/PRA structure are applied as follows.

- For **dual-regulated** (ie, FCA/PRA regulated) firms, the applicant must have the **legal status** to carry on certain regulated activities. This requirement looks at the legal structure of the business.

- Another condition concerns the **location of offices** of the applicant. If the applicant is a UK company, its head and registered offices must be located in the UK. For an applicant that is not a company, if it has its head office in the UK, then it must carry on business in the UK.

- Firms will need to ensure that no impediment to their **effective supervision** arises from: the nature and complexity of regulated activities undertaken, products offered, and the business organisation. This condition also covers the effect of **close links** of the applicant with other entities, eg other members of the same group, and whether these have an effect on effective supervision by the regulator.

- An applicant for FCA authorisation must have **appropriate resources** for the activities they seek to undertake. Such resources would not only include capital, but also non-financial resources such as personnel. Adequacy of resources will be determined by reference to the scale and nature of business, risk to the continuity of services, and the effect of a firm's membership of a group if applicable.

- The new threshold condition of **appropriate non-financial resources** – for dual-regulated firms –covers the nature and scale of the firm's business, risks to the continuity of services, the skills and experience of the firm's management, and whether the non-financial resources of the firm are sufficient for the firm to comply with the FCA's requirements.

- Another threshold condition relates to the **suitability** of the applicant. The firm must be considered to be 'fit and proper', ie it must have integrity, be competent and have appropriate procedures in place to comply with regulations. Suitability to carry on one regulated activity does not mean that the applicant is suitable to carry on all regulated activities. FCA-authorised firms must ensure that their affairs are conducted in an appropriate manner with regard to the interest of consumers and the integrity of the UK financial system. Those responsible for managing the affairs of a firm are to act with probity, in order to satisfy the regulators that the firm is fit and proper – in making their assessments, the regulators will consider the entirety of a firm's board and non-board senior management. Management will be required to minimise the extent to which their business could be used for financial crime. Firms must be pro-active and co-operative when asked to provide information to the PRA or FCA.

- The FCA's **business model** threshold condition refers to the risk that might be posed for a firm, for its customers and for the integrity of the UK financial system. This threshold condition demonstrates the importance that the FCA places on a firm's ability to put forward an appropriate, viable and sustainable business model, given the nature and scale of business it intends to carry out. The regulator will expect firms to demonstrate adequate contingency planning in their business models. Firms will be expected to make clear how their business model meets the needs of clients and customers, not placing them at undue risk, or placing at risk the integrity of the wider UK financial services industry.

- The PRA's **business to be conducted in a prudent manner** threshold condition is closely equivalent to the FCA's appropriate resources and business model conditions, which we have described above. PRA-authorised firms must hold appropriate financial and non-financial resources. Financial resources include appropriate capital and liquidity. Non-financial resources include having appropriate resources to monitor, manage and mitigate risk. Appropriate resources are evaluated by reference to complexity of activities, the liabilities of the firm, effective management, and the ability to reduce risks to the safety and soundness of the firm.

- Relevant only to **motor insurers** is the threshold condition of **appointment of claims representatives** to handle claims in each EEA state.

## 2.4.4 Application procedure

As we have already seen, if a firm wishes to undertake a regulated activity by way of business in the UK, it must be authorised or exempt. Earlier, we considered the scope of the exemptions (eg appointed representatives and RIE/RCHs).

A firm wishing to obtain permission (**Part 4A permission**) from the regulator to perform a regulated activity will be sent an application pack requiring detailed information from the firm and the payment of a fee. The amount of detailed information that the applicant will have to submit will be related to the risks posed to the active elements of the four regulatory objectives.

The regulator will view the application in accordance with the regulatory objectives and must be proportional in the information it requires, having regard to the nature of the applicant's business. Therefore, although some applicants will have to complete all sections of the pack, other sections are specific to certain types of business. The regulator has **six months** to determine an authorisation from the date of receipt.

The **information** an applicant must provide includes the following:

- A UK address for the service of documents
- General information about the applicant, intended activities, proposed/current unregulated activities
- How the firm will comply with the regulatory requirements
- Business plan
- Financial budget and projections
- Details of systems to be used including compliance systems
- Details of individuals managing the business, including details of any outsourcing of functions
- For insurance activities, details of the risks being underwritten

The relevant regulator will determine whether the threshold conditions have been met including whether the applicant is ready, willing and organised to comply with the regulatory obligations that will apply if it is given permission to conduct those regulated activities. The regulator may, in addition to the information provided, carry out any further enquiries about the applicant, including requiring the applicant to attend meetings to give further information, requiring information supplied to be verified (eg by an auditor or accountant) and visiting the applicant's premises. In addition, the regulator may have regard to any person (including **firms**) who is **connected** to the applicant.

If the application is successful, permission is granted and the direct consequence is that the applicant is authorised to carry out those activities. The firm will receive a written notice of the decision and the regulator's register of authorised persons is updated.

The regulator may, however, consider that the permissions applied for need to be modified based on the regulator's review of the applicant. They will recommend the application be granted subject to limitations or requirements or to a narrower scope of activities than the applicant originally requested.

The initial determination of the application is taken by the regulator's staff. When the firm is given permission to do a regulated activity it will be recorded on the **public register** of authorised persons maintained by the regulator. If the applicant does not accept these limitations or if the regulator simply decide to refuse the application in its entirety then the case is passed to the **Regulatory Decisions Committee (RDC)** for review. The process may result in a final reference to the Tribunal if the RDC's decision is not agreed by the applicant.

### 2.4.5 Ready, willing and able

The regulator must be satisfied that the firm will be able, once authorised, to comply with the rules and regulations applicable to it. This will therefore require the applicant to show that they have processes and procedures to implement and monitor compliance with the provisions of FSMA 2000, secondary legislation and the regulatory Handbooks.

For example, can the firm show that it has procedures to comply with the regulator's rules on systems and controls including money laundering, approved persons, training and competence, prudential regulation, market abuse, conduct of business, client assets and complaints?

# 3 Approved persons and controlled functions

## 3.1 Procedure for obtaining approval

Certain **individuals** within an authorised firm will require **approval** from the regulator because they carry out **controlled functions**. We explain what the controlled functions are below.

It is important to appreciate that the process of an **individual** obtaining **approved person** status is different from the process of a **firm** obtaining **authorisation**.

To obtain and to retain approval, a person must satisfy the regulator that they are **fit and proper** to carry out the controlled function. The suitability of a member of staff who performs a controlled function is covered in the **Fit and Proper Test for Approved Persons** (part of the High Level Standards section of the regulatory Handbook).

The most important considerations are as follows.

- **Honesty, integrity and reputation.** The regulator will examine whether the person's reputation might have an adverse impact on the firm they are doing a controlled function for. This will include looking at a number of factors including whether they have had any criminal convictions, civil claims, previous disciplinary proceedings, censure or investigations by any regulator, exchange, governing body or court; any other previous contraventions of regulations; any complaints which have been upheld; any connection with any body which has previously been refused a registration, authorisation or licence or had such registrations, authorisations or licences revoked or been expelled by a regulatory or governmental body; whether they have had any management role within any entities which have gone into liquidation; whether they have been dismissed or asked to resign from a similar position or position of trust; any disqualifications as a director, and finally whether they have been candid and truthful in their dealings with all regulatory bodies and demonstrated a willingness to comply with the regulatory and legal standards applicable to them. When looking at previous convictions, even old (i.e. spent) convictions, as defined in the Rehabilitation of Offenders Act 1974, can be taken into account.

- **Competence and capability.** The regulator will examine whether the Training and Competence requirements in the FCA Handbook have been complied with and whether they have demonstrated by training and experience that they are able to perform the controlled function. If a person has been convicted of, or dismissed or suspended from employment due to drug or alcohol abuse this will be considered in relation only to their continuing ability to perform that function. In addition, S61 FSMA 2000 emphasises that the fit and proper test for approved persons includes assessing qualifications, training and competence. It is not a requirement that a person has experience in order to be approved.

- **Financial soundness.** The regulator will look at whether the applicant has any outstanding judgement debts, has filed for bankruptcy or been involved in any similar proceedings. The fact that a person is of limited financial resources will not in itself affect their suitability to perform a controlled function.

These criteria must be met on a continuing basis. Individuals performing a controlled function must obtain approval **before** they take up the role. Approved persons must adhere to the seven **Statements of Principle**, which we look at in Chapter 8 of this Study Text.

### Case example

*Terence Boyd was bankrupt 12 years ago. Does this mean that he cannot be approved?*

*Not necessarily. If we are told something which suggests that an individual might not be fit and proper, understand that the regulator will consider how relevant and how important it is. It does not automatically mean that the individual will not be approved. The regulator will consider the full circumstances of each case before deciding. If the regulator has concerns, it will give the individual a Warning Notice setting out these concerns and the individual will have the opportunity to make representations about these concerns in writing and/or in person before the regulator makes a final decision.*

## 3.2 Application procedure

It is the obligation of the authorised firm for which the person works (and not the individual) to apply to the regulator for approval for each controlled function to be undertaken. But, if a person performs an FCA-controlled function without approval, it is not only the firm that is accountable. If a person knowingly performs a controlled function without approval, the FCA may impose a penalty on the individual. (SUP 10A.13.2&3)

To apply for approval, the firm must complete **Form A**. Where a firm outsources a controlled function it should ensure that no person performs a controlled function without the regulator's approval.

The applying firm will need to complete the following sections in its application.

- **Candidate Details**, e.g. name and address of individual

- **Arrangements and Controlled Functions**, e.g. nature of relationship to firm (employee/appointed representative) and controlled function(s) to be undertaken

- **Employment History** for the last five years – this should leave no gaps and the reason for leaving each job

- **Fitness and Propriety**, e.g. any criminal or civil convictions, County Court Judgements, bankruptcy proceedings or regulatory censures

- **Supplementary Information** – if any

- **Declarations and Signatures** – the individual and the firm must declare their reasonable belief of the accuracy of the contents of the form. The applicant is asked to print a copy of the application ensuring original signatures are obtained for both individual (where necessary) and firm

FSMA 2000 allows the regulator **three months** to review and determine the application, although most straightforward applications are dealt with in a matter of a few days.

Where a person ceases to perform a controlled function, the firm must notify the regulator **within seven business days** using **Form C**. However, where a firm is effecting a 'dirty withdrawal', e.g. where an employee has been dismissed, or there are concerns relating to their fitness and propriety, this information should be passed to the regulator immediately. Any material changes to an individual's personal details should also be notified to the regulator. Where an individual is to be internally transferred and will undertake different controlled functions within the firm, this should also be notified to the regulator. Failure to comply with the requirements relating to approval may result in disciplinary action against the authorised firm.

It is possible in very limited circumstances for an employee to undertake a significant influence function without approval to cover a temporary absence or in an emergency.

Where approval is given, the regulator's register of approved persons will be updated. Where the regulator rejects an application for approval, this is referred to the **Regulatory Decisions Committee (RDC)** and may be further referred to the **Upper Tribunal** where agreement is not reached.

When an authorised firm is recruiting employees, while the rules do not specifically require it, the firm will usually obtain a reference from the previous employer. In respect of **customer functions** only, a former employer who is an authorised firm must give all relevant information as soon as it is reasonably practicable to the new employer. This can create legal difficulties relating to the accuracy of references that should be carefully considered. The former employer must be frank and honest but should verify facts set out in the reference and act with due care and skill towards its former employee.

## 3.3 Controlled functions

The **FCA** may specify a function as a **controlled function** if the individual performing it is:

- Exerting a significant influence on the conduct of the firm's affairs
- Dealing directly with customers, or
- Dealing with the property of customers

The **PRA** may specify a function as a **controlled function** if, in relation to carrying on a regulated activity by a PRA-authorised firm, it is a SIF.

For an individual who performs **both PRA and FCA-related SIFs**, application for approval may need only to be made to the PRA, provided that there is a single application for both roles. The PRA approval will cover the approval of the FCA functions. In such a case, the PRA must get the consent of the FCA before granting approval.

In **dual-regulated firms**, controlled functions that are **'significant-influence functions' (SIFs)** are divided between the PRA and the FCA, so as to reduce the duplication of approvals by each of the regulators.

The specific controlled functions are split into groups as shown in the following Table. (The numbering is discontinuous because of past re-categorisations of functions.)

As shown in the following Table, there are:

- FCA-controlled functions for FCA-authorised firms (**FCAcont FCAauth** below)
- FCA-controlled functions for PRA-authorised firms (**FCAcont PRAauth**), and
- PRA-controlled functions for PRA-authorised firms (**PRAcont PRAauth**)

(The functions have discontinuous numbering because of re-categorisation of functions.)

| Group | Function (CF) | FCAcont FCAauth | FCAcont PRAauth | PRAcont PRAauth |
|---|---|:---:|:---:|:---:|
| **Governing functions** | 1. Director | • | | • |
| | 2 (PRA). PRA firm Non-executive Director | | | • |
| | 2 (FCA). FCA firm Non-executive Director | • | | |
| | 3. Chief executive | • | | • |
| | 4. Partner | • | | • |
| | 5. Director of unincorporated association | • | | • |
| | 6. Small Friendly Society | • | | • |

| Group | Function (CF) | FCAcont FCAauth | FCAcont PRAauth | PRAcont PRAauth |
|---|---|:---:|:---:|:---:|
| Required functions | 8. Apportionment and oversight | • | • | |
| | 10. Compliance oversight | • | • | |
| | 10a. CASS operational oversight | • | • | |
| | 11. Money laundering reporting | • | • | |
| | 12. Actuarial | | | • |
| | 12A. With-profits actuary | | | • |
| | 12B. Lloyd's actuary | | | • |
| | 40. Benchmark submission | • | • | |
| | 50. Benchmark administration | • | • | |
| Systems and controls function | 28. Systems and controls | • | | • |
| Significant management function | 29. Significant management | • | • | |
| Customer functions | 30. Customer function | • | • | |

The overall scope of the approved persons regime is not changed with the changeover from the FSA to the FCA and PRA. Future changes are anticipated, following consultations.

Individuals who fall within all of the categories in the Table **except** customer functions would be considered to be exerting a **significant influence** on the conduct of the firm's affairs. The previous regulator (the FSA) strengthened its approach to 'significant-influence' functions (**SIFs**) by ensuring that those likely to exert a significant influence on a firm fall within the scope of the approved persons regime.

In adopting a **more 'intrusive' approach**, the regulators are coming to focus more on the **competence and capability** of candidates for **SIFs**. For example, the regulators have carried out interviews for 'significant influence' posts at high impact firms. Once in post, where individuals fail to meet the required standards, the regulator will consider enforcement action. The regulators are placing greater emphasis on the role of senior management, including non-executive directors (NEDs). The regulators consider that it is important that directors and senior managers at firms understand their regulatory obligations and have the relevant competencies and experience to carry out their roles with integrity.

Note the following points about particular groups of functions.

- **Governing functions**. A firm will have one or more approved persons responsible (e.g. the Board of Directors) for directing its affairs. An insurance intermediary that is not a sole trader must have a director or senior manager responsible for insurance mediation activities of the firm.

- **Required functions: Apportionment and oversight function**. A director or senior manager will be responsible for either or both of the functions of apportionment of responsibilities, and oversight of systems and controls.

- **Systems and controls function**. This is the function of acting in the capacity of an employee of the firm with responsibility for reporting to the governing body of a firm, or the audit committee (or its equivalent) in relation to (1) its financial affairs, (2) setting and controlling its risk exposure, and (3) adherence to internal systems and controls, procedures and policies.

- **Significant management function**. In many firms, those approved for the governing functions, required functions and the systems and controls function are likely to exercise all the significant influence at senior management level.

- **Customer function**. This applies to activities carried on from a UK establishment and has to do with giving advice on, dealing and arranging deals in and managing investments. (It does not apply to banking business such as deposit taking and lending.)

An adviser who is promoted to a role involving significant-influence function may still advise clients.

**What if an approved person moves within a group?** If an approved person moves from a firm to another firm, whether or not the firms are within the same group, then the new firm will need to make a **fresh application** for that person's approved person status, even if the controlled functions performed are the same (SUP 10A.14).

## 3.4 Which controlled functions must be covered?

Not all controlled functions apply to all firms, so firms do not need to have individuals covering all controlled functions.

**Examples**

- A firm that only does mortgage and/or general insurance business, does not need to apply for individuals to be approved for customer functions (for example, advising on mortgage and general insurance products)

- A retailer whose main business is not financial services but who sells insurance policies will only need to seek approval for the person who allocates responsibility for its business to senior management and oversees systems and controls

If more than one controlled function applied to a firm, then a single individual can perform more than one controlled function. For example, a director can perform the Director function and the Compliance Oversight function.

## 3.5 Directors of appointed representatives

Anyone performing a governing function for an appointed representative must be an **approved person**.

However, for **appointed representatives** that carry on general insurance business incidental to their main business (for example, a vet recommending specific pet insurance), only one person in the firm needs to be an approved person. That person should be a director (or equivalent) and perform one of the following governing functions:

- Director
- Chief Executive
- Partner
- Director of unincorporated association

The individual does not apply to the regulator on their own behalf to be an approved person of an appointed representative. The individual's Principal (the authorised firm responsible for their actions) must apply for the individual.

# 4 Training and competence

## 4.1 Overview

**Principle 3** of the **Principles for Businesses** requires firms to take reasonable care to organise and control its affairs responsibly and effectively, with adequate risk management systems. This implies having appropriate systems of control, including ensuring that **employees maintain and enhance competence**.

SYSC states that a firm's systems and controls should enable it to satisfy itself of the suitability of anyone who acts for it. A requirement under **MiFID** is that firms must employ personnel with the skills, knowledge and expertise necessary for the discharge of the responsibilities allocated to them.

The **Training and Competence (TC)** sourcebook within the FCA Handbook applies only to firms whose employees advise **retail clients, customers or consumers**.

The TC Sourcebook does not apply to firms 'passported-in' from other EEA countries.

Appropriate examination requirements no longer apply to **wholesale business** in the financial services sector.

A contravention of the TC rules does not give rise to a **right of action by a private person** under s138D of FSMA 2000.

## 4.2 The competent employees rule

**Competence** means having the skills, knowledge and expertise needed to discharge the responsibilities of an employee's role. This includes achieving a good standard of **ethical behaviour**.

- The **competent employees rule** is now the main Handbook requirement relating to the competence of employees. The purpose of the TC Sourcebook is to support the regulator's supervisory function by supplementing the competent employees rule for **retail activities**.

- The **competent employees rule** is that firms must employ personnel with the skills, knowledge and expertise necessary for the discharge of the responsibilities allocated to them. This rule applies to non-MiFID firms as well as **MiFID** firms.

## 4.3 Assessment of competence and supervision

A firm must not assess an employee as competent to carry on an activity until the employee has demonstrated the necessary competence to do so and passed each module of an **appropriate examination** (where required). This assessment need not take place before the employee starts to carry on the activity. However, if the employee carries on the activity, the firm must ensure that the employee gains an appropriate qualification **within 30 months** of starting to carry on that activity. (Different rules apply for certain specialist roles, as outlined later below.)

- If the adviser does not complete the qualification within 30 months, they must stop carrying out the activity until they have passed.

- This rule started on 1 January 2011 and so the earliest that this will apply to anyone is 30 June 2013.

- In calculating the 30 months, periods of time spent on the activity during different periods of employment are aggregated, and periods of 60 business days or more of an employee's continuous absence from work are excluded.

For retail advisers within the scope of the **RDR**, there are different deadlines for those who were assessed as competent at an earlier date – i.e., before 1 January 2011 (see later in this Section).

A firm must not allow an employee to carry on an activity without appropriate **supervision**.

A firm must ensure that an employee – such as a trainee adviser – does not carry on an activity (other than an overseeing activity) for which there is an examination requirement without first passing the relevant **regulatory module** of an appropriate examination.

## 4.4 Ongoing assessment

Firms should ensure that their employees' training needs are assessed at the outset and at regular intervals (including if their role changes). Appropriate training and support should be provided to ensure that training needs are satisfied. The quality and effectiveness of such training should be reviewed regularly.

Firms must review regularly and frequently employees' competence and take appropriate action to ensure that they remain competent for their role.

An employee is, of course, additionally subject to the **fit and proper test** on becoming an **approved person**.

A firm should ensure that **maintaining competence** for an employee, for example through a formal programme of **Continuing Professional Development (CPD)**.

## 4.5 Appropriate examinations

Under the 'RDR Professionalism' rules, requirements for a **QCF Level 4** appropriate examination apply to advising **retail clients** on **retail investment products (RIPs)**, whether advisers are engaged in providing **independent advice** or **restricted advice. Qualifications at Level 4** within the national **Qualifications and Credit Framework (QCF)** are at a higher standard than the previous benchmark Level 3. They involve greater understanding and require more hours of learning than Level 3 qualifications.

Requirements to hold an 'appropriate qualification' apply to individuals carrying out one or more of the following regulated activities for **retail clients**:

- Advising on (but not dealing in) securities (which are not stakeholder pension schemes or broker funds) (Activity number 2)

- Advising on (but not dealing in) derivatives (Activity number 3)

- Advising on retail investment products (RIPs) (which are not broker funds) (Activity number 4)

- Advising on Friendly Society tax-exempt policies(Activity number 6)

- Advising on, and dealing in securities (which are not stakeholder pension schemes or broker funds) (Activity number 12)

- Advising on and dealing with or for clients in derivatives(Activity number 13)

There is not a qualification requirement for:

- 'Basic' advice on stakeholder products

- Advice on friendly society life policies where the employee's annual remuneration from them will not exceed £1,000

- Advice on non-investment insurance contracts

If an individual acts as a **retail investment adviser (RIA)** in respect of any of these regulated activities – even if this is only on one occasion – then they will still need an **appropriate RDR qualification** and also need to become an **approved person** to carry out the controlled function: **CF30 Customer Function**.

**Appropriate Qualification Tables** in the FCA's **Training and Competence Sourcebook** (TC, Appendix 4E) detail which are the appropriate qualifications for the various activities requiring qualifications. For example, the **CII's Diploma in Regulated Financial Planning** is an 'appropriate qualification' for **advising on retail investment products** that are not broker funds (Activity number 4).

A **waiver** to the RDR qualification rules, in the form of an extension to the firm, may be granted by the regulator where there are exceptional circumstances that prevent an individual from attaining their qualification by the required date.

Advisers who did not achieve an appropriate Level 4 qualification by 31 December 2012, and who either do not qualify for the **30 month rule** or are not awarded a waiver by the regulator against the rule, are not allowed to advise under supervision. Such an adviser must '**de-authorise**'.

Under the RDR qualifications rules, there are two important deadlines for those who were previously assessed as competent:

- Advisers who were deemed competent on or before 30 June 2009 must have attained an **appropriate RDR-compliant qualification** by the **end of 2012** – the first **RDR qualification deadline**.

- For advisers who are assessed as competent between 1 July 2009 and 1 January 2011, the **second RDR deadline** of **1 July 2013** applied for obtaining their RDR qualification.

- Those who **started giving advice** on or after 1 January 2011 will have a rolling qualification deadline of 30 months from the date they begin the activity.

Advisers already holding certain appropriate qualifications do not need to take further exams to meet RDR standards, but are likely to need to carry out qualifications **gap-fill** using relevant structured **continuing professional development (CPD)**. CPD activity carried out in the past can be used towards this gap filling, where it meets a learning outcome set out in the gap fill template.

Some advisers may choose to reach the required standards (e.g., if they do not want to take the exam route) by undertaking an alternative assessment available from some providers.

**Supervisors** are required to hold an appropriate examination if they supervise advisers who give advice to retail clients on packaged products but are not yet signed off as competent. The rationale for this is that the supervisor will generally be responsible for the advice given.

## 4.6 Specialist examinations

**Specialist examinations** must be completed in addition for giving advice in the areas shown below. (Activity numbers are as listed in the FCA Handbook, TC Sourcebook, Appendix 1.)

Pensions transfer / opt-out specialists and broker fund advisers must attain the specialist examinations before acting in those roles. For other specialist roles listed below, advisers must be monitored by a competent person until an appropriate exam is passed.

- Regulated mortgage contracts advice (Activity number 20)
- Equity release (Activity number 21)
- Long-term care insurance contracts (Activity number 7)
- Pension transfer and specialist (Activity number 11)
- Broker fund adviser (Activity number 10)

## 4.7 Notification requirements for firms

As part of the regulator's new **risk-based supervisory strategy for individuals,** since **July 2011** firms have been required to notify the regulator of adviser competence issues.

A firm must notify the regulator as soon as they become aware, or have information that suggests any of the following has occurred, or **may have** occurred, in relation to any of its retail investment advisers (RIAs):

- An RIA who has been assessed as competent is no longer considered competent.

- An RIA has failed to attain an appropriate qualification within the prescribed time limit.

- An RIA has failed to comply with a Statement of Principle in carrying out his/her controlled function.

- An RIA has performed an activity to which the training and competence (TC) requirements apply before having demonstrated the necessary competence and without appropriate supervision.

Why does the regulator need this information? The information gathered will be fed, along with data from other sources, into an adviser database that has the objective of identifying the highest risk advisers.

## 4.8 Maintaining competence

**Continuing Professional Development (CPD)** is a term used to describe the process an individual needs to go through to keep their knowledge and skills up to date.

The FCA Handbook (TC2.1.13G) states that a firm should ensure that **maintaining competence** for an employee takes into account such matters as:

- Technical knowledge and its application
- Skills and expertise

- Changes in the market and to products, legislation and regulation

These aspects may vary, for example according to whether an individual is independent or tied, is a general financial planner or specialist, or whether they have any managerial responsibilities within the firm. For example, a supervisor attending a coaching course could reasonably use this as CPD – it is not restricted just to technical knowledge.

Firms should have systems in place to be able to monitor an individual's competence. This is likely to focus on either the activities undertaken to maintain competence, e.g. **CPD records**, or **tests** used to ensure that knowledge is acceptable at any point. In practice, both methods are likely to be used.

Under the **RDR requirements** applying since the end of 2012, advisers need to carry out at least **35 hours** of **CPD** annually, of which **21 hours** must be structured. **Structured CPD** is an activity that has a defined learning outcome and must take a **minimum of 30 minutes**. Both structured and unstructured CPD must be capable of being **independently verified**.

## 4.9 T&C records

A firm must make appropriate records to demonstrate compliance with the rules in TC and keep them for the following periods after an employee stops carrying on the activity:

- At least five years for MiFID business
- Three years for non-MiFID business, and
- Indefinitely for a pension transfer specialist

The precise contents of **records** to be held within a training and competence scheme are not prescribed by the regulator, and will be decided by the firm.

**T&C records** kept for each individual are likely to include:

- Copies of completed exam certifications
- Details of training programmes completed
- Agreed personal development plans
- Dates when adviser started work on regulated activities
- Performance review and appraisal documents
- Logs of continuing professional development (CPD) completed
- Key performance indicators (KPIs)

# 5 Record keeping and reporting

## 5.1 Record keeping

Firms are required to arrange for orderly records to be kept, which must be sufficient to enable the regulators (or other competent authority) to:

- Monitor compliance with the requirements under the regulatory system
- Ascertain that the firm has complied with all obligations with respect to clients and potential clients

A firm must take reasonable care to make and retain adequate records of matters and dealings (including accounting records) which are the subject of requirements and standards under the regulatory system.

Records should be capable of being reproduced in English, on paper, or alternatively in the official language of a different country for records relating to business done there.

**MiFID** requires firms to keep records for **five years**, for MiFID business generally.

For **non-MiFID business**, a retention period of five years also commonly applies, but note the following exceptions.

**Record keeping requirements** (set out in **COBS Schedule 1**) are, in summary, as follows.

- **Indefinitely**, for pension transfers, pension opt-outs and FSAVCs (Free-Standing Additional Voluntary Contributions arrangements, for pensions)

- **Five years**, for life policies and pension contracts, but **six years** for financial promotions for these products

- **Five years** in most other cases, including (as mentioned earlier) **MiFID business**, but **three years** in some circumstances, for example for suitability reports for non-MiFID business regarding products not mentioned above

## 5.2 Reporting executions

In respect of **MiFID** and equivalent third country business, a firm must ensure that clients receive **adequate reports** on the services provided to it by the firm and their costs.

A firm must provide promptly in a durable medium the **essential information** on **execution of orders** to clients in the course of **designated investment business**, when it is not managing the investments. The information may be sent to an agent of the client, nominated by the client in writing.

For retail clients, a notice confirming execution must be sent as soon as possible and no later than the first business day following receipt of confirmation from the third party.

Firms must supply information about the **status of a client's order** on request.

For **series of orders** to buy units or shares in a collective undertaking (such as a **regular savings plan**), after the initial report, further reports must be provided at least at six-monthly intervals.

Where an order is executed in tranches, the firm may supply the price for each tranche or an average price. The price for each tranche must be made available on the request of a retail client.

For business that is not MiFID or equivalent third country business, confirmations need **not** be supplied if:

- The client has agreed not to receive them (with informed written consent, in the case of retail clients), or
- The designated investment is a life policy or a personal pension scheme (other than a SIPP), or
- The designated investment is held in a CTF and the information is contained in the annual statement

**Copies of confirmations** dispatched must be **kept** for at least **five years**, for MiFID and equivalent third country business, and for at least **three years** in other cases.

**Information to be included in trade confirmations to a retail client**

- Reporting firm identification
- Name / designation of client
- Trading day and time
- Order type (e.g. limit order / market order)
- Venue identification
- Instrument identification
- Buy / sell indicator (or nature of order, if not buy/sell)
- Quantity
- Unit price
- Total consideration
- Total commissions and expenses charged with, if requested, itemised breakdown
- Currency exchange rate, where relevant
- Time limit for payment, and appropriate account details
- Details if counterparty was in firm's group or was another client, unless trading was anonymous

## 5.3 Periodic reporting

A firm **managing investments** on behalf of a client must provide a periodic statement to the client in a durable medium, unless such a statement is provided by another person. The statement may be sent to an agent nominated by the client in writing.

**Information to be included in a periodic report**

- Name of the firm

- Name / designation of retail client's account

- Statement of contents and valuation of portfolio, including details of:
    - Each designated investment held, its market value or, if unavailable, its fair value
    - Cash balance at beginning and end of reporting period
    - Performance of portfolio during reporting period

- Total fees and charges, itemising total management fees and total execution costs

- Comparison of period performance with any agreed investment performance benchmark

- Total dividends, interest and other payments received in the period

- Information about other corporate actions giving rights to designated investments held

For a **retail client**, the **periodic statement** should be provided once every **six months**, except that:

- In the case of a leveraged portfolio, it should be provided at least **once a month**

- It should be provided every **three months** if the client requests it. (The firm must inform clients of this right.)

- If the retail client elects to receive information on a transaction-by-transaction basis and there are no transactions in derivatives or similar instruments giving rise to a cash settlement, the periodic statement must be supplied at least once every **12 months**

A firm managing investments (or operating a retail client account that includes an uncovered open position in a contingent liability transaction – involving a potential liability in excess of the cost) must report to the client any **losses** exceeding any **predetermined threshold** agreed with the client.

Periodic statements for **contingent liability transactions** may include information on the **collateral value** and **option account valuations** in respect of each option written by the client in the portfolio at the end of the relevant period.

For **non-MiFID business**, a firm need not provide a periodic statement to a client habitually resident outside the UK if the client does not wish to receive it.

## 5.4 Persistency reports

**Persistency** is a measure of the proportion of contracts that have not been cancelled by the customer and thus remain in force at the end of a period. Product providers of regular and single premium life and pension contracts must submit to the FCA **persistency reports** (as set out in the FCA Handbook SUP Chapter 16 Annex 6). Term assurance, and contracts cancelled during the standard 'cooling off' cancellation period, are excluded.

Persistency figures must be reported annually over the first four years of contracts, broken down by sales channel and type of contract. The regulator compiles the data into an aggregated report.

# 6 Financial crime and counter-terrorism

## 6.1 Money laundering

Money laundering is a key target of the law and regulation regarding financial crime as it affects the financial services industry. UK anti-money laundering legislation applies to the proceeds of all crimes no matter how small.

What is money laundering? **Money laundering** is the process by which money that is illegally obtained is made to appear to have been legally obtained. By a variety of methods, the nature, source and ownership of these criminal proceeds are concealed.

- Criminal conduct is any crime that constitutes an offence in the UK, or any act abroad that would constitute an offence if it had occurred in the UK.

- Property is criminal property if it constitutes a person's benefit from criminal conduct and the alleged offender knows or suspects that it constitutes this benefit.

There are three typical phases in the laundering of money: **placement**, **layering** and **integration**.

- If the money launderer is able to deposit illicit proceeds within an institution or a state (**placement**), which requires little or no disclosure concerning the ownership of those funds, it may be difficult, if not impossible, to trace the property back to its criminal source.

- In the second instance, if property is passed through a complicated series of transactions (**layering**), involving legitimate as well as illegitimate enterprises, it may again be impossible to identify the owner or origin of that property.

- If the ownership or origin of the funds cannot be ascertained, it is virtually impossible to establish that they are the product of criminal activity. The funds can then be reused in legitimate activity (**integration**).

The following are the definitions of **money laundering** employed in the 1991 European Union Council Directive. They have, in the main, been adopted in subsequent UK legislation.

- The conversion or transfer of property for the purpose of concealing or disguising the origin of the property.

- The concealment or disguise of the true nature, source, location, disposition, movement, rights with respect to, or ownership of, illicitly gained property.

- The acquisition, possession or use of property derived from criminal activity or participation in criminal activity.

## 6.2 Action to combat money laundering

In recognition of the scale and impact of money laundering globally, various national governments have in recent years collaborated on an international scale to combat money laundering. Action taken has concentrated not only on the law enforcement process, but also on recommendations to banks and financial institutions to put in place practices and procedures that will assist in the detection of money laundering activity.

In the **EU**, it has been envisaged that the **Money Laundering Directives** would enable the financial sector to play a powerful role in combating money laundering and, consequently, criminal activity. Additionally, it was anticipated that regulation of this kind would maintain public confidence in the soundness and stability of the European financial system.

## 6.3 EU Money Laundering Directives

In 1991, the EU adopted Council Directive 91/308 (**First EU Money Laundering Directive**) on the prevention of the use of the financial system for the purpose of money laundering.

- The Directive required all EU Member States to create criminal offences applicable to individuals to prohibit money laundering activity. This was enacted into UK legislation via the **Criminal Justice Act 1993 (CJA 1993).** More recently the money laundering offences within CJA 1993 have been repealed and replaced with the **Proceeds of Crime Act 2002 (POCA 2002)** which we shall discuss in detail later.

- The Directive also stated that all EU Member States should ensure that all financial and credit institutions located within the Member States should implement certain internal procedures and controls.

The aim of these internal procedures is threefold.

1. **Deterrence:** to prevent credit and financial institutions being used for money laundering purposes

2. **Co-operation:** to ensure that there is co-operation between credit and financial institutions and law enforcement agencies

3. **Detection:** to establish customer identification and record-keeping procedures within all financial and credit institutions which will assist the law enforcement agencies in detecting, tracing and prosecuting money launderers

In 2001, a **Second EU Money Laundering Directive** was adopted to cure some of the deficiencies in the first Directive. Then, a **Third Money Laundering Directive** came into force on **15 December 2007**. The Third Directive more fully incorporates into EU law the **Forty Recommendations** of the international **Financial Action Task Force (FATF)**.

The latest **Money Laundering Regulations 2007 (MLR 2007)** repeal earlier regulations and implement the Third Directive.

The main changes brought about by the Third Directive are as follows.

- The term '**occasional transaction**' (with a monetary limit of transactions of a value below €15,000) is now used, instead of 'one-off' transaction as in earlier Regulations.

- A **risk-based approach** is mandatory, in respect of risk management generally, and in applying customer due diligence.

- There is detailed coverage of **customer due diligence** in the 2007 Regulations, with substantial guidance on how firms should meet their obligation of identifying customers, and mandatory monitoring of customer relationships.

- There is **enhanced** due diligence on a **risk-sensitive basis**, including for 'politically exposed persons' ('PEPs') from outside the UK.

- There is additional scope for **relying on other appropriately qualified regulated firms**, although the 'relying firm' retains ultimate responsibility for meeting the obligations under the Regulations.

In February 2013, the European Commission announced that it had adopted proposals for the framework of a **Fourth EU Money Laundering Directive (4MLD)**. As well as the Directive, there is a separate proposed regulation which sets out new information requirements for transfers of funds. 4MLD seeks to make changes in line with international standards promulgated by the FATF and to strengthen international co-operation. 4MLD stresses the risk-based approach that has been the cornerstone of UK AML/CTF (Anti-Money Laundering/Counter-Terrorism Financing) measures for many years. Most of the requirements implemented in the 4MLD proposals are already included within the UK AML/CTF regime.

4MLD was finally published in June 2015. It is currently expected that member states will be required to put its provisions into effect by mid-2017.

## 6.4 Money Laundering Regulations 2007: Institutional liability

Under MLR 2007, there are a number of **supervising agencies** with whom businesses of different types are required to register.

- For the purposes of the Regulations, the FCA is responsible for the supervision of authorised firms and also certain other firms including leasing companies, commercial finance providers and safe custody services. FCA-authorised firms are automatically supervised by the FCA but other such businesses must register with the FCA under MLR 2007.

- Various other types of business falling under the regulations are supervised by other authorities: for example, auctioneers accepting cash of €15,000 or more and foreign exchange bureaux must register with HMRC, estate agents must register with the Office of Fair Trading and casinos must register with the Gambling Commission.

- Members of Designated Professional Bodies not conducting mainstream regulated activities are supervised by their professional bodies.

The **Money Laundering Regulations 2007 (MLR 2007)** relate to institutional liability generally. They require internal systems and procedures to be implemented to deter criminals from using certain institutions to launder money. They also aim to enable money laundering to be more easily detected and prosecuted by the law enforcement agencies.

The following 'risk-sensitive' policies and procedures must be established.

- Customer due diligence measures and ongoing monitoring

- Internal reporting

- Record-keeping procedures (for five-year period)

- Internal control

- Risk assessment and management

- Compliance monitoring, management and communication of the policies and procedures

- Recognition of suspicious transactions and reporting procedures, including appointing a Money Laundering Reporting Officer (MLRO)

- Staff training programmes

### Offence

Failure to implement the MLR 2007 measures is a **criminal offence**. The **FCA** may institute proceedings (other than in Scotland) for money laundering regulation breaches. This power is not limited to firms or persons regulated by the FCA. Whether a breach of the Money Laundering Regulations has occurred is not dependent on whether money laundering has taken place: firms may be sanctioned for not having adequate **anti-money laundering (AML)/counter-terrorism financing (CTF)** systems.

### Penalty

Failure to comply with any of the requirements of the ML Regulations constitutes an offence punishable by a maximum of two years' imprisonment, or a fine, or both when tried in a Crown Court. If this case was tried in a Magistrates Court the maximum penalty is 6 months plus a £5,000 fine.

Where a UK business **outsources** certain operations to an overseas jurisdiction, the business is still effectively carried on in the UK. For example, if an investment bank moved its call centre to India, it would still have to comply with money laundering requirements and staff in India would need proper training.

## 6.5 The Proceeds of Crime Act 2002: Individual liability

The following are offences under this Act.

- Assistance
- Failure to report
- Tipping off

### 6.5.1 Assistance (POCA S327, S328, S329)

**Offence**

If any person knowingly helps another person to launder the proceeds of criminal conduct, he or she will be committing an offence. This covers obtaining, concealing, disguising, transferring, acquiring, possessing, investing or using the proceeds of crime. The legislation historically covered the laundering of the proceeds of **serious crime**, however as a result of the POCA it now covers the proceeds of **all crimes**, no matter how small. This could include evasion of tax.

**Possible defences**

- It is a defence to the above offence that a person **disclosed** his knowledge or belief concerning the origins of the property either to the police or to the appropriate officer in his firm.

- Under changes made by the **Serious Organised Crime and Police Act 2005 (SOCPA)**, there may also be a defence if the person knew or believed on reasonable grounds that the relevant criminal conduct occurred outside the UK and the conduct was not at the time unlawful in the overseas jurisdiction.

**Penalty**

The maximum penalties for any offence of assisting a money launderer are **14 years' imprisonment and/or an unlimited fine** when tried in a Crown Court. If tried in a Magistrates Court the maximum penalty is reduced to 6 months' imprisonment and a £5,000 fine.

### 6.5.2 Failure to report

**Offence**

If a person discovers information during the course of his employment that makes him **believe or suspect** money laundering is occurring, he must inform the police or the appropriate officer (usually the **Money Laundering Reporting Officer (MLRO)**) of the firm as soon as possible. If he fails to make the report as soon as is reasonably practicable, he commits a criminal offence.

For those working in the **regulated sector** (for an authorised firm), this offence covers not only where the person had actual suspicion of laundering (i.e. subjective suspicions) but also where there were **reasonable grounds for being suspicious**. The grounds are when a hypothetical **reasonable person** would in the circumstances have been suspicious (i.e. **objective suspicions**).

**Possible defences**

The only defences to this charge are if a person charged can prove one of the following.

- He had a **reasonable excuse** for failing to disclose this information. Whether an excuse is reasonable will depend on the circumstances of the case, but it is noteworthy that the person charged has the burden of proving that he had a reasonable excuse for his failure to disclose.

- Where the person had no subjective suspicion but is deemed to have objective suspicions, they had not been provided by their employer with appropriate **training** to recognise and report suspicions.

- Under changes made by the Serious Organised Crime and Police Act 2005 (SOCPA), there may also be a defence if the person knew or believed on reasonable grounds that the relevant criminal conduct occurred outside the UK and the conduct was not at the time unlawful in the overseas jurisdiction.

The relevant legislation specifically provides that any person making a disclosure of this kind will not be in breach of any **duty of confidentiality** owed to a customer.

**Penalty**

This offence is punishable with a maximum of **five years' imprisonment** and/or an **unlimited fine** when tried in a Crown Court. If tried in a Magistrates Court the maximum penalty is reduced to 6 months' imprisonment and a £5,000 fine.

## 6.5.3 Tipping off (POCA s333A)

**Offence**

Even where suspicions are reported, the parties must generally be careful not to alert the suspicions of the alleged launderer since, within the regulated sector, this can itself amount to an offence.

Under s333A, a person within the regulated sector commits an **offence** if, based on information they acquire in the course of business that is likely to prejudice any investigation, they disclose:

- That information has been passed to the police, HMRC, a Nominated Officer (generally, the firm's MLRO) or the National Crime Agency (NCA) (the successor body to the Serious Organised Crime Agency), or
- That an investigation into money laundering allegations is being contemplated or carried out

The mischief that s333A seeks to prevent is the mischief of acting so as to frustrate an investigation, and there are a number of **exceptions**. An offence is **not** committed for disclosures within the EEA or territories with anti-money laundering regimes, broadly if the disclosure is:

- Within an EEA financial institution or credit institution or its group
- Between professional advisers within the same group
- Between financial and credit institutions or between advisers generally, for disclosure with the purpose of preventing a money laundering offence
- To the supervisory authority under the Money Laundering Regulations – which, for FCA-authorised firms, is the FCA
- By a professional adviser to their client if for the purpose of dissuading the client from committing an offence

**Possible defence**

It is a defence if the person charged can prove that he neither knew nor suspected that the disclosure would be likely to prejudice an investigation.

**Penalty**

Tipping off is punishable with a maximum of **two years' imprisonment** and/or an **unlimited fine** in the Crown Court, or three months' imprisonment and a maximum fine of £5,000 in the Magistrates' Court.

## 6.5.4 Prejudicing an investigation (s342 POCA, as amended)

For a person **outside the regulated sector**, the offence of **prejudicing an investigation** is similar to tipping off. It involves the offence, for those who know or suspect that a money laundering investigation is being carried out, of either:

- In the **non-regulated sector** (s342 (2)(a)), making a disclosure which is likely to prejudice the investigation, or

- For **all persons** (s342 (2)(b)), falsifying, concealing or destroying documents relevant to the investigation

There is a **defence** if the person charged can prove that he neither knew nor suspected that the disclosure would be likely to prejudice an investigation.

Section 342 carries a maximum custodial penalty of **five years** and/or a **fine** in the Crown Court, or six months' imprisonment and a maximum fine of £5,000 in the Magistrates' Court.

## 6.6 Senior management arrangements, systems and controls (SYSC)

### 6.6.1 Systems and controls in relation to compliance, financial crime and money laundering

SYSC provides that a firm must take reasonable care to establish and maintain effective systems and controls for compliance with applicable regulations and for countering the risk that the firm might be used to further financial crime. Applicable regulations include the Proceeds of Crime Act 2002, the Money Laundering Regulations 2007 and the Terrorism Act 2000.

The systems and controls laid down should enable the firm to identify, assess, monitor and manage **money laundering risk**, which is, the risk that a firm may be used to further money laundering. In addition, the systems and controls should be **comprehensive** and **proportionate** to the **nature**, **scale** and **complexity** of its activities and be regularly assessed to ensure they remain adequate. Failure by a firm to manage money laundering risk will effectively increase the risk to society of crime and terrorism.

In identifying its **money laundering risk** and in establishing the nature of the systems and controls required, a firm should consider a range of factors, including:

- Its customer, product and activity profiles
- Its distribution channels
- The complexity and volume of its transactions
- Its processes and systems
- Its operating environment

The SYSC rules require firms to ensure that their systems and controls include:

- Allocation to a director or senior manager (who may also be the MLRO) overall responsibility within the firm for the **establishment** and **maintenance** of effective anti-money laundering systems and controls.

- Appropriate provision of information to its governing body and senior management, including a report at least annually by that firm's **MLRO** on the operation and effectiveness of those systems and controls.

- **Appropriate training** for its employees in relation to money laundering.

- Appropriate **documentation** of its risk management policies and risk profile in relation to money laundering, including documentation of its application of those policies.

- Appropriate measures to ensure that **money laundering risk** is taken into account in its day-to-day operation, e.g. in the development of new products, the taking on of new customers and changes in its business profile.

- Appropriate measures to ensure that **identification procedures** for customers do not unreasonably deny access to its services.

## 6.6.2 The Money Laundering Reporting Officer (MLRO)

The MLRO which each authorised firm must appoint has responsibility for oversight of its compliance with the regulators' SYSC rules on money laundering.

The MLRO:

- Must act as the focal point for all activity within the firm relating to anti-money laundering
- Must have a level of authority and independence within the firm
- Must have access to sufficient resources and information to enable them to carry out that responsibility
- Should be based in the UK

A **nominated officer** is someone who has been nominated by their employer to receive reports of suspected money laundering. In practice, this will be the **MLRO** or **his deputy**.

Employers will have reporting processes in place for staff with suspicions to disclose to the MLRO. The nominated officer will act as a filter for reporting, and is placed under a duty to disclose to the **National Crime Agency (NCA)**, if he knows or suspects, or has reasonable grounds to suspect, that another person is engaged in money laundering.

## 6.6.3 The compliance function

Depending on the nature, scale and complexity of its business, it may be appropriate for a firm to have a separate **compliance function**. The organisation and responsibilities of the compliance function should be documented.

The compliance function should:

- Be staffed by an appropriate number of competent staff who are sufficiently independent to perform their duties objectively
- Have unrestricted access to the firm's relevant records
- Have ultimate recourse to its governing body

A firm which carries on designated investment business with or for customers must allocate to a director or senior manager the function of having responsibility for oversight of the firm's compliance and reporting to the governing body in respect of that responsibility. This will be the person carrying out the controlled function '**Compliance oversight**' under the regulators' approved persons regime. As a minimum, this individual will have to oversee compliance with COBS, CASS and COLL, however, firms are free to give additional responsibilities to this person.

**FCA'S FINANCIAL CRIME: A GUIDE FOR FIRMS**

The FCA has issued, in two Parts, its **Financial Crime: A Guide for Firms** (sometimes referred to as the Financial Crime Guide). The Guide provides practical examples and information for firms on the actions they can take to counter the risk that they might be used to further financial crime. The Guide also contains guidance on rules and principles that are included in the FCA Handbook. The regulator aims, through this Guide, to help firms to adopt an effective risk-based, outcomes-focused approach to mitigating the risk of financial crime.

The Guide seeks to increase awareness of what the regulator expects, and to help firms to evaluate the adequacy of their control systems in respect of financial crime and to remedy any deficiencies. The Guide does not contain rules and its contents are not binding.

**Part 1: A firm's guide to preventing financial crime** (April 2014) addresses the issues of: financial crime systems and controls; money laundering and terrorist financing; fraud; data security; bribery and corruption; sanctions and asset freezes.

**Part 2: Financial crime thematic reviews** (April 2013) contains summaries of, and links to, the thematic reviews of various financial crime risks that have been undertaken by the regulator (the FSA, before the FCA was established) since 2006. It includes the consolidated examples of good and poor practice that were included with the reviews' findings.

The Guide comes with some caveats. It does not include guidance on all the financial crime risks a firm may face. The good practice examples present ways, but not the only ways, in which firms might comply with applicable rules and requirements. There are many practices we would consider poor that we have not identified as such in the Guide.

## 6.7 Joint Money Laundering Steering Group Guidance

### 6.7.1 Status

The JMLSG is made up of representatives of trade bodies such as the British Bankers Association. The purpose of the guidance notes is to outline the requirements of the UK money laundering legislation, provide a practical interpretation of the MLR 2007 and provide a base from which management can develop tailored policies and procedures that are appropriate to their business.

The JMLSG Guidance Notes advise the UK financial services industry on how to take the required **risk-based approach** to the fight against crime.

The courts must take account of industry guidance, such as the MLSG Guidance, which have been approved by a Treasury Minister, when deciding whether:

- A person has committed the offence of failing to report money laundering under POCA 2002
- A person has failed to report terrorist financing under the Terrorism Act 2000, or
- A person or institution has failed to comply with any of the requirements of the MLR 2007

When considering whether to take disciplinary action against an authorised firm for a breach of SYSC, the regulator will have regard to whether a firm has followed relevant provisions in the JMLSG Guidance Notes. The guidance will therefore be significant for individuals or companies subject to regulatory action.

The Guidance Notes provide a sound basis for firms to meet their legislative and regulatory obligations when tailored by firms to their particular business risk profile. Departures from good industry practice, and the rationale for so doing, should be documented and may have to be justified to the regulator.

### 6.7.2 Directors' and senior managers' responsibility for money laundering precautions

Senior management of regulated firms must provide direction to, and oversight of, the firm's **anti-money laundering (AML)** and **combating the financing of terrorism (CFT)** systems and controls.

Firms' senior management have a responsibility to ensure that the firm's control processes and procedures are appropriately designed, implemented and effectively operated to manage the firm's risks. This includes the risk of the firm being used to further financial crime.

Senior management must also meet the following specific requirements.

- Allocate to a director or senior manager (who may or may not be the MLRO) overall responsibility for the establishment and maintenance of the firm's AML/CTF systems and controls

- Appoint an appropriately qualified senior member of the firm's staff as the MLRO

### 6.7.3 High level policy statement and risk-based approach

The regulator requires firms to produce adequate documentation of its risk management policies and risk profile in relation to money laundering, including documentation of the application of those policies.

A statement of the firm's AML/CFT policy and the procedures to implement it will clarify how the firm's senior management intend to discharge their legal responsibility. This will provide a framework of direction to the firm and its staff, and will identify named individuals and functions responsible for implementing particular aspects of the policy. The policy will also set out how senior management makes its assessment of the money laundering and terrorist financing risks the firm faces, and how these risks are to be managed.

The **policy statement** should be tailored to the circumstances of the firm and might include, but is not limited to, the following.

| Guiding principles |
| --- |
| An unequivocal statement of the culture and values to be adopted and promulgated throughout the firm towards the prevention of financial crime |
| A commitment to ensuring that customers' identities will be satisfactorily verified before the firm accepts them |
| A commitment to the firm 'knowing its customers' appropriately at acceptance and throughout the business relationship – through taking appropriate steps to verify the customer's identity and business, and his reasons for seeking the particular business relationship with the firm |
| A commitment to ensuring that staff are trained and made aware of the law and their obligations under it, and to establishing procedures to implement these requirements |
| Recognition of the importance of staff promptly reporting their suspicions internally |
| **Risk mitigation approach** |
| A summary of the firm's approach to assessing and managing its money laundering and terrorist financing risk |
| Allocation of responsibilities to specific persons and functions |
| A summary of the firm's procedures for carrying out appropriate identification and monitoring checks on the basis of their risk-based approach |
| A summary of the appropriate monitoring arrangements in place to ensure that the firm's policies and procedures are being carried out |

### 6.7.4 The risk-based approach

As already explained, a **risk-based approach** to anti-money laundering (AML) procedures is mandatory under MLR 2007. The approach requires the full commitment and support of senior management, and the active co-operation of business units. The risk-based approach needs to be part of the firm's philosophy, and as such reflected in its procedures and controls. There needs to be a clear communication of policies and procedures across the firm, together with robust mechanisms to ensure that they are carried out effectively, any weaknesses are identified and improvements are made wherever necessary.

**Steps in adopting the risk-based approach**

- Identify the money laundering and terrorist financing risks that are relevant to the firm.
- Assess risks presented by the firm's customers, products, delivery channels, geographical areas.
- Design and implement controls to manage and mitigate these assessed risks.
- Monitor and improve the effective operation of these controls, and
- Record appropriately what has been done, and why.

What is the **rationale** of the risk-based approach? To assist the overall objective to prevent money laundering and terrorist financing, a risk-based approach:

- Recognises that the money laundering/terrorist financing threat to firms varies across customers, jurisdictions, products and delivery channels.

- Allows management to differentiate between their customers in a way that matches the risk in their particular business.

- Allows senior management to apply its own approach to the firm's procedures, systems and controls, and arrangements in particular circumstances, and

- Helps to produce a more cost-effective system.

## 6.7.5 Risk assessment and 'Know Your Customer'

Firms are expected to 'know their customers'. The **Know Your Customer (KYC)** requirements:

- Help the firm, at the time customer due diligence is carried out, to be reasonably satisfied that customers are who they say they are, to know whether they are acting on behalf of others, whether there are any government sanctions against serving the customer, and

- Assist law enforcement with information on customers or activities under investigation.

Based on an **assessment of the money laundering / terrorist financing risk** that each customer presents, the firm will need to:

- **Verify the customer's identity (ID)** – determining exactly who the customer is.

- **Collect additional 'KYC' information**, and keep such information **current and valid** – to understand the customer's circumstances and business, and (where appropriate) the sources of funds or wealth, or the purpose of specific transactions.

Many customers, by their nature or through what is already known about them by the firm, carry a **lower** money laundering or terrorist financing **risk**. These might include:

- Customers who are employment-based or with a regular source of income from a known source which supports the activity being undertaken; (this applies equally to pensioners or benefit recipients, or to those whose income originates from their partners' employment).

- Customers with a long-term and active business relationship with the firm.

- Customers represented by those whose appointment is subject to court approval or ratification (such as executors).

Firms should not, however, judge the level of risk solely on the nature of the **customer** or the **product**. Where, in a particular customer/product combination, either or both the customer and the product are considered to carry a higher risk of money laundering or terrorist financing, the overall risk of the customer should be considered carefully. Firms need to be aware that allowing a higher risk customer to acquire a lower risk product or service on the basis of a verification standard that is appropriate to that lower risk product or service, can lead to a requirement for further verification requirements, particularly if the customer wishes subsequently to acquire a higher risk product or service.

## 6.8 Due diligence

One of the most important ways in which money laundering can be prevented is by establishing the identity of clients, thus making it difficult for those trading under assumed names or through bogus companies to gain access to the financial markets. This emphasises, again, the obligation to '**know your customer**'.

In the context of **conduct of business rules**, the firm may generally accept at face value information which customers provide. The **money laundering regulations**, however, require that the firm takes positive steps to verify the information that they receive. The **JMLSG** Guidance Notes lay down some basic, but not exhaustive, procedures that can be followed.

## 6.9 CDD, EDD and SDD

### 6.9.1 Customer due diligence

MLR 2007 regulations require detailed **customer due diligence (CDD)** procedures and these are explained in the **JMLSG** guidance.

**CDD** involves:

- Identifying the customer and verifying his identity.

- Identifying the beneficial owner (taking measures to understand the ownership and control structure, in the case of a company or trust) and verifying his identity.

- Obtaining information on the purpose and intended nature of the business relationship.

A firm must apply CDD when it:

- Establishes a business relationship
- Carries out an occasional transaction, of €15,000 or more
- Suspects money laundering or terrorist financing
- Doubts the veracity of identification or verification documents

Firms' information demands from customers need to be '**proportionate, appropriate and discriminating**', and to be able to be **justified to customers**.

Identification is not required for the following '**simplified transactions**':

- Life policies with an annual premium of no more than €1,000 or a single premium of no more than €2,500

- Pension schemes where members cannot assign their rights

- Pension contracts without a surrender value that cannot be used as loan collateral

As well as standard CDD there is:

- **Enhanced due diligence (EDD)** – for higher risk situations, customers not physically present when identities are verified, correspondent banking and **politically exposed persons (PEPs)**

- **Simplified due diligence (SDD)** – which may be applied to certain financial sector firms, companies listed on a regulated market, UK public authorities, child trust funds and certain pension funds and low risk products

## 6.9.2 Enhanced due diligence

**EDD** measures when a customer is not present include obtaining additional documents, data or information to those specified below, requiring certification by a financial services firm, and ensuring that an initial payment is from a bank account in the customer's name.

The category '**politically exposed persons**' **(PEPs)** comprises higher-ranking **non-UK** public officials, members of parliaments other than the UK Parliament, and such persons' immediate families and close associates. Prominent PEPs can pose a higher risk because their position may make them vulnerable to corruption. Senior management approval (from an immediate superior) should be sought for establishing a business relationship with such a customer and adequate measures should be taken to establish sources of wealth and of funds.

## 6.9.3 Simplified due diligence

**SDD** means not having to apply CDD measures. In practice, this means not having to identify the customer, or to verify the customer's identity, or, where relevant, that of a beneficial owner, nor having to obtain information on the purpose or intended nature of the business relationship.

## 6.9.4 Evidence of identity

How much identity information to ask for in the course of CDD, and what to verify, are matters **for the judgement of the firm**, based on its **assessment of risk**.

**Documents** offering evidence of identity are seen in the JMLSG Guidance Notes as forming the following broad hierarchy according to who has issued them, in the following order:

- Government departments or a court
- Other public sector bodies
- Regulated financial services firms
- Other firms subject to MLR 2007 or equivalent legislation
- Other organisations

For **private individuals**, the firm should obtain full name, residential address and date of birth of the personal customer. Verification of the information obtained should be based either on a document or documents provided by the customer, or electronically by the firm, or by a combination of both. Where business is conducted face-to-face, firms should request the original documents. Customers should be discouraged from sending original valuable documents by post.

Firms should therefore obtain the following in relation to **corporate clients**: full name, registered number, registered office in country of incorporation, and business address.

The following should also be obtained for private companies:

- Names of all directors (or equivalent)
- Names of beneficial owners holding over 25%

The firm should verify the identity of the corporate entity from:

- A search of the relevant company registry, or
- Confirmation of the company's listing on a regulated market, or
- A copy of the company's Certificate of Incorporation

## 6.9.5 Ongoing monitoring

As an obligation separate from CDD, firms must conduct ongoing **monitoring of the business relationship**, even where SDD applies. Ongoing monitoring of a business relationship includes scrutiny of transactions undertaken including, where necessary, sources of funds.

**CDD** and **monitoring** is intended to make it more difficult for the financial services industry to be used for money laundering or terrorist financing, but also helps firms guard against fraud, including impersonation fraud.

### 6.9.6 Reporting of suspicious transactions

All institutions must appoint an 'appropriate person' as the MLRO, who has the following functions.

- To receive reports of transactions giving rise to knowledge or suspicion of money laundering activities from employees of the institution

- To determine whether the report of a suspicious transaction from the employee, considered together with all other relevant information, does actually give rise to knowledge or suspicion of money laundering

- If, after consideration, he knows or suspects that money laundering is taking place, to report those suspicions to the appropriate law enforcement agency: the National Crime Agency (NCA)

For the purpose of each individual employee, making a report made to the MLRO concerning a transaction means that the employee has fulfilled his statutory obligations and will have **no criminal liability** in relation to any money laundering offence in respect of the reported transaction.

## 6.10 Terrorism

### 6.10.1 Terrorist activities

Acts of terrorism committed since 2001 have led to an increase in international efforts to locate and cut off funding for terrorists and their organisations.

There is a considerable overlap between the movement of terrorist funds and the laundering of criminal assets. Terrorist groups are also known to have well-established links with organised criminal activity. However, there are two major differences between terrorist and criminal funds.

- Often only small amounts are required to commit a terrorist atrocity, therefore increasing the difficulty of tracking the funds.

- Whereas money laundering relates to the proceeds of crime, terrorists can be funded from legitimately obtained income.

The **Terrorism Act 2000 (TA 2000)** defines **terrorism** in the UK as the use or threat of action wherever it occurs, designed to influence a government or to intimidate the public for the purpose of advancing a political, religious or ideological cause where the action:

- Involves serious violence against a person, or
- Involves serious damage to property, or
- Endangers a person's life, or
- Creates a serious risk to the health or safety of the public, or
- Is designed seriously to interfere with, or seriously to disrupt an electronic system, e.g. a computer virus

### 6.10.2 Offences

TA 2000 sets out the following terrorist offences.

- **Fund raising**, which covers inviting another to provide money or other property to fund terrorism

- **Use and possession**, which covers using money or other property for the purposes of terrorism

- **Funding arrangements**, which covers involvement in funding arrangements as a result of which money or other property is made available for terrorism

- **Money laundering**, which covers any arrangement which facilitates the retention or control by any person of terrorist property by means of concealment, removal from the jurisdiction, transfer to nominees or in any other way

An offence will be committed if the action or possession of terrorist funds occurs in the UK. It will also be an offence if the action or possession occurs outside the UK but would have constituted an offence in the UK if it had occurred here.

### 6.10.3 Terrorist property

**Terrorist property** is defined as money or other property which is likely to be used for the purposes of terrorism, proceeds of the commission of acts of terrorism and proceeds of acts carried out for the purposes of terrorism.

### 6.10.4 Preventative measures

Although **MLR 2007** focuses on firms' obligations in relation to the prevention of money laundering, **POCA 2000** updated and reformed the obligation to report to cover involvement with any criminal property, and the **TA 2000** extended this to cover terrorist property.

The JMLSG Guidance states that the risk of terrorist funding entering the financial system can be reduced if firms apply satisfactory money laundering strategies and, in particular, **know your customer** procedures. Firms should assess which **countries** carry the highest risks and should conduct careful scrutiny of transactions from countries known to be a source of terrorist financing.

For some countries, public information about known or suspected terrorists is available. For example, terrorist names are listed on the US Treasury website.

### 6.10.5 Sanctions and the Consolidated List

There is no single Act of Parliament that sets out the **UK financial sanctions regime**. The regime reflects the requirements of various UN Security Council resolutions, and is implemented by way of EU Regulations and UK Statutory Instruments. There are also EU investment ban and trade sanctions regimes that apply in the UK.

**Sanctions** can take the form of any of a range of restrictive or coercive measures against selected countries, organisations and individuals. They can include arms embargoes, travel bans, asset freezes, reduced diplomatic links, withdrawal of aid, trade embargoes, and military, sporting and other restrictions. Here we are concerned with financial sanctions, although financial firms need also to keep aware of asset freezes and trade embargoes. The JMLSG gives guidance to the financial services sector on implementing financial sanctions.

A **Consolidated List** of all targets to whom financial sanctions apply is maintained by HM Treasury, and includes all individuals and entities that are subject to financial sanctions in the UK. Each financial sanctions order is set out in a statutory instrument and/or European Community Regulation.

This list can be found at: www.hm-treasury.gov.uk/financialsanctions. HM Treasury directions can be found on the web sites of HM Treasury and JMLSG (www.jmlsg.org.uk). The obligations under the UK financial sanctions regime apply to all firms, and not just to banks.

It is generally a criminal offence directly or indirectly to make funds or economic resources available to or for the benefit of targets on the Consolidated List, or to deal with targets' funds or resources, unless a licence is obtained from HM Treasury.

HM Treasury (HMT) is responsible for implementing, administering and enforcing compliance with UK financial sanctions. In 2007, HMT set up a dedicated **Asset Freezing Unit**, designed to increase the expertise and operational focus that the Government can bring to bear on asset freezing. **Firms must inform HMT's Asset Freezing Unit** as soon as practicable where it has identified an actual match with a person or entity on the HMT list, or where it knows or suspects that a customer or a person with whom the firm has had business dealings has committed a breach, and supply any information that would facilitate compliance.

In line with SYSC, firms should have **proportionate systems and controls** in place to reduce the risk of a breach of UK financial sanctions occurring. Some firms, for example large firms with millions of customers or firms which process many millions of transactions every day, will use automated screening systems. Other firms with smaller numbers of customers and transactions may achieve compliance through other processes.

### 6.10.6 Duty to report terrorism

A **duty to report** occurs where a person believes or suspects that another person has committed a terrorist offence and where the belief or suspicion has arisen in the course of a trade, profession, business or employment.

An individual commits an offence of failing to report if he does not disclose the suspicion and the information on which it is based to a constable (i.e. the police) as soon as is reasonably practicable.

The following are possible defences to the offence of the failure to report.

- The firm has an established procedure for making disclosures, and the individual properly disclosed the matters in accordance with this procedure.

- The person had a reasonable excuse for not making the disclosure.

A person guilty of failing to report will face a **maximum penalty** of **six months in jail** and/or **£5,000 fine** in the **Magistrates Court** and **five years in jail** and/or an **unlimited fine** in the **Crown Court**.

## 6.11 Failure to disclose: regulated sector (s21A Terrorism Act 2000)

In addition to the offences in POCA 2002, there is specific UK legislation relating to terrorism. The main legislation is the **Terrorism Act 2000** which is supplemented by the **Anti-Terrorism Crime and Security Act 2001** and the **Terrorism Act 2000 and Proceeds of Crime Act 2000 (Amendment Regulations) 2007**.

**Offence**

Under s21A TA 2000 (as amended), it is an offence for those working in the **regulated sector** to fail to report (as soon as practicable) knowledge, suspicion or reasonable grounds for suspicion of offences or attempted offences relating to the following.

- Terrorist fund raising
- Use and possession of funds for terrorism
- Arrangements facilitating the retention or control of terrorist property

Thus, as with POCA 2002, there is an objective test for reporting. Reports should be made to the police or MLRO as soon as practicable.

**Defences**

There is a **defence** where person had a **reasonable excuse** for not making such a disclosure, and also where a professional adviser (i.e. a lawyer, accountant or auditor) receives the information in privileged circumstances.

**Penalty**

The offence is punishable (as in POCA 2002) with a maximum of **five years' imprisonment and/or an unlimited fine**, or 6 months' imprisonment and a fine of £5,000 in the Magistrates' Court.

**Protected disclosures**

There is clearly a concern that where a disclosure is made in accordance with the above requirements the client may claim this is a breach of client confidentiality. However, the rules state that where disclosures are made in accordance with the reporting rules there will not be a breach of client confidentiality.

## 6.12 Counter-Terrorism Act 2008

### 6.12.1 Overview

The **Counter-Terrorism Act 2008 (CTA 2008)** provides additional tools in the range of legislation addressing the risks of money laundering, terrorist financing and the proliferation of nuclear, biological, biological or chemical weapons.

### 6.12.2 Directions

Schedule 7 of CTA 2008 gives powers to the Treasury to issue **directions** to **firms in the financial sector**, which may relate to:

- Customer due diligence
- Ongoing monitoring
- Systematic reporting
- Limiting or ceasing business

The requirements to carry out CDD and ongoing monitoring build on similar obligations under MLR 2007. The requirements for **systematic reporting** and **limiting or ceasing business** are introduced by CTA 2008.

A Treasury direction under CTA 2008 must relate to a **non-EEA country**. A direction may be given only if the Financial Action Task Force advises that measures be taken, **or** if the Treasury reasonably believes that production or facilitation of nuclear, radiological, biological or chemical weapons, or terrorist financing or ML activities are being carried on in the country, **and** that this poses a significant risk to UK national interests.

A direction may impose an obligation to carry out EDD, or to undertake **ongoing monitoring** of a business relationship, which may involve retention of documentation or scrutiny of transactions.

**Systematic reporting** of **prospective transactions** may be required. A firm may also be required not to enter into a specified transaction or business relationship (**limiting or ceasing business**).

### 6.12.3 Penalties

A failure to comply with a direction could lead to a **civil penalty** (fine) imposed by the FCA as the enforcement authority, or to **criminal prosecution** (carrying a prison term of up to two years and/or a fine) – but not both for the same failure. No civil penalty will be applied and no criminal offence is committed if the firm took all reasonable steps and exercised all due diligence.

## 6.13 Law on bribery

### 6.13.1 Bribery Act 2010

The **Bribery Act 2010 (BA 2010)** came into effect on **1 July 2011**. BA 2010 replaces existing anti-corruption legislation and introduces a new offence for commercial organisations of negligently failing to prevent bribery.

A commercial organisation will commit an offence if a person acting for it, or on its behalf, makes corrupt payments.

Organisations and individuals will face heavy **penalties** if prosecuted and convicted under BA 2010. Under BA 2010, the maximum jail term for bribery by an individual is 10 years. A company that is convicted of failing to prevent bribery is subject to an unlimited fine.

It will be a defence for a firm if it can demonstrate that it has '**adequate procedures**' to prevent such conduct by persons associated with it.

Only firms with a '**demonstrable business presence' in the UK** are subject to BA 2010, and a 'common sense approach' will be adopted in interpreting this. Having a UK subsidiary will not necessarily mean that the parent company is subject to BA 2010. The Serious Fraud Office (SFO) has expressed the opinion that a UK listing would mean that a company would fall under BA 2010.

The **FCA** will not have responsibility for enforcing the criminal offences in BA 2010 for authorised firms. Where the regulator finds evidence of criminal matters, it will refer them to the Serious Fraud Office, who are the UK lead agency for criminal prosecutions for corruption. However, authorised firms who fail to address corruption and bribery risks adequately remain liable to regulatory action by the FCA.

## 6.13.2 Bribery offences

There are four **main offences** under BA 2010:

- **Section 1: Active bribery** – Offering, promising or giving a bribe
- **Section 2: Passive bribery** – Requesting, agreeing to receive or accepting a bribe (passive bribery)
- **Section 6: Bribing a foreign public official** – A breach of this section may also breach s1 BA 2010, and prosecutors will need to decide which is the more appropriate offence for the case
- **Section 7: Failure of firms to prevent bribery** – Failure by a commercial organisation to prevent persons associated with it from bribing another person on its behalf

Note that, as well as a company's agents and consultants in overseas countries potentially being '**associated persons**' under BA 2010, a company's own employees are also associated persons, and so their actions could make a company criminally liable. Firms should take this into account in establishing their anti-bribery policy or code of conduct.

## 6.13.3 Adequate procedures as a defence

An organisation has a defence against the s7 offence (failure to prevent bribery) if it can prove that, despite a particular instance of bribery having occurred, the organisation had **adequate procedures** in place to prevent persons associated with the organisation from committing bribery.

**Associated persons** include anyone performing services for the commercial organisation, but suppliers of goods are not necessarily 'associated persons'. The legal relationship between a joint venture entity and its members does not automatically mean that they are associated: this would depend on the degree of control the joint venture has over a bribe paid by its employee or agent.

Under s9 BA 2010, the **Minister of Justice** is required to publish **Adequate Procedures Guidance** on the defence. After much discussion, the final Guidance was published on 30 March 2011, and is supplemented by a Quick Start Guide aimed at smaller businesses, which does not form part of the statutory guidance.

- The guidance seeks to reassure senior management of properly organised businesses that BA 2010 is not intended to bring the force of the criminal law to bear in relation to single instances isolated incident. The guidance seeks instead to assert the importance of the matter of bribery and to encourage effective procedures to be established.

- The guidance also seeks to define the circumstances in which bribery may or may not have been committed. For example, it makes clear that genuine client entertainment, for example at sporting events, would not be caught by the legislation.

### 6.13.4 Ministry of Justice Guidance: principles

The **Ministry of Justice's Guidance** sets out **six principles** to help firms, which can be summarised as follows.

- **1: Proportionate procedures.** Procedures should be proportionate to the risks faced by the organisation, with tailored procedures based on a **risk assessment**.

- **2: Top-level commitment.** Senior management in the organisation need to help create a **culture of integrity** with a **commitment to zero tolerance to bribery**.

- **3: Risk assessment.** The organisation's assessment of the risks it faces should be periodic, informed and documented.

- **4: Due diligence.** In alignment with the requirement for a **proportionate** and **risk-based** approach, the extent of due diligence for different relationships will vary greatly depending on the particular relationship and the associated risks.

- **5: Communication (including training).** Internal communications should include a clear **statement of the policies and procedures** of the organisation, and of how concerns about instances of bribery can be raised.

- **6: Monitoring and review.** An organisation must be able to demonstrate that it regularly monitors and reviews the adequacy and suitability of policies and procedures and adapts them to reflect organisational changes.

# 7 Data protection

## 7.1 Data Protection Act 1998

Everyone is familiar nowadays with the fact that there is **data protection** legislation.

The **Data Protection Act 1998** replaced the earlier Data Protection Act 1984 and put into UK law the provisions of the **EU Data Protection Directive 1995**. The objective of the Data Protection Act is to **regulate the use of personal information**.

Some of the important features of the legislation are as follows.

- (a) Clarification of conditions under which data processing is lawful.

- (b) Right given to everyone to seek redress at court for breach of the Act.

- (c) Paper-based, microfilm and microfiche filing systems are encompassed by the Act, which covers information recorded in a 'relevant filing system' as well as in a computer system.

- (d) The case of **Durant v FSA (2003)**, dealt with the definition of a '**relevant filing system**'. This is a system that is so referenced or indexed as to enable the **data controller** to identify with reasonable certainty and speed relevant files and personal data without having to make a manual search for them. This means that some manual files will not be subject to the Data Protection Act.

## 7.2 Data protection obligations

### 7.2.1 General provisions

There are various obligations for any organisation that keeps personal information, as follows.

- The organisation must have a **data protection policy**.
- **Personal data** must have been **obtained lawfully and fairly** and shall not be processed unless at least one of the **Schedule 2 conditions** is met (see below).
- In the case of **sensitive personal data** (see below for what this includes), the data subject's explicit consent is normally required.
- Data must be **held and used** only for **lawful purposes**.
- Data should be used only **for the purposes for which it was originally obtained**.
- The data must not exceed what is **necessary** for the purpose for which it was obtained.
- Data must be **accurate** and must be **updated regularly**.
- Data must **not be kept longer than is necessary** for its lawful purpose.
- The person whose data is held is entitled to **access** to that information and has the right to correct it where appropriate. The **data subject** may be charged a **maximum fee of £10 for access** to their records, with a **maximum fee of £2** in the case of credit reference agency records. The person is also entitled to be told the source, purposes and recipients of the data. The 1998 Act requires **requests to be dealt with** 'promptly' and, in any event, within **40 days** of the request (along with any fee) being received.
- The data must be **protected** by appropriate technical and organisational measures against unauthorised or unlawful access and against accidental loss, destruction or damage.
- Unless the data is **exempt**, a data controller (such as a firm) processing personal data must **register** the holding of data with the **Public Register of Data Controllers** (the **Data Protection Register**), maintained by the **Information Commissioner**. Each register entry includes the name and address of the data controller, details of the data processed, the purpose and source for which it is held, and who has the right to see it.

  (As an *Exercise*, you could look up your firm, or your bank or another organisation, in the public register at www.informationcommissioner.gov.uk)
- Personal data must not be transferred outside the European Economic Area unless to a country or territory that ensures an adequate level of protection for the rights and freedoms of data subjects in respect of processing of personal data.

The **Schedule 2 conditions** (see above) are that:

(a) The data subject has given consent to the processing of the data

(b) The processing is necessary in connection with a contract entered into by the data subject

(c) The processing is necessary for the data controller to comply with legal obligations

(d) The processing is necessary for public functions exercised in the public interest

(e) The processing is necessary in pursuing the data controller's legitimate interests, provided that the processing does not prejudice the data subject's rights, freedoms or legal interests

### 7.2.2 Personal data

**Personal data** is any data relating to an identifiable living individual (the **data subject**).

There are **exemptions** for data controllers who only process personal data for:

- Staff administration (including payroll)

- Advertising, marketing and public relations (for their own business)
- Accounts and records of some not-for-profit organisations

There are also exemptions for:

- Processing personal data for personal, family or household affairs (including recreational purposes)
- Maintenance of a public register

**Sensitive personal data** which, as stated above, may normally only be processed with the explicit consent of the data subject, comprises the following.

- The racial or ethnic origin of the data subject
- Their political opinions
- Their religious beliefs or other beliefs of a similar nature
- Whether they are a member of a trade union
- Their physical or mental health or condition
- Their sexual life
- The commission or alleged commission by them of any offence
- Any proceedings for any offence committed or alleged to have been committed by him, the disposal of such proceedings or the sentence of any court in such proceedings

If collecting sensitive personal data from an individual, the person collecting it should:

- Make the individual aware of the intended purposes of collecting it
- Provide the individual with any details that are reasonably fair
- Obtain the explicit consent of the individual to process the data

## 7.3 Enforcement of the Data Protection Act

The working of the Data Protection Act is overseen by the **Information Commissioner**.

If the Information Commissioner considers that a data controller is in contravention of any of the data protection principles, the Commissioner can serve an **enforcement notice**. If the data controller fails to comply with the enforcement notice, he is committing an offence and could be subject to a **fine** of **£5,000**.

An offence is also committed if data is processed without prior notification.

An individual should take a **complaint** about a firm to the firm itself, in the first instance. If not satisfied with the outcome, the individual can approach the Information Commissioner with a **Request for Assessment**.

As mentioned earlier, the individual ultimately has the right to seek redress for a breach under the Act **through the courts**.

## 7.4 Record-keeping and DPA 1998

As a result of DPA 1998, regulated firms should be aware that **records** required to be obtained and kept under the regulators' rules (including money laundering identification requirements) must also comply with the requirements of DPA 1998.

# 8 Complaints and compensation

## 8.1 General points

Firms carrying on regulated activities may receive complaints from their clients about the way the firm has provided financial services or in respect of failure to provide a financial service. This could include allegations of financial loss whether or not such losses have actually yet occurred: for example, in the case of a mis-sold pension contract, future losses may be involved. A firm is required to have **written procedures** to ensure complaints from eligible complainants are properly handled.

A **complaint** is defined as 'any **oral or written** expression of dissatisfaction, whether justified or not, from, or on behalf of, a person about the provision of, or failure to provide, a financial service, which alleges that the complainant has suffered (or may suffer) financial loss, material distress or material inconvenience'.

Firms are permitted to **outsource complaints handling**, or to arrange a 'one-stop shop' for handling complaints with other firms.

## 8.2 Eligible complainants

The rules on how firms must handle complaints apply to **eligible complainants**. An eligible complainant is a person eligible to have a complaint considered under the Financial Ombudsman Service.

An eligible complainant must be:

- A **consumer**
- A smaller business – that is, with fewer than 10 employees and turnover or annual balance sheet not exceeding €2 million (called a '**micro-enterprise**')
- A **charity with annual income of less than £1 million**, or
- A **trust with net asset value of less than £1 million**

The rules do not apply to **authorised professional firms** (such as firms of accountants or solicitors) in respect of their **non-mainstream regulated activities**.

For **MiFID business**, the **complaints handling and record rules** apply to:

- Complaints from **retail clients**, but not those who are not retail clients
- Activities carried on from a **branch** of a UK firm in another EEA state, but not to activities carried on from a branch of an EEA firm in the UK
- If a firm takes responsibility for activities **outsourced** to a third party processor, the firm is responsible for dealing with complaints about those activities

## 8.3 Consumer awareness rule

To aid **consumer awareness** of the complaints protection offered, firms must:

- Publish a **summary** of their internal processes for dealing with complaints promptly and fairly.
- Refer eligible customers in writing to this summary at, or immediately after, the point of sale.
- Provide the summary on request, or when acknowledging a complaint.

## 8.4 Complaints handling

Firms, and UK firms' branches in the EEA, must establish procedures for the reasonable handling of complaints which

- Are effective and transparent
- Allow complaints to be made by any reasonable means (which might include email messages, or telephone calls, for example)
- Recognise complaints as requiring resolution

In respect of non-MiFID business, firms must seek to identify the root causes of complaints, and any **recurring or systemic problems** revealed by complaints. For MiFID business, the requirement is that firms must use complaints information to detect and minimise risk of '**compliance failures**'.

There is an expectation that firms should maintain standards of ethics and professional integrity in their handling of complaints:

- Having regard to the regulators' **Principle for Businesses 6** (*Customers' Interests*), which requires that firms **treat customers fairly**, firms should consider acting on their own initiative in respect of customers who may have been disadvantaged but have not complained.
- This is an example of how, in line with its emphasis on 'principles-based regulation', the regulator expects firms to adopt an **ethical stance** and to consider themselves how to apply the Principles for Businesses.

## 8.5 Complaints resolution

For all complaints received, the firm must:

- Investigate the complaint competently, diligently and impartially
- Assess fairly, consistently and promptly:
  - Whether the complaint should be upheld
  - What remedial action and/or redress may be appropriate
  - Whether another respondent may be responsible for the matter (in which case, by the complaints forwarding rule, the complaint may be forwarded to that other firm, promptly and with notification of the reasons to the client)
- Offer any redress or remedial action
- Explain the firm's assessment of the complaint to the client, its decision, including any offer of redress or remedial action made – in a fair, clear and not misleading way

### Factors relevant to assessing a complaint

- All the available evidence and circumstances
- Similarities with other complaints
- Guidance from the FCA, FOS or other regulators

The firm should aim to resolve complaints as early as possible, minimising the number of unresolved complaints referred to the FOS – with whom the firm must cooperate fully, complying promptly with any settlements or awards.

## 8.6 Complaints resolved the next day

Complaints **time limit, forwarding and reporting rules** do not apply to complaints which are **resolved by the next business day** after the complaint is made.

## 8.7 Time limit rules

**On receiving a complaint**, the firm must:

- Send to the complainant a prompt written acknowledgement (no specific time limit is stated) providing 'early reassurance' that it has received the complaint and is dealing with it, and

- Ensure the complainant in kept informed of progress on the complaint's resolution thereafter.

By the end of **eight weeks** after receiving a complaint which remains unresolved, the firm must send:

- A final response, or

- A holding response, which explains why a final response cannot be made and gives the expected time it will be provided, informs the complainant of his right to complain directly to the FOS if he is not satisfied with the delay, and encloses a copy of the FOS explanatory leaflet.

The regulator expects that, **within eight weeks of their receipt**, almost all complaints will have been **substantively addressed**.

## 8.8 Time barring

Complaints received outside the FOS **time limits** (see below) may be rejected without considering their merits in a final response, but this response should state that the FOS may waive this requirement in exceptional circumstances.

## 8.9 Complaints record-keeping

**Records** of complaints and of the measures taken for their resolution must be retained for:

- **Five years**, for MiFID business
- **Three years**, for other complaints

after the date the complaint was received.

## 8.10 Complaints reporting

Firms must provide a complete **report to the regulator** on complaints received, **twice a year**. There is a standard format for the report, which must show, for the reporting period:

- Complaints broken down into categories and generic product types

- Numbers of complaints closed by the firm: within four weeks of receipt; within four to eight weeks; and more than eight weeks from receipt

- Numbers of complaints: upheld; known to have been referred to and accepted by the FOS; outstanding at the beginning of reporting period; outstanding at the end of the reporting period

- Total amount of redress paid in respect of complaints

## 8.11 The Financial Ombudsman Service

A **complainant** must first go to the authorised firm against which the complaint is being made. If the authorised firm does not resolve the complaint to his satisfaction, the complainant may refer it to the **Financial Ombudsman Service (FOS)**.

The FOS offers an informal method of independent adjudication of disputes between a firm and its customer, which is relatively cheap compared with the alternative of taking action through the Courts.

## 8.12 Powers of the FOS

The FOS is a body set up by statute and, while its Board is appointed by the FCA, it is **independent** from the regulator and authorised firms. The FOS is, however, accountable to the FCA and is required to make an annual report to the regulator on its activities. The Board is all non-executive – and so, they have no involvement with individual complaints.

- The FOS can consider a complaint against an authorised firm for an act or omission in carrying out any of the firm's regulated activities together with any ancillary activities that firm does. This is known as the **Compulsory Jurisdiction** of the FOS.

- In addition to the Compulsory Jurisdiction, the FOS can consider a complaint under its **'Voluntary Jurisdiction'**. Firms or businesses can choose to submit to the voluntary jurisdiction of the FOS by entering into a contract with the FOS. This is available, for example, to unauthorised firms, and can cover activities such as credit and debit card transactions and ancillary activities carried on by that voluntary participant where they are not regulated activities.

- A further **Consumer Credit Jurisdiction** applies under the Consumer Credit Act 2006, which gives to the FOS powers to resolve certain disputes regarding loans against holders of licences issued by the Office of Fair Trading under the Consumer Credit Act 1974.

## 8.13 Eligible complainants

Only **eligible complainants** who have been customers of authorised firms or of firms which have voluntarily agreed to abide by the FOS rules may use the FOS. (The scope of what is meant by 'eligible complainants' was explained **earlier in this section of the Chapter**.)

Where an eligible complainant refers a matter to the Ombudsman, a firm has no definitive right to block the matter being referred, but may dispute the eligibility of the complaint or the complainant. In such circumstances, the Ombudsman will seek representations from the parties. The Ombudsman may investigate the merits of the case and may also convene a hearing if necessary.

## 8.14 FOS time limits

The following **time limits** apply to taking a complaint to the FOS.

- When **six months** have passed since the firm sent the consumer a final response (which has to mention the six-month time limit)

- When more than **six years** have passed **since the event** complained about, **or**

- More than **three years** since the person became aware of or could reasonably be expected to have become **aware** of the problem

After these time limits have expired, the firm complained about can choose to object to the Ombudsman looking at the complaint on the grounds that it is 'time-barred'.

## 8.15 Outcome of FOS findings

Where a complaint is determined in favour of the complainant, the Ombudsman's determination may include one or more of the following.

- A **money award** against the respondent
- An **interest award** against the respondent
- A **costs award** against the respondent

- A **direction** to the respondent

The Ombudsman may give a **direction** to the firm to take just and appropriate steps to remedy the position including to pay a money award of up to a **maximum of £150,000** plus reasonable costs (although awards of costs are not common). This figure will normally represent the financial loss the eligible complainant has suffered but can also cover any pain and suffering, damage to their reputation and any distress or inconvenience caused. If the Ombudsman considers that a sum greater than the specified maximum would be fair, he can recommend that the firm pays the balance, although he cannot force the firm to pay this excess.

An **interest award** may provide for interest from a specified date to be added to the money award.

Once the Ombudsman has given a decision, the complainant may decide whether to accept or reject that decision.

- If the complainant accepts the Ombudsman's decision, the authorised firm is bound by it
- If the complainant rejects the decision, they can pursue the matter further through the Courts

## 8.16 Claims management services

There are companies that offer the service of handling certain types of claims for compensation relating to financial services, for example in respect of mis-sold payment protection insurance or unfair bank charges.

Any business that handles such claims must be authorised by the **Claims Management Regulator**, unless they are covered by an exemption. There are exemptions for certain groups such as solicitors and advice agencies.

## 8.17 The Financial Services Compensation Scheme

The **Financial Services Compensation Scheme (FSCS)** is set up under FSMA 2000. The FSCS is designed to compensate **eligible claimants** where a relevant firm is unable or likely to be unable to meet claims against it. Generally speaking, therefore, the scheme will apply where the firm is **insolvent or bankrupt**. The FSCS is part of the 'toolkit' the FCA will use to meet its statutory objectives.

The compensation scheme is independent, but accountable, to the FCA and HM Treasury for its operations and works in partnership with the regulator in delivering the FCA's objectives, particularly that of consumer protection. The FSCS is funded by **levies on authorised firms**.

In the case of bank defaults during the **2008 financial crisis**, the FSCS **borrowed** funds through separate short-term facilities from the Bank of England and from HM Treasury. By 16 December 2008, the total amount of the FSCS's borrowings had reached £19.7 billion, representing amounts to fund deposit book transfers and compensation costs relating to Bradford & Bingley plc, Heritable Bank plc and Kaupthing Singer & Friedlander Limited, Landsbanki 'Icesave' and London Scottish Bank plc.

The legal framework of the FSCS was strengthened by the **Banking Act 2009**, which received royal assent in February 2009. This Act made permanent the **Special Resolution Regime (SRR)**, in order to deal with crises in the banking system, protect depositors and maintain financial stability.

Consumer awareness of the FSCS is promoted by a rule requiring firms to **provide information** on the existence of the **FSCS** and on the level of **protection** it offers to depositors, as well as proactively informing customers of any **additional trading names** under which the firm operates.

## 8.18 Entitlement to compensation

To be entitled to compensation from the scheme, a person must:

1. Be an **eligible claimant**. This covers most individuals and small businesses. Broadly, an eligible claimant is defined as a claimant who is **not**:

- A director of the insolvent firm or someone who contributed to the default

- A large company or large partnership/mutual association. What is meant by a large company and partnership will depend on rules established under the UK Companies Acts, which are amended from time to time

- An authorised firm, unless they are a sole trader/small business and the claim arises out of a regulated activity of which they have no experience, i.e. do not have permission to carry out

- An overseas financial services institution, supranational body, government and local authority

2. Have a '**protected claim**'. This means certain types of claims in respect of deposits and investment business. Protected investment business means **designated investment business**, the activities of the manager/trustee of an authorised unit trust and the activities of the authorised corporate director/depository of an ICVC. These activities must be carried on either from an establishment in the UK or in an EEA State by a UK firm which is passporting their services there.

3. Be claiming against a '**relevant person**' who is **in default**. A relevant person means:

- An authorised firm, except an EEA firm passporting into the UK (customers who lose money as a result of default by an EEA firm must normally seek compensation from the firm's Home State system, unless the firm has **top-up cover** provided by the FSCS in addition to, or in the absence of, compensation provided by the Home State)

- An appointed representative of the above

4. Make the claim within the relevant **time limits** (normally six years from when the claim arose)

The scheme will normally award financial compensation in cash. The FSCS may require the eligible claimant to assign any legal rights to them in order to receive compensation as they see fit.

## 8.19 Compensation limits

Maximum compensation levels for failures of firms occurring since 31 December 2010 are shown in the Table below. The limits are per person and per claim, and not per account or contract held.

| | Compensation limits |
|---|---|
| **Protected investments and home finance** | £50,000 (i.e. 100% of the first £50,000) |
| **Protected deposits** | £85,000 (i.e. 100% of the first £85,000) (This is the sterling equivalent of the €100,000 limit for deposits applying across the EEA.) |
| **Long-term insurance policies** | 90% of the claim (no upper limit) |
| **General insurance** | 100% for compulsory insurance; in other cases, 90% of the claim |

The **Deposit Guarantee Schemes Directive (DGSD)** requires payout of compensation within 20 days. The FCA aligns its rules with that requirement but expects that payout will be faster, with a target of seven days.

## 8.20 Consumer redress power

In October 2010, a new **consumer redress power** of the regulator came into effect, as provided for in the **Financial Services Act 2010**. It is envisaged that this power would be used in cases when there is evidence of **widespread or regular failings that have caused consumer detriment**. This is a rule making power, and so the regulator must undertake cost-benefit analysis and consult each time it wants to establish a redress scheme.

A **consumer redress scheme** is a set of rules under which a firm is required to take one or more of the following steps:

- Investigate whether, on or after a specific date, it has failed to comply with particular requirements that are applicable to an activity it has been carrying on

- Determine whether the failure has caused (or may cause) loss or damage to consumers

- Determine what the redress should be in respect of the failure, and

- Make the redress to the consumers

The **trigger** for the regulator making a consumer redress scheme is set out in s404(1) of FSMA 2000 and it provides that the power can be used if it appears to the regulator that:

- There may have been a **widespread or regular failure** by relevant firms to comply with requirements applicable to the carrying on by them of any activity

- As a result, consumers have suffered (or may suffer) loss or damage in respect of which, if they brought legal proceedings, **a remedy or relief would be available** in the proceedings, and

- It is **desirable** to make rules for the purpose of securing that redress is made to consumers in respect of the failure, having regard to the other ways in which consumers may obtain redress

The requirements that can be included in a consumer redress scheme include both **regulatory rules** and the **general law** (eg the tort of negligence, or the Unfair Terms in Consumer Contracts Regulations 1999).

Consumer redress schemes cannot be used to require redress in relation to those failures in respect of which a consumer would not have a **right of action in court**. Therefore, such a scheme could not be used to require redress for breaches of the Principles for Business because, as we saw in Chapter 1, breaches of **Principles** (as opposed to regulatory **rules**) do not give rise to a right of action by private persons under s138D FSMA 2000.

## 8.21 Super-complaints and mass detriment references

The **Financial Services Act 2012** introduced two new mechanisms by which potentially significant matters can be brought to the attention of the FCA.

- Certain designated consumer bodies can make what are known as **'super-complaints'**. The aim is to provide consumer bodies with a way of raising competition and consumer issues with the FCA. The Treasury will designate which organisations can make super-complaints.

  As set out in the amended FSMA 2000 (s234C), a super-complaint is a complaint that a feature or combination of features of the UK financial services industry is, or appears to be, significantly damaging the interests of consumers and should therefore be investigated. Super-complaints must relate to the interests of consumers generally or to those of a specific class or classes of consumer.

- Regulated firms and the Financial Ombudsman Service (FOS) can bring **mass detriment references** to the attention of the FCA.

  This type of reference (under s234D FSMA 2000) is one alleging that a failure by a regulated firm is or appears to be giving rise to consumer detriment. The 'failure' may involve non-compliance with regulatory requirements such that consumers have suffered losses or damage for which they could sue in a court; or it may involve actions that would be likely to result in awards by the FOS.

The FCA will look into the issues raised in a super-complaint or mass detriment reference and must publish a response **within 90 days**, setting out how it has dealt with it and whether it has decided to take any action.

## 8.22 Whistle blowing

Part of the regulatory Handbooks relating to Senior Management Arrangements, Systems and Controls covers procedures relating to '**whistle blowing**'.

The rules and guidance serve:

- To remind firms that there is legislation covering whistle blowing which applies to authorised firms **(Public Interest Disclosure Act 1998 (PIDA))**

- To encourage firms to adopt and communicate procedures for employees to raise concerns about the risk management arrangements of the firm

Whistle blowing is the process whereby a worker seeks to make a **protected disclosure** to a regulator or law enforcement agency outside the firm, in good faith, of information which tends to show that one or more of the following activities is, or is likely, to be committed or is being deliberately concealed by their employer.

- A criminal offence
- A failure to comply with a legal obligation
- A miscarriage of justice
- A breach of health and safety rules
- Damage to the environment

A firm cannot include a clause in the employee's contract preventing the employee from making such a disclosure, i.e. from 'blowing the whistle' on their employer's practices. The rules apply even if the activity listed above occurs outside the UK.

In addition, if the firm or member of staff of an authorised firm were to discriminate against an employee who made a disclosure in any way, the regulators would regard this as a serious matter. In particular, the regulators could question the firm's **'suitability'** under **Threshold Condition 5** and the individual's **fitness and propriety**. In serious cases, the regulator could withdraw the firm's authorisation and an individual's approval.

# Key chapter points

- Specified regulated activities relating to specified investments are covered by FSMA 2000. The regulated activity must be carried on 'by way of business' for regulation to apply.

- Those exempt from authorisation include appointed representatives and, in respect of non-mainstream activities, members designated professional bodies.

- Those carrying out a controlled function need to meet a 'fit and proper' test to be approved persons. This test covers honesty, integrity and reputation; competence and capability; and financial soundness. Controlled functions include exerting significant influence on the firm, and dealing with customers or their property.

- A firm is responsible for ensuring that there is appropriate training for employees and that employees remain competent.

- Minimum periods are set down for retaining records (five years for MiFID business) and there are requirements on reporting executions of trades, complaints and persistency, as well as on periodic reporting.

- Money laundering has three typical stages: placement, layering, integration. Those in the financial services industry must keep alert to possible offences relating to the proceeds of any crime.

- Joint Money Laundering Steering Group 2007 guidance requires firms to assess risks when implementing money laundering precautions. The 'Know Your Customer' principle implies that firms should, where appropriate, take steps to find out about the customer's circumstances and business.

- It is a criminal offence to assist laundering the proceeds of crime, to fail to report it satisfactorily or, in the regulated sector, to tip off someone who is involved in laundering the proceeds of crime.

- Fund raising, use and possession, funding arrangements and money laundering are offences under the Terrorism Act 2000. There is a duty to report suspected terrorism to the police.

- The Bribery Act 2010 makes it an offence to give a bribe or to accept a bribe. It is also an offence for a firm to fail to prevent bribery, and firms should have adequate procedures in place, which will constitute a defence against this offence.

- The Data Protection Act 1998 sets out eight Data Protection Principles with which data controllers must comply. The principles are designed to ensure that firms are open with individuals about the information they hold about them, and should be careful about passing it on.

- Firms must have transparent and effective complaints procedures, and must make customers aware of them. Firms must investigate complaints competently, diligently and impartially. Time limits apply to complaints processing, and the firm must report data on complaints to the regulator twice-yearly.

- If the firm does not resolve a customer's complaint to the customer's satisfaction, the Financial Ombudsman Service is available to adjudicate the dispute. The FOS has a Compulsory Jurisdiction (covering authorised firms' regulated activities) and a Voluntary Jurisdiction (for unregulated activities where a firm opts for it).

- The Financial Services Compensation Scheme – set up under FSMA 2000 – will pay out within the claim limits to eligible depositors and investors if a firm becomes insolvent.

- The FCA has a power, introduced to FSMA 2000 by the Financial Services Act 2010, to create special consumer redress schemes, in instances where there is evidence of widespread or regular failings that have caused consumer detriment.

- A 'whistle blowing' employee can make a protected disclosure to a regulator or law enforcement agency of wrongdoing.

# Chapter Quiz

1 Gerard publishes an investment tip sheet called 'Investment Directions'. Does this activity require regulatory authorisation? ................................................................................................................. (see para 1.4)

2 No person can carry on a regulated activity in the UK, nor purport to do so, unless they are either .......... or .......... *[Fill in the blanks]* ............................................................................................................(2.1)

3 What is the purpose of the Threshold Conditions? ............................................................................(2.4)

4 What are the important attributes a person must show to the regulator in order to become approved? ..........(3.1)

5 Outline the significant influence functions. ....................................................................................(3.3)

6 For how long must a firm keep records to demonstrate compliance with the training and competence rules for MiFID business? ..........................................................................................................................(4.9)

7 What does a persistency report show? .........................................................................................(5.4)

8 What are the three typical stages of money laundering? ...................................................................(6.1)

9 Explain what is meant by the 'Nominated Officer' in money laundering prevention provisions. ....................(6.6.2)

10 A direction by HM Treasury under the Counter-Terrorism Act 2008 must relate to a threat to the UK from within the EEA. True or False? ....................................................................................................................(6.12.2)

11 Outline the main offences under the Bribery Act 2010. .....................................................................(6.13.2)

12 Within what time period does the regulator expect almost all complaints to have been substantively addressed?

...............................................................................................................................................(8.7)

13 What is the maximum award the Financial Ombudsman Service may make? ..........................................(8.15)

14 What is the compensation limit for protected deposits? ....................................................................(8.19)

15 Who may initiate: (a) a super-complaint, and (b) a mass detriment reference? .....................................(8.21)

chapter

7

# Client relationships

7 **Apply the regulatory framework in practice for the consumer**

    7.1    **Apply** client relationships, regulated advice standards, and the adviser responsibilities in terms of these.

    7.2    **Monitor** and **review** client plans and circumstances.

8 **Understand the range of skills required when advising clients**

    8.1    **Examine** the range of skills required when advising clients.

# 1 Accepting customers for business

## 1.1 Conduct of Business Sourcebook (COBS)

Classifying clients into different types allows different regulatory rules to be applied to each type of client, who may therefore be afforded different degrees of protection under the regulatory system. The main corpus of rules affected by the categorisation of any particular client is that found in the regulators' **Conduct of Business Sourcebook (COBS)**, included within the regulatory Handbooks.

Before looking at how clients are categorised, we explain the activities to which COBS applies.

## 1.2 General application rule

The **general application rule** is that **COBS** applies to an authorised **firm** in respect of the following activities when carried out from one of its (or its **appointed representative's**) **UK** establishments.

- Accepting deposits
- Designated investment business
- Long-term life insurance business

Many rules (except the financial promotion rules) only apply when the firm is doing **designated investment business** with customers.

The term **'designated investment business'** has a narrower meaning than the concept of **'regulated activities'** by excluding activities relating to Lloyd's business, deposits, funeral plans, mortgages, pure protection policies and general insurance contracts. Following the implementation of MiFID, operating a **multilateral trading facility (MTF)** is designated investment business.

There are **modifications** to the general application rule. Only some of the COBS rules apply to **eligible counterparty business** which is MiFID or equivalent third country (that is, **non-EEA**) business. The term 'eligible counterparty' is explained later in this Chapter. The following COBS rules **do not** apply to such business.

- Conduct of business obligations, except 'Agent as client' and 'Reliance on others' rules
- Communicating with clients (including financial promotions rules)
- Rules on information about the firm and its services
- Client agreements
- Appropriateness rules (for non-advised sales)
- Best execution and client order handling
- Information about designated investments
- Reporting information to clients

## 1.3 Territorial scope provisions

The **territorial scope** of COBS is modified to ensure compatibility with European law: this is called the '**EEA territorial scope rule**'. One of the effects of the EEA territorial scope rule is to override the application of COBS to the overseas establishments of EEA firms in a number of cases, including circumstances covered by MiFID, the Distance Marketing Directive or the Electronic Commerce Directive. In some circumstances, the rules on financial promotions and other communications will apply to communications made by UK firms to persons located outside the United Kingdom and will not apply to communications made to persons inside the United Kingdom by EEA firms.

## 1.4 Communications by electronic media

Where a rule requires a notice to be delivered in writing, a firm may comply using **electronic media**. The COBS rules often specify that communication must be in a **durable medium**.

'Durable medium' means:

- Paper, or

- Any instrument (e.g., an email message) which enables the recipient to store information addressed personally to him in a way accessible for future reference for a period of time adequate for the purposes of the information and which allows the unchanged reproduction of the information stored. This will include the recipient's computer hard drive or other storage devices on which the electronic mail is stored, but not internet websites unless they fulfil the criteria in this definition.

Some communications are allowed to be delivered either in a durable medium or via a website, where the **website conditions** are satisfied.

The **website conditions** are specified as follows:

- The provision of the information in that medium must be appropriate to the context in which the business between the firm and the client is, or is to be, carried on (i.e. there is evidence that the client has regular access to the internet, such as the provision by the client of an e-mail address).

- The client must specifically consent to the provision of that information in that form.

- The client must be notified electronically of the address of the website, and the place on the website where the information may be accessed.

- The information must be up-to-date.

- The information must be accessible continuously by means of that website for such period of time as the client may reasonably need to inspect it.

## 1.5 Levels of protection for clients

Within any cost-effective regulatory system, protection provided ought to be **proportionate** to the need for protection. This is because there is not only a cost element to protection but also an inverse relationship with freedom. It is desirable that those who do not require high protection are given more freedom to trade without the restrictions that the rules inevitably bring.

The **size** and **financial awareness** of **clients** will determine the level of protection. As the size/knowledge increases, protection will decrease. A system of categorising clients can help determine that the level of protection is appropriate to the client.

While this might ideally be a continuous spectrum, gradually moving from full protection to no protection, in practical terms this is an impossibility and so there are discrete client categories.

## 1.6 Client categories

### 1.6.1 Overview

The terms used to classify clients has changed following the 2007 implementation of the European Markets in Financial Instruments Directive (**MiFID**) and the introduction of the new COBS.

Firms (unless they are providing only the special level of **basic advice** on a **stakeholder product**) are obliged to classify all clients who are undertaking **designated investment business,** before doing such business.

MiFID creates three client categories:

- **Eligible counterparties** – who are either *per se* or **elective** eligible counterparties
- **Professional clients** – who are either *per se* or **elective** professional clients
- **Retail clients**

As well as setting up criteria to classify clients into these categories, MiFID provides for clients to **change** their initial classification, on request.

A **customer** is a client who is not an eligible counterparty. The scheme of categorisation is summarised in the following diagram.

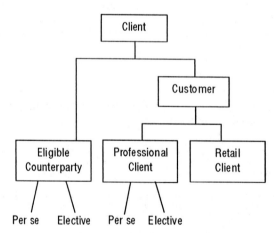

### 1.6.2 Clients

A **client** is a person to whom an authorised **firm** provides a service in the course of carrying on a **regulated activity** or, in the case of MiFID or equivalent third country business, a person to whom a firm provides an **ancillary service**.

### 1.6.3 Retail clients

**Retail clients** are defined as those clients who are not professional clients or eligible counterparties.

### 1.6.4 Professional clients

Some undertakings are automatically recognised as **professional clients**. Accordingly, these entities may be referred to as *per se* professional clients. (An **undertaking** is a company, partnership or unincorporated association.)

The following types of client are *per se* **professional clients**.

- Entities that **require authorisation or regulation** to operate in the financial markets, including: credit institutions, investment firms, other financial institutions, insurance companies, collective investment schemes and pension funds and their management companies, commodity and commodity derivatives dealers, 'local' derivatives dealing firms, and other institutional investors.

- In relation to **MiFID** or equivalent third country business, a **large undertaking** – meaning one that meets two of the following size requirements:

    - €20,000,000      Balance sheet total
    - €40,000,000      Net turnover
    - €2,000,000      Own funds

- In relation to business that is not **MiFID** or equivalent third country business, a **large undertaking** meeting **either** of the following requirements:

    - Called-up share capital or net assets of at least £5,000,000 or equivalent, or

    - Two of the three following size tests:

        - €12,500,000 balance sheet total
        - €25,000,000 net turnover
        - 250 average number of employees in the year

- Central banks, international institutions, and national and regional government bodies.

- Institutional investors whose main activity is to invest in financial instruments.

A firm may treat a retail client as an **elective professional client** if the following tests are met.

- **Qualitative test.** The firm must assess adequately the client's **expertise, experience** and **knowledge** and thereby gains reasonable assurance that, for the transactions or services envisaged, the client is capable of making his own investment decisions and understanding the risks involved.

- **Quantitative test.** In the case of **MiFID** or equivalent third country business, at least **two** of the following three criteria must apply.

    - The client has carried out at least ten 'significant' transactions per quarter on the relevant market, over the last four quarters

    - The client's portfolio, including cash deposits, exceeds €500,000

    - The client has knowledge of the transactions envisaged from at least one year's professional work in the financial sector

**Additionally**, for opting up to professional client status:

- The client must agree in writing to be treated as a professional client.

- The firm must give written warning of the protections and compensation rights which may be lost.

- The client must state in writing, separately from the contract, that it is aware of the consequences of losing protections.

The professional client is responsible for keeping the firm informed about changes (e.g. in portfolio size or company size) which could affect their categorisation.

COBS states that an elective professional client should not be presumed to have market knowledge and experience comparable to a *per se* professional client.

## 1.6.5 Eligible counterparties

In relation to MiFID (or equivalent third country business), a client can **only** be an **eligible counterparty** in relation to **eligible counterparty business**.

The following, and their non-EEA equivalents, are ***per se* eligible counterparties** (i.e. they are automatically recognised as eligible counterparties).

- Investment firms
- Credit institutions
- Insurance companies
- UCITS collective investment schemes, and their management companies
- Pension funds, and their management companies
- Other financial institutions authorised or regulated under the law of the EU or an EEA state
- Certain own-account commodity derivatives dealers and 'local' derivatives firms
- National governments
- Central banks
- Supranational organisations

A firm may treat an undertaking as an **elective eligible counterparty** if the client:

- Is a *per se* professional client (unless it is such by virtue of being an institutional investor), or

- Is an elective professional client and requests the categorisation, but only in respect of the transactions and services for which it counts as a professional client, and

- In the case of MiFID or equivalent third country business, provides 'express confirmation' of their agreement (which may be for a specific transaction or may be general) to be treated as an eligible counterparty.

If the prospective counterparty is established in another EEA state, for MiFID business the firm should defer to the status determined by the law of that other state.

## 1.7 Agent as client

One area that has proved complicated in the past is where a firm is dealing with an **agent**. For example, suppose that a solicitor is acting for his client and approaches a firm to sell bonds on his client's behalf. Clearly, it is important that the firm establish whether it owes duties to the solicitor or to the solicitor's client.

The agent is the client of the firm, unless an agreement in writing treats the other person as the client.

The relevant COBS rule applies to designated investment business and ancillary services. The rule states that the firm may treat the agent as its client if the agent is another authorised firm or an overseas financial services institution **or** if the agent is another person, provided that the arrangement is not to avoid duties which the firm would otherwise owe to the agent's clients.

An agreement may however be made, in writing, to treat the other person (in the above example, the solicitor's client) as the firm's client.

## 1.8 Providing a higher level of protection to clients

Firms must allow **professional clients** and **eligible counterparties** to re-categorise in order to get more protection. Such clients are themselves responsible for asking for higher protection if they deem themselves to be **unable** to assess properly or manage the risks involved.

Either on its own initiative or following a client request or written agreement:

- A *per se* eligible counterparty may be re-categorised as a professional client or retail client
- A *per se* professional client may be re-categorised as a retail client

The **higher level of protection** may be provided through re-categorisation:

- On a general basis
- Trade by trade
- In respect of specified rules
- In respect of particular services, transactions, transaction types or product types

The client should (of course) be notified of a re-categorisation.

Firms must have written internal policies and procedures to categorise clients.

## 1.9 Client agreements

If a firm carries on **designated investment business**, other than advising on investments, for a **new retail client,** the firm must enter into a **basic agreement** with the client. Thus, for example, there should be a client agreement when discretionary investment management services are provided. Although little guidance is given in the rules as to the contents, the agreement will set out the essential rights and obligations of the firm – the **terms of business**. The agreement must be in writing – on paper or other durable medium. For a **professional client**, there is no requirement for an agreement, although most firms will wish there to be one.

In good time, normally **before** the client is bound by any agreement relating to designated investment business or ancillary services, the firm must provide to the retail client – either in a durable medium or on a website, if the website conditions are satisfied:

- The terms of the agreement

- Information about **the firm and its services** (see below), including information on communications, conflicts of interest and authorised status

The agreement and information may be provided **immediately after** the client is bound by the agreement if the agreement was concluded using a means of distance communication (e.g. telephone).

Relevant material changes to the information provided must be notified to the client in **good time**.

A **record** of the client agreement should be kept for five years, or for the duration of the relationship with the client if longer. For pension transfers or opt-outs, or FSAVCs, the record should be kept indefinitely.

# 2 Financial promotions and communications

## 2.1 Introduction

A **financial promotion** is an **invitation** or **inducement** to **engage** in investment activity. The term therefore describes most forms and methods of marketing financial services. It covers traditional advertising, most website content, telephone sales campaigns and face-to-face meetings. The term is extended to cover **marketing communications** by MiFID.

The purpose of regulation in this area is to create a regime where the quality of financial promotions is scrutinised by an authorised firm who must then comply with lengthy rules to ensure that their promotions are **clear, fair and not misleading** (Principle 7) and that customers are treated **fairly** (Principle 6).

The **financial promotions rules** within COBS apply to a firm:

- Communicating with a client in relation to designated investment business

- **Communicating** or **approving** a **financial promotion** (with some exceptions in respect of: credit promotions, home purchase plans, home reversion schemes, non-investment insurance contracts and unregulated collective investment schemes)

Firms must also apply the rules to promotions issued by their **appointed representatives**.

## 2.2 FCA's financial promotions power

The FCA has a new **power** under the Financial Services Act 2012 (s137R FSMA 2000, as amended) **to ban misleading financial promotions**.

- The regulator can give a **direction** to firms requiring them immediately to withdraw or to modify promotions which it deems to be misleading, and to publish such decisions.

- The firm can make **representations** to the FCA to challenge the Authority's decision. The FCA may then decide to amend or revoke its decision, or it may confirm its original decision. After having given the firm the opportunity to challenge the decision, the FCA can publish: (1) Its direction, (2) A copy of the promotion, and (3) The regulator's reasons for banning it. The FCA may publish details even if it has decided to revoke its decision.

## 2.3 Territorial scope

For financial promotions, the **general application rule** applies. This indicates that the rules apply to a firm in respect of designated investment business carried out from an establishment maintained by the firm or its appointed representative in the UK. Additionally, in general the rules apply to firms carrying on business with a client in the UK from an establishment overseas.

The financial promotions rules also apply to:

- Promotions communicated to a person in the UK

- Cold (unsolicited) calling to someone outside the UK, if the call is from within the UK or is in respect of UK business

## 2.4 Fair, clear and not misleading

A firm must ensure that a communication or financial promotion is **fair, clear and not misleading**, and is **appropriate** and **proportionate** considering the means of communication and the information to be conveyed.

This rule applies to **communications** in relation to designated investment business other than a third party prospectus.

It applies to **financial promotions** approved by the firm, and to retail financial promotions communicated by the firm, but not to excluded communications, nor to third party prospectuses.

The **fair, clear and not misleading rule** is specifically interpreted in COBS as it applies to financial promotions in some aspects, as follows.

- If a product or service places a client's capital at risk, this should be made clear

- Any yield figure quoted should give a balanced impression of both short-term and long-term prospects for the investment

- Sufficient information must be provided to explain any complex charging arrangements, taking into account recipients' needs

- The regulator (FCA) should be named, and any non-regulated aspects made clear

- A fair, clear and not misleading impression should be given of the producer for any packaged product (a term explained later) or stakeholder products not produced by the firm

The British Bankers' Association / Building Societies Association **Code of Conduct for the Advertising of Interest Bearing Accounts** is also relevant in the case of financial promotions relating to deposits.

## 2.5 Identifying promotions as such

A firm must ensure that a **financial promotion** addressed to a **client** is clearly **identifiable as such**.

- This rule does not apply to a third party prospectus in respect of **MiFID** (or equivalent third country) business.

- There are also some exceptions in respect of **non-MiFID** business, including prospectus advertisements, image advertising, non-retail communications, deposits and pure protection long-term care insurance (LTCI) products.

## 2.6 Exceptions

As mentioned earlier, the **financial promotions rules** in COBS do **not apply** to promotions of qualifying credit, home purchase plans, home reversion schemes, non-investment insurance contracts, and certain unregulated collective investment schemes whose promotions firms may not communicate or approve.

Except in regard to disclosure of compensation arrangements, the COBS rules on communications (including financial promotions) do **not** apply when a firm communicates with an **eligible counterparty**.

The financial promotions rules also do **not** apply to incoming communications in relation to **MiFID business** of an investment firm **from another EEA state** that are, in its home state, regulated under MiFID.

## 2.7 Excluded communications

A firm may rely on one or more of the following aspects which make a communication into an **excluded communication** for the purposes of the rules.

- A financial promotion that would benefit from an exemption in the Financial Promotion Order (see below) if it were communicated by an unauthorised person, or which originates outside the UK and has no effect in the UK

- A financial promotion from outside the UK that would be exempt under articles 30, 31, 32 or 33 of the Financial Promotion Order (Overseas communicators) if the office from which the financial promotion is communicated were a separate unauthorised person

- A financial promotion that is subject to, or exempted from, the Takeover Code or to the requirements relating to takeovers or related operations in another EEA state

- A personal quotation or illustration form

- A **'one-off' financial promotion** that is not a cold call. The following conditions indicate that the promotion is a 'one-off', but they need not necessarily be present for a promotion to be considered as 'one-off'.

  (i)   The financial promotion is communicated only to one recipient or only to one group of recipients in the expectation that they would engage in any investment activity jointly

  (ii)  The identity of the product or service to which the financial promotion relates has been determined having regard to the particular circumstances of the recipient

  (iii) The financial promotion is not part of an organised marketing campaign

## 2.8 Financial Promotions Order

**Section 21** FSMA 2000 makes it criminal for someone to undertake a financial promotion, i.e. invite or induce another to engage in investment activity, unless they are either

- An authorised firm (i.e. issuing the financial promotion), or
- The content of the communication is **approved** by an authorised firm

**Conviction** under this section is **punishable** by two years' imprisonment and an unlimited fine in the Crown Court, or six months' imprisonment and a statutory maximum of £5,000 in the Magistrates' Court.

There are a number of exemptions from s21 set out in the **Financial Promotions Order**. The effect of being an **exemption** is that the promotion would **not** need to be issued or approved by an authorised firm. It would therefore not have to comply with the detailed financial promotion rules.

The main examples are as follows. (Other exemptions cover certain one-off and purely factual promotions.)

| Exemption | Comments |
|---|---|
| 1. Investment professional | A communication to an authorised or exempt person. |
| 2. Deposits and insurance | Very limited application of COBS. |
| 3. Certified high net worth individuals (FPO Article 48), and sophisticated investors (FPO Article 50(A)) | These exemptions apply only to certain types of investment, principally: **unlisted securities**, collective investment schemes whose underlying investments are unlisted securities, and options, futures and contracts for differences (CfDs) relating to unlisted securities. |
| | A firm may make a promotion, accompanied by a **prescribed warning**, for such securities to persons whom the firm reasonably believes is a **high net worth individual** and who has signed within the last 12 months a certificate of high net worth, for which there is a highly prescribed format. A high net worth individual is a person with a net income in the year prior to the certification of £100,000 or more, or net assets (excluding principal property) of £250,000 or more. |
| | A similar provision relates to those whom the firm believes are **sophisticated investors**. (The definition of a sophisticated investor was amended in 2014.) As for high net worth individuals, the promotion must be accompanied by a warning and the individual must have signed a prescribed certificate during the previous 12 months. |
| | A **sophisticated investor** is someone who: |
| | • Has been a member of a network or syndicate of business angels for at least the six months preceding the date of the certificate, or |
| | • Has made more than one investment in an unlisted company in the two years preceding, or |
| | • Has worked, in the two years preceding, in a professional capacity in the private equity sector, or in providing finance for SMEs, or |
| | • Has been, in the two years preceding that date, a director of a company with an annual turnover of at least £1 million |
| 4. Takeover Code | Promotions subject to the Takeover Code. |

## 2.9 Communicating with retail clients

### 2.9.1 General rule

The general rule on **communicating with retail clients** in relation to **designated investment business** states that firms must ensure that the information:

- Includes the **name of the firm** (which may be the **trading name** or **shortened name**, provided the firm is identifiable)

- Is accurate and does not emphasise potential benefits of investment without also giving a **fair and prominent indication of relevant risks**

- Is **sufficient** for and presented so as to be **likely to be understood** by the **average member** of the group to whom it is directed or by whom it is likely to be received

- Does not disguise, diminish or obscure important items, statements or warnings

In deciding whether and how to communicate to a target audience, the firm should **consider**: the nature of the product/business, risks, the client's commitment, the average recipient's information needs and the role of the information in the sales process.

The firm should consider whether omission of a relevant fact will result in information being **insufficient, unclear, unfair** or **misleading**.

## 2.9.2 Comparative information

Information comparing business / investments / persons must

- Present **comparisons** in a meaningful, fair and balanced way

- In relation to MiFID or equivalent third country business, specify **information sources**, key facts and assumptions

## 2.9.3 Tax treatment

If **tax treatment** is referred to, it should be stated prominently that the tax treatment depends on the individual circumstances of the client and may be subject to change in future. (One of a couple of exceptions to this rule is that it does not apply to deposits other than cash ISAs or CTFs.)

## 2.9.4 Consistency

The firm should ensure that information in a financial promotion is **consistent** with other information provided to the retail client. (**Deposits** are an exception to this rule.)

## 2.9.5 Promotion of collective investment schemes

There are restrictions on promoting **unregulated collective investment schemes (UCIS)** to retail clients.

A legislative order permits promotion of UCIS to:

- Certified high net worth individuals (HNW)
- Certified sophisticated investors

FCA rules allow UCIS to be marketed to certain categories of client:

- Category 1 – those who are already investors in UCIS (in the last 30 months)
- Category 2 – clients for whom UCIS are suitable
- Category 7 – professional clients and eligible counterparties
- Category 8 – experienced clients

The regulator has provided **guidance** that **traded life policy investments (TLPIs)** are high risk products that should not be promoted to the vast majority of retail investors in the UK. TLPIs invest in life insurance policies, typically of US citizens. Investors hope to benefit by buying the right to the insurance payouts upon the death of the original policyholder. Many TLPIs take the form of unregulated collective investment schemes (UCIS). Basically, a TLPI investor is betting on when a particular set of US citizens will die and, if these people live longer than anticipated, the investment may not function as expected. Many of these products have failed, causing loss for UK retail investors.

**Land banks** are another concern of the regulator in the area of collective investments. The FCA does not regulate the sale of land, but land banking may amount to a collective investment – something that does require regulatory authorisation. Some land banks have operated without authorisation, selling plots of land unlawfully, in the regulator's judgement, to UK consumers.

## 2.10 Financial promotions containing offers or invitations

A **direct offer financial promotion** is a form of financial promotion which enables investors to purchase investments directly 'off the page' without receiving further information.

A direct offer financial promotion to retail clients must contain whatever **disclosures** are relevant to that offer or invitation (as outlined earlier, such as information about the firm and its services, and costs and charges) and, for non-MiFID business, additional appropriate information about the relevant business and investments so that the client is reasonably able to understand their nature and risks, and consequently to take investment decisions on an informed basis. This information may be contained in a separate document to which the client must refer in responding to the offer or invitation. Alternatively, information disclosures may be omitted if the firm can demonstrate that the client referred to the required information before making or accepting the offer.

A firm may wish to include in a direct offer financial promotion a summary of **tax** consequences, and a statement that the recipient should seek a **personal recommendation** if he has any doubt about the suitability of the investments or services.

## 2.11 Unwritten promotions and cold calling

An **unwritten financial promotion** outside the firm's premises may only be initiated if the person communicating it:

- Does so at an appropriate time of day
- Identifies himself and his firm, and makes his purpose clear
- Clarifies if the client wants to continue or terminate the communication, and terminates it on request at any time
- If an appointment is arranged, gives a contact point to a client

Firms may only make **cold (unsolicited) calls** if:

- The recipient has an established client relationship with the firm, such that the recipient envisages receiving them, or
- The call is about a generally marketed packaged product (not based on a high volatility fund), or
- The call relates to controlled activities by an authorised person or exempt person, involving only readily realisable securities (not warrants)

Note that the rules on unwritten promotions and cold calling apply only to **retail clients**.

## 2.12 Financial promotions for the business of overseas persons

An 'overseas person' here means a firm carrying on regulated activities who does not do so within the UK.

Any financial promotion for the business of such an **overseas person** must:

- Make clear which firm has approved or communicated it
- Explain that rules for protection of retail clients do not apply
- Explain the extent and level of any available compensation scheme (or state that no scheme applies)
- Not be issued if the firm has any reason to doubt that the overseas person will deal with UK retail clients in an honest and reliable way

## 2.13 Promotions targeted at investment professionals

2012 guidance from the regulator states that promotions can be specifically **targeted at investment professionals**, but they must:

- Be effectively targeted through the publication or medium used

- Be fair, clear and not misleading

- Clearly state the target audience – reasonably prominently, and not in 'small print' at the foot of the advertisement

Authorised firms should use language appropriate to the promotion.

**Investment professionals** are defined as (broadly):

- Authorised persons
- Exempt persons (for the relevant controlled activity)
- Other persons who carry on the relevant controlled activity for business purposes
- Government, local authority or an international organisations, and
- Directors, officers or employees of any of the above, acting in that capacity

Investment professionals is a term used in the relevant legislation, which gives an exemption from the financial promotion restrictions. But these exemptions are usually only relevant for unauthorised firms or unregulated Collective Investment Schemes (CIS), and those in the FPO are not available for MiFID business.

## 2.14 Image advertising

**Image advertising** is a communication consisting **only** of one or more of:

- The name of the firm
- A logo or other image associated with the firm
- A contact point
- A reference to the types of regulated activities provided by the firm, or to its fees or commissions

**Image advertising: exempt from financial promotions rules**. The regulator has issued guidance in 2012. The treatment of image advertising varies depending on the type of product and therefore on which sourcebook applies. For example, image advertising for investment products is exempt from most detailed financial promotions rules, but it still needs to comply with the high-level 'fair, clear and not misleading' rule.

**Brand advertising** is something different. Brand advertising is advertising that focuses on the firm's brand, to raise awareness, but which may, for example, refer to and promote particular products and services.

## 2.15 Approving financial promotions

The rules in **SYSC** require that a firm which communicates with a client regarding designated investment business, or communicates or approves a financial promotion, puts in place **systems and controls** or **policies and procedures** in order to comply with the COBS rules.

As explained earlier in this Section of the Chapter, s21 FSMA 2000 prohibits an unauthorised person from communicating a financial promotion, unless either an exemption applies or the financial promotion is approved by an authorised firm.

Approval of a financial promotion by an **authorised firm** enables it to be communicated by an **unauthorised firm**.

A firm **approving** a financial promotion must confirm that it **complies** with the **financial promotion rules**. The firm must withdraw its approval, and notify anyone it knows to be relying on its approval, if it becomes aware that it no longer complies with the financial promotion rules.

A promotion made during a personal visit, telephone conversation or other interactive dialogue cannot be approved.

Approval given by the firm may be '**limited**', e.g. limited to communication to **professional clients** or **eligible counterparties**.

In communicating a financial promotion, a firm is permitted to **rely on another firm's confirmation of compliance** with the financial promotions rules. The firm must take reasonable care to ensure that the promotion is only communicated to types of recipients for whom it was intended.

## 2.16 Past, simulated past and future information

### 2.16.1 Introduction

Rules on **performance information** apply to information disseminated to retail clients, and to financial promotions. In the case of non-MiFID business, the rules do not apply to deposits generally nor to pure protection long-term care insurance (LTCI) contracts.

### 2.16.2 Past performance information

**Past performance information** must:

- Not normally be the **most prominent feature** of the communication (although it could be in a periodic statement for managed investments)

- Include appropriate information covering at least the **five preceding years**, or the whole period the investment/service has been offered/provided or the whole period the financial index has been established, if less than five years

- Be based on and must show complete **12-month periods**

- State the reference period and source of the information

- Contain a **prominent warning** that the figures refer to the past and that past performance is not a reliable indicator of future results

- If denominated in a foreign **currency**, state the currency clearly, with a warning that the return may increase or decrease as a result of currency fluctuations

- If based on gross performance, disclose the effect of **commissions**, fees or other charges

The above provisions are to be interpreted in a way that is '**appropriate and proportionate**' to the communication.

For a **packaged product** (except a unitised with-profits life policy or a stakeholder pension scheme), information should be given on:

- An **offer to bid** basis (which should be stated) for an actual return or comparison with other investments, or

- An **offer to offer**, **bid to bid** or **offer to bid** basis (which should be stated) if there is a comparison with an index or with movements in the price of units, or

- A **single pricing** basis with allowance for charges.

### 2.16.3 Simulated past performance information

**Simulated past performance information** must

- Relate to an investment or a financial index

- Be based on actual past performance of investments/indices which are the same as, or underlie, the investment concerned
- Contain a **prominent warning** that figures refer to simulated past performance and that past performance is not a reliable indicator of future performance

## 2.16.4 Future performance information

**Future performance information** must:

- **Not** be based on nor refer to simulated past performance
- Be based on reasonable assumptions supported by objective data
- If based on gross performance, disclose the effect of **commissions**, fees or other charges
- Contain a **prominent warning** that such forecasts are not a reliable indicator of future performance
- Only be provided if **objective data** can be obtained

## 2.17 Record keeping requirements relating to financial promotions

A firm must make an adequate record of any financial promotion it communicates or approves. The record must be retained for:

- indefinitely for a pension transfer, opt-out or FSAVC
- Six years for a life policy, occupational pension scheme, SSAS, personal pension scheme or stakeholder scheme
- Five years for MiFID or equivalent third country business
- Three years for other cases

## 2.18 Distance marketing communications

### 2.18.1 Overview

The EU **Distance Marketing Directive (DMD)** covers the distance marketing of financial services and has been enacted in the UK via the **Financial Services (Distance Marketing) Regulations 2004**.

**COBS** Chapter 5 on *Distance communications* includes provisions conforming to the DMD. COBS clarifies how the **Distance Marketing Directive (DMD)** and the Regulations should be interpreted by authorised firms. It requires that certain product disclosures are given to **consumers** who conclude contracts at a distance.

The UK financial regulator has taken the view that responsibility for the DMD requirements applies to the Home State except in the case of a branch, in which case responsibility rests with the EEA State in which the branch is located. This means that the relevant COBS rules will apply to branches in the UK, including branches of foreign (EEA or non-EEA) firms.

### 2.18.2 Disclosure requirements

The DMD introduced requirements to provide consumers with certain **detailed information** before a contract is concluded, including information about:

- The identity of the supplier (including geographical address)
- Product details (including price and fees), and
- Particulars of the contract (including rights of cancellation)

During **voice telephony** communications, only specified abbreviated distance marketing information needs to be provided. However, the standard distance marketing information must still be provided on a durable medium in good time before the customer is bound by any distance contract or offer.

### 2.18.3 Consumer

The DMD provides protections for any individual who is a **consumer**, meaning a natural person (i.e. an individual) who concludes a **distance contract** outside of their trade, business or profession.

The Directive covers individuals acting, for example:

- As personal representatives, including executors, unless they are acting in a professional capacity, e.g. a solicitor acting as executor, or
- In personal or other family circumstances for example, as trustee of a family trust.

but excludes individuals acting, for example:

- As trustee of a trust, such as a housing or NHS trust, or
- As member of the governing body of a club or other unincorporated association, such as a trade body or a student union, or
- As a pension trustee.

### 2.18.4 Distance contract

A **distance contract** is one which is concluded under an '**organised distance sales or service-provision scheme**' – meaning that there has been no '**simultaneous physical presence**' of the firm and the **consumer** throughout the offer, negotiation and conclusion of the contract.

Concluding a contract by **means of distance communication** includes by post, telephone, fax or the internet.

### 2.18.5 Use of intermediaries

The mere fact that an intermediary (acting for the firm or for the **consumer**) is involved does not make the sale of a financial product or service a **distance contract**.

### 2.18.6 Distance contracts for intermediation services

In a small number of cases, intermediaries will themselves fall within the scope of DMD, e.g. where the intermediary agrees to provide continuing advisory, broking or portfolio management services for a **consumer**.

However, the DMD is only relevant if:

- There is a contract between the intermediary and the consumer in respect of the intermediary's mediation services, and
- The contract is a distance contract, and
- The contract is concluded other than merely as a stage in the provision of another service by the intermediary or another person.

## 2.19 Information about the firm

**Information about a firm and its services** which must be provided to a **retail client** comprises the following general information.

- The firm's **name, address** (permanent place of business) and **contact details** which allow effective communication

- For MiFID and equivalent third country business, the **languages** the firm uses for documents and other communication

- **Methods of communication with clients** which are used by the firm, including those for sending and receiving orders where relevant

- Statement that the firm is **authorised**, and the name of the authorising **competent authority** (e.g. the Financial Conduct Authority) – with the authority's contact address, in the case of MiFID business

- If the firm is acting through an **appointed representative or tied agent**, a statement of this fact specifying the EEA State in which the representative/agent is registered

- The nature, frequency and timing of **performance reports** provided by the firm (in accordance with rules on reporting to clients)

- The firm's **conflicts of interest policy** (or a summary of it)

- For other firms, details of **how the firm will ensure fair treatment** of clients when material interests or conflicts of interest arise

## 2.20 Information about compensation

For MiFID business, the firm must tell the client about the applicable **investor compensation scheme** (generally, **FSCS**), giving information in a durable medium or via a web site meeting the web site conditions and in the language of the EEA State:

- On the amount and scope of cover offered
- At the client's request, on conditions and formalities involved in claiming compensation

## 2.21 Financial promotions in social media

FCA guidance issued in March 2015 aims to help firms in using social media and ensuring that they are complying with the regulator's general requirements on financial promotions. Each communication – for example, a web page, a Facebook page, or a tweet – must be considered individually, on a **stand-alone** basis, for its compliance with the relevant rules. As with other financial promotions, there should be an adequate system in place for an appropriately competent and senior person in the firm to **sign off** digital media communications.

Social media communications can be disseminated to a wide audience very quickly, for example through retweeting on **Twitter** or sharing on **Facebook**, and so firms should ensure that their communications will remain fair, clear and not misleading even if they reach a non-intended recipient.

Where a recipient shares or forwards a firm's communication, for example by retweeting it, responsibility lies with the communicator and not with the firm. However, any breaches of FCA rules in the original communication remain the responsibility of the originating firm, and not the 'retweeter'. Sharing or forwarding by a third party does not 'cure' any original non-compliance.

Media with limited character length, such as Twitter, will generally be unsuitable for communicating complex features of products, and their risks as well as benefits. Signposting may be possible by including a link to more comprehensive information. As an alternative, **image advertising** (see above) to promote the firm more generally may be more appropriate.

## 2.22 Electronic Commerce Directive

### 2.22.1 Purpose and scope

The Electronic Commerce Directive has been implemented in the UK and aims to provide freedom for EEA firms to carry out Electronic Commerce Activity (ECA) freely into other EEA states. The Directive simplified previous rules so that an EEA firm doing ECA generally only has to comply with its **home state** conduct of business rules, therefore introducing a **country of origin** approach to regulation.

**Electronic Commerce Activity (ECA)** is defined as any electronic financial service which would be a regulated activity if it were provided by non-electronic means, e.g. the provision of electronic broking services.

The rules apply to three types of ECA provider:

- Incoming
- Outgoing
- Domestic

### 2.22.2 Incoming ECA providers

An **incoming ECA provider** is an EEA firm (other than a UK firm) carrying out ECA with or for a UK consumer. This would, for example, cover a French firm providing ECA to a UK consumer.

An incoming ECA provider has to comply with the applicable laws in the country of origin (home state) from which the service is provided, e.g. France, and not FSMA 2000 or the UK regulators' Handbooks.

This makes it easier for firms to provide cross-border services, but the general rule is subject to certain derogations. These derogations would allow the host State, in our example the UK, to impose certain 'host State' (i.e. UK) requirements. These derogations are allowed as the host state has continuing responsibility for consumer protection and include requirements to provide basic terms and conditions in English. Therefore subject to certain derogations set out in the regulators' rules, the FCA/PRA Handbooks and FSMA 2000 do not apply to incoming ECA providers.

### 2.22.3 Outgoing ECA providers

An **outgoing ECA provider** is one which carries on electronic commerce activity with an EEA recipient (other than a UK recipient) from a UK establishment, whether or not the recipient is a consumer. This would, for example, cover a UK firm providing ECA to a French consumer.

There are minimum additional information requirements on outgoing ECA providers such as information about the firm.

The electronic commerce rules relate to all regulated firms in relation to a financial promotion which is an outgoing electronic commerce communication.

### 2.22.4 Domestic ECA providers

From the UK perspective, a **domestic ECA provider** is a UK-authorised firm which provides ECA from an establishment which it has in the United Kingdom, with or for a UK recipient or a recipient outside the EEA. This would, for example, cover a UK firm providing ECA to a UK or a Canadian consumer.

In the first scenario, not surprisingly, UK rules apply to the relationship. In the second scenario, the UK firm would have to comply with Canadian rules as the recipient is not in the EEA. So the rules revert to a 'host State' position. However, as well as considering the host state rules, the UK firm is required to supply certain minimum information requirements to the ECA recipient regardless of the recipient's location.

# 3 Identifying client needs

## 3.1 Assessing suitability

Suitability rules apply when a firm makes a **personal recommendation** in relation to a **designated investment** (but not if the firm makes use of the rules on basic scripted advice for stakeholder products).

The firm has obligations regarding the assessment of **suitability**: the firm must take reasonable steps to ensure that, in respect of designated investments, a personal recommendation or a decision to trade is **suitable for its client**.

To meet this obligation, the firm must **obtain necessary information** regarding the client's:

- **Knowledge and experience** in the relevant investment field (including: types of investment or service with which the client is familiar; transactions experience; level of education and profession or former profession; understanding of risks)

- **Investment objectives** (including: length of time he wishes to hold the investment; risk preferences; risk profile; purposes of the investment)

- **Financial situation** (including: extent and source of regular income; assets including liquid assets; investments and real property; regular financial commitments) (Is he able to bear any investment risks, consistent with his investment objectives?)

The firm is entitled to **rely** on **information provided by the client**, unless it is aware that the information is out of date, inaccurate or incomplete.

A **transaction** may be **unsuitable** for a client because of

- The risks of the designated investments involved
- The type of transaction
- The characteristics of the order
- The frequency of trading
- It resulting in an unsuitable portfolio (in the case of **managing investments**)

For non-MiFID business, these rules apply to business with **retail clients**. When making personal recommendations or managing investments for **professional clients**, in the course of MiFID or equivalent third country business, a firm is entitled to assume that the client has the necessary experience and knowledge, in relation to products and services for which the professional client is so classified.

A provider must not make a recommendation unless there is a **suitable product within its range** of products.

## 3.2 Suitability report

### 3.2.1 Requirement

A firm must provide a **suitability report** to a retail client if the firm makes a personal recommendation and the client:

- Buys or sells shares/units in a regulated collective investment scheme
- Buys or sells shares through an investment trust savings scheme or investment trust ISA or PEP
- Buys, sells, surrenders, cancels rights in or suspends contributions to a personal or stakeholder pension
- Elects to make income withdrawals from a short-term annuity
- Enters into a pension transfer or pension opt-out

A suitability report is required for all personal recommendations in relation to **life policies**.

A suitability report is **not** required:

- If the firm acts as investment manager and recommends a regulated collective investment scheme
- If the client is habitually resident outside the EEA and is not in the UK when consenting to the proposal
- For small life policies (not > £50 p.a.) recommended by friendly societies
- For recommendations to increase regular premiums on an existing contract
- For recommendations to invest further single contributions to an existing packaged product

### 3.2.2 Timing

The suitability report must generally be provided to the client **as soon as possible after the transaction is effected**. For personal or stakeholder pension schemes requiring notification of cancellation rights, the report must be provided no later than 14 days after the contract is concluded.

### 3.2.3 Contents

The suitability report is based on 'knowing your customer' and must, at least:

- Specify the client's **demands and needs**

- Explain the firm's **recommendation** that the transaction is suitable, having regard to information provided by the client

- Explain any possible **disadvantages** of the transaction to the client

The firm should give details appropriate to the **complexity** of the transaction.

For **income withdrawals** from a **short-term annuity**, the explanation of possible disadvantages should include **risk factors** involved in income withdrawals or purchase of a short-term annuity.

If a **personal pension** plan is recommended, an explanation should be included of why it is at least as suitable as a stakeholder pension.

## 3.3 Appropriateness test – for non-advised sales

The central aim of the appropriateness rules – which were introduced under **MiFID** – is to prevent complex products from being sold on an **execution only** basis (that is, without advice) to **retail clients** who do not have the experience and/or the knowledge to understand the risks of such products.

The **appropriateness** rules we outline here apply to a firm providing **investment services** in the course of **MiFID** investment services, **other than** making a personal recommendation and managing investments ('non-advised' sales). (Note that, as we have seen, the **suitability** rules apply where there is a personal recommendation.) The rules thus apply to '**execution only**' services which are available in the UK, where transactions are undertaken at the initiative of the customer without advice having been given.

The rules apply to arranging or dealing in **derivatives** or **warrants** for a **retail client**, when in response to a **direct offer financial promotion**. (Direct offer financial promotions were explained earlier in this Chapter.) The glossary of the regulators' Handbook defines **derivatives** as comprising **contracts for differences (CfDs), futures and options**.

Except for the case of direct offer business, the appropriateness test is not required for **non-MiFID** business: therefore, it does not apply to non-MiFID products such as insurance policies, deposits (including structured deposits) and pension plans.

To **assess appropriateness**, the firm must ask the client to provide information on his knowledge and experience in the relevant investment field, to enable the assessment to be made.

The firm will then:

- Determine whether the client has the necessary **experience and knowledge** to understand the **risks** involved in the product/service (including the following aspects: nature and extent of service with which client is familiar; complexity; risks involved; extent of client's transactions in designated investments; level of client's education and profession or former profession).

- Be entitled to assume that a **professional client** has such experience and knowledge, for products/services for which it is classified as 'professional'.

Unless it knows the information from the client to be out-of-date, inaccurate or incomplete, the firm may rely on it. Where reasonable, a firm may infer knowledge from experience.

The firm may seek to increase the client's level of understanding by providing appropriate information to the client.

If the firm is satisfied about the client's experience and knowledge, there is **no duty to communicate** this to the client. If, in doing so, it is making a personal recommendation, it must comply with the **suitability** rules. But if the firm concludes that the product or service is **not appropriate** to the client, it must **warn** the client. The warning may be in a standardised format.

If the client provides insufficient information, the firm must **warn** the client that such a decision will not allow the firm to determine whether the service or product is appropriate for him. Again, the warning may be in a standardised format.

If a client who has received a warning asks the firm to go ahead with the transaction, it is for the firm to consider whether to do so 'having regard to the circumstances'.

A firm **need not assess appropriateness**:

- For an execution-only service in listed shares provided on the initiative of the client, if the client is warned that there will be no suitability assessment and the firm meets conflict of interest requirements

- If it is receiving or transmitting an order in relation to which it has assessed suitability

- If it is able to rely on a recommendation made by an investment firm

- On each occasion, in new dealings with a client engaged in a course of dealings

## 3.4 Referring to specialists

Very few financial advisers have extensive or sufficient knowledge in all areas of financial planning.

If dealings with a client involve actions that are beyond the authority of the adviser, either as a result of the firm's rules or the regulator's requirements and rules, then the adviser should seek authority from an appropriate person.

The adviser should be able to refer to other specialists within the firm, and should be willing to do so if necessary. Advisers may also need to refer to specialists outside their business in certain areas of advice and should explain to the client when it would be necessary.

## 3.5 Reliance on others

Suppose that a firm (**F1**) carrying out MiFID or equivalent third country business receives an instruction from an investment firm (**F2**) to perform an investment or ancillary service on behalf of a client (**C**).

**F1** may rely on:

- Information about the client **C** which firm **F2** provides
- Recommendations about the service provided to **C** by **F2**

**F2** remains responsible for the completeness and accuracy of information provided and the appropriateness of its advice.

More generally, a firm is taken to be in **compliance with COBS** rules which require it to obtain information, if it can show it was **reasonable** for it to rely on information provided by others in writing. It is reasonable to rely on written information provided by another where that person is **competent** and **not connected** with the firm.

This rule links with Principle 2 *Skill, Care and Diligence*. Note that this rule has no impact on the requirements laid down in the Money Laundering Regulations, which require a firm to identify its clients for money laundering purposes.

# 4 Advice standards

## 4.1 Overview

In Chapter 2, we examined in detail the changes arising from the **Retail Distribution Review (RDR)** which took effect from 31 December 2012. Refer back to that Chapter for the detail on these provisions, which we summarise here.

**Independent advice** and **restricted advice** are distinguished. If an adviser declares themselves to offer **independent advice**, they will need to consider a broader range of **retail investment products (RIPs)**, a more widely defined category than packaged products. Advice which is not independent must be labelled as **restricted advice**, for example as advice on a limited range of products or providers.

As you will recall, under the new regime, a firm making a personal recommendation to a retail client to **invest in a retail investment product**, or providing **related services** will not receive commission from the product provider. The firm will instead receive an **adviser charge** that has been agreed with the client in advance.

These new rules represent a fundamental change and necessitate many firms re-thinking their business models. However, the regulator considers that removing the potential for commission to bias product recommendations means that consumers can be more confident that they are being sold the product that best fits their needs.

## 4.2 Disclosure requirements

A firm must prepare a **key features document** for each packaged product, cash deposit ISA and cash deposit CTF it produces, in good time before that document has to be provided.

The firm does **not** have to prepare the document if **another firm** has agreed to prepare it. There are some further **exceptions**, including certain collective investment schemes for which a simplified prospectus is produced instead of a key features document, and stakeholder and personal pension schemes if the information appears prominently in another document.

A **single document** may be used as the key features document for **different schemes**, if the schemes are offered through a **platform** service and the document clearly describes the difference between the schemes.

## 4.3 Key Features Document

A **key features document** must:

- Be produced / presented to **at least** the quality / standard of **sales and marketing material** used to promote the product
- Display the **firm's brand** as prominently as any other
- Include the **keyfacts logo** prominently at the top
- Include the following **statement**, in a prominent position:

'The Financial Conduct Authority is a financial services regulator. It requires us, [provider name], to give you this important information to help you to decide whether our [product name] is right for you. You should read this document carefully so that you understand what you are buying, and then keep it safe for future reference.'

- Not include anything that might reasonably cause a retail client to be **mistaken** about the **identity** of the firm that produced, or will produce, the product

**Required headings** in a **key features document** are as follows. (The **order** shown below must be followed.)

- *Title:* 'key features of the [name of product]'

- *Heading:* **'Its aims'** – followed by a brief description of the product's aims

- *Heading:* **'Your commitment'** or **'Your investment'** – followed by information on what a retail client is committing to or investing in and any consequences of failing to maintain the commitment or investment

- *Heading:* **'Risks'** – followed by information on the material risks associated with the product, including a description of the factors that may have an adverse effect on performance or are material to the decision to invest

- *Heading:* **'Questions and answers'** – (in the form of questions and answers) about the principal terms of the product, what it will do for a retail client and any other information necessary to enable a retail client to make an informed decision

The **key features document** must:

- Include **enough information** about the nature and complexity of the product, any minimum standards / limitations, material benefits / risks of buying or investing for a retail client to be able to make an **informed decision** about whether to proceed

- Explain arrangements for handling **complaints**

- Explain the **compensation** available from the FSCS if the firm cannot meet its liabilities

- Explain whether there are **cancellation / withdrawal rights**, their duration and conditions, including amounts payable if the right is exercised, consequences of not exercising, and practical instructions for exercising the right, including the address to which any notice must be sent

- For personal pension schemes, explain clearly and prominently that **stakeholder pension schemes** are available and might meet the client's needs as well as the scheme on offer

The declared **reduction in yield** included in the key features document for a product indicates the amount by which the investment yield is reduced, in percentage terms, by the effect of charges. The reduction in yield figures for different providers can be reviewed, to compare the effect of each provider's charges.

These rules apply to a UK firm's business carried out in another EEA State for a retail client in the UK, subject to certain exclusions. They also apply to business carried out in the UK for a client in another EEA State.

## 4.4 Disclosure documents for retail clients

The regulator has given guidance on the format of appropriate disclosures in the form of the **Services and Costs Disclosure Document (SCDD)** or the alternative **Combined Initial Disclosure Document (CIDD)**. Firms have flexibility about how they explain the cost of their services: the use of these documents remains as guidance rather than being mandatory.

The **CIDD** may be used for insurance and home finance services and provides information to the consumer about the type of advice given, and the nature and costs of the services offered by the firm.

The **SCDD** contains the following sections.

- **Financial Conduct Authority**. This section explains the purpose of the document to consumers.

- **Which service will we provide you with?** This section tells consumers the type of advice they are receiving – independent advice; restricted advice; or no advice.

- **What will you have to pay us for our services?** This section explains the charging arrangements, and how the consumer will pay the firm for its services. (For non-advised sales, firms can instead explain that clients will be told how much they get paid before they carry out any business for the client.)

- **Who regulates us?** Details of the regulator, and the relevant activities for which the firm has permission.

- **Loans and ownership**. This section tells consumers of interests held in (share capital, voting rights or both) and/or loans provided to firms by product providers, and *vice versa*.

- **What to do if you have a complaint**. Contact details for the firm's complaints department, and mention of the Financial Ombudsman Service.

- **Are we covered by the Financial Services Compensation Scheme?** Explanation of the compensation arrangements and the relevant limit.

The regulators consider that disclosure requirements are met if the firm's representatives provide the information '**in good time**' before the client is bound by an agreement to provide a personal recommendation, or the firm performs an act preparatory to providing a recommendation.

## 4.5 Cancellation and withdrawal rights

### 4.5.1 Introduction

**Cancellation and withdrawal rights** are relevant to firms that enter into a cancellable contract, which means most providers of retail financial products, including distance contracts, based on deposits or designated investments.

### 4.5.2 Cancellation periods

Minimum **cancellation periods** where a consumer has a right to cancel are summarised below (and are subject to certain exemptions in special situations which are beyond the syllabus). (Note that a **wrapper** means an ISA or CTF. Personal pension contracts, including SIPPs, and pension contracts based on regulated collective investment schemes, fall within the definition of a **pension wrapper**.)

- Life and pensions contracts: 30 calendar days
- Cash deposit ISAs: 14 calendar days
- Non-life and non-pensions contracts (advised non-distance contracts): 14 calendar days
- Non-life and non-pensions contracts (distance contracts): 14 calendar days

If one transaction attracts more than one right to cancel, the longest period applies.

The **cancellation period begins**

- **Either:** From the day the contract is concluded (but, for life policies, when the consumer is informed that the contract has been concluded),

- **Or:** From the day when the consumer receives the contract terms and conditions, if later

### 4.5.3 Disclosure of rights to cancel or withdraw

Where the consumer would not already have received similar information under another rule, the firm must **disclose** – in a durable medium and in good time or, if that is not possible, immediately after the consumer is bound – the right to cancel or withdraw, its duration and conditions, information on any further amount payable, consequences of not exercising the right, practical instructions for exercising it, and the address to which notification of cancellation or withdrawal should be sent.

### 4.5.4 Exercising a right to cancel

A consumer's notification of exercise of a right to cancel is deemed to have observed the deadline if it is **dispatched**, in a durable medium, before the deadline expires. A method other than mail may be used, if the provider states that it is acceptable.

The consumer need **not** give any **reason** for exercising the right to cancel.

# 5 Dealing and managing

## 5.1 Application of rules

COBS rules on **dealing and managing** (except for the rules on personal account dealing – see below) apply to **MiFID business** carried out by a **MiFID investment firm**, and to equivalent third country business.

## 5.2 Best execution

The basic COBS rule of **best execution** is as follows.

A firm must take all reasonable steps to obtain, when executing orders, the best possible result for its clients taking into account the execution factors.

When a firm is **dealing on own account with clients**, this is considered to be execution of client orders, and is therefore subject to the best execution rule.

If a firm provides a best quote to a client, it is acceptable for the quote to be executed after the client accepts it, provided the quote is not manifestly out of date.

The obligation to obtain best execution needs to be interpreted according to the particular type of financial instrument involved, but the rule applies to **all types of financial instrument**.

The **best execution criteria** are that the firm must take into account **characteristics of**:

- The client, including categorisation as retail or professional
- The client order
- The financial instruments
- The execution venues

The '**best possible result**' must be determined in terms of **total consideration** – taking into account any costs, including the firm's own commissions in the case of competing execution venues, and not just quoted prices. (However, the firm is not expected to compare the result with that of clients of other firms.) Commissions structure must not discriminate between execution venues.

## 5.3 Inducements

For MiFID business, **inducements rules** apply to all fees, other payments and non-monetary benefits. These fees, payments or non-monetary benefits must enhance the quality of the service provided to clients, in accordance with the client's best interests. Firms within the scope of MiFID must disclose to clients the essential details or the existence, nature and amount of fees, payments or non-monetary benefits. The disclosure must be made before services are provided and must be clear, comprehensive and accurate.

These rules supplement Principles 1 and 6 of the *Principles for Businesses*. They deal with the delicate area of inducements and seek to ensure that firms do not conduct business under arrangements that may give rise to conflicts of interest.

**Inducements** could mean anything from gifts to entertainment to bribes. The rules provide a test to help judge whether or not something is acceptable.

In relation to the sale of **RIPs**, the following are among those deemed to be **reasonable non-monetary benefits**.

- Gifts, hospitality and promotional prizes of reasonable value, given by product provider to the firm
- Assistance in promotion of a firm's RIPs
- Joint marketing exercises, such as the provision of product literature, and articles for publication
- Generic product literature which enhances client service, with costs borne by the recipient firm
- Generic technical information
- Training facilities
- Reasonable travel and accommodation expenses, e.g. to meetings or training

If a product provider makes benefits available to one firm but not another, this is more likely to impair compliance with the rule of acting in the **client's best interests**. Most firms deliver against the inducements requirements by drafting detailed 'gifts policies' (although the rule does **not** explicitly require firms to have a gifts policy). These contain internal rules regarding disclosure, limits and clearance procedures for gifts.

## 5.4 Personal account dealing

Personal account dealing relates to trades undertaken by the staff of a regulated business for themselves. As a matter of good practice, a firm's policy on personal account dealing should generally be extended to immediate family members. Such trades can create **conflicts of interest** between staff and customers.

A firm conducting **designated investment business** must establish, implement and maintain adequate **arrangements** aimed at preventing employees who are involved in activities where a conflict of interest could occur, or who has access to inside information, from:

- Entering into a transaction which is prohibited under the **Market Abuse Directive**, or which involves misuse or improper disclosure of confidential information, or conflicts with an obligation of the firm to a customer under the regulatory system

- Except in the course of his job, advising or procuring anyone else to enter into such a transaction

- Except in the course of his job, disclosing any information or opinion to another person if the person disclosing it should know that, as a result, the other person would be likely to enter into such a transaction or advise or procure another to enter into such a transaction

The **firm's arrangements** under these provisions must be designed to ensure that:

- All relevant persons (staff involved) are aware of the personal dealing restrictions

- The firm is informed promptly of any personal transaction

- A service provider to whom activities are outsourced maintain a record of personal transactions and provides it to the firm promptly on request

- A record is kept of personal transactions notified to the firm or identified by it, including any related authorisation or prohibition

The rule on personal account dealing is **disapplied** for personal transactions:

- Under a discretionary portfolio management service where there has been no prior communication between the portfolio manager and the person for whom the transaction is executed

- In UCITS collective undertakings (e.g. OEICs and unit trusts) where the person is not involved in its management

- In life policies

- For successive personal transactions where there were prior instructions in force, nor to the termination of the instruction provided that no financial instruments are sold at the same time

## 5.5 Churning and switching

Churning and switching are similar wrongs. They involve the cynical **overtrading** of customer accounts for the purpose of generating commission. This would clearly contravene the **client's best interests rule**.

Churning or switching will often be difficult to isolate, unless blatant. Much would depend upon the market conditions prevailing at the time of dealing.

The **COBS guidance** on churning and switching state that:

- A series of transactions that are each suitable when viewed in isolation may be unsuitable if the recommendations or the decisions to trade are made with a frequency that is not in the best interests of the client

- A firm should have regard to the client's agreed investment strategy in determining the frequency of transactions. This would include, for example, the need to switch within or between packaged products

Note also the following section on CIPs and replacement business.

## 5.6 Guidance: CIPs and replacement business

In July 2012, the regulator issued **guidance** for retail firms when they offer a **Centralised Investment Proposition (CIP)**. This is part of how investment advisory firms are **changing their business models** as a result of the **Retail Distribution Review (RDR)**, with many choosing to offer a CIP.

A CIP is where a firm offers a standardised approach to providing investment advice, including portfolio advice services, distributor influenced funds (DIFs) and discretionary fund management.

The regulator believes there are benefits from CIPs for both clients and firms.

- **Clients** can benefit from more structured and better researched investments
- **Firms** can benefit from efficiencies in the management of risks associated with investment selection

However, the regulator is concerned that, in certain circumstances, CIPs are **unsuitable** for retail investors, for example because of:

- **'Shoe-horning'** – firms might recommend a 'one size fits all' solution which is not suitable for the individual needs and objectives of a client

- **Churning** – firms might advise clients to switch their existing investments into a CIP without adequate consideration of whether the switch is both suitable and in the client's best interest, and

- **Additional costs** – the use of a CIP might result in higher (and potentially less transparent) charges than the client's existing investments and with few additional, actual benefits

Of course, firms should not recommend CIPs in cases where they are unsuitable for clients.

**Replacement business** is a term for switching: the regulator is concerned with the suitability of recommendations to switch any existing investment into a new investment solution. While the regulator acknowledges that firms cannot be precise about the potential for higher returns, where improved performance is an objective of the client, firms should clearly demonstrate **why they expect improved performance to be more likely** in the new investment.

# 6 Giving investment advice

## 6.1 The financial planning process

The **financial planning** process can be summarised as comprising the following six stages.

1. **Obtaining relevant information** – sometimes termed fact finding
2. **Establishing and agreeing** the client's financial objectives
3. **Processing and analysing the data** obtained
4. **Formulating recommendations** in a comprehensive plan with objectives
5. **Implementing the recommendations** as agreed with the client
6. **Reviewing and regularly updating** the plan

It is helpful to consider **client objectives** below (stage **2** in the process as set out above) before we go on to discuss the **fact-find** (stage **1** in the process).

## 6.2 Client objectives

### 6.2.1 Overview

Broadly speaking, the requirements of clients fall into one of two categories:

- To **maximise returns**, e.g. positive net worth individuals looking for a portfolio to match their risk/return preferences

- To **match liabilities**, e.g. pension funds, where the aim is to match assets and liabilities or minimise any mismatch

### 6.2.2 Return maximisation

Given the choice, most investors would elect to have a high performance fund with minimal risk. However, this is not achievable and some trade-off between the two will have to take place. Understanding the **risk/reward trade-off** is crucial to understanding the overall objectives of a return maximising fund and then to establishing the policy of a fund.

Lower risk aversion or greater risk tolerance will tend to result in greater allowable portfolio risk, along with greater potential gains (and potential losses).

The primary concern in this type of fund is, therefore, to fully understand the client's risk tolerance, whether the clients are private or institutional clients.

### 6.2.3 Liability matching

The only way to guarantee the matching of any liability is through investment in government bonds where the income and capital inflows exactly match those liabilities.

If the return from bonds is insufficient to achieve this required return, then we must use other assets. The result of the use of other assets is that we may achieve the higher return required. However, the risk associated with the use of these other assets means that the liabilities may not be exactly met – there may be a **mismatch**.

Again, a key requirement here will be to establish the client's attitude to risk, though here we have more specific financial objectives to meet, i.e. a future liability to satisfy.

### 6.2.4 Mixed requirements

For most institutional clients, the primary requirement will be quite clear-cut – collective investments are generally return-maximising funds whereas pension funds are liability-driven.

For many private clients, however, the requirements may be more mixed. A wealthy private client may have certain liabilities to meet such as paying for children's/grandchildren's school and college fees, repaying loans/mortgages or providing financial protection for relatives/dependents, but may wish that any 'spare' resources be managed to maximise returns.

There are a number of stages that need to be undertaken when considering client objectives.

## 6.3 Quantifying and prioritising clients' objectives

The first stage is to determine all of the objectives that the client is looking to meet and to prioritise and quantify those objectives, especially quantifying any liability targets since they will invariably be the top priorities.

From a priority viewpoint, this will clearly be specific to and determined by the client.

From a quantification viewpoint, the fund liabilities may include such factors as school/college fees, loans, dependent pensions, and a primary consideration here will be whether those liabilities are nominal or real.

* A **nominal liability** is one that is fixed in monetary terms irrespective of future inflation. An example of a nominal liability would be a bank loan or mortgage where the monetary sum borrowed must be paid off at the end of the term and does not alter with inflation over that time.

* In contrast, a **real liability** is one which changes in monetary terms as we experience inflation. For example, in order to maintain a standard of living a pension needs to pay out the same amount each year in real terms, i.e. a rising monetary amount to cover the impacts of inflation, and this sum needs to be paid for the remaining life from the retirement – an indeterminate term.

Whatever the liability, assessment will involve a **present value analysis** of the anticipated future liabilities that the fund is aiming to meet. For example, to pay a pension of £20,000 pa for a period of 20 years when real returns (asset returns in excess of inflation) are 3% will require a fund value at retirement of almost £300,000 and so we would be looking to achieve this fund value at the retirement date.

## 6.4 Affordability of client's objectives

Based on the quantification, the portfolio manager will be able to determine any lump sum or annual contributions that needs to be paid into the fund in order to establish the required pool and at this stage the issue of affordability needs to be considered. **Affordability** is the primary issue since if a client cannot afford a proposal then it is not suitable.

If the current assets and/or disposable income of the client are more than sufficient to meet the liability needs then the surplus funds are available for (return-maximising) savings. If, on the other hand, there is a deficit or shortfall then the client's targets and, potentially, priorities will need to be reconsidered.

## 6.5 The fact find process

### 6.5.1 General points

Key to the assessment of the affordability, therefore, is the client's current personal and financial circumstances which may be determined through the fact find.

The fact find will seek to establish both personal and financial information. **Personal information** detailed in the fact find would, for a retail client, include family names and addresses, dates of birth, marital status, employment status, tax status. **Financial information** would include current income and expenditure levels, levels of savings and investments, the scale of any financial liabilities (usually mortgages, loans and credit cards), and the existence of any life assurance policies and pensions.

The client will have much of this information easily to hand, however certain information may need to be obtained from third parties. For example, the current performance and value of any pension schemes or life policies such as endowments will probably need to be obtained from the relevant pension fund manager or life assurance fund manager. The overall financial plan will need to take account of any payments that are committed to such funds, any receipts that may be expected from them and whether it is worth considering changing providers.

Other areas that may be considered at this stage are current mortgage terms and the terms of other loans as it may again be appropriate to refinance at better rates.

In order to obtain this information from a third party, the fund manager will require a **letter of authority** from the client that authorises the release of the information. Such enquiries typically take several weeks to get resolved and may cause a substantial delay in finalising the fund investment plan.

What if a **client declines to provide some of the information** requested by the adviser? In that case, the adviser should record the refusal on the fact-find.

### 6.5.2 Hard facts and soft facts

The objective information regarding the client's personal and financial situation may be referred to as **hard facts**. One final aim of the fact find will be to seek to understand the more subjective information that may be relevant, such as client aspirations, risk tolerances and any other subjective factors such as their attitude towards issues such as socially responsible investment. This subjective information may be referred to as **soft facts**.

Understanding such soft facts requires face-to-face meeting with the client to discuss and consider the issues alongside them. Establishing a client's risk tolerance, for example, is far from straight forward as standard risk measures are far from familiar to most retail clients and approaches are covered below.

## 6.6 Risks affecting clients

### 6.6.1 Overview

The main risks that a **client** faces and that they need to understand are as follows.

- **Capital risk** – the potential variability in investment values
- **Inflation risk** – the potential variability in inflation rates, which will impact significantly on return requirements for funds looking to finance real liabilities
- **Interest rate risk** – the risk of changes in bank base rates and the knock-on effect that this may have on asset returns
- **Shortfall risk** – the risk of a fund failing to meet any specified liabilities. This can be reduced by minimising targets, increasing sums invested or extending investment terms.

## 6.6.2 Diversification

One of the key benefits of employing a fund manager is that the investor's funds are being pooled with those of other investors. This pooling allows the investor's money to be spread over a range of assets.

Consider an **investment** in shares (equities). Two sorts of risk can be distinguished:

- The general **market risk** of investing in shares or bonds
- The **specific risk** of any individual investment

For example, if an investor were to put all their money into the shares of a company, there would firstly be the risk that the market in all shares would fall, causing the value of the investment to fall, and secondly the risk that the specific company itself may suffer from a specific incident causing the share price to fall.

If an investor is able to buy more investments, he will be taking on board specific risks of different companies. Eventually, there will be a situation where, because of specific risks, some of the investments will fall but others will rise. Overall, through this process of **diversification**, investors are able to rid themselves of the specific risk of a stock. It is, however, impossible to remove the market risk.

Having established the general principle of diversification, we can see that there are the following different types of diversification:

- **Diversification by asset class.** This is achieved by holding a combination of different kinds of asset within a portfolio, possibly spread across: cash, fixed interest securities, equity investments, property-based investments, and other assets.

- **Diversification within asset classes.** An investor can diversify a portfolio by holding a variety of investments within the particular asset types that he holds. This may be achieved by holding various fixed interest securities, by holding equities in a number of different companies, by spreading investments across different industry sectors and geographical markets, and by holding a number of different properties or property-based investments.

- **Diversification by manager.** Diversifying risk across different funds with different managers reduces the risks from a manager performing poorly. This is one of the attractions of '**manager of manager**' and '**fund of fund**' structures.

The **principle of diversification** should be clearly explained to the client as it will have a significant impact on the potential asset allocations. As part of the fact find, the fund manager will probably illustrate various possible asset allocations and discuss in detail the potential returns and risks of each.

## 6.6.3 Timescales

A client's attitude to risk may be influenced by **investment timescales**.

If, for example, we are managing a pension fund, our attitude to risk will be highly dependent on timescales. If the fund is a young scheme with 30 or 40 years to client retirement then it can afford to take a reasonably aggressive attitude to capital risk and invest in what may be regarded as the riskier assets. By taking a high risk, we may experience some poor years but we are also likely to experience some very good years. The effect is that risk averages out over time, giving rise to a good overall long-term return, thus minimising shortfall risk.

If, on the other hand, the scheme is very mature and retirement is imminent, then there is insufficient time for this averaging effect to take place. As a result, any poor performance this year may have a significantly adverse effect on the fund, i.e. a high capital risk in this circumstance increases the shortfall risk.

The fund managers approach will, therefore, be very much affected by investment timescales.

## 6.6.4 Client's risk tolerance

There are two approaches that a fund manager will utilise in order to get an understanding of the clients risk tolerance, specifically the fact find soft facts discussion and undertaking a review of any current investments. Since a full appreciation of risk is essential to how the fund is managed, the fund manager will investigate both.

The process will probably start with a review of the client's current investments and risks, which will clearly illustrate the client's historical attitude to risk. As we noted above, however, risk tolerance changes over time, so this historical information, whilst a very useful insight, is not of itself sufficient for a full understanding of the client's risk tolerance.

To augment this, the fund manager will also undertake the fact find soft facts review. The standard fact find approach is to ask the client to select a mix of, say, equities and bonds, to give an idea of the normal mix (and hence risk) that the client wishes to face. We noted above that as part of the fact find process the fund manager will illustrate various possible asset allocations and discuss in detail the potential returns and risks of each. Such targeted discussions should enable the manager to get an understanding of the clients general risk tolerance. The fund manager will also be looking to establish limits for each asset class, maximum and minimum holdings of the different assets available, representing investment risk limits.

## 6.6.5 Investment risks and rewards

We have already mentioned the trade-off between risk and potential reward. This is fundamental to an understanding of investment management.

- **Low risk** investments offer low returns, but low probability of loss
- **High risk** investments offer the possibility of high returns, and a high probability of loss

The following table gives a broad indication of where various investments can be placed in a 'spectrum' of overall investment risk.

| Negligible risk | NS&I deposit products<br>Gilts (income)<br>Gilts (redemption) |
|---|---|
| Low risk | Bank deposits<br>Building society deposits<br>Cash ISAs<br>Annuities |
| Low / medium risk | Gilts (pre-redemption capital)<br>With-profits funds |
| Medium risk | Unit-linked managed funds<br>Unit trusts and OEICs/ICVCs (UK funds)<br>Investment trusts (UK)<br>Residential and commercial property |
| Medium / high risk | Unit-linked overseas funds<br>Unit trusts and OEICs/ICVCs (overseas funds)<br>UK single equities<br>Commodities |
| High risk | Unlisted shares<br>Warrants<br>Futures and Options when used to speculate<br>Venture Capital Trusts<br>Enterprise Investment Scheme<br>Enterprise Zone Property |

Before offering any investment advice, it is vital to ensure that the risk and returns of proposed investments match the client's preferences and circumstances.

# 7 Advising individuals

## 7.1 Client questionnaire

Information collected about the client should be **recorded carefully and meticulously**. The standard method of doing this is the use of a **questionnaire** designed to ensure that all relevant information is sought.

**Comprehensive information gathering** can serve the function of helping to generate business for the adviser but it is also important from the compliance point of view. It ensures that a proper record is kept, that information was sought from a client, that it was either given or refused and, combined with documents recording recommendations made to a client, can confirm that the advice given to the client was sound and suitable.

## 7.2 Client's attitudes

The following questions concern attitudes of the client.

- What is the client's attitude to existing savings/investment/protection?

- Are existing arrangements **sufficient**?

- Are they **suitable**?

- Have they been **reviewed recently**?

- Is the level of **investment risk acceptable** to a client?

- Is the client prepared to accept **more or less risk**?

- Are there any **constraints** on investment, e.g. ethical investments?

- Does the client consider that the existing investments meet current needs?

- **Do you consider that they meet current and existing needs**? (Remember that with long-term contracts such as life policies, surrender is not precluded but it must be recommended only when such a course is obviously suitable. This is likely to happen in very few cases, except perhaps with term assurance, where better terms may be obtained if premium rates have fallen.)

## 7.3 Client's objectives

The **client's objectives** and **expected liabilities** should be considered under headings such as the following.

- Is the client expecting to buy **property** or move house?
- Is any **change of job / work** expected?
- Could the client incur **major expenses** for school fees, new cars, or face major repairs?
- What is the client's **timespan** for investments, i.e. short-term or long-term or both?
- How **accessible** must the client's funds be?
- What is the client's current and future tax position?
- Are the client's needs for **income or growth** or both?
- Does the client want any **personal involvement** in the direction of investment?
- Does the client have **ethical views or preferences** which could influence their investment choices?

## 7.4 Present client circumstances

The analysis of a client's current circumstances begins with an analysis of the financial figures for the client's current circumstances. For a typical retail client, this would show a list of the client's **assets and liabilities**, and reveal whether there is a surplus or a deficit. It will also include an **income and expenditure** account to reveal whether there is **surplus** income or a **shortfall**: this is effectively a **budget**.

- If there is a **surplus**, it will enable the client to put into effect at least some of any recommendations which involve an additional outlay.

- If there is a **shortfall**, this reveals the need for the client to take action not to increase liabilities and perhaps to reduce existing liabilities.

**Current income needs** should be measured and this will enable you to check whether or not the **protection** against death and disability is adequate to meet those needs.

## 7.5 Future client circumstances

The adviser must also analyse the client's possible **changing circumstances** and **lifestyle**.

- What are the consequences, for example, of moving to another house or a prospective job change or children approaching fee paying school age? There may be additional housing or education costs, for example.

- If the client is employed and is planning to become self-employed, are any arrangements in hand for replacing company group life and disability cover with personal life and disability cover?

- Are arrangements in hand to ensure that finance is available to enable the move to take place?

## 7.6 Analysing client needs

In order to formulate a **recommendation** for a client, an adviser must always **identify** and **analyse** the **client's needs**.

By now, you have all the information necessary regarding the client and you can quantify a client's protection needs against the existing provision and compare future income needs against expectations.

You can also assess the client's current and future **tax position** and evaluate the tax efficiency of existing investments.

After all this has been done, the chances are that **most clients will not be able to achieve all of their objectives**. This will mean prioritising their objectives according to their resources.

An adviser must take into account all the **regulatory compliance requirements** that apply before dealing with the client (such as giving to the client a **business card**, a **services and costs disclosure document (SCDD)**, and **terms of business letter**) through the process to the stage where recommendations are given, when the reasons for those recommendations are required.

## 7.7 Discretionary and non-discretionary portfolio management

If the client is to own a portfolio, we should be clear about the nature of the advice being given.

- With **discretionary portfolio management**, the investment manager makes and implements decisions to buy and sell investments in the portfolio without asking the client each time.

- The **non-discretionary portfolio manager** provides advice to the client to assist the client in making their own investment decisions.

## 7.8 Execution-only customers

**Execution-only** customers are those who are not given any advice by the firm when they make investment decisions. The main responsibility of the firm to such customers is one of 'best execution': to implement the customer's investment decisions at the best price available.

## 7.9 Client needs and circumstances

It is possible to characterise individual investors by their situation, which may cover:

- Source of wealth
- Amount of wealth
- Stage of the life cycle

## 7.10 Wealth and investment exposure

When considering investment, the **wealth** of the investor is clearly an important consideration. If there is free capital to invest, then clearly it is sensible for the individual to take steps to make the best use of that capital.

It is possible, although not generally advisable, for someone with little wealth to gain exposure to investment markets, for example by **borrowing money to invest**, or by using investments such as derivatives or spread betting to gain a greater exposure than the individual's free resources. When investing in **risky assets** such as **equities**, a good principle is the often-stated one that **someone should only invest what they can afford to lose**. Someone who borrows to invest without having other capital to back it up if things go wrong, has the problem that they may end up with liabilities in excess of their assets.

An investor who uses instruments such as derivatives to increase their exposure should maintain other accessible resources (for example, cash on deposit) that can be used to meet losses that may arise. Clearly, it is also important that they understand the risks they are undertaking.

**Major investments**, including housing, should be appropriately **safeguarded**. For investments, the soundness of institutions holding funds, and any compensation arrangements where applicable, should be considered. Good title to housing should be ensured, and appropriate insurance taken out against risks such as fire.

## 7.11 Source of wealth

The way in which people received their wealth may affect their characteristics as investors. Investors may have acquired their wealth **actively** or **passively**.

**Passive wealth**

- People who have acquired their wealth passively, for example, through inheritance, or those who have acquired savings gradually from their salaries.

- These people are frequently less experienced with risk and do not believe that they could rebuild their wealth were they to lose it.

- They have a greater need for security and a lower tolerance for risk.

**Active wealth**

- People who have earned their own wealth, often by risking their own capital in the process.
- These types of people are assumed to be more confident and familiar with risk.
- They have a higher tolerance for risk.
- They dislike losing control over anything, including their investments.

## 7.12 Amount of wealth

The amount or **measure** of someone's wealth will affect his views on risk, since it will affect a person's sense of financial health. However, this sense of financial health is highly subjective. This makes it difficult to use this approach as a means of categorising investors.

Generally, if people perceive their wealth to be small, they are less inclined to take risks with their portfolios.

A portfolio that is only just sufficient to cover lifestyle needs could be viewed as small. A portfolio that is well in excess of that needed for the person's lifestyle could be considered large.

## 7.13 Factors shaping individual circumstances

There are various **life stages**, and people have differing financial needs. Every case is different, and there may be many variations in individual circumstances that cannot easily be fitted into easily formulated categories.

As an individual gets older, different priorities and needs take effect. Each person will clearly be different and therefore it is difficult to generalise to any degree. However, analysing by reference to where someone is in their life cycle will give some insight into investor characteristics.

Typically, but not always, **risk tolerance** declines as someone passes through his life cycle. Younger people have a long time horizon and a lower net worth. They may be more willing and able to take risk as a result.

As a person gets older, his net worth may increase and long-term spending goals will start to appear. The investor is still investing for the long term, but risk tolerance has declined, reflecting a fear of capital losses. These will be harder to recover over the shorter time available.

Later in a person's life, when they have paid off all their liabilities (e.g. mortgage), they will find that their personal net worth increases more quickly. The person who is close to retirement age has the prospect that earnings will no longer be able to counterbalance falls in the portfolio value. As a result, risk tolerance will fall even more.

## 7.14 Life cycle, age and commitments

The **age** of an investor, the stage of **life cycle** that he is at, and his **commitments**, all affect the investor's **risk profile**.

Adventurous risk-taking may be unwise for someone with heavy financial **commitments**, for example to children and other dependants. Another aspect of an investor's commitments is that of how much time he has available: if he works full-time and has a family, there may be little time left for him to manage his own investments even if he has an interest and knowledge to do so, and his commitments may mean that he is more likely to wish to seek professional financial advice.

## 7.15 An individual's risk profile

The financial adviser must recognise that each client has their own views, aspirations and attitudes. **Attitudes to risk** vary widely, and accordingly investment choices vary widely too. Some individuals will be reluctant to take on any significant risk of loss of their capital while others are prepared to 'gamble' with their savings.

People are likely to take notice of the growth potential of an investment while some could be less willing to appreciate the risk involved. The adviser needs to take especial care to make such a client aware of risks.

Attitudes to risk vary according to the different objectives of the investor. An investor may have a core holding of deposits that he wishes to keep as an emergency fund, while he may be prepared to take greater risks with other funds he holds. If a client has a specific target for a particular investment – for example, to pay for children's education, or to pay for a vacation – then he may choose lower risk investments for the funds intended to reach that target than for other his other investments.

One way of classifying investors is to look at an investor's views on risk and the way that investor makes decisions. This will give a classification system based on how **cautious**, **methodical**, **spontaneous** or **individualistic** the investor is.

| | Decision making is rational/based on thought | Decision making is emotional/based on feeling |
| --- | --- | --- |
| **High risk aversity** | Methodical | Cautious |
| **Low risk aversity** | Individualist | Spontaneous |

*Source: Bronson, Scanlan, Squires*

The following is a general guide to typical characteristics.

**Cautious investors**

- Highly loss averse
- Need for security
- Want low-risk investments with safe capital
- Do not like making decisions but do not listen to others
- Tend not to use advisers
- Portfolios are low risk and with low turnover

**Methodical investors**

- Analytical and factual
- Make decisions slowly
- Little emotional attachment to investments and decisions
- Tend to be conservative in investment approach

**Spontaneous investors**

- High portfolio turnover

- Do not trust the advice of others

- Some are successful investors, but most do less well, particularly because of high transaction costs due to high turnover

- Make decisions quickly and are fearful of missing out on opportunities

**Individualist investors**

- Self-confident
- Prepared to do analysis and will expect to achieve their long-term goals

## 7.16 Customer understanding

It is a basic regulatory requirement that a firm should not recommend a transaction or act as an investment manager for a customer unless it has taken reasonable steps to help the customer **understand the nature of the risks** involved.

In the case of **warrants** and **derivatives**, the firm should provide to the customer any appropriate **warrants and derivatives risk warnings**.

If recommending to a retail customer transactions in investments that are not readily realisable, the adviser should explain the difficulties in establishing a market price.

Following the recording of recommendations in a **report**, the adviser can check whether the client has read and understood the contents of the report, and can be asked whether he has any **questions** to ask about it.

## 7.17 Affordability and accessibility

The **affordability** of any investments and protection policies to be recommended for the client must be considered. The client's prospective disposable income should be ascertained in order to assess the affordability of regular contributions to policies and investment plans. Existing assets and policies, such as life assurance contracts and other savings need to be taken into account in quantifying the sizes of investments needed to meet client needs.

## 7.18 Client reviews

The adviser is concerned with identifying and satisfying client needs. This is not just a 'one-off' process. Clients will have a continuing need for financial advice. Their circumstances will change, and there may need to be a review of whether products initially recommended continue to be suitable.

Regular **reviews** of client circumstances will enable the adviser to make best use of future business opportunities with that client. For the client, there are the benefits of the advice arising from the review.

## 7.19 Review dates

Many financial advisers conduct client reviews **annually**. This may fit well with the client's needs, if pay or bonuses are reviewed annually for example, or to fit in with the accounting cycle of a business. A review at the time of a client's birthday is another possibility: some life assurance risks are assessed in annual steps linked to the birth date.

Client reviews should not be restricted to **pre-determined review dates**. Clients' circumstances may change in unpredictable ways. An individual may be made redundant, or may start a new job. There could be a change in family health circumstances, or a new baby may be expected. These are examples of changes that could have a significant impact on financial planning, and so the client should be encouraged to seek advice and appropriate review of their circumstances, when such events occur.

Events in the financial world may produce an opportunity for the adviser to contact the client to review their effect on his or her circumstances.

- For example, **new tax rules** may be announced, or investment conditions may change, for example if there are significant movements in share prices.
- A **new tax year** can present possible **tax planning** opportunities, for example relating to ISA investments and pension contributions.

It may be most appropriate for an adviser to agree with the client that there will be an annual review date, but with the proviso that either client or adviser may make contact if an additional review is appropriate.

# 8 Client interaction

## 8.1 The financial adviser

The adviser must work within the scope of the activities for which their firm is **authorised** or for which they are individually **approved**. The adviser needs to be aware of the extent of their own **professional competence** and not attempt to work outside this, or beyond the **job description** laid out by their firm.

## 8.2 Communication techniques

Good **communication skills** are important for the financial adviser and wealth manager. Much of the information the adviser acquires is likely to be by interviewing – asking questions of – the client.

You should appreciate the difference between objective **factual information** and evaluative statements which express opinions or feelings. The latter type of statement may be expressed in terms of someone's hopes, wants or plans.

**Examples of factual information**

- Disregarding dividends, the Clearfield Unit Trust has grown in value by more than the FTSE 100 benchmark index over the three-year period to 31 December 2011.

- Brenda has fallen into two months' arrears on her mortgage payments.

**Examples of non-factual statements**

- Graham thinks that he should invest more of his portfolio in foreign stocks, in order to diversify risk.
- Matilda was disappointed by the service provided by her previous financial adviser.

**Closed questions** ask for a **specific** piece of **information**, for example a National Insurance number or a figure for the value of a property. Examples could be:

- Could you please tell me your address?
- Do you have any ISAs?

The answer to a closed question is typically a single word, or a short phrase, or 'Yes' or 'No'. The client may tire of having too much of this form of questioning quickly, and the questioner will not find out much about the client's views or feelings in the process.

**Open questions** give the client more opportunity to **express his views** or **feelings** in a **longer response**. Examples of open questions are:

- How do you feel about taking risks with your investments?
- What do you think are the most immediate financial needs to be addressed?

## 8.3 'Know your customer'

You will be well aware of the need to possess a lot of **information** about your client before you can give them advice. This need is reflected in one of the basic requirements of the regulatory regime: to '**know your customer**' **(KYC)**. This is one of the basic requirements of the regulatory regime as well as being part of the **fiduciary duty** of the adviser.

This includes obtaining sufficient information about a customer's personal and financial situation, before giving advice or (if applicable) before constructing a portfolio for the customer. The process of obtaining this information is not only essential in ensuring that you give suitable advice on a current issue. It can also reveal further areas where you might help your clients in the future.

A further aspect of knowing one's customer is to know the **customer's capabilities**, so that one can **adapt** one's communication to suit the customer. Such adaptation should cover the extent of use of technical terminology and the extent of quantitative analysis presented to the customer. The adaptation should cover both **spoken and written communication**.

Earlier, we mentioned initiatives such as the **Money Advice Service**, which targets consumers generally, many of whom may have had limited if any contact with financial services firms. Firms themselves can help to widen their customer base and be more inclusive through initiatives to write **printed and website content** in plain English, and to train advisers in communicating with a range of consumers.

In **presentations** to clients, the adviser who is an effective communicator will be checking for indications that the client understands what is being said as the presentation develops, so that the adviser can explain a point again if necessary, perhaps simplifying aspects of the explanation. Checks on understanding can be made by asking open questions. Just to ask 'Do you follow what I am saying?' will not be sufficient: the less assertive client may say 'Yes' even if they do not fully understand.

## 8.4 Written reports to clients

Providing a **written report** to clients is an important part of the process of giving financial advice.

The **parts of a financial planning report** to a client are typically as follows.

- A statement of the client's objectives

- A summary of the client's income and assets and other relevant circumstances or problems

- Recommendations, including any proposals for immediate action as well as longer-term suggestions for the client to consider in the future

- Appendices, including any data that is best presented separately, if appropriate

**Product quotations, illustrations and brochures** should be presented in an orderly way, possibly with an index listing the various items being sent to the client.

The **language** in the report should be phrased as concisely as possible and, again, with explanations to suit the capabilities of the particular client while also meeting all regulatory requirements. Jargon should be avoided except where necessary to explain points being made.

When a client has agreed a set of recommendations, there will be a considerable amount of work involved in arranging investments, along with any pension arrangements and protection policies also being taken out.

## 8.5 Formulating a plan

The prime objective of the **comprehensive plan** is to make **recommendations** regarding the action needed to meet the client's stated and agreed objectives.

As well as **regulatory considerations,** the plan must **take account of economic conditions** which could affect the client, such as the possibility of redundancy, the prospects for a self-employed person's business and the effect of inflation.

The plan should take account of a client's **current financial position**. Is there a surplus of assets over liabilities? If so, is the surplus in a form where it can be better used?

If liabilities exceed assets then can **liabilities be rearranged**? For example, if part of the reason is an expensive loan, can the loan be repaid (provided any repayment charges are acceptable) and replaced by a more effective loan such as borrowing on the security of a with profits policy where interest rates tend to be below average?

**How liquid are the client's assets**? How much of the client's assets is in a form which can be turned into cash quickly, if necessary?

The client's current **tax position** is of prime importance.

The client's protection requirements will be affected not only by current needs but by **changing economic conditions**.

Full account must be taken of the **client's attitude and understanding of risk** when it comes to arranging investments. Widows with small capital sum and whose only income is the state pension should not be advised to invest in futures and options! Equally, high net worth individuals with substantial excess of income over expenditure could spread their investments in a way which provides a balanced mix of caution, medium risk and high risk.

## 8.6 Ethical preferences

In taking account of any **ethical preferences** affecting investment choice that a client may have, the adviser needs to bear in mind the differences between funds. As we have seen, there are many **'ethical' funds**, but these cover a range of criteria, for example between 'dark green' funds that use **negative criteria** to exclude companies to other 'lighter green' funds that use **positive criteria** to include companies that pursue positive policies on the environment or social factors. The adviser should ensure that funds chosen match the expressed concerns of the client.

# Key chapter points

- The regulators' Conduct of Business Sourcebook (COBS) generally applies to authorised firms engaged in designated investment business carried out from their (or their appointed representatives') UK establishments. Some COB rules do not apply to eligible counterparty business.

- 'Designated investment business' is business involving regulated activities, except mortgages, deposits, pure protection policies, general insurance, Lloyd's business and funeral plans.

- The level of protection given to clients by the regulatory system depends on their classification, with retail clients being protected the most. Professional clients and eligible counterparties may both be either *per se* or elective. Both professional clients and eligible counterparties can re-categorise to get more protection.

- Firms doing designated investment business, except advising, must set out a basic client agreement. Firms must provide to clients appropriate information about the firm and its services, designated investments and their risks, execution venues and costs. Firms managing investments must establish a performance benchmark and must provide information about valuations and management objectives.

- It is generally acceptable for a firm to rely on information provided by others if the other firm is competent and not connected with the firm placing the reliance.

- A financial promotion inviting someone to engage in investment activity must be issued by or approved by an authorised firm. Communications must be fair, clear and not misleading. Prospectus advertisements must clearly indicate that they are not a prospectus. Communications with retail clients must balance information about benefits of investments with information about risks.

- Unwritten financial promotions rules cover cold calling, which must be limited to an 'appropriate time of day'.

- Rules on assessing suitability of a recommendation apply when a firm makes a personal recommendation in relation to a designated investment.

- For certain packaged products, a suitability report is required, specifying the client's demands and needs and explaining the firm's recommendation.

- There are obligations to assess 'appropriateness' – based on information about the client's experience and knowledge – for MiFID business where personal advice is not given, and managing investments.

- Key Features Documents, which must be produced to at least the same quality as marketing material, disclose product information.

- Retail clients must be given the opportunity to change their mind (cancel) after agreeing to the purchase of investment products.

- Inducements must not be given if they conflict with acting in the best interests of clients.

- Firms must make adequate arrangements to safeguard clients' money, and to prevent the use of client money for the firm's own account.

- A firm must in general take all reasonable steps to obtain, when executing orders, the best possible result for its clients. This is the requirement of best execution.

- Firms must establish arrangements designed to prevent employees entering into personal transactions which are prohibited forms of market abuse. Staff must be made aware of the personal dealing restrictions.

- Churning and switching are forms of unsuitable overtrading of customer accounts in order to generate commission.

- The financial planning process involves six stages: 1: Obtaining relevant information – fact finding. 2: Establishing and agreeing the client's financial objectives. 3: Processing and analysing the data obtained. 4: Formulating recommendations in a comprehensive plan with objectives. 5: Implementing the recommendations as agreed with the client. 6: Reviewing and regularly updating the plan.

- Clients' objectives may need to be prioritised and quantified, resulting in a present value analysis of anticipated future liabilities. Affordability should be assessed.

- Information on the client's current personal and financial circumstances is collected through the fact find process.

- Higher risk investments are needed to produce the potential of high returns, but also bring the chance of loss. Specific risks of investments can be diversified away, but general market risk will remain. A client's attitude to risk may be influenced by investment timescales.

- Differences in individuals' circumstances may include variability in sources of wealth (whether passively or actively acquired), amount of wealth and the current life cycle stage of the individual. The level of an individual's tolerance to risk needs to be considered by an adviser.

- Regular (e.g. annual) client review is a valuable process for both client and adviser, and ideally both client and adviser should get in contact with the other if changing circumstances suggest the need for a review at any time.

- Advisers need to employ good communication skills. The desirability of avoiding social exclusion underlines the idea that communications with consumers be adapted suit the capabilities of the consumer to which the communication is directed.

## Chapter Quiz

1   Name the three main categories of client. ............................................................ (see para 1.6.1)

2   Name three types of *per se* eligible counterparty. ...........................................................(1.6.5)

3   A firm's communications and financial promotions must be '...................... , ...................... and not
    ......................'. *[Fill in the blanks]* ....................................................................(2.4)

4   What information will the firm need to obtain from the client to enable it to assess the appropriateness of a
    product or service to the client? .................................................................................(3.3)

5   List the main cancellation periods for retail clients. .........................................................(4.5.2)

6   What does the rule on best execution require? ................................................................(5.2)

7   Outline the six stages of the financial planning process. ..................................................(6.1)

8   What different types of diversification might an investor or adviser consider? ...........................(6.6.2)

9   What is meant by client review, and why should an adviser conduct a review? ............................(7.18)

10  In the context of communicating verbally with a client, give examples of closed questions and open questions.
    ........................................................................................................................(8.2)

# 8

# Principles and outcomes based regulation

## Chapter topic list

9 **Understand the financial regulators' use of principles and outcomes based regulation to promote ethical and fair outcomes**

9.1 **Examine** the Principles for Businesses and the discretionary obligations these place on firms

9.2 **Examine** the impact of corporate culture and leadership

9.3 **Examine** the responsibilities of approved persons and the need for integrity, competence and fair outcomes for clients

# 1 Principles for Businesses

## 1.1 Application of the Principles for Businesses

The **High Level Standards** known as the **Principles for Businesses** apply in whole or in part to every **authorised firm** carrying out a regulated activity. **Approved persons** are individuals, who subject to a separate set of principles known as **Statements of Principle** – to which we turn later in this chapter.

The Principles for Businesses state firms' fundamental obligations under the regulatory system. They are formulated to require honest, fair and professional conduct from firms.

The Principles for Businesses are included in the **FCA Handbook**. They are referred to as **PRIN** in the Handbooks. The PRA has its own set of Fundamental Rules (see below).

While the Principles for Businesses apply to regulated activities generally, with respect to the activities of accepting deposits, general insurance and long-term pure protection policies (i.e., that have no surrender value and are payable upon death), they apply only in a 'prudential context'. This means the regulator will only proceed against a contravention where it is a serious or persistent violation of a principle that has an impact on confidence in the financial system, the fitness and propriety of the firm or the adequacy of the firm's financial resources.

## 1.2 The Principles

The **11 Principles for Businesses** are as follows.

| Principles for Businesses |
|---|
| **1.** **Integrity** |
| A firm must conduct its business with integrity. |
| **2.** **Skill, care and diligence** |
| A firm must conduct its business with due skill, care and diligence. |
| **3.** **Management and control** |
| A firm must take reasonable care to organise and control its affairs responsibly and effectively, with adequate risk management systems. |
| **4.** **Financial prudence** |
| A firm must maintain adequate financial resources. |

| Principles for Businesses |
|---|
| **5.** **Market conduct** <br><br> A firm must observe proper standards of market conduct. |
| **6.** **Customers' interests** <br><br> A firm must pay due regard to the interests of its customers and treat them fairly. |
| **7.** **Communications with clients** <br><br> A firm must pay due regard to the information needs of its clients, and communicate information to them in a way which is clear, fair and not misleading. |
| **8.** **Conflicts of interest** <br><br> A firm must manage conflicts of interest fairly, both between itself and its customers and between a customer and another client. |
| **9.** **Customers: relationships of trust** <br><br> A firm must take reasonable care to ensure the suitability of its advice and discretionary decisions for any customer who is entitled to rely upon its judgement. |
| **10.** **Clients' assets** <br><br> A firm must arrange adequate protection for clients' assets when it is responsible for them. |
| **11.** **Relations with regulators** <br><br> A firm must deal with its regulators in an open and co-operative way and must disclose to the appropriate regulator appropriately anything relating to the firm of which that regulator would reasonably expect notice. |

## 1.3 Scope of the Principles

Some of the principles (such as Principle 10) refer to **clients**, while others (such as Principle 9) refer to **customers**. This difference affects the scope of the relevant principles.

- **'Client'** includes everyone from the smallest retail customer through to the largest investment firm. It therefore includes, under the terminology of MiFID, eligible counterparties, professional customers and retail customers.

- **'Customer'** is a more restricted term that includes professional and retail clients but excludes 'eligible counterparties'. 'Customers' are thus clients who are not **eligible counterparties**. Principles 6, 8 and 9, and parts of Principle 7, apply only to **customers**.

In line with MiFID, a firm will not be subject to a Principle to the extent that it is contrary to the EU Single Market Directives. Principles 1, 2, 6 and 9 may be disapplied for this reason, in the case of:

- **Eligible counterparty business**
- Transactions on a regulated market (e.g. the London Stock Exchange), and member transactions under a **multilateral trading facility** – a system that enables parties (e.g. retail investors or other investment firms) to buy and sell financial instruments

Note that Principle 3 would not be considered breached if the firm failed to prevent **unforeseeable** risks.

## 1.4 Breaches of the Principles

The consequence of breaching a Principle makes the firm liable to **enforcement or disciplinary sanctions**. In determining whether a Principle has been breached it is necessary to look to the standard of conduct required by the

Principle in question. Under each of the Principles, the onus will be on the relevant regulator to show that a firm has been at fault in some way.

The definition of 'fault' varies between some of the different Principles.

- Under **Principle 1 (Integrity)**, for example, the regulator would need to demonstrate a lack of integrity in the conduct of a firm's business.

- Under **Principle 2 (Skill, care and diligence)** a firm would be in breach if it was shown to have failed to act with due skill, care and diligence in the conduct of its business.

- Similarly, under **Principle 3 (Management and control)** a firm would not be in breach simply because it failed to control or prevent unforeseeable risks, but a breach would occur if the firm had failed to take reasonable care to organise and control its affairs responsibly or effectively.

**S138D FSMA 2000** (as amended) creates a right of action in damages for a '**private person**' who suffers loss as a result of a contravention of certain **rules** by an authorised firm. However, a 'private person' may not sue a firm under S138D FSMA 2000 for the breach of a **Principle**.

## 1.5 The PRA's Fundamental Rules

The **Prudential Regulation Authority** has set out the following **Fundamental Rules** for **PRA-authorised firms**, as follows.

| PRA: Fundamental Rules | |
|---|---|
| 1. | **Integrity** |
| | A firm must conduct its business with integrity. |
| 2. | **Skill, care and diligence** |
| | A firm must conduct its business with due skill, care and diligence. |
| 3. | **Prudence** |
| | A firm must act in a prudent manner. |
| 4. | **Financial resources** |
| | A firm must maintain adequate financial resources. |
| 5. | **Risk** |
| | A firm must have effective risk strategies and risk management systems. |
| 6. | **Organisation and control** |
| | A firm must organise and control its affairs responsibly and effectively. |
| 7. | **Relations with regulators** |
| | A firm must deal with its regulators in an open and co-operative way and must disclose to the PRA appropriately anything relating to the firm of which the PRA would reasonably expect notice. |
| 8. | **Resolution** |
| | A firm must prepare for resolution so, if the need arises, it can be resolved in an orderly manner with the minimum disruption of critical services. |

You will note that there are similarities between the **PRA's Fundamental Rules and the FCA's Principles for Businesses**. The key **differences** are as follows.

- The FCA's Principles for Businesses include a number of principles that deal with **conduct** and are not covered In the PRA Fundamental Rules: that is, Principles 5, 6, 7, 8, 9, and 10.

- Unlike the FCA's Principles for Businesses, the PRA's Fundamental Rules contain a rule concerning **Resolution**, which refers to the restructuring of failing banks and other credit institutions.

# 2 Principles-based regulation

## 2.1 Principles, outcomes and supervision

The principles-based approach to regulation requires compliance with principles, but leaves firms with discretion as to how to comply with the principles. In the wake of the financial crisis of the late 2000s, the Chief Executive of the FSA, Hector Sants, commented in a 2009 speech that 'a principles-based approach does not work with individuals who have no principles'.

Mr Sants said: 'In future, we will seek to make judgements on the judgements of senior management and take actions if, in our view, those actions will lead to risks to our statutory objectives'.

This was a fundamental change in the regulator's approach to supervision, moving from **evidence-based regulation** (based on observable facts) to regulation based on judgements about the future.

The new 'intrusive and direct' approach proposed by the regulator would, Mr Sants continued, 'carry significant risk and our judgements will necessarily not always be correct'. It did however appear that society expected regulators to behave in this way.

Writing in the Chief Executive's Overview to the FSA's **2009/10 Business Plan**, Hector Sants complained that the regulatory philosophy of **more principles-based regulation** had often been misunderstood. The focus of the Authority's philosophy, he wrote, is not *per se* on our principles, but rather on judging the consequences of the actions of the firms and the individuals we supervise. Given this philosophy, Sants argued, a better 'strapline' would be **outcomes-focused regulation**.

An example of this developing emphasis on **outcomes** is found in the regulators' approach to the principle of treating customers fairly (TCF): In Chapter 2 of this Study Text, we explain the TCF **consumer outcomes** against which firms are expected to measure their progress in meeting the TCF principle.

## 2.2 Turner Review (2009)

The role of the FSA had come under heavy criticism, from the House of Commons Treasury Committee as well as more widely, following the run on the **Northern Rock** bank in the autumn of 2007. While the directors of the mortgage lender had 'pursued a reckless business model', in the words of the Committee, the regulator had, the Committee asserted, 'systematically failed in its regulatory duty to ensure that Northern Rock would not pose a systemic risk'.

In the light of this and other aspects of the financial turmoil of 2007 and 2008, Lord Adair Turner, Chairman of the FSA, prepared a report commissioned by the Chancellor of the Exchequer to review the events that had led to the financial crisis and to recommend reforms. The **Turner Review** was published in March 2009 as a *'Regulatory response to the global banking crisis'*, and extended to approximately 120 pages.

The FSA's regulatory and supervisory approach, before the crisis, was based on a philosophy that was sometimes characterised – although not by the regulator itself – as a '**light touch**' regulatory regime.

This philosophy seemed to have been broadly based on the beliefs that:

- **Markets are in general self-correcting**, with market discipline a more effective tool than regulation or supervisory oversight through which to ensure that firms' strategies are sound and **risks** contained

- The **primary responsibility for managing risks lies with the senior management** and boards of the individual firms, who are better placed to assess business model risk than bank regulators, and who can be relied on to make appropriate decisions about the balance between risk and return, provided appropriate systems, procedures and skilled people are in place

- **Customer protection is best ensured** not by product regulation or direct intervention in markets, but **by ensuring that wholesale markets** are as **unfettered** and **transparent** as possible, and that the **way in which firms conduct business** is appropriate

The philosophy had resulted in a **supervisory approach** which involved:

- A **focus**, evident also in supervisory systems across the world, on the supervision of individual **institutions** rather than on the whole **system**

- A more **intrusive and 'direct'** style of supervision referred to as the **Intensive Supervisory Model**, requiring the supervisor to have a more integrated or 'holistic' and 'macro-' view of firms and the markets in which they operate

- A focus on ensuring that **systems and processes** were correctly defined, rather than on challenging **business models and strategies**

- A focus within the regulator's oversight of '**approved persons**' (e.g. those proposed by firms for key risk management functions) on checking that there were **no issues of probity** raised by past conduct, **rather than assessing technical skills**, with the presumption that management and boards were in a better position to judge the appropriateness of specific individuals for specific roles

- A balance between conduct of **business regulation** and **prudential regulation** which, with the benefit of hindsight, now appeared **biased towards the former** in most sectors

The Review emphasised the importance of regulation and supervision being based on a '**macro-prudential**' **(system-wide) approach** rather than focusing solely on specific firms. The overall approach continues in the FCA's regulatory work.

# 3 Conflicts of interest

## 3.1 Principle 8

Inevitably, authorised firms, particularly where they act in dual capacity (both broker and dealing for the firm itself), are faced with **conflicts** between the firm and customers or between one customer and another.

**Principle 8** of the *Principles for Businesses* states: 'A firm must manage conflicts of interest fairly, both between itself and its customers and between a customer and another client'.

Principle 8 thus requires that authorised firms should seek to ensure that when **conflicts of interest** do arise, the firm **manages** the conflicts to ensure that customers are treated **fairly**.

One way in which a potential conflict of interest may be dealt with is, of course, by declining to act for the client.

## 3.2 SYSC 10

**SYSC 10** in the regulatory Handbooks requires firms to take all **reasonable steps** to **identify conflicts of interest** between the firm, its managers, employees and appointed representatives or tied agents, or between clients, which may arise in providing a service.

The firm must take into account, as a minimum, likely financial gains, or avoidance of losses, at the expense of a client, interests in the outcome of a service which are different from the client's interest, financial incentives to favour some clients or groups of client, and whether the firm carries on the same business as the client, or receives inducements in the form of monies, goods and services other than the standard commission or fee for that service.

Regularly updated records must be kept of where conflicts of interest have or may arise.

The firm must maintain and operate effective **organisational and administrative arrangements** to prevent conflicts of interest from giving rise to material risk of damage to clients' interests. **'Chinese walls'** are administrative and physical barriers and other internal arrangements, designed to contain **sensitive information**.

Where conflicts are not preventable by any other means, as a last resort the firm must **disclose** them to clients – in a durable medium, in sufficient detail for the client to take an informed decision – before undertaking business.

Firms should aim to **identify** and **manage** conflicts under a **comprehensive conflicts of interest policy**. That firms actively manage conflicts is important: 'over-reliance on disclosure' without adequate consideration of how to manage conflicts is not permitted.

## 3.3 Conflicts policy

Firms must maintain an effective **conflicts of interest policy**, in **writing** and appropriate to the size and type of firm and its business.

The conflicts of interest policy must:

- Identify circumstances constituting or potentially giving rise to conflicts materially affecting clients
- Specify procedures and measures to manage the conflicts

The procedures and measures must:

- Be designed to ensure that activities are carried on with an appropriate **level of independence** (this part of the procedures is often called a **policy of independence**)

- As and where necessary, include procedures to **prevent and control exchange of information** between persons involved, to **supervise persons separately**, to remove **links in remuneration** producing possible conflicts, to prevent exercise of **inappropriate influence**, and to **prevent and control simultaneous and sequential involvement** of persons in separate services or activities

# 4 Corporate culture and leadership

## 4.1 Societal and corporate values

The concept of **societal values** is of values that are generally agreed by reasonable people and that are widely accepted. At a **corporate** level, reference to values or the **corporate culture** suggests that particular ways of acting can become prevalent throughout a firm, whether by design or not. A 'culture' of pursuing short-term profit or revenue even if customers are misled ('having the wool pulled over their eyes') may pervade through a firm, either at the instigation of an aggressive if short-sighted and unethical senior management team, or as the unintended consequence of mis-judged target-setting incentive structures for employees.

## 4.2 Corporate culture

Firms have to follow the law and regulations, or else they will be subject to fines and their officers might face similar charges. **Ethics** in organisations relates to **social responsibility** and **business practices.**

People who work for organisations bring their own **values** into work with them. Organisations encompass a variety of ethical frameworks.

- **Personal ethics** deriving from a person's upbringing, religious or non-religious beliefs, political opinions, personality and so on.

- **Professional ethics**, for example the CII's Code of Ethics.

- **Corporate culture** (e.g. 'Customer first'). Culture, in denoting what is normal behaviour, also denotes what is the right behaviour in many cases.

- **Organisation systems**. Ethics might be contained in a formal code, reinforced by the overall statement of values. A problem might be that good ethics does not always save money, and there is a real cost to ethical decisions. Equally, there can be substantial risk, and costs, if poor ethics results in loss of reputation for the firm.

As the financial regulator has stated (in CP10/12), promoting **standards of ethical behaviour** improves outcomes for consumers and their perception of the financial services industry. Consumer perception stems from their view of the behaviour and culture established by senior management in large firms as much as that of a sole trader.

## 4.3 Leadership

It is recognised that, beyond mere compliance with rules, organisations and firms must – through their **leaders** – foster a corporate culture that is congruent with the purpose of regulatory rules and principles, if regulation is to be effective.

For example, this is recognised in respect of financial crime. One of the suggested guiding principles for a firm's anti-money laundering and anti-terrorist financing policy statement is:

'An unequivocal statement of the culture and values to be adopted and promulgated throughout the firm towards the prevention of financial crime.'

Senior management must use their **leadership** positions to move the culture of their firm in the desired direction. A programme to imprint a corporate culture on the firm should be backed up by:

- Communicating the principles to all levels of the organisation, and possibly external stakeholder groups
- Leaders (senior management, and team leaders) setting an example
- Appropriate training of staff

# 5 Approved persons: Statements of Principle

## 5.1 Approved persons

Section 59 FSMA 2000 states that a person (an individual) cannot carry out certain **controlled functions** unless that individual has been approved by the regulators. This requirement gives rise to the term '**approved person**', and the regulators' Supervision Manual (SUP) covers the approval process. We looked at the approval process, and at what are controlled functions, earlier in this Study Text.

## 5.2 Statements of Principle for Approved Persons

The regulators' **Statements of Principle** apply generally to all **approved persons** (i.e. to relevant employees of regulated firms) when they are performing a **controlled function**.

Under the Financial Services Act 2012 (FSA 2012), the Statements of Principle relate not only to an individual's conduct in relation to the **controlled functions** they perform, but also to any **other regulated activities** functions they perform which relate to the firm within which they hold their approved person status. The term '**accountable functions**' is used in the Statements of Principle to cover both controlled functions and the other regulated activities that an approved person performs.

The Statements of Principle will not apply where it would be contrary to the UK's obligations under EU Single Market Directives. Under **MiFID** rules, the requirement to employ personnel with the necessary knowledge, skills and expertise is reserved to the firm's **Home State**. As a result, the UK financial regulators do not have a role in assessing individuals' competence and capability in performing a controlled function in relation to an **incoming EEA firm** providing MiFID investment services.

There are **seven Statements of Principle**.

- The first four Principles apply to all approved persons (which includes those doing a **significant influence function (SIF)** as well as those not performing a SIF).

- As noted in the following Table, the final three Principles (5-7) only apply to approved persons performing a SIF. The PRA has the primary responsibility for the designation and regulation of significant-influence functions.

| Statements of Principle for Approved Persons | |
|---|---|
| 1  **Integrity**. An approved person must act with integrity in carrying out his accountable functions. | **Apply to all approved persons** |
| 2  **Due skill, care and diligence**. An approved person must act with due skill, care and diligence in carrying out his accountable functions. | |
| 3  **Proper standards of market conduct**. An approved person must observe proper standards of market conduct in carrying out his accountable functions. | |
| 4  **Open and co-operative dealings with regulators**. An approved person must deal with the FCA, the PRA and other regulators in an open and co-operative way and must disclose appropriately any information of which the FCA or the PRA would reasonably expect notice. | |
| 5  **Effective organisation of business**. An approved person performing an accountable significant-influence function must take reasonable steps to ensure that the business of the firm for which he is responsible in his accountable function is organised so that it can be controlled effectively. | **Apply only to those with a significant-influence function** |
| 6  **Due skill, care and diligence in management**. An approved person performing an accountable significant-influence function must exercise due skill, care and diligence in managing the business of the firm for which he is responsible in his accountable function. | |
| 7  **Compliance with regulatory requirements**. An approved person performing an accountable significant-influence function must take reasonable steps to ensure that the business of the firm for which he is responsible in his accountable function complies with the relevant requirements and standards of the regulatory system. | |

## 5.3 The Code of Practice for Approved Persons

As required under FSMA 2000, the **Code of Practice for Approved Persons** (**APER** in the regulatory Handbooks) helps approved persons to determine whether or not their conduct complies with the Statements of Principle. The Code sets out descriptions of conduct which, in the regulators' opinion, does not comply with any of the statements, and factors which will be taken into account in determining whether or not an approved person's conduct does comply with the Statements of Principle. These descriptions have the status of **evidential provisions**.

Thus, the Code is not conclusive – it is only evidential towards indicating that a Statement of Principle has been breached. Account will be taken of the context in which the course of conduct was undertaken. In determining whether there has been a breach of Principles 5 to 7, account will be taken of the nature and complexity of the business, the role and responsibilities of the approved person, and the knowledge that the approved person had (or should have had) of the regulatory concerns arising in the business under their control. The examples in the Code that would breach a principle are not exhaustive.

The Code may be amended from time to time and the current published version at the time of the approved person's conduct will be the Code that the regulator will look to in determining whether or not there has been a breach. The regulator will examine all the circumstances of a particular matter and will only determine that there has been a breach where the individual is '**personally culpable**', i.e. deliberate conduct or conduct below the reasonable standard expected of that person in the circumstances.

We now look at the **seven Statements of Principle** in detail, taking into account the treatment of each by the **Code of Practice for Approved Persons**.

## 5.4 The Statements of Principle (1-7) in detail

**1:** An approved person must act with integrity in carrying out his accountable functions.

The Code of Practice provides examples of behaviour that would not comply with this Statement of Principle. These include an approved person:

- **Deliberately misleading clients**, his firm or the regulators, or

- Deliberately failing to inform a customer, his firm, or the regulators, that their understanding of a material issue is incorrect.

**2:** An approved person must act with due skill, care and diligence in carrying out his accountable functions.

Examples of non-compliant behaviour under Statement of Principle 2 include failing to inform a **customer**, or his firm, of material information or failing to control client assets.

The coverage of Statement of Principle 2 is similar to Principle 1. The difference is that Principle 1 states that each act needs to be **deliberate**. Principle 2 may be breached by acts which, while not deliberate wrongdoing, are **negligent**.

**3:** An approved person must observe proper standards of market conduct in carrying out his accountable functions.

Examples of non-compliant behaviour under Statement of Principle 3 include:

- A breach of market codes and exchange rules
- A breach of the *Code of Market Conduct*

The regulators expect all approved persons to meet proper standards, whether they are participating in organised markets such as exchanges, or trading in less formal over-the-counter markets.

**4:** An approved person must deal with the FCA, the PRA and other regulators in an open and co-operative way and must disclose appropriately any information of which the FCA or the PRA would reasonably expect notice.

This Statement of Principle concerns the requirement to co-operate, not only with the FCA and/or the PRA, but also with other bodies such as an overseas regulator or an exchange.

Approved persons do not have a duty to report concerns directly to the regulator unless they are responsible for such reports. The obligation on most approved persons is to report concerns of '**material significance**' in accordance with the firm's **internal procedures**. If no such procedures exist, the report should be made direct to the regulator.

It would also be a breach of this Statement of Principle if an approved person did not attend an interview or meeting with the relevant regulator, answer questions or produce documents when requested to do so and within the time limit specified.

**5:** An approved person performing an accountable significant-influence function must take reasonable steps to ensure that the business of the firm for which he is responsible in his accountable function is organised so that it can be controlled effectively.

As stated above, Principles 5 to 7 relate only to those approved persons performing a significant influence function. This principle requires those performing a significant influence function to **delegate** responsibilities responsibly and effectively. Paramount to this is a requirement that they should delegate only where it is to a suitable person. In addition, they must provide those persons with proper reporting lines, authorisation levels and job descriptions. Clearly, all of these factors (and in particular the suitability requirement) should be regularly reviewed.

Principle 5 will be particularly relevant to the person whose responsibility it is to ensure appropriate apportionment of responsibilities under the Senior Management Arrangements, Systems and Controls (SYSC) section of the regulatory Handbooks.

**6:** An approved person performing an accountable significant-influence function must exercise due skill, care and diligence in managing the business of the firm for which he is responsible in his accountable function.

This principle requires those performing a significant influence function to inform themselves about the affairs of the business for which they are responsible. They should not permit transactions or an expansion of the business unless they fully **understand the risks** involved. They must also take care when monitoring highly profitable or unusual transactions and in those or other cases, must never accept implausible or unsatisfactory explanations from subordinates.

This principle links to Principle 5 as it makes it clear that **delegation is not an abdication** of responsibility. Therefore, where delegation has been made, a person must still monitor and control that part of the business and, therefore, should require progress reports and question those reports where appropriate.

**7:** An approved person performing an accountable significant-influence function must take reasonable steps to ensure that the business of the firm for which he is responsible in his accountable function complies with the relevant requirements and standards of the regulatory system.

This has a clear link to Principle 3 of the *Principles for Businesses – Management and Control*. Those exerting a significant influence on the firm must take reasonable steps to ensure that the requirements set out therein are implemented within their firm. They should also review the improvement of such systems and controls, especially where there has been a breach of the regulatory requirements. Principle 7 will be particularly relevant to the person whose responsibility it is to ensure appropriate apportionment of responsibilities under the Senior Management Arrangements, Systems and Controls section of the regulatory Handbooks.

# Key chapter points

- The High Level Standards known as the Principles for Businesses apply in whole or in part to every authorised firm carrying out a regulated activity. Approved persons are subject to a separate set of principles, known as Statements of Principle.

- Breaching a Principle makes the firm liable to enforcement or disciplinary sanctions. Additionally, S138D FSMA 2000 creates a right of action in damages for a 'private person' who suffers loss as a result of a contravention of certain rules by an authorised firm. However, a 'private person' may not sue a firm under S138D FSMA 2000 for the breach of a Principle.

- Although the regulators stress the Principles for Businesses over and above compliance with detailed rules, the emphasis of the regulators' philosophy is on the actual consequences of what firms do. Increasingly, the term used for the regulators' approach has been outcomes-focused regulation.

- The 2009 Turner Review acknowledged that there are limits to the degree to which risks can be identified and offset at the level of the individual firm. As well stressing a more intensive and direct regulatory style, the regulators have been seeking to focus regulatory effort on emphasising outcomes.

- Ethical conduct by all team members should be a major concern for management. Incorporating ethics in the organisation's values and corporate culture is promoted through leadership.

- The regulators' Statements of Principle apply generally to all approved persons (i.e. relevant employees of regulated firms) when they are performing a controlled function. The Code of Practice for Approved Persons sets out types of conduct breaching the Statements of Principle.

# Chapter Quiz

1    List six of the regulators' Principles for Businesses. .......................................................... (see para 1.2)

2    'Section 138D FSMA 2000 creates a right of action in damages for a private person who suffers loss from contravention of a rule or principle by an authorised firm.' Is this statement *True* or *False*? ........................... (1.4)

3    What do the Principles for Businesses say about conflicts of interest? ........................................................ (3.1)

4    State three methods by which senior management might seek through leadership to ensure adoption of a corporate culture throughout a firm.  . ................................................................................. (4.3)

5    Which Statements of Principle apply to all approved persons? ...................................................... (5.2)

6    State the first Statement of Principle for Approved Persons. ........................................................ (5.4)

7    Give two examples of behaviour that would breach Statement of Principle 1. ............................................. (5.4)

## Chapter topic list

|   |  | Page |
|---|---|---|

# Ethical behaviour and professional standards

10 **Apply the Code of Ethics and professional standards to business behaviour of individuals**

    10.1 **Apply** the Code of Ethics and the professional principles and values on which the code is based

    10.2 **Identify** ethical dilemmas and apply the steps involved in managing ethical dilemmas

11 **Critically evaluate the outcomes that distinguish between ethical and compliance-driven behaviours**

    11.1 **Evaluate** the positive indicators of ethical behaviour

    11.2 **Evaluate** the negative indicators of limiting behaviour to compliance within the rules

    11.3 **Critically evaluate** the outcomes that distinguish ethical and compliant behaviours

# 1 Ethics and professional integrity

## 1.1 Framework of rules

The society we live in could not exist without **rules and standards**.

What would life be like if everyone went about doing exactly what they felt like? People may decide not to turn up for work. This would mean shops not opening, and that you could not buy food. What we consider **crime would spiral out of control** as members of the public decide to take what they want and the police would only tackle criminals if they felt like it. **Businesses would not function** and the **financial markets** could not operate.

As society developed from prehistoric tribes to the complex interrelationships we have today, rules regulating behaviour had also to evolve. This is because humans recognised the need for everyone to work together for the good of the group.

## 1.2 Development of society and law

Back in prehistoric times, there were no laws, no courts and no police. Rules would have **developed through need**. The tribe would have a collective idea of what was **right** and **wrong** for the good of the group and would have **punished** a group member who stepped out of line, for example by taking food from others.

Further rules developed as society grew and eventually the first **laws** were laid down to control the larger populations.

**Business law** is relatively new, and has only developed over the last couple of hundred years with **industrialisation** and the needs that grew from it.

## 1.3 Values – personal, corporate, societal

Beyond merely developing rules, human groups and individuals have formulated **values** which, if followed by all, result in a better outcome than if individuals acted only out of their own **self-interest**.

For example, a commonly espoused **personal value** is that of **concern for others**, or acting towards others in the way that you would wish them to act towards you. Some have associated the rules, principles and values they have personally sought to live by with **religion**, while others have seen the rules, principles and values as having a **rational** basis.

The concept of **societal values** is of values that are generally agreed by reasonable people and that are widely accepted. At a corporate level, reference to values or the corporate culture suggests that particular ways of acting can become prevalent throughout a firm, whether by design or not. A 'culture' of pursuing short-term profit or revenue even if customers are misled ('having the wool pulled over their eyes') may pervade through a firm, either at the instigation of an aggressive if short-sighted and unethical senior management team, or as the unintended consequence of mis-judged target-setting incentive structures for employees.

## 1.4 Societal values and business

**Social attitudes**, such as a belief in the merits of education, progress through science and technology, and fair competition, are significant for the management of a business organisation. Other beliefs have either gained strength or been eroded in recent years.

- There is a growing belief in preserving and improving the **quality of life** by reducing working hours, reversing the spread of pollution, developing leisure activities and so on. Pressures on organisations to consider the environment are particularly strong because most environmental damage is irreversible and some is fatal to humans and wildlife.

- Many pressure groups have been organised in recent years to protect social minorities and under-privileged groups. Legislation has been passed in an attempt to prevent racial discrimination and discrimination against women and disabled people.

- Issues relating to the environmental consequences of corporate activities are currently debated, and respect for the environment has come to be regarded as an unquestionable good.

- There remains a debate about whether consumers should be protected by a comprehensive set of rules with the objective of making sure that they do not enter into bad deals or transactions, or whether the rule of *caveat emptor* ('let the buyer beware') should guide all transactions.

## 1.5 Sources of rules and principles

The rules or principles that regulate behaviour of individuals and businesses derive from:

- The **law**
- The requirements of **rules and regulations**
- Regulatory **guidance** that is not mandatory
- **Professional standards** and **codes of conduct**
- **Ethics** and ethical **values**

## 1.6 Ethics: moral principles to guide behaviour

Whereas the political environment in which an organisation operates consists of laws, regulations and government agencies, the social environment consists of the customs, attitudes, beliefs and education of society as a whole, or of different groups in society; and the ethical environment consists of a set (or sets) of well-established rules of personal and organisational behaviour.

## 1.7 Rights

The idea that individuals have natural **inherent rights** that should not be abused is a further, long-established influence on Western ethical thinking and one that has led to the development of law to protect certain 'human rights'.

## 1.8 Reasons for unethical behaviour

Unethical behaviour can arise for a number of different reasons. The regulator's **Discussion Paper 18** *An ethical framework for financial services* (2002) suggested some of them, as outlined below.

- The pressure of short-term gain could be seen to encourage undesirable behaviour. Staff bonus payments may often seem to be geared to pure bottom line success. How risks and tensions can be identified is a constant issue – e.g. truth versus loyalty, one person versus the many? In all of this, it is usual for the values and actions of senior management to influence employee levels.

- Some individuals behave unethically because they think it is worth the risk. This may be related to a short-termist agenda, or may simply be personally selfish. People weigh up the pros and cons and take a chance. It is a deliberate risk/reward trade off. Others may believe they are behaving ethically but come to operate by a different yardstick to that used by others. They might do something which is deemed unethical, but which seems acceptable from their own perspective.

- Others (and some of these groups are not mutually exclusive) may be unaware of the values embedded in existing regulatory standards. So, they comply (or do not comply!) blindly with the 'letter of the law', rather than thinking about the wider effects their behaviour might have.

## 1.9 Ethical principles

Much of the practical difficulty with ethics lies in the absence of an **agreed basis** for decision-making. Effective **legal systems** are certain in their effects upon the individual. While the complexity of such matters as tax law can make it difficult to determine just what the law says in any given case, it is still possible to determine the issue in court. Once the law is decided, it is definite and there is little scope for argument.

The **certainty of legal rules** does not have a counterpart in ethical theory. Different ideas apply in different cultures.

Ethics and morality are about right and wrong behaviour. Western thinking about ethics tends to be based on ideas about **duty** and **consequences**. Unfortunately, such thinking often fails to indicate a single clear course of action. Ethical thinking is also influenced by the concepts of **virtue** and **rights**.

## 1.10 Ethics based on consequences

This approach judges actions by reference to their outcomes or consequences.

**Utilitarianism**, propounded by Jeremy Bentham, is the best known version of this approach and can be summed up as choosing the action that is likely to result in the **greatest good for the greatest number of people**.

This approach has been refined by other moral philosophers who distinguish this 'act utilitarianism' with an alternative 'rule utilitarianism' which involves choosing and living by the **rules** that are most likely to result in the greatest good for the greatest number of people.

## 1.11 Ethics based on duty

We use **duty** as a label for the ethical approach technically called **deontology** (which means much the same thing as 'duty' in Greek). This set of ideas is associated with the German thinker Immanuel Kant and is based upon the idea that behaviour should be governed by **absolute moral rules** that apply in all circumstances.

## 1.12 Ethics based on virtue and personal qualities

**Virtue ethics** continues to exert a subtle influence. The idea is that if people cultivate certain **values / principles** or **virtues / qualities**, their **behaviour** is likely to be inherently ethical. Today it is suggested that managers should attempt to incorporate such **personal qualities** as firmness, fairness, objectivity, charity, forethought, loyalty and so on into their daily behaviour and decision-making.

## 1.13 Two approaches to business ethics

### 1.13.1 Overview

*Lynne Paine* (*Harvard Business Review*, March-April 1994) suggests that ethical decisions are becoming more important as penalties, in the US at least, for companies which break the law become tougher. Paine suggests that there are two approaches to the management of ethics in organisations:

- Compliance-based (or 'rules-based'), and
- Integrity-based

### 1.13.2 Compliance-based approach

A rules-based compliance approach is primarily designed to ensure that the company **acts within the letter of laws and regulations**, and that violations are prevented, detected and punished. Some organisations, faced with the legal consequences of unethical behaviour, take legal precautions such as:

- Compliance procedures to detect misconduct
- Audits of contracts
- Systems for employees to report criminal misconduct without fear of retribution
- Disciplinary procedures to deal with transgressions

### 1.13.3 Integrity-based approach

An integrity-based approach combines a concern for the law with an **emphasis on managerial responsibility** for ethical behaviour. Integrity strategies strive to define companies' guiding values, aspirations and patterns of thought and conduct. When integrated into the day-to-day operations of an organisation, such strategies can help prevent damaging ethical lapses, while tapping into powerful human impulses for moral thought and action.

### 1.13.4 Comparison of the two approaches

The integrity-based approach, as compared with a rules-centred or compliance-based approach, echoes the financial regulators' **principles-based approach** to regulation. The principles-based approach requires firms to act with integrity and to treat customers fairly, for example. Unlike rules, such principles require senior management to apply higher-level professional values in how they run their business.

A compliance-based approach suggests that bureaucratic control is necessary; an integrity-based or principles-based approach relies on cultural control.

Basing our professional work on integrity, instead of asking 'Show me where it says we can't...', we ask 'How can we improve our standards and conduct our business with integrity?'

## 1.14 Professional integrity

### 1.14.1 The principle of integrity

Financial services is an important industry, affecting the lives of most people. The industry needs not simply to provide the necessary expertise, but to do so with integrity.

The regulators' first **Principle for Businesses** is **Integrity**:

'A firm must conduct its business with integrity.'

The first Statement of Principle for Approved Persons also deals with **Integrity**:

'An approved person must act with integrity in carrying out his controlled functions.'

We covered which functions are categorised as 'controlled' functions earlier in this Study Text (Chapter 6).

What do we mean by professional integrity? Among the attributes that contribute to integrity are:

- **Honesty** – which will mean that the person will not deliberately mislead another

- **Reliability** – meaning that the person can be relied upon to maintain appropriate levels of competence and skill in practice

- **Impartiality** – this means treating different people fairly, where the people involved could be customers, or employees

- **Openness** – which implies transparency, where appropriate and where justified confidentiality is not breached

### 1.14.2 Examples of behaviour lacking integrity

The **Code of Practice for Approved Persons (APER)** includes examples of behaviour that would breach the Statement of Principle.

The regulator has stated (Policy Statement PS10/18, December 2010) that **adherence to APER** is a **vital part of retaining approved persons status**. The Authority was disappointed to note that knowledge of APER among the approved persons population appeared to be low.

The integrity principle will be contravened, in the view of the regulators, and indeed on any commonsense interpretation of the principle, if the approved person **deliberately misleads**, or **attempts to mislead**, by act or omission, a client, his firm, its auditors or actuaries, or the regulators.

The following examples of behaviour of this type are provided in APER:

- Falsifying documents

- Misleading a client about the risks of an investment

- Misleading a client about the charges or surrender penalties of investment products

- Misleading a client about the likely performance of investment products by providing inappropriate projections of future investment returns

- Misleading a client by informing him that products require only a single payment when that is not the case

- Mismarking the value of investments or trading positions

- Procuring the unjustified alteration of prices on illiquid or off-exchange contracts, or both

- Misleading others within the firm about the credit worthiness of a borrower

- Providing false or inaccurate documentation or information, including details of training, qualifications, past employment record or experience

- Providing false or inaccurate information to the firm (or to the firm's auditors or an actuary appointed by the firm

- Providing false or inaccurate information to the regulators

- Destroying, or causing the destruction of, documents (including false documentation), or tapes or their contents, relevant to misleading (or attempting to mislead) a client, his firm, or the regulators

- Failing to disclose dealings where disclosure is required by the firm's personal account dealing rules

- Misleading others in the firm about the nature of risks being accepted

- Deliberately recommending an investment to a customer, or carrying out a discretionary transaction for a customer where the approved person knows that he is unable to justify its suitability for that customer

- Deliberately failing to inform, without reasonable cause a customer, the firm or its auditors or actuary, or the regulators, of the fact that their understanding of a material issue is incorrect, despite being aware of their misunderstanding, including failing to disclose false documents

- Deliberately preparing inaccurate or inappropriate records or returns, including performance reports for customers and training records

- Deliberately misusing the assets or confidential information of a client or of his firm

- Deliberately designing transactions so as to disguise breaches of requirements and standards of the regulatory system

- Deliberately failing to disclose the existence of a conflict of interest

- Deliberately not paying due regard to the interests of a customer

- Deliberate acts, omissions or business practices that could be reasonably expected to cause consumer detriment

## 1.14.3 Behaviour reflecting professional integrity

The following types of behaviour reflect professional integrity.

- **Commitment and capacity to work to accepted professional values and principles, beyond professional norms**. Firstly, employees and prospective employees should receive training about professional values, either through professional or company training programmes. Individuals' capacity to abide by these values can be tested through employee selection (e.g. at interview). Employees' technical and professional training needs to be sufficient to enable the employee to understand how the application of professional values affects consumers, the firm and its stakeholders, and the industry.

- **Relating professional values to personally held beliefs**. Ideally, the professional standards required in an employee's workplace should be congruent with his or her personally held beliefs and ethical standards. If this is not the case, tensions may result. An adviser who values regulatory compliance highly may find it difficult to work in a firm where a 'blind eye' may be turned to some rule breaches. If the professional finds themselves in a difficult ethical situation they cannot easily resolve alone, or if they are aware of failings in the organisation that are not within their immediate control, they should consider and take further action, which may include discussion with a superior, with their professional body or possibly with the regulator. If the situation remains unresolved, the individual will need to consider the position further, ultimately resigning if appropriate.

- **Giving a coherent account of beliefs and actions**. When holding discussions with a client, the ethical beliefs of an adviser with professional integrity are likely to show through. Where contraventions of ethical standards are at issue, the ability of employees to give a coherent account of actions is key to resolving this issue. A professional adviser should be disciplined in note-taking and in recording their actions, so that an accurate account of events can be assembled if necessary.

- **Strength of purpose and ability to act on values**. The qualities of a positive attitude and an assertive personality can be cultivated to promote a strong sense of purpose. The firm can help to promote an environment in which strength of purpose will thrive if it is clear about its objectives, which may be expressed in a mission statement.

## 1.14.4 Professional integrity and ethics in financial services

Professional integrity and ethical issues within financial services can be demonstrated in various ways.

- **The workings of financial markets**. There are various wrongs that can occur. Trading on inside information is an offence and corrodes confidence in markets. If investors believe that price movements may be caused by such practices, then they perceive that the market is rigged against them, and they may suffer financial losses as a result. Research analysis firms are showing lack of integrity if they or their employees deal ahead of publication of research, which could take an unfair advantage of price movements caused by publication of research.

- **The operation of institutions**. Organisations need to make arrangements that ensure as far as possible that employees, and the firm, will operate with integrity. These arrangements can take various forms, and should include training in matters of ethics. Conflicts of interest should be avoided, wherever possible, before they become a problem. This can sometimes be achieved by 'Chinese walls' which are organisational or physical barriers separating departments or employees where exchange of information between them could be unethical.

- **Personal conduct of finance professionals and representatives**. Professional employees, and appointed representatives who may be acting as **agents**, should act with integrity, and there should be transparency: they should be *seen* to act with integrity, to encourage **consumer** confidence. As individuals, they must play their part in complying with conduct of business rules of the regulator, and also rules set out by the firm.

## 1.15 Questioning our values

The financial regulator (in Discussion Paper 18 (2002)) suggested the following framework of questions that are designed to help professionals to recognise, apply and balance values in everyday decisions and actions.

### Openness, honesty, responsiveness and accountability

- Who is left out or kept in the dark? Why?
- How happy are we to be associated with our decisions/actions?
- Are we listening or just hearing?
- What can we learn? How do we help others to understand us?
- How do we recognise and deal with conflicts of interest?

### Relating to colleagues and customers fairly and with respect

- Do we treat everyone as we would like to be treated?
- Do we deal with people with respect and without prejudice?
- How do we keep rights and obligations in balance and proportionate?
- When do we hold to our commitments and resist 'fudging'?
- Who benefits and who loses out? Should they?

### Committed to acting competently, responsibly and reliably

- Do we do what we say we will do?
- Under pressure do we swap co-operation for coercion?

- Do we dither or delay? How is error treated?
- Do people trust us? If not, why not?
- Can we meet our commitments and plans?

To embed these values, the regulator concluded, needs:

**Developing vision and a values-led approach**

- What needs changing? What prevents change?
- What is the long-term outcome? What is sustainable?
- Do we sufficiently recognise and act on our stakeholder responsibilities?
- How do we develop shared purpose, loyalty and fulfilment?
- Do we apply ethical criteria simply to gain an advantage or because we believe we should?

# 2 Ethics in organisations

## 2.1 Ethical and unethical behaviour

The **ethical environment** can be said to refer to justice, respect for the law and a moral code. The conduct of an organisation, its management and employees will be measured against ethical standards by the customers, suppliers and other members of the public with whom they deal.

An example of unethical behaviour is to **present misleading information** to a customer which wrongly claimed that they would be likely to be better off transferring from a work-based pension scheme to a personal pension, when this is not the case. Such pension transfers led to the widespread pensions mis-selling scandal in recent years.

More recently, excessively zealous selling of 'sub-prime' and 'undocumented' or 'self-certified' mortgages to those who lacked the resources to meet future payments has been seen by many as a root cause of the **financial crisis of the late 2000s**, particularly in the US housing market. However, views vary about which behaviours are unethical in such a situation, and attributing 'blame' for such a crisis is complex.

- Were consumers to blame for over-committing themselves?

- Were mortgage brokers to blame for selling mortgages to those who were likely to default?

- Were lenders to blame for making the funds available, while knowing that the mortgages could be 're-packaged' and sold on to investors in securitised form?

Because of differences about where to draw the line between ethical and unethical behaviour, there is much to be said for formulating clearly stated **principles** and **codes** that will apply to particular professional groups or to particular regulated activities.

## 2.2 Responsibilities to stakeholders

Managers have a duty (in most enterprises) to aim for profit. At the same time, modern ethical standards impose a duty to guard, preserve and enhance the value of the enterprise for the good of all touched by it, including the general public. The various groups with an interest of some kind in the business and its activities are termed **stakeholders** in the business and include shareholders, employees, customers and suppliers. Large organisations tend to be more often held to account over this duty than small ones.

In the area of **products and production**, managers have responsibility to ensure that the public and their own employees are protected from danger. Attempts to increase profitability by cutting costs may lead to dangerous working conditions or to inadequate safety standards in products. In the United States, **product liability litigation** is so common that this legal threat may be a more effective deterrent than general ethical standards.

Business ethics are also relevant to competitive behaviour. This is because a market can only be free if competition is, in some basic respects, fair. There is a distinction to be drawn between competing aggressively and competing unethically.

In **Discussion Paper 18** *An ethical framework for financial services* (2002), the regulator commented on how the highest ethical standards can generate significant benefits for all stakeholders, for example with the following potential benefits.

- **Market confidence.** High ethical standards offer the potential of differentiating the UK financial services sector as being renowned for good ethical practice. A good ethical track record for the sector could help it (and its regulator) to absorb some 'shocks'.

- **Consumer protection.** Improved ethical standards might include a better relationship between firms and consumers which would be reflected in, for example, improved financial promotions.

- **Financial crime.** High ethical standards could change the perception that it is easy to launder money in the UK, and reduce the scope for our firms and markets to be targeted by criminals in the first place. This can be done by developing individual responsibility and a sense of involvement by all staff.

- **Public awareness and confidence.** Higher business and individual standards of behaviour promote the integrity and the general probity of all working in financial services, enhancing public perceptions and trust in the firms and individuals concerned.

## 2.3 Social responsibility in business

Arguably, institutions like public hospitals, schools and so on exist because health care and education are seen to be desirable social objectives by government at large, if they can be afforded.

However, where does this leave businesses? How far is it reasonable, or even appropriate, for businesses to exercise 'social responsibility' by giving to charities, voluntarily imposing strict environmental objectives on themselves and so on?

Social responsibility action is likely to have some adverse effects on shareholders' interests.

- **Additional costs** such as those of environmental monitoring
- **Reduced revenues** as a result of refusing to supply certain customers
- **Diversion of employee effort** away from profitable activities
- **Diversion of funds** into social projects

However, it is possible to argue that being socially responsible is in shareholders' interests, particularly over the longer term. This is primarily because it may enhance reputation and people's trust in the business, thus developing confidence among would-be customers of the business.

## 2.4 Self-interest in the organisational context

The **free market model** of society is based on the idea that individuals act to maximise their own utility. They seek to do this by making decisions to enter into transactions based on the utility gained compared with the opportunity cost on the transaction: the opportunity cost is typically the utility to be gained from spending the same amount of money on the next best alternative. The basic economic model assumes that the economic actor makes decisions out of **self-interest**, as well as being in possession of full **information**.

By and large, we can expect that people will act to better their own interests. But how is this best achieved?

In the *Harvard Business Review*, it was reported that the US retailer, Sears Roebuck was deluged with complaints that customers of its car service centre were being charged for unnecessary work: apparently this was because mechanics had been given targets of the number of car spare parts they should sell. The mechanics were seeking to advance their own self-interest in trying to meet the targets set by the organisation.

When targets are set, the key consideration may be to enhance revenues, in the interests of shareholders of the firm. Sales targets for the sale of financial products might, for example, encourage advisers, acting out of self-interest, to advise unnecessary **switching** of client's investments in order to generate commission.

- As well as attracting regulatory sanctions, excessive switching of customers' investments by a firm may, as soon as it becomes known to customers or the media, damage the **firm's reputation**. A poorer reputation could hit sales significantly, thus hurting the business and shareholders' profits that the targets were originally seeking to enhance.

- The adviser responsible for unnecessary switching of customer investments is also liable to damage **his or her own reputation** as a professional. Through the practice of excessive switching having been discovered, the adviser has in fact damaged the self-interest he or she was seeking to promote.

Such examples illustrate how the interaction of self-interest with motivation and with a firm's rules can be complex. Self-interest can be a powerful motivator, encouraging employees to do a better job, but the wrong incentives can lead to sub-optimal outcomes arising.

## 2.5 Role of the agent

**Agency**, as we have seen, is a contractual relationship where one party hires or engages another party to act on his behalf in transactions with a third party. There are many examples of agency within the world of financial services. Clients and their financial adviser or their stockbroker are two obvious relationships, with solicitors and estate agents being other agency situations in the world of commerce.

A person who enlists the services of another is the principal and the person so engaged is the agent.

The **duties of an agent** are usually set out in an agreement between principal and agent. However, where there is no agreement or where the agreement does not expressly cover all matters, there are certain duties implied by law which apply – a duty to:

- **Obey instructions** – if the agent exceeds his authority, he may be personally liable to the third party
- **Exercise skill and care**
- **Act in person** – the duties must not be delegated to someone else
- Account and to **keep accounts**
- **Act in good faith** – conflicts of interest must be disclosed to the principal, with everything the agent does being for the principal's benefit

# 3 Professional codes and standards

## 3.1 The regulator's requirements

In 2009, the financial regulator at the time – the FSA – published a draft **Code of Ethics** for investment advisers in **Consultation Paper 09/18** *Distribution of financial services: delivering the RDR* (the Retail Distribution Review).

The Authority declared that its objective was to deliver standards of professionalism that inspire consumer confidence and build trust so that, in time, financial advice is seen as a profession on a par with other professions. Achievement of this objective is linked closely to the wider package of RDR changes, in particular on adviser charging.

The code was to apply to all investment advisers who are giving advice, whether giving independent or restricted advice. However, as reported in Consultation Paper **CP10/12**, further consideration of this approach and feedback to CP09/18 led the regulator to decide that constructing an ethical code aimed solely at the retail investment sector was not the most effective way forward. The Consultation Paper stated that ethics apply at all levels. Thus, attempts to ring-fence certain behaviours or individuals may give a misleading impression that others do not have to follow ethical behaviours, which would be an unsatisfactory outcome.

The regulators' preferred approach is to make amendments to the **Code of Practice for Approved Persons** in **APER** (discussed earlier in this Chapter) – which will apply to all approved persons – instead of the regulator producing a separate Code of Ethics for investment advisers. Additionally, advisers will be expected to subscribe to a code of ethics adopted by their professional body, as evidenced in each adviser's Statement of Professional Standing (SPS).

## 3.2 Statement of Professional Standing (SPS)

Retail investment advisers are required to hold a **Statement of Professional Standing (SPS)** if they want to give independent or restricted advice. This requirement has applied since 31 December 2012, when the **Retail Distribution Review (RDR)** changes came into effect.

The SPS provides customers with evidence that the adviser subscribes to a **code of ethics**, is qualified, and has kept their knowledge up to date. The SPS will be issued by **FCA-accredited bodies** that will be subject to **FCA oversight** in relation to their investment adviser members' activities.

## 3.3 Accredited body requirements

The SPS must be issued by **FCA-accredited bodies** which satisfy the following criteria:

- They act in the public interest and further the development of the profession

- They carry out effective verification services

- They have appropriate systems and controls in place and provide evidence to the regulator of continuing effectiveness, and

- They cooperate with the regulator on an ongoing basis

The **accredited bodies** are subject to **FCA oversight** in relation to their investment adviser members' activities, and must ensure that all advisers who use their services:

- Are appropriately qualified

- Have made an **annual** written declaration that they have complied with the Statements of Principle and Code of Conduct for Approved Persons (APER)

- Have completed Continuing Professional Development (CPD) requirements

The **Chartered Insurance Institute (CII)** is an approved **accredited body**.

## 3.4 CII Code of Ethics

As a professional body in the financial sector, the Chartered Insurance Institute has issued a **Code of Ethics** (new version, 2009) which its members are bound to follow.

The Institute has stated: 'The CII encourages the highest professional and ethical standards in insurance and financial services worldwide. Consumers and the membership of the CII expect all members to meet these standards and maintain the reputation of the CII by following the Code of Ethics.'

The code sets down the principles which all members of the CII should follow in the course of their professional duties. Members are obliged to comply with this code. If they do not comply, this may result in the CII taking disciplinary action against them.

The **CII Code of Ethics** covers the following aspects.

1.  The Code requires members to **comply with all relevant laws and regulations** as well as the Code itself

2.  Members must act with the **highest ethical standards and integrity**

3.  Members must **act in the best interests of each client**

4.  Members must **provide a high standard of service**

5.  Members must **treat people fairly** regardless of race or racial group, sex or sexual orientation, religion or belief, age, and disability

# Key chapter points

- Ethics is about rules, principles and standards to be observed, by people, by firms, and in society generally.

- The conduct of an organisation, its management and employees will be measured against ethical standards by the customers, suppliers and other members of the public with whom they deal. Perceptions of its conduct will determine the reputation of the organisation, which can take time to build up, while it can be reduced quickly.

- There are rules-based and compliance-based approaches to business ethics. Professional integrity encompasses such attributes as honesty, reliability, impartiality and openness.

- Ethical conduct by all team members should be a major concern for management. Inside the organisation, a compliance based approach highlights conformity with the law. An integrity based approach suggests a wider remit, incorporating ethics in the organisation's values and culture. Organisations sometimes issue codes of conduct to employees. Many employees are bound by professional codes of conduct.

- The financial regulator – the FSA, succeeded by the FCA – declared that its objective was to deliver standards of professionalism that inspire consumer confidence and build trust so that, in time, financial advice is seen as a profession on a par with other professions. However, as reported in CP10/12, following consultations, the regulator decided that constructing an ethical code aimed solely at the retail investment sector is not the most effective way forward. Ethics apply at all levels, and so attempts to ring fence certain behaviours or individuals might give a misleading impression that others do not have to follow ethical behaviours.

- Retail investment advisers must hold a Statement of Professional Standing (SPS) if they want to give either independent or restricted advice. The SPS provides customers with evidence that the adviser subscribes to a code of ethics, such as the CII's Code of Ethics, is qualified, and has kept their knowledge up-to-date.

## Chapter Quiz

1   Give examples of how unethical behaviour may arise in a financial services organisation. ...............(see para 1.8)

2   What measures might organisations take to protect themselves against the legal consequences of unethical behaviour? ...........................................................................................................(1.13.2)

3   How do Principle for Businesses 1 and Statement of Principle 1 relate to professional standards? ..............(1.14)

4   How could high ethical standards in financial services firms help in the fight to stop financial crime? ...........(2.2)

5   Outline the duties of an agent. ...............................................................................................(2.5)

6   What is the regulators' preferred approach, in place of the now-abandoned project of producing a separate Code of Ethics for investment advisers?.............................................................................................(3.1)

7   What does an adviser's Statement of Professional Standing demonstrate to the retail customer? ................(3.2)

8   Outline the main elements of the CII's Code of Ethics. ................................................................(3.4)

# Index